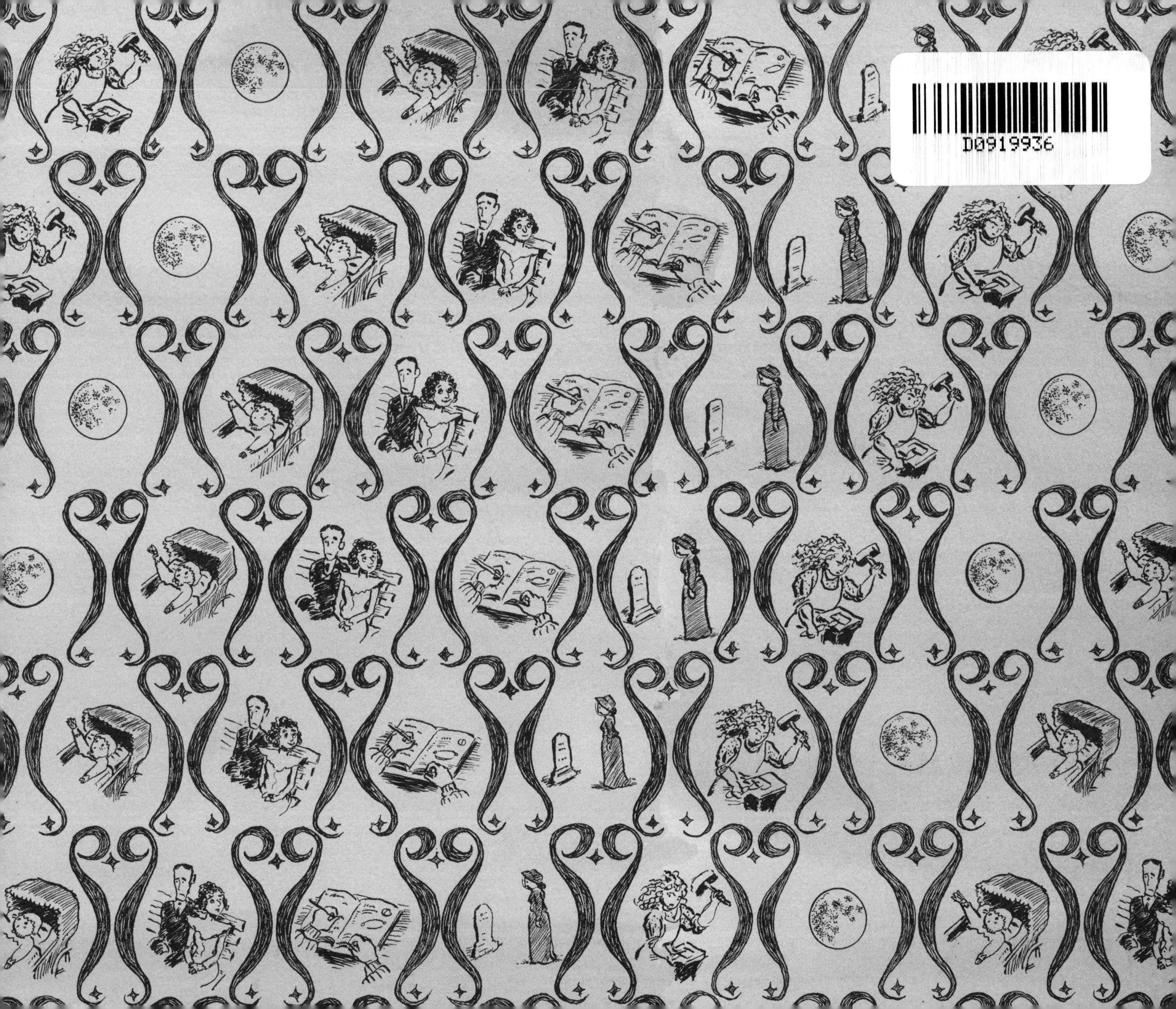

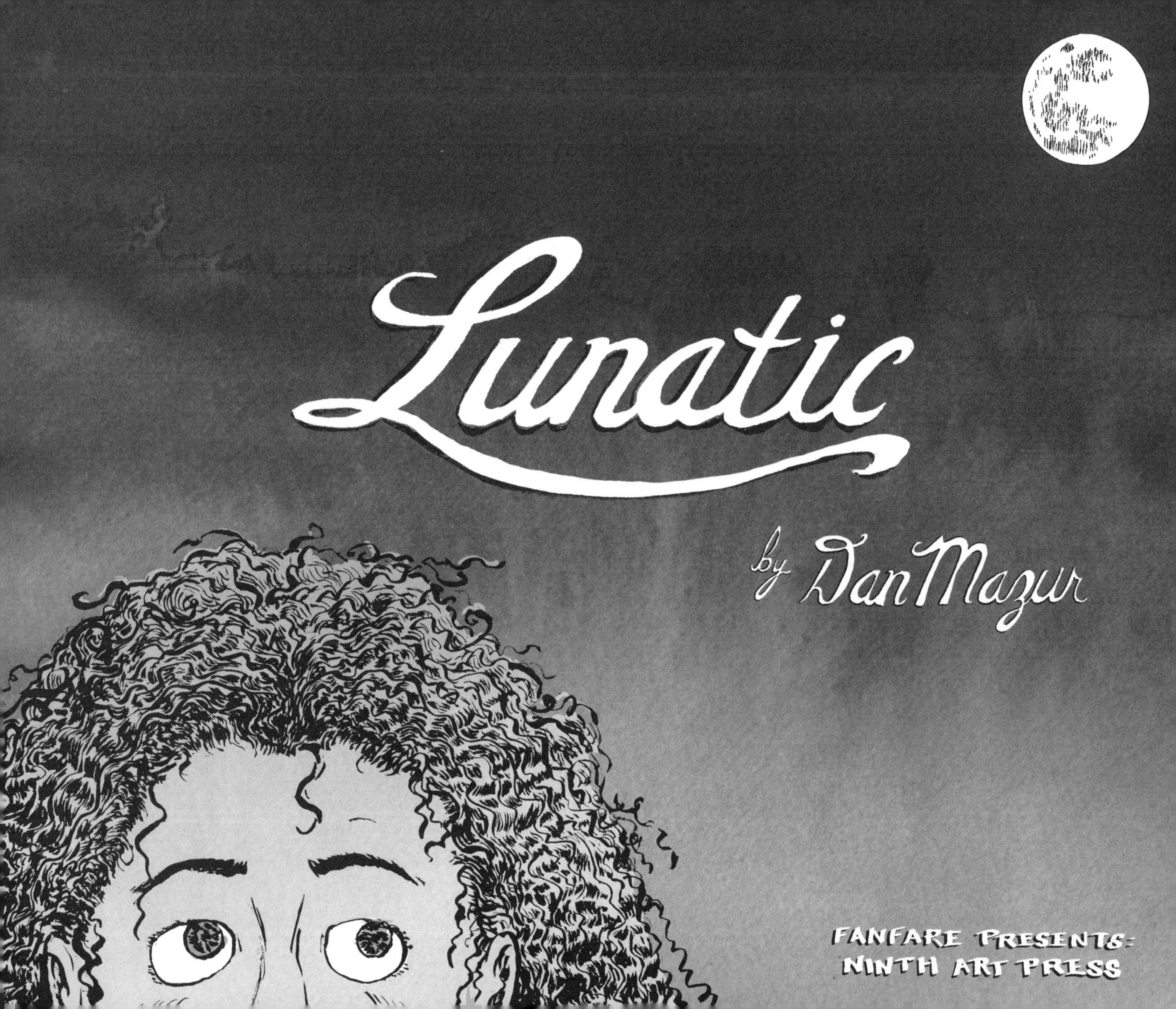
Lunatic
by Dan Mazur
FANFARE PRESENTS:
NINTH ART PRESS

© DAN MAZUR 2020
© Fanfare Presents & Ninth Art Press for the bound edition 2020

Edited by Dan Mazur and Stephen Albert

www.danmazurcomics.com
www.ninthartpress.com
www.fanfareuk.com

A C.I.P. catalogue record for this book is available from the British Library
ISBN 978-0-9932112-2-5
Printed and bound in the European Union by Spauda, LT

For Susan (Dan)
To Heidi Sen, my Moonlight on La Mesa (Stephen)

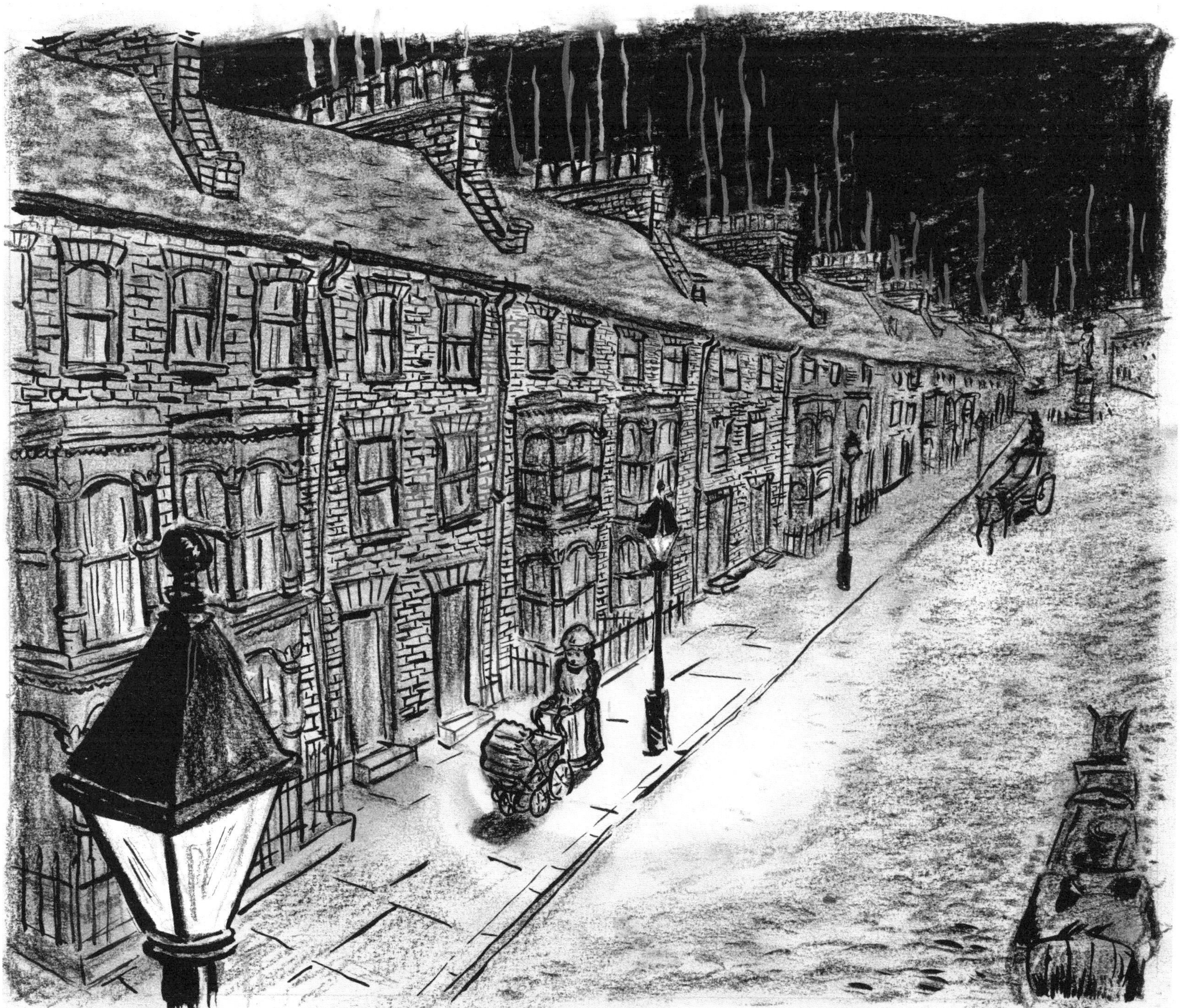

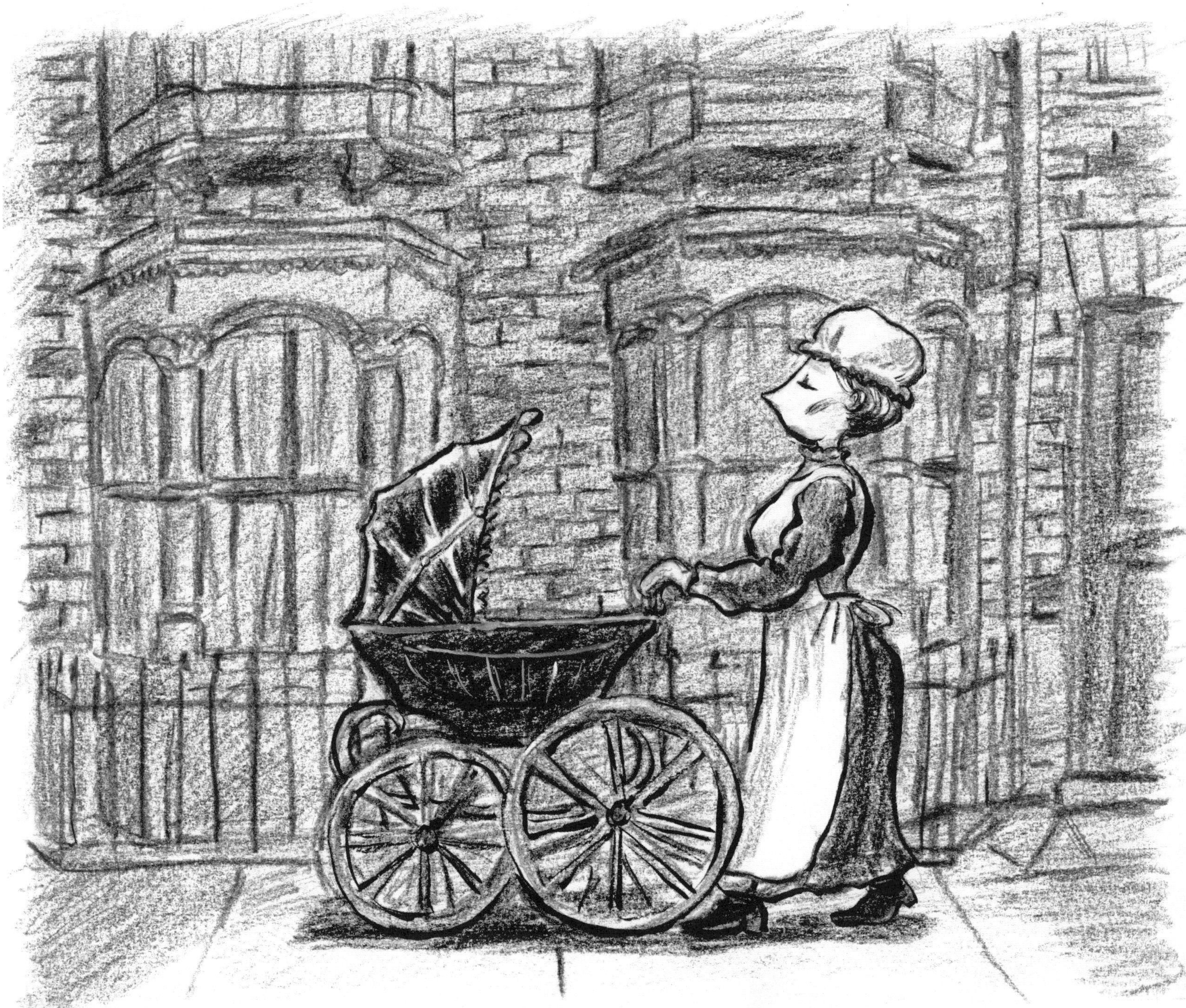

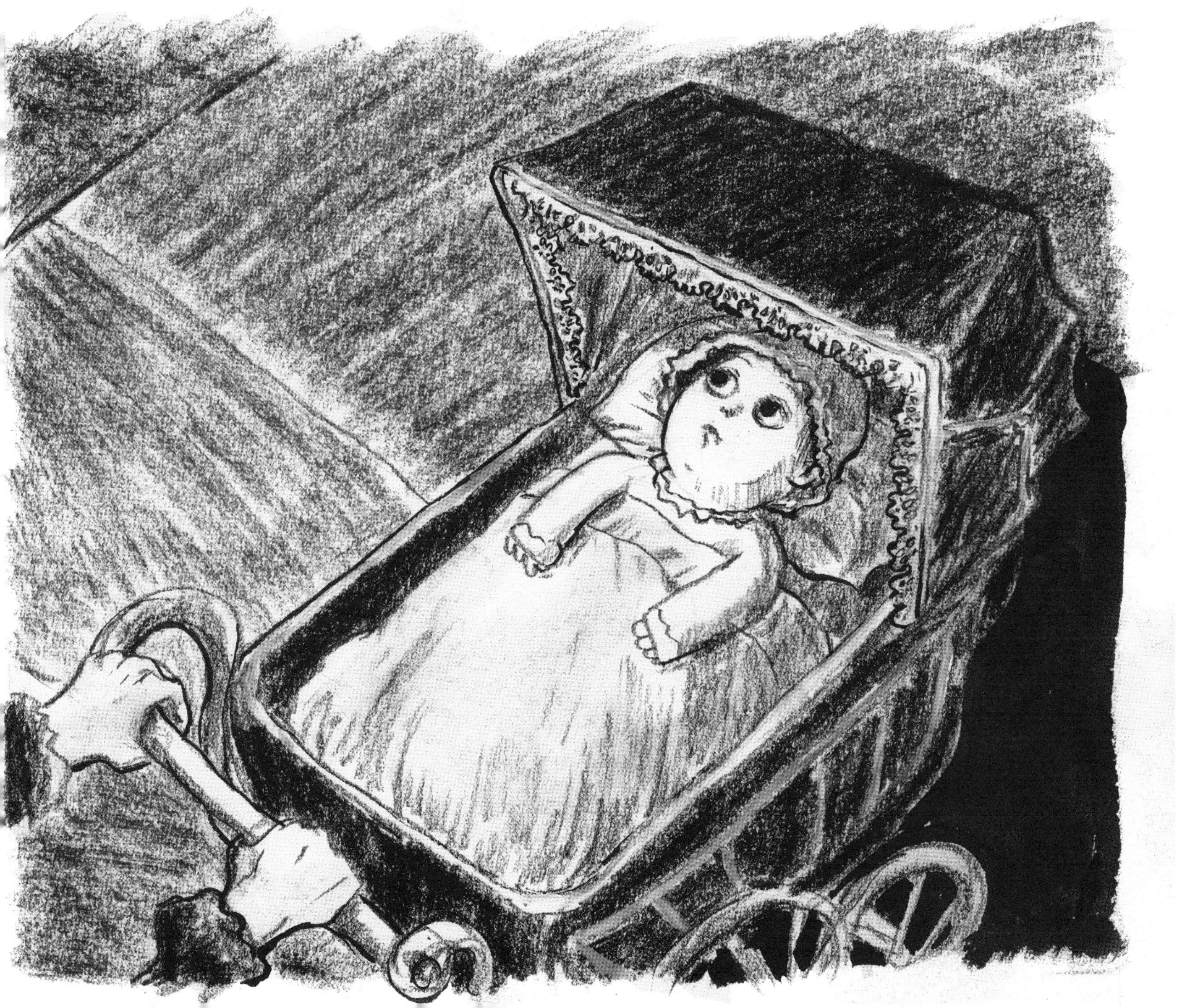

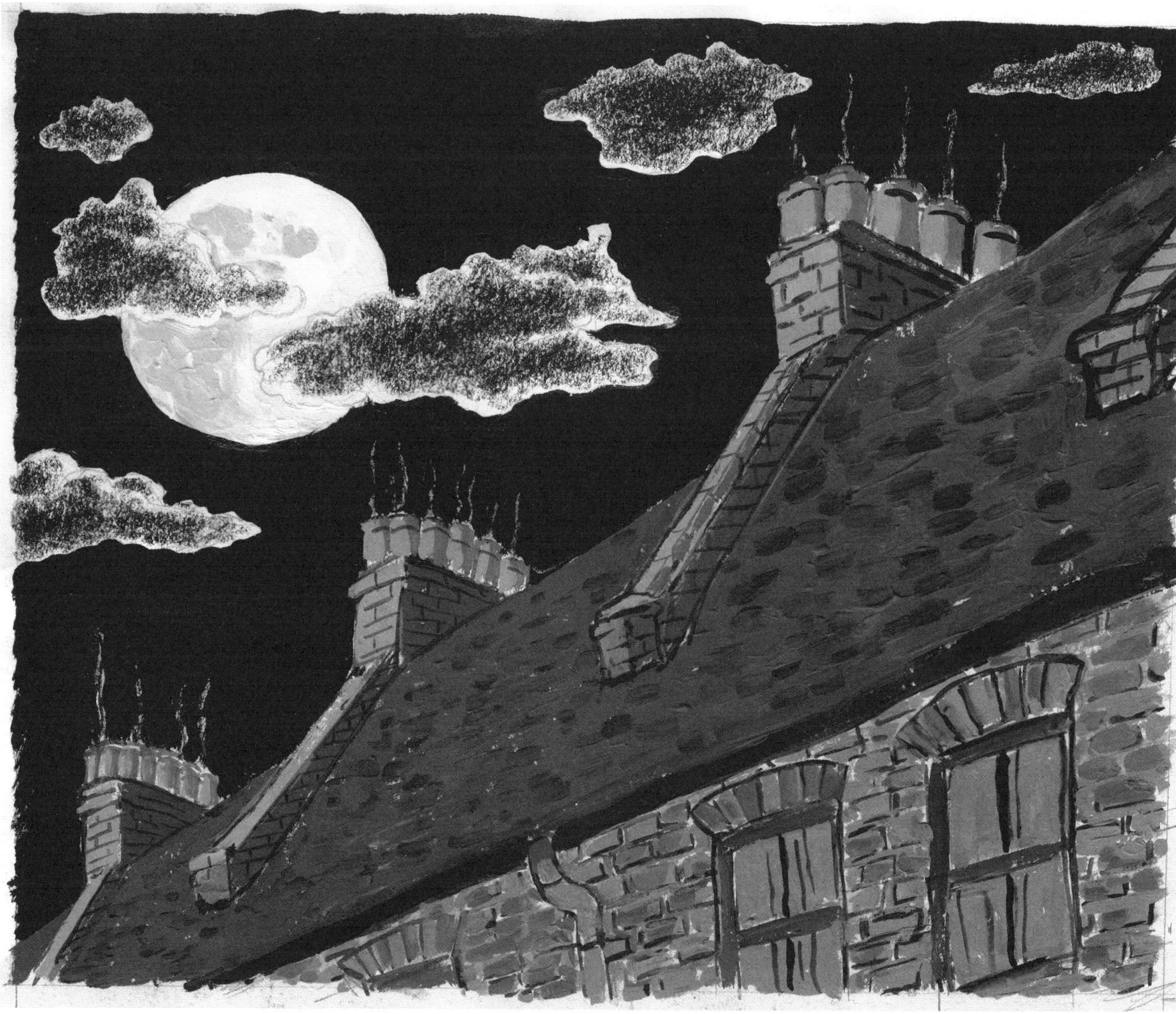

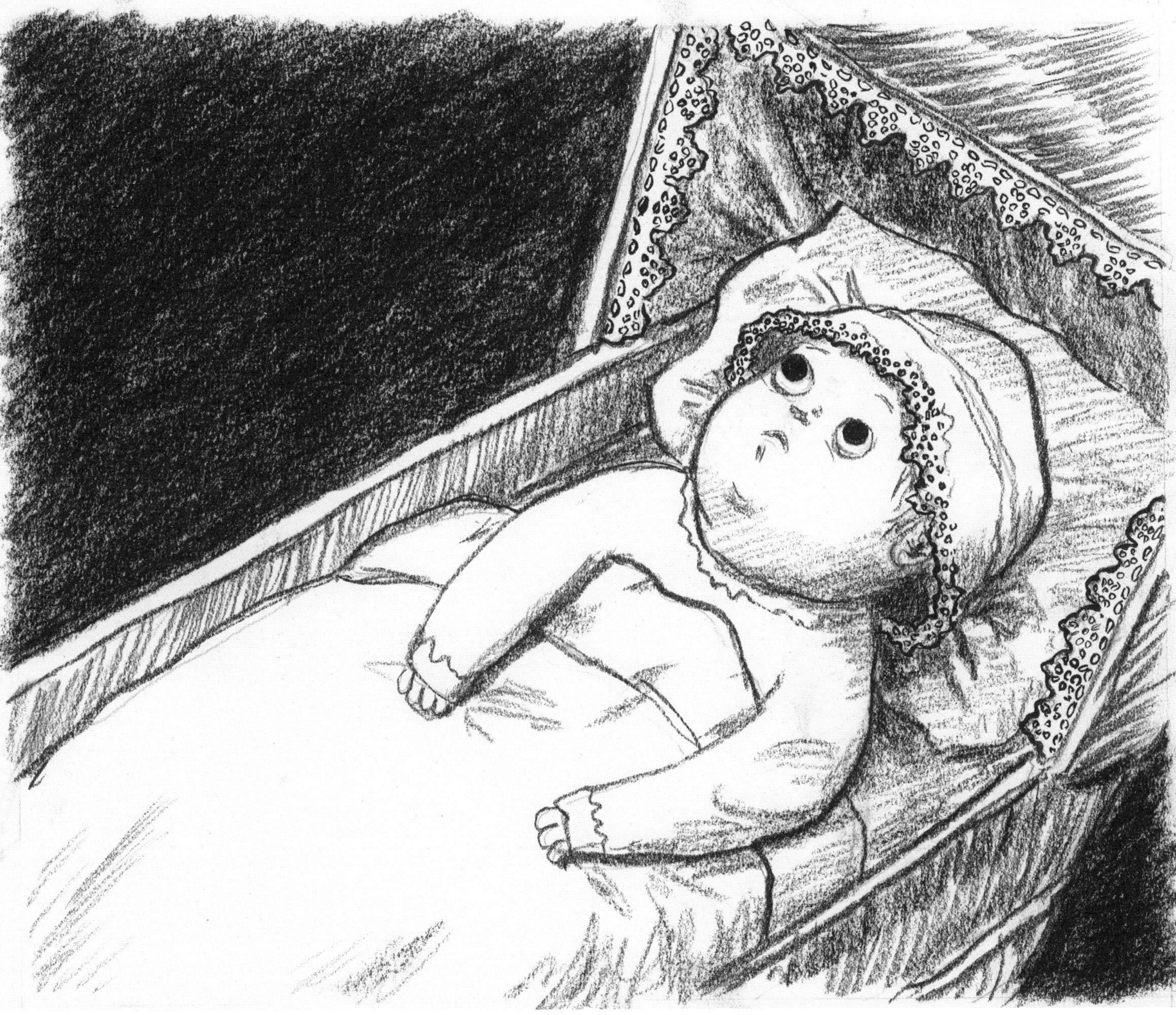

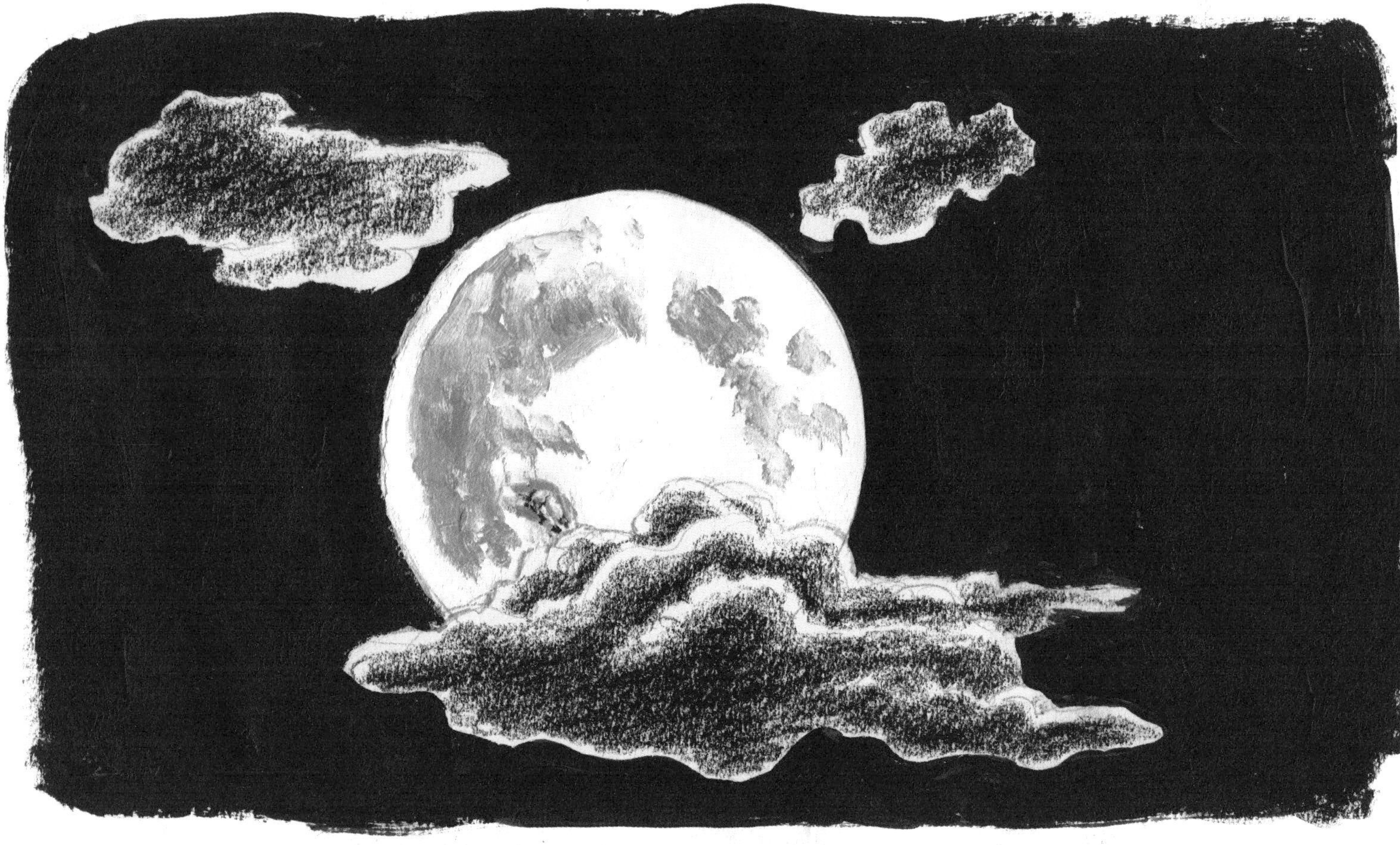

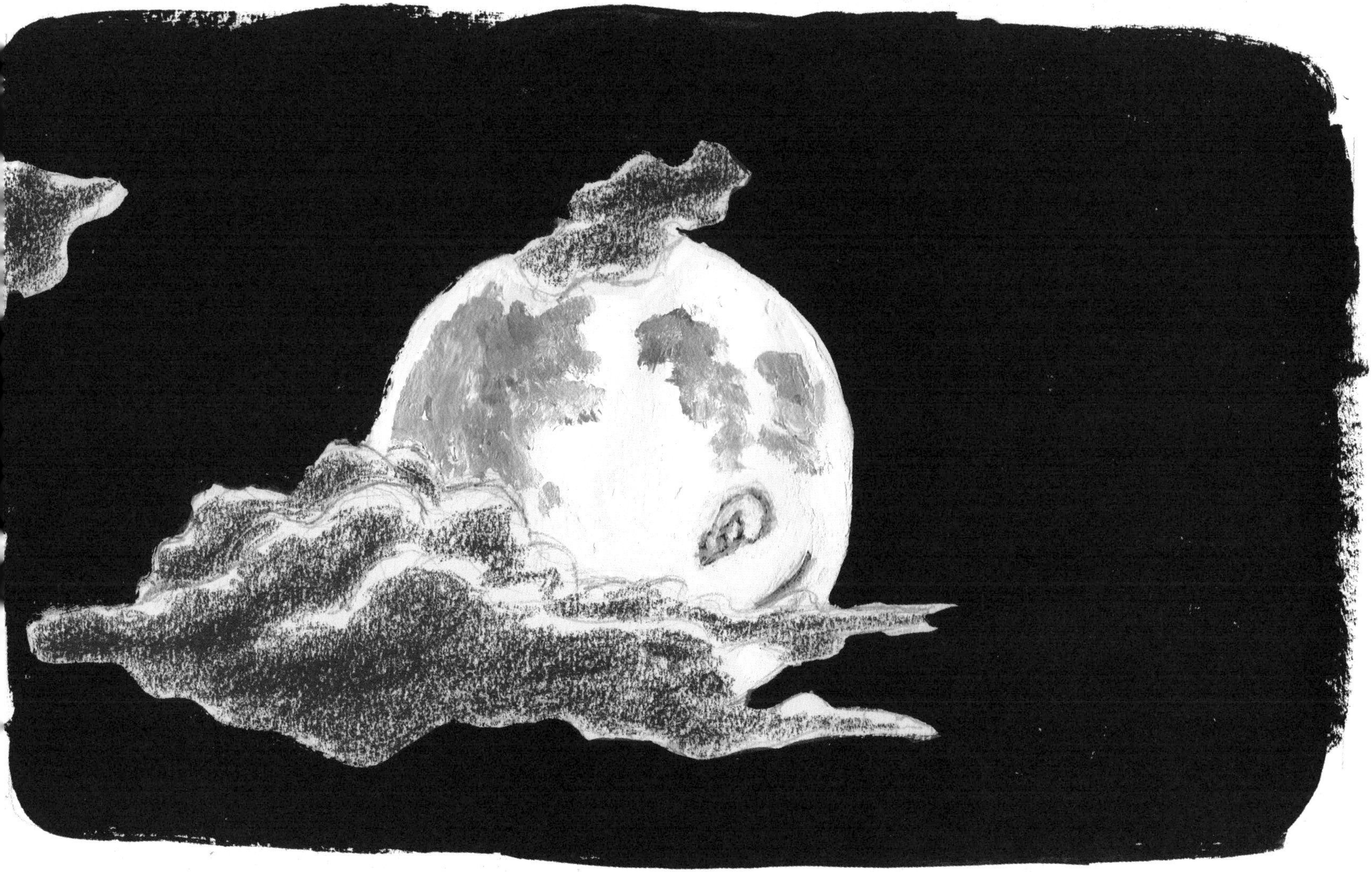

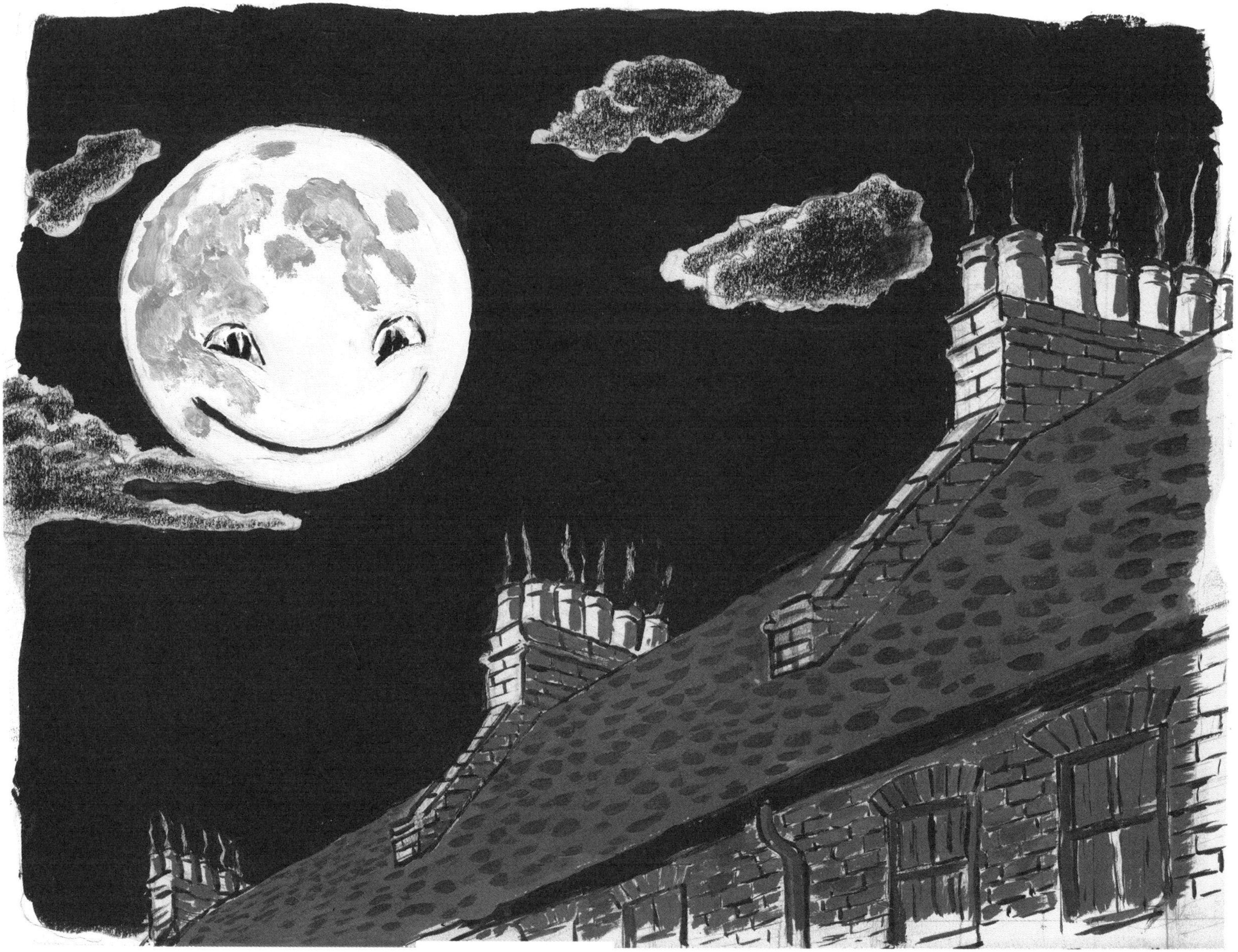

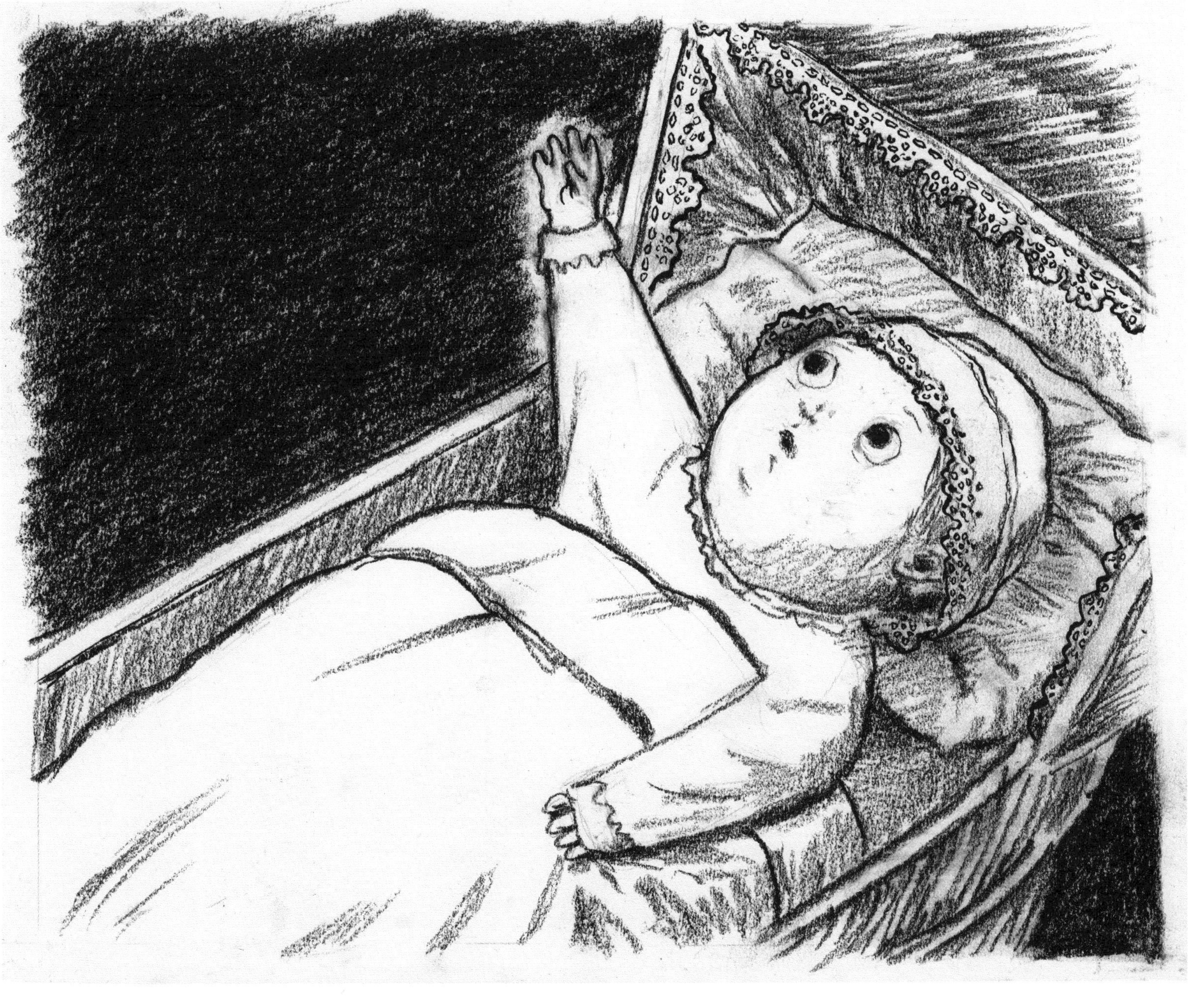

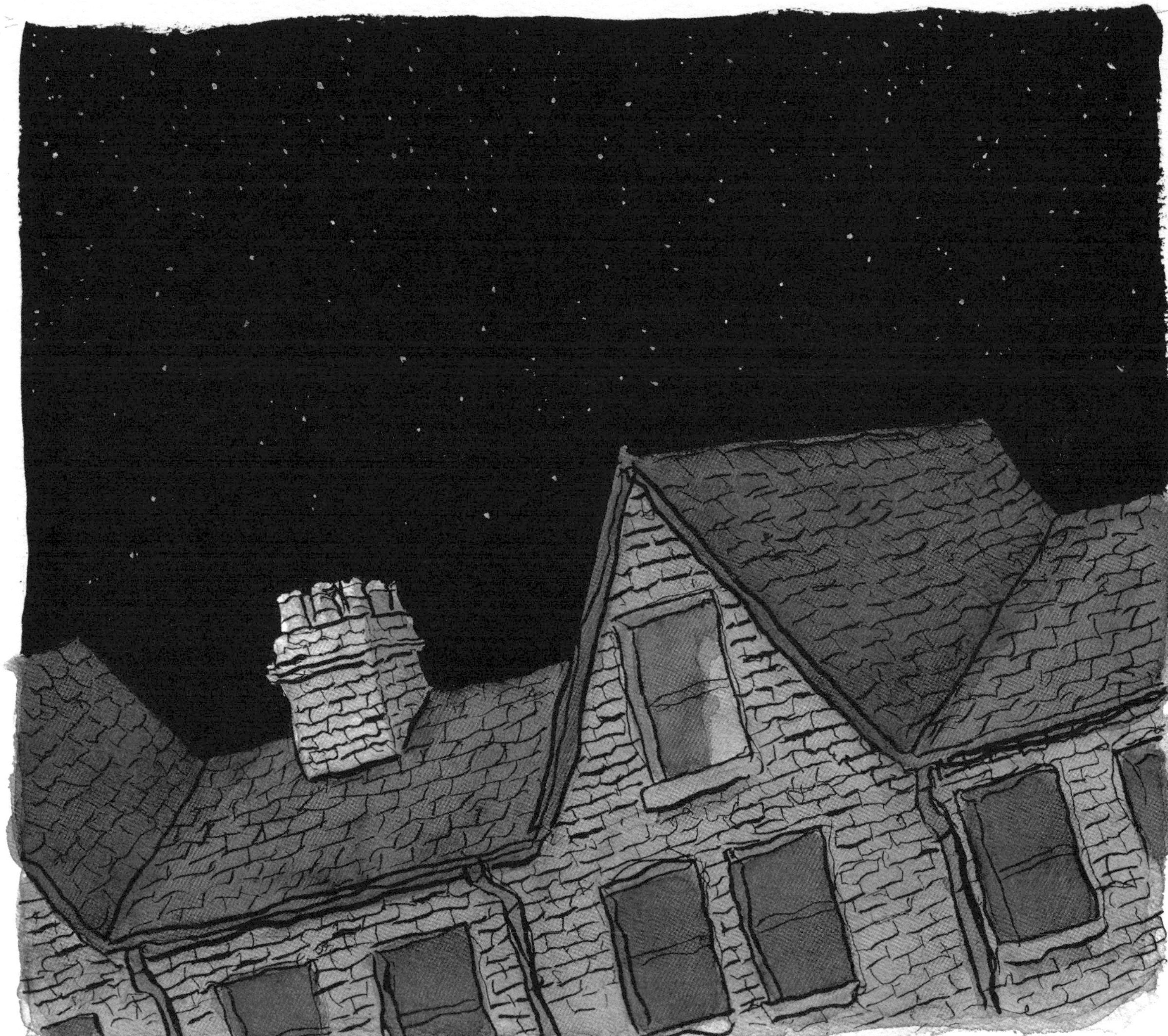

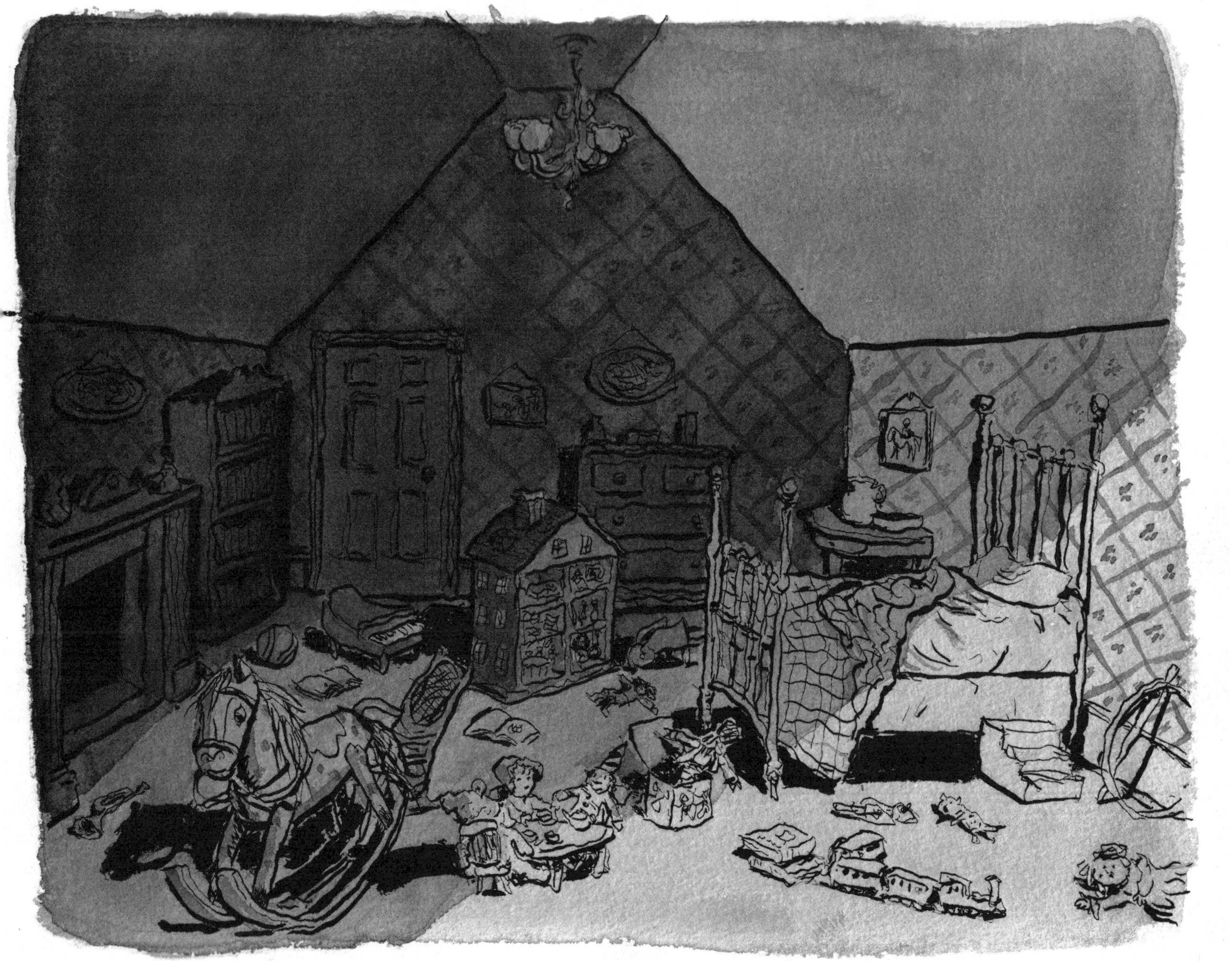

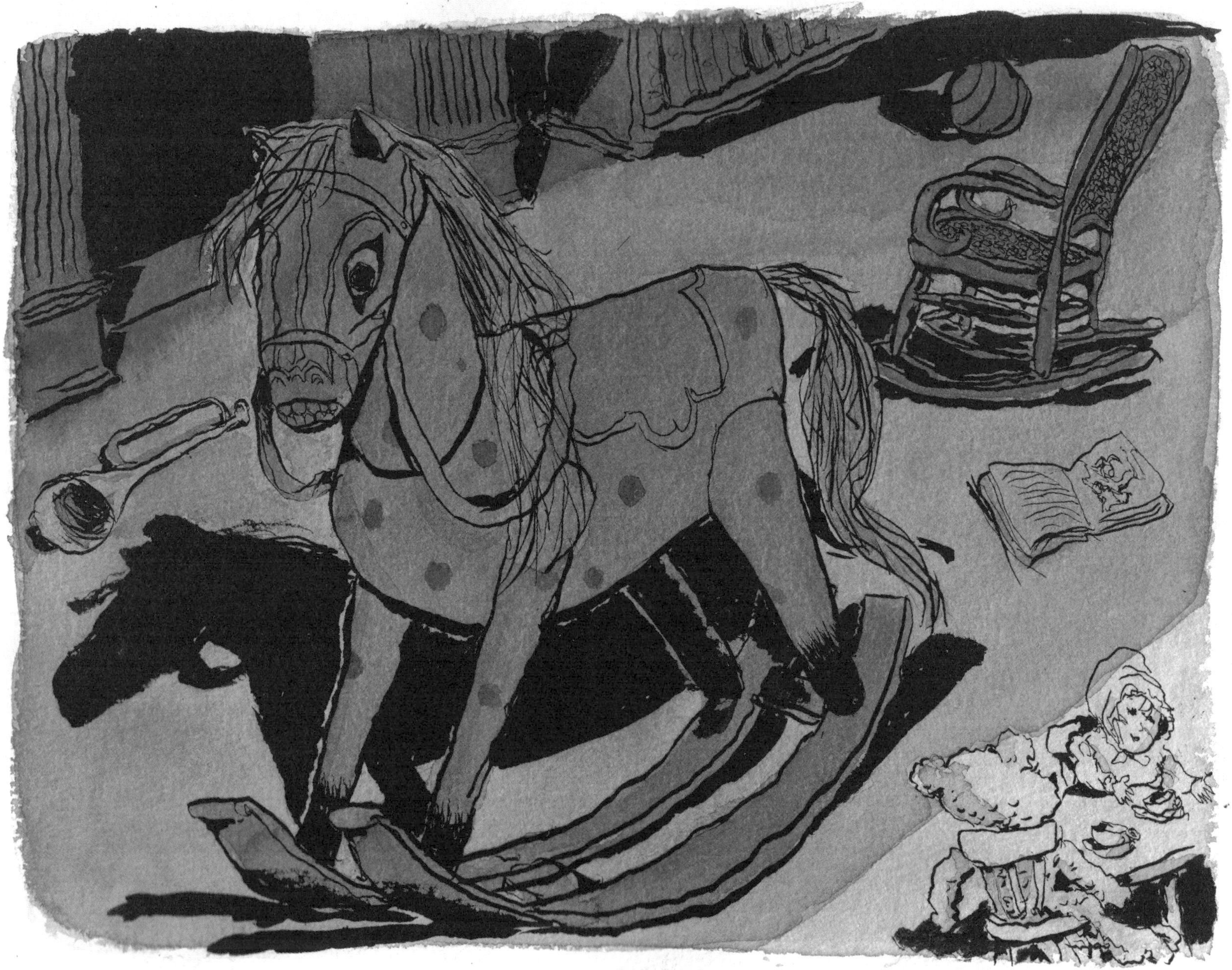

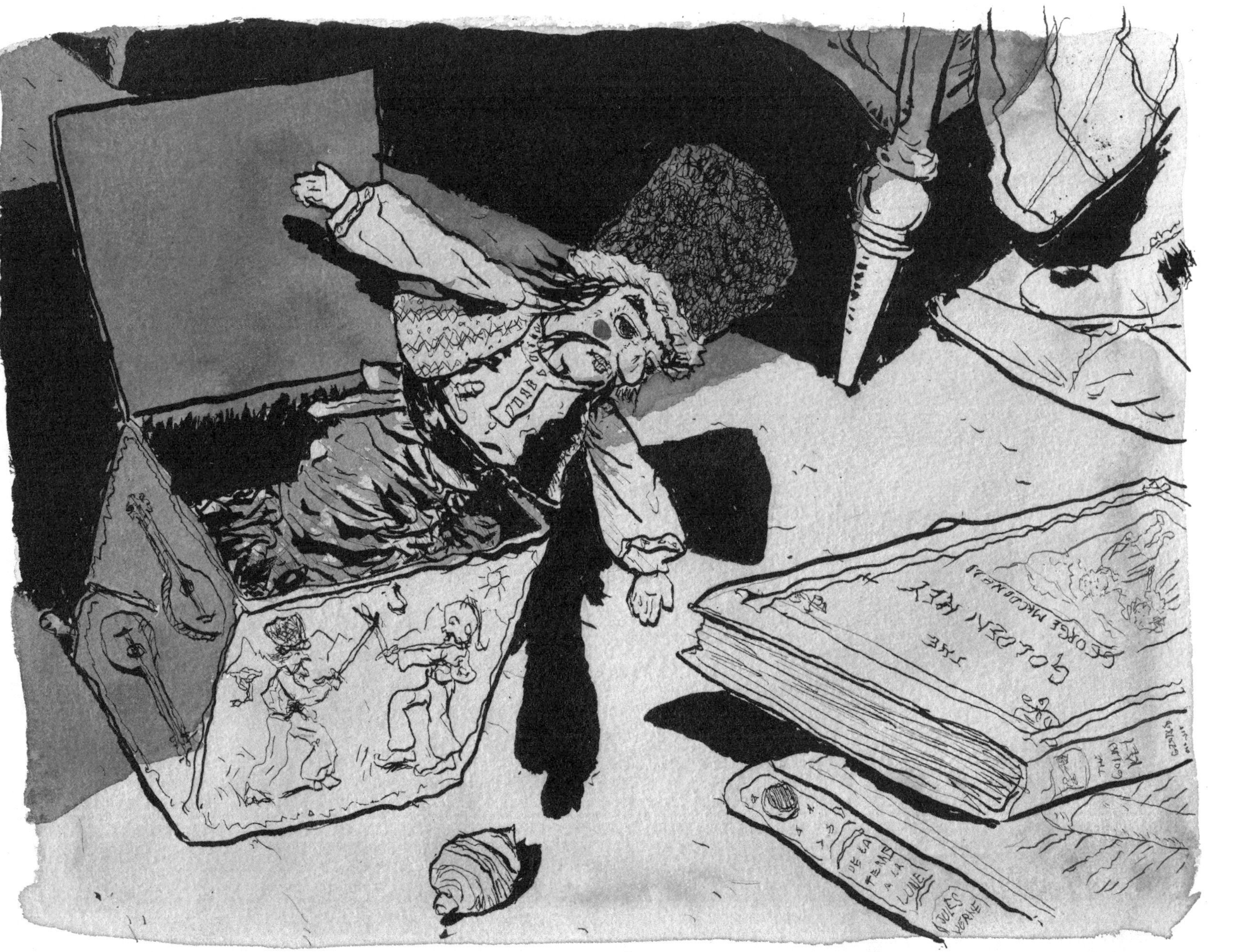
THE GOLDEN KEY
GEORGE MACDONALD
DE LA TERRE A LA LUNE
JULES VERNE

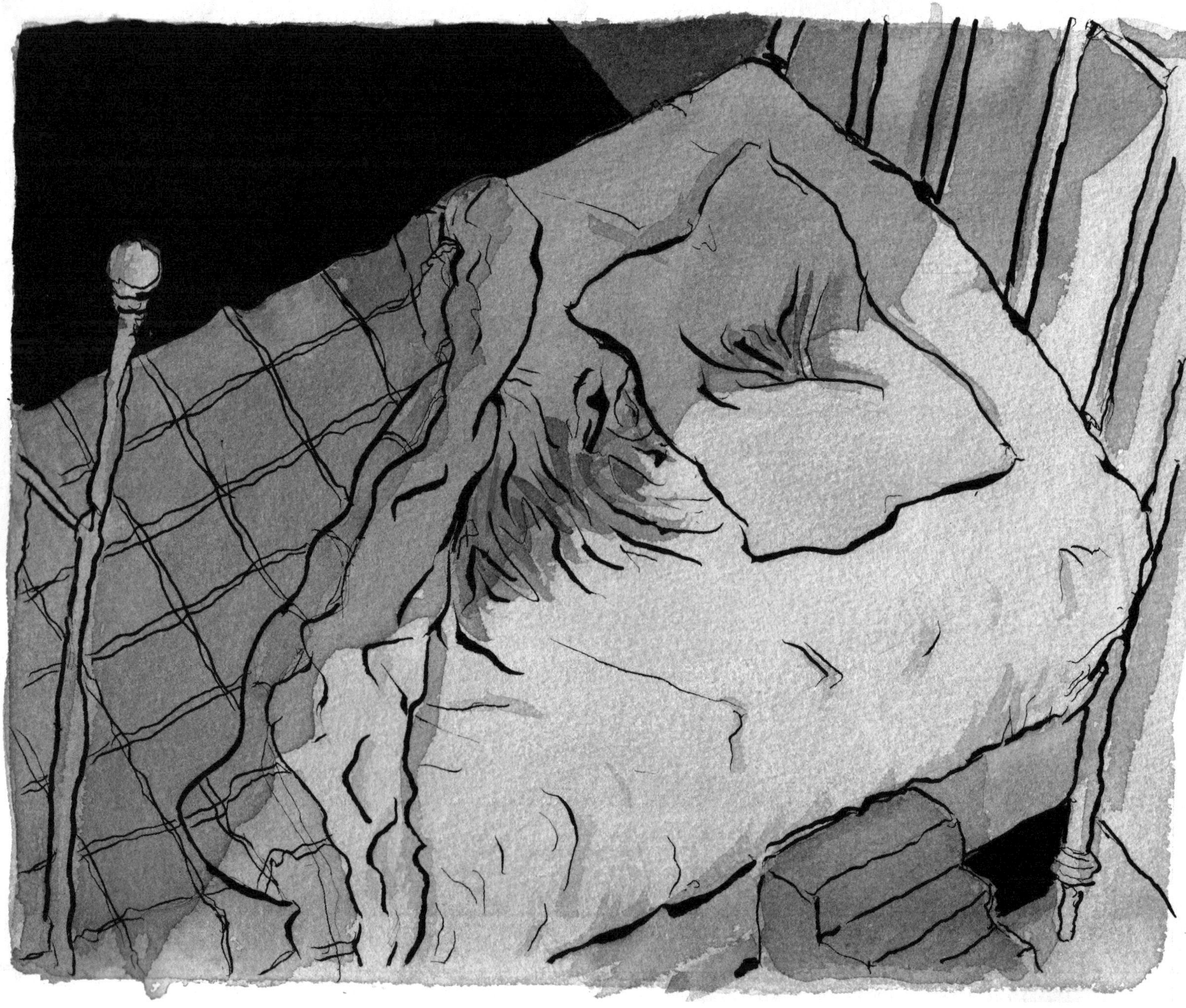

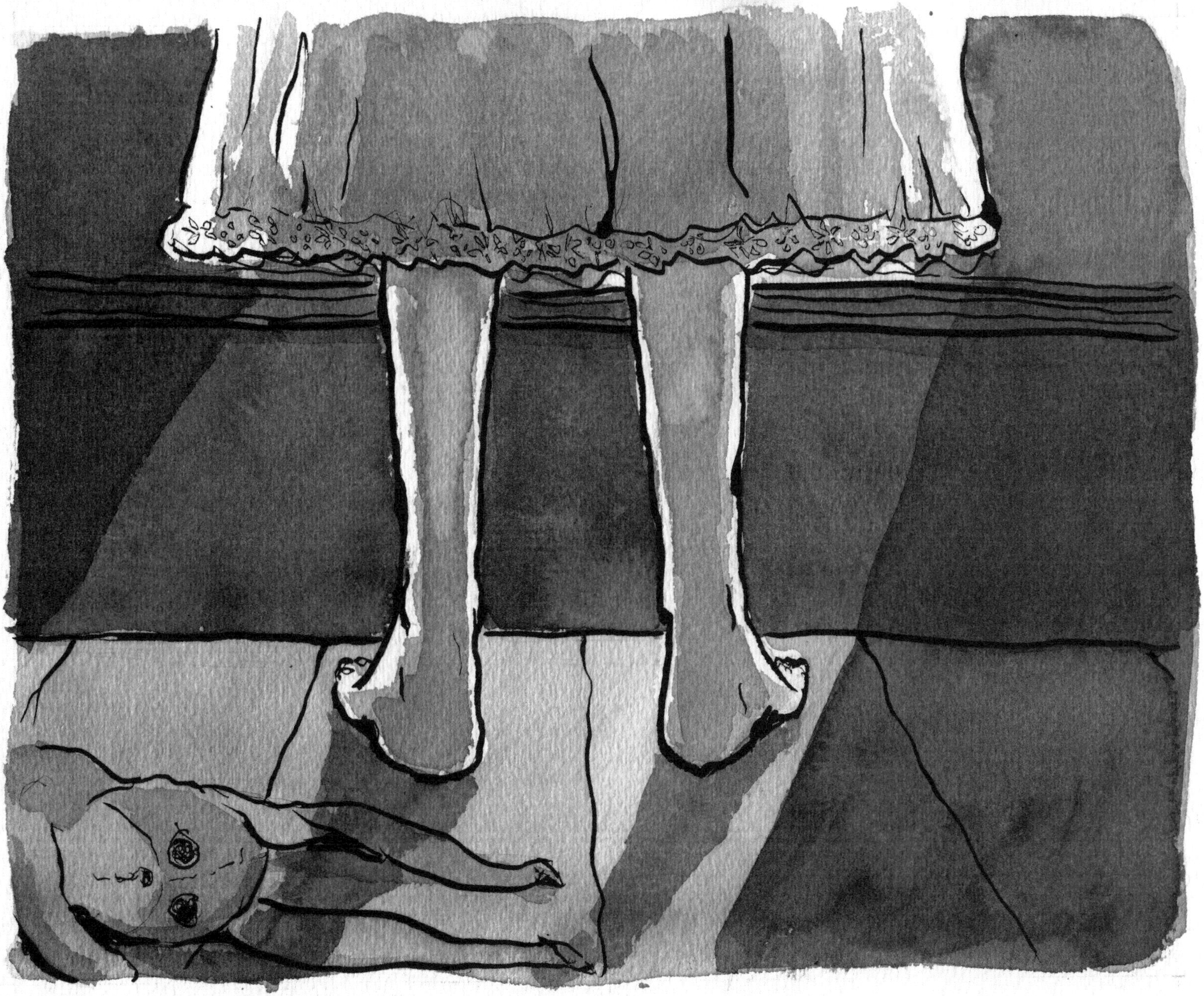

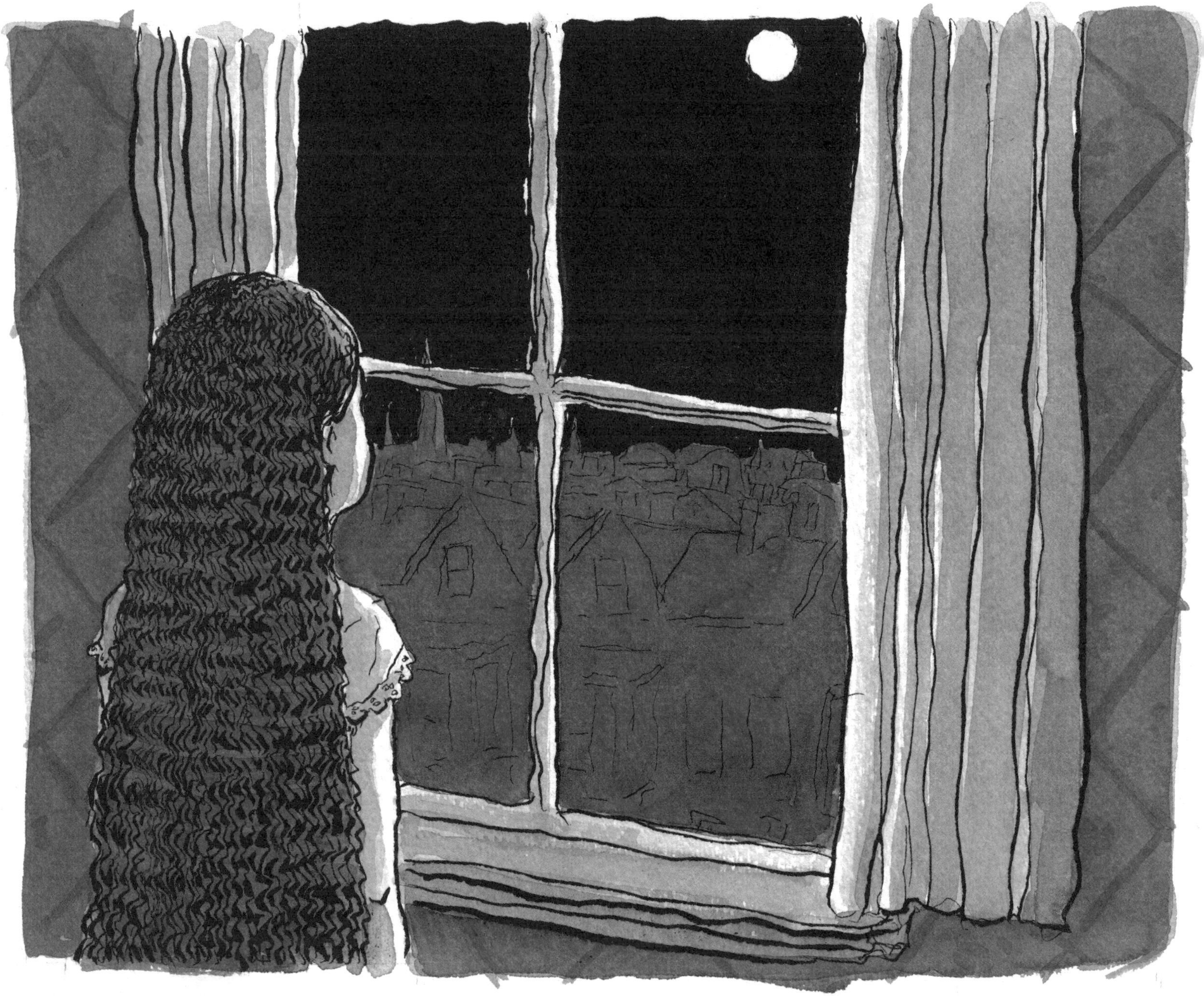

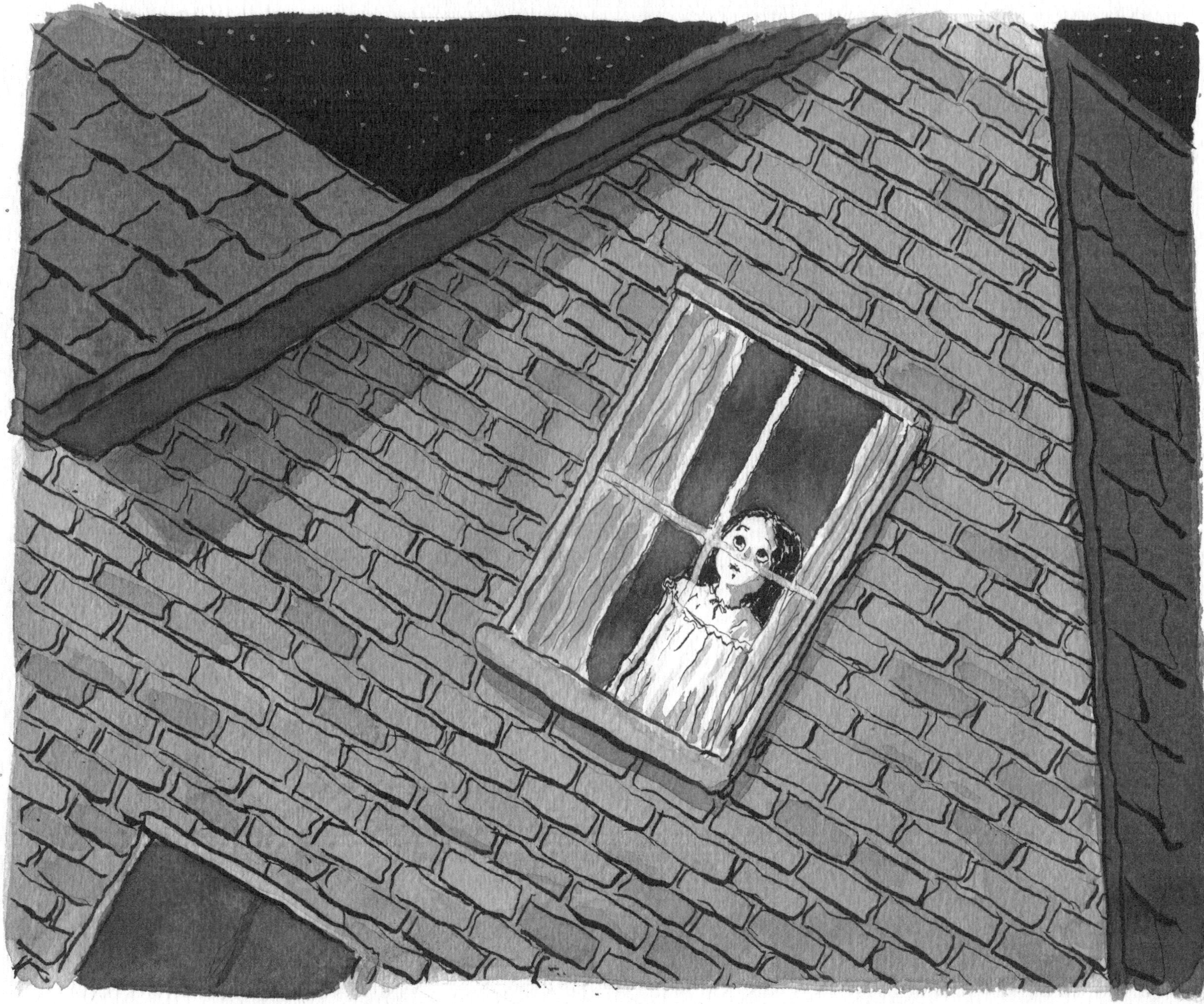

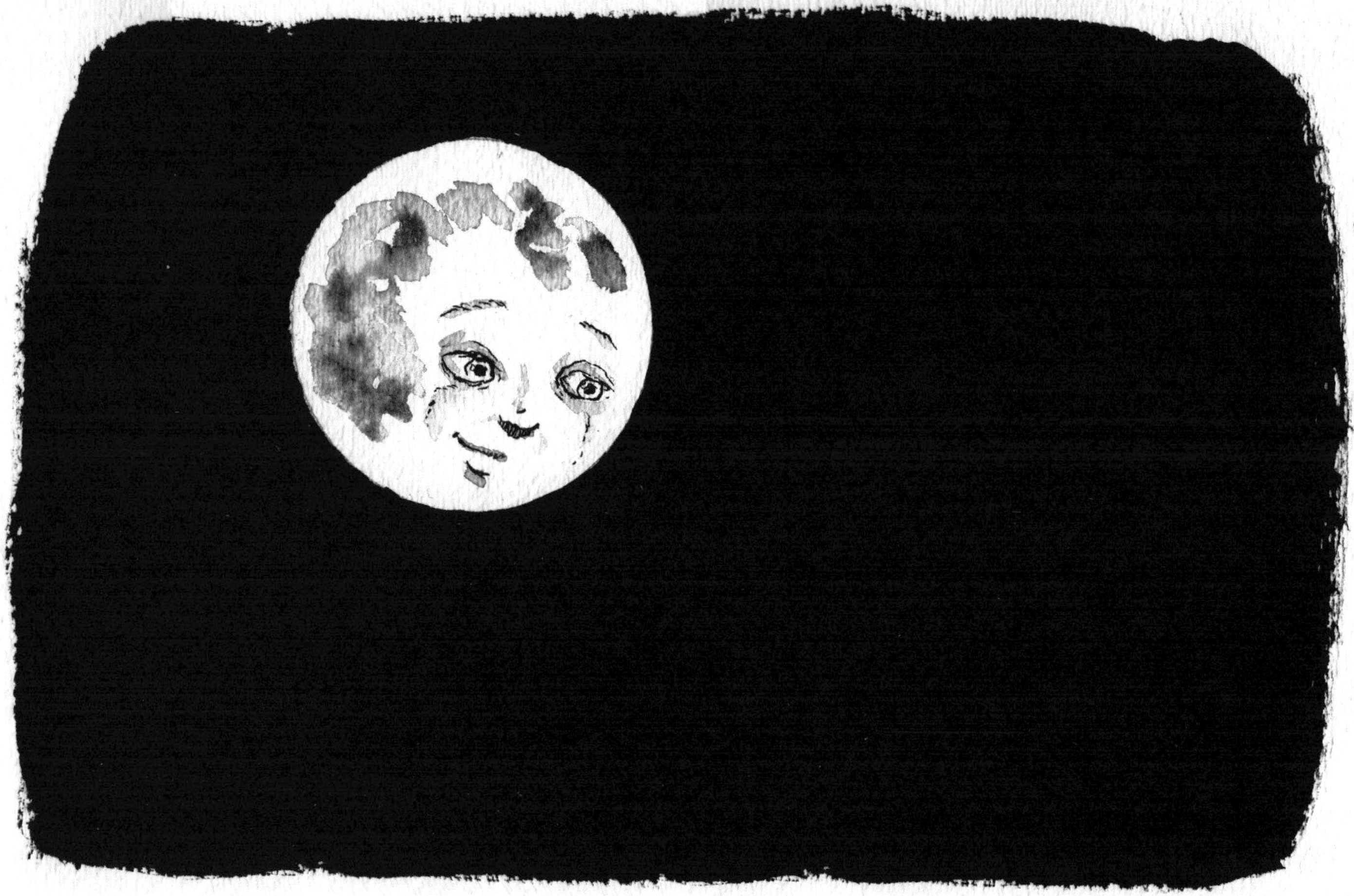

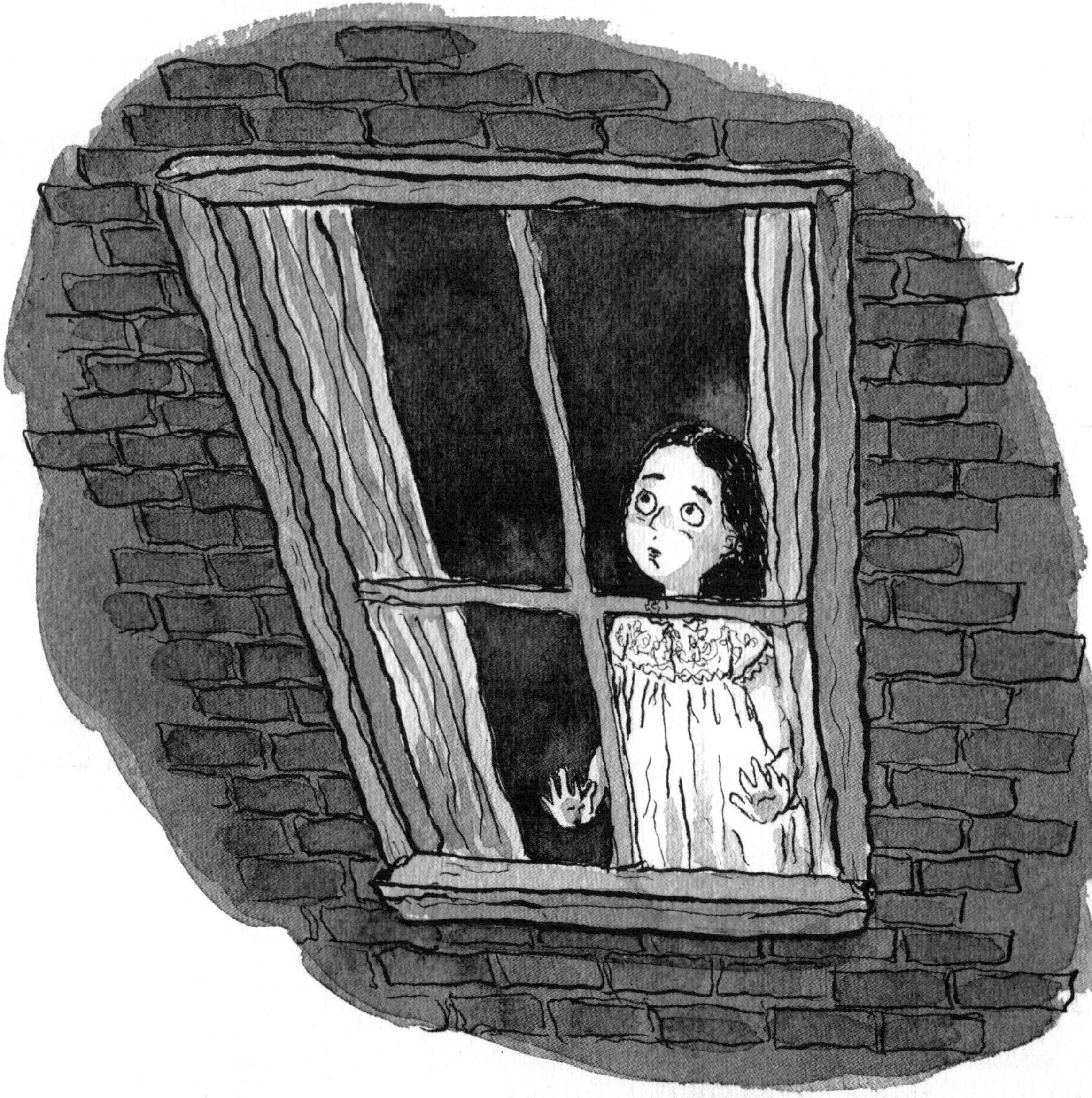

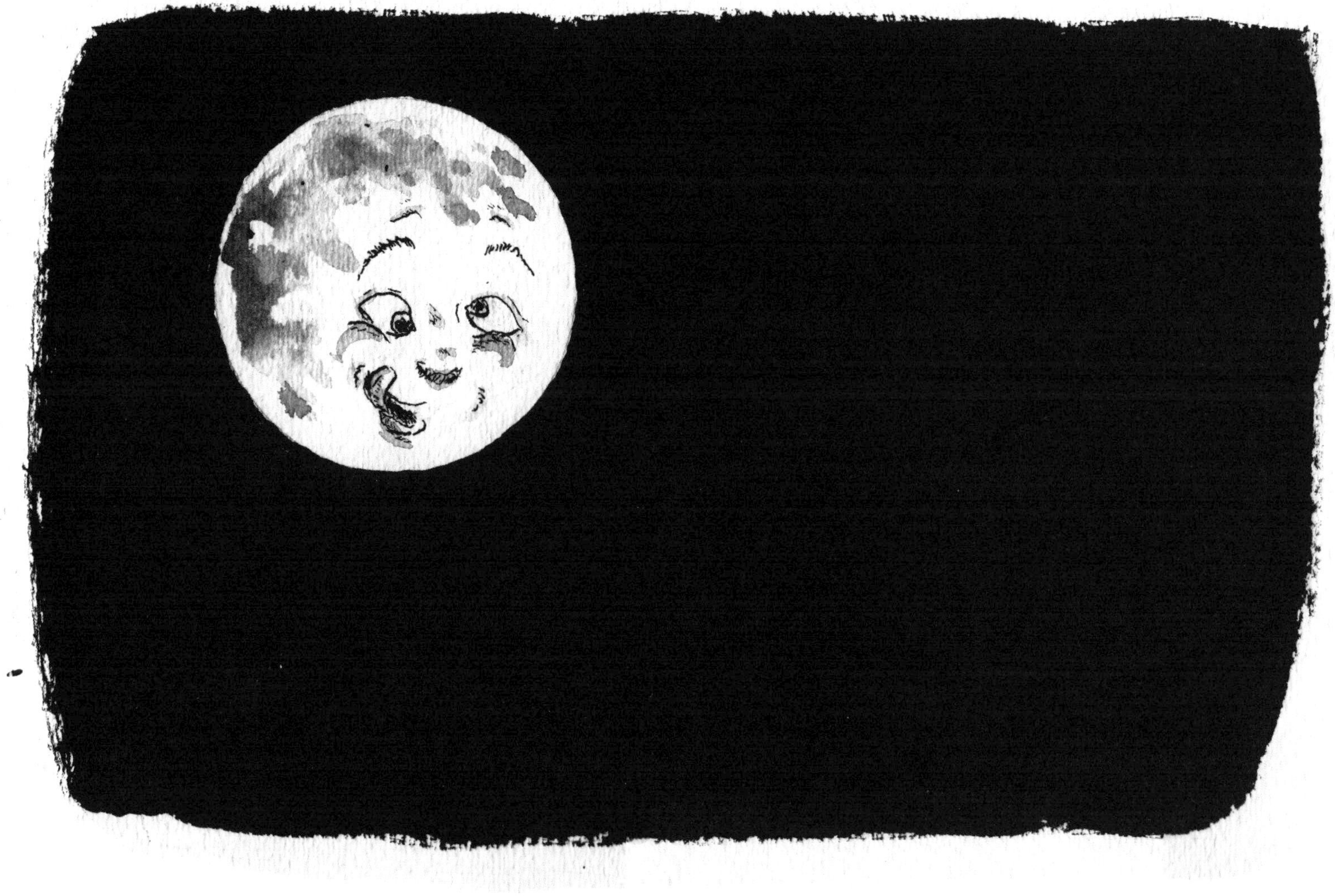

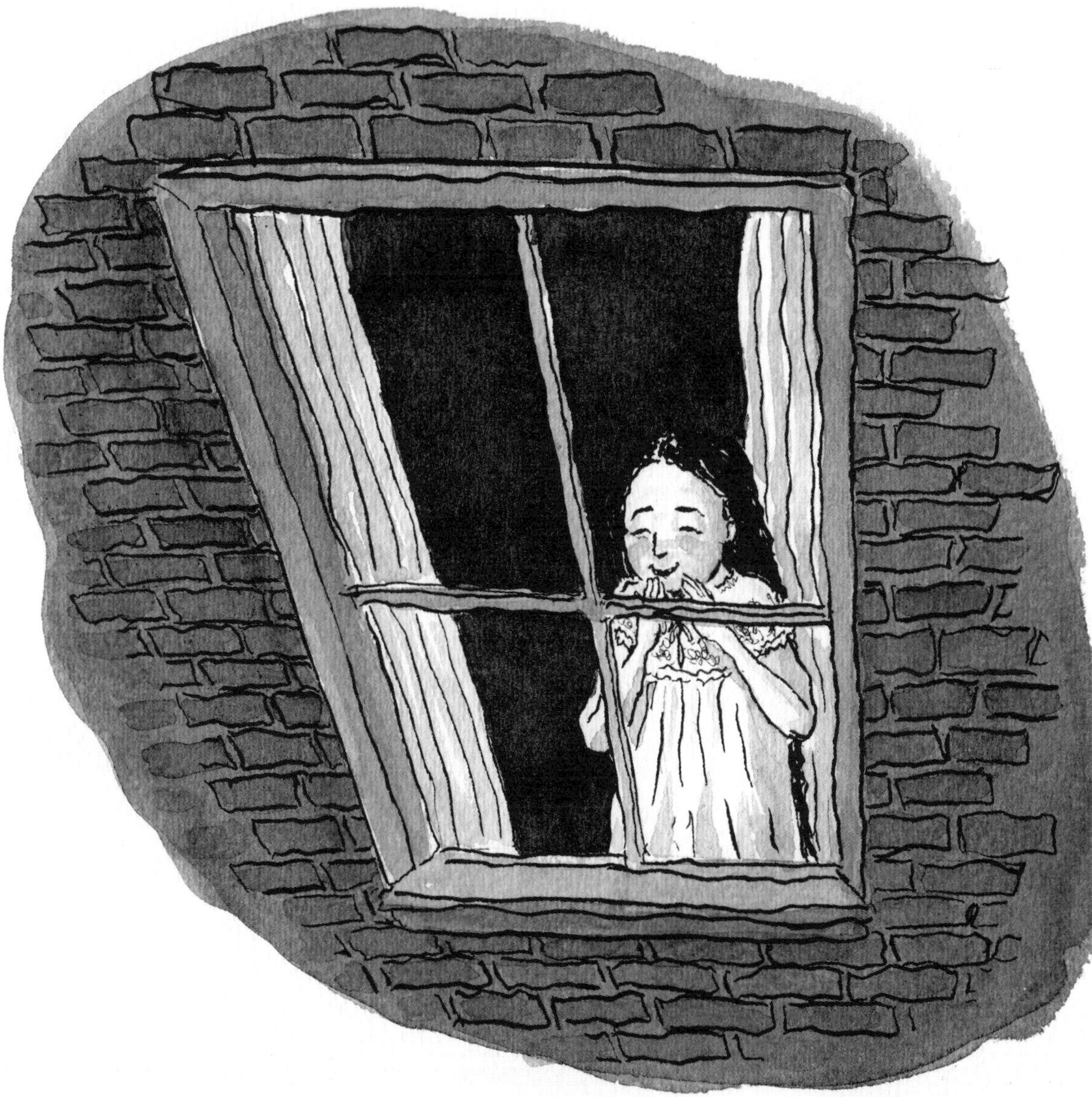

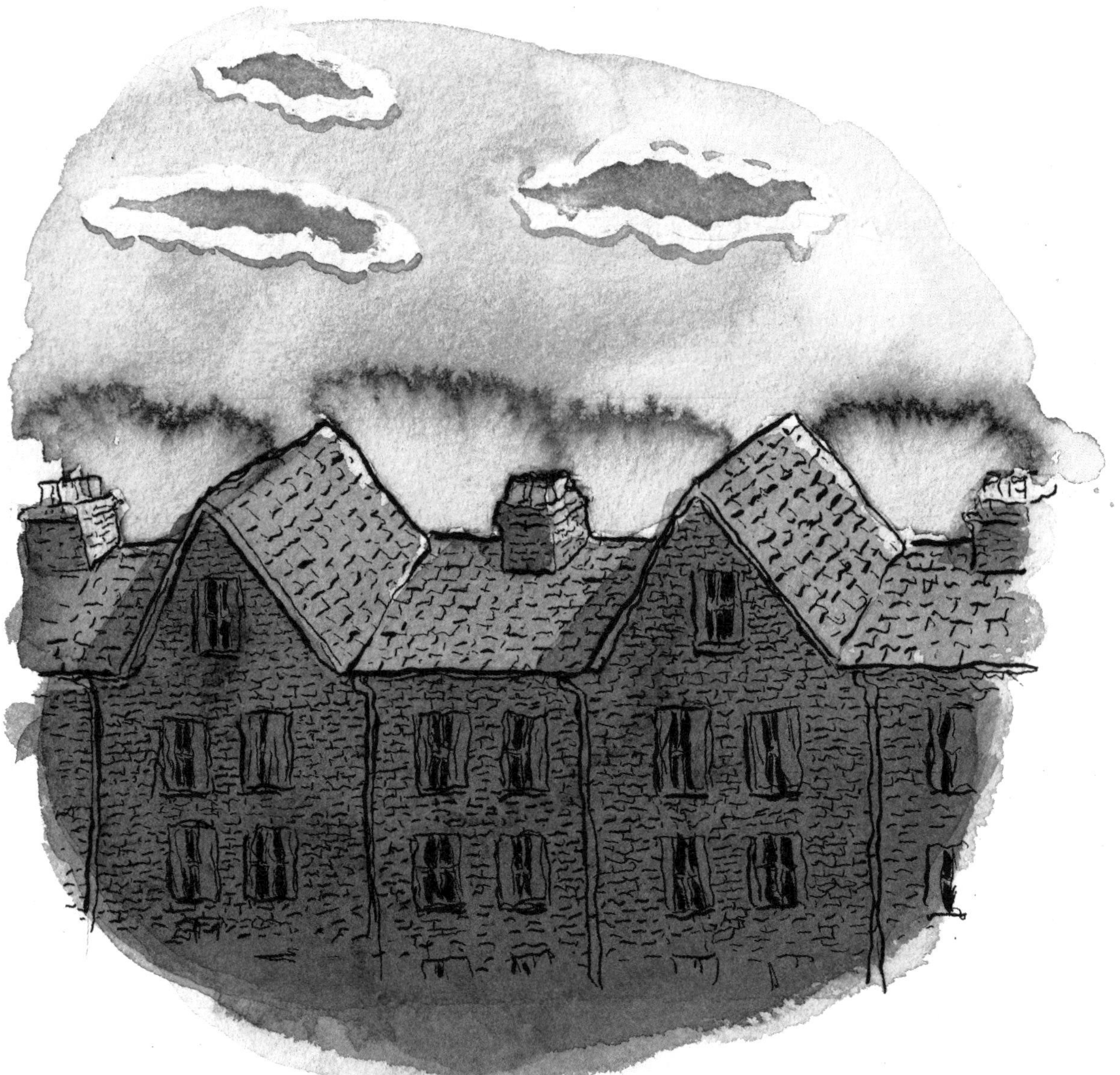

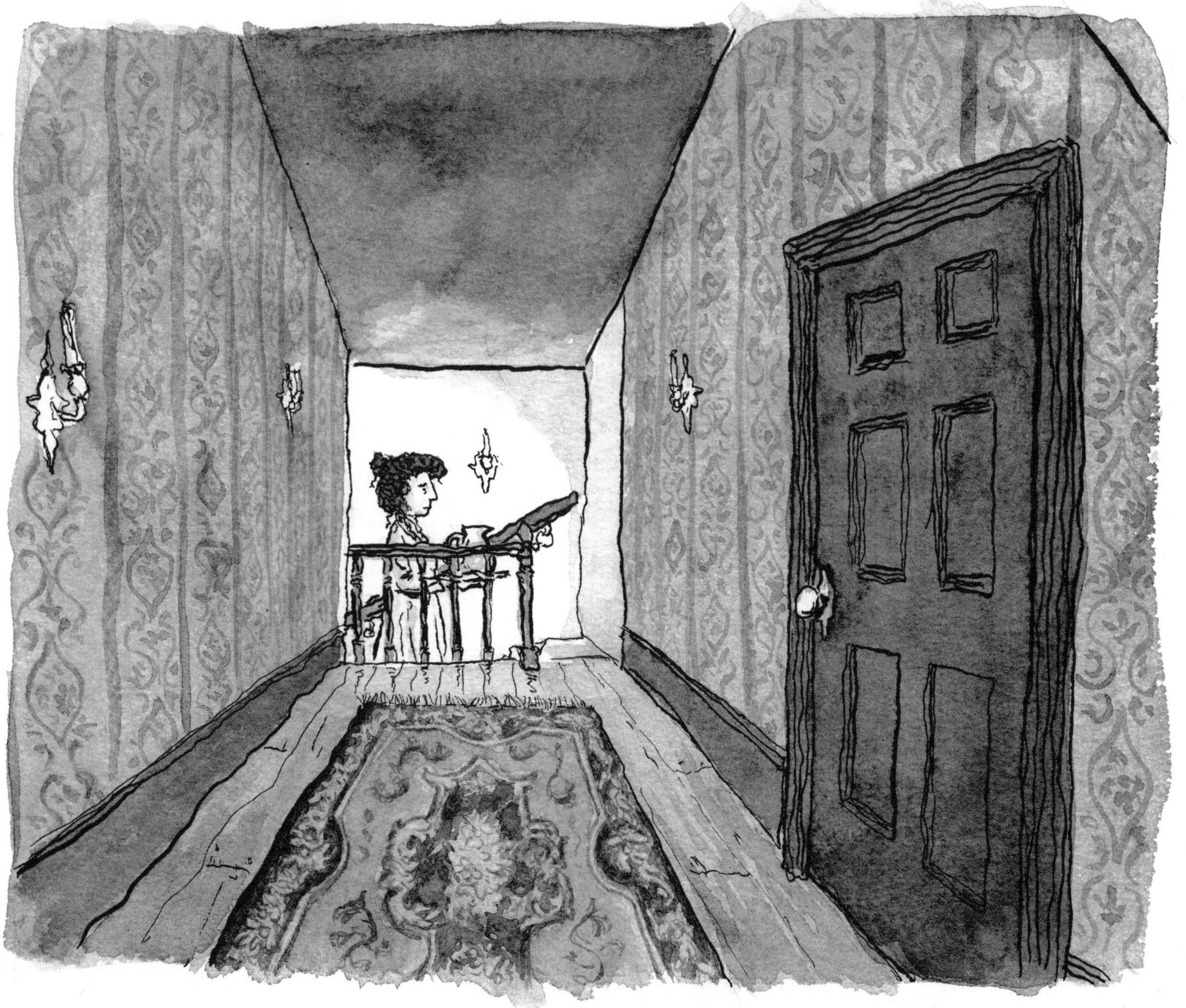

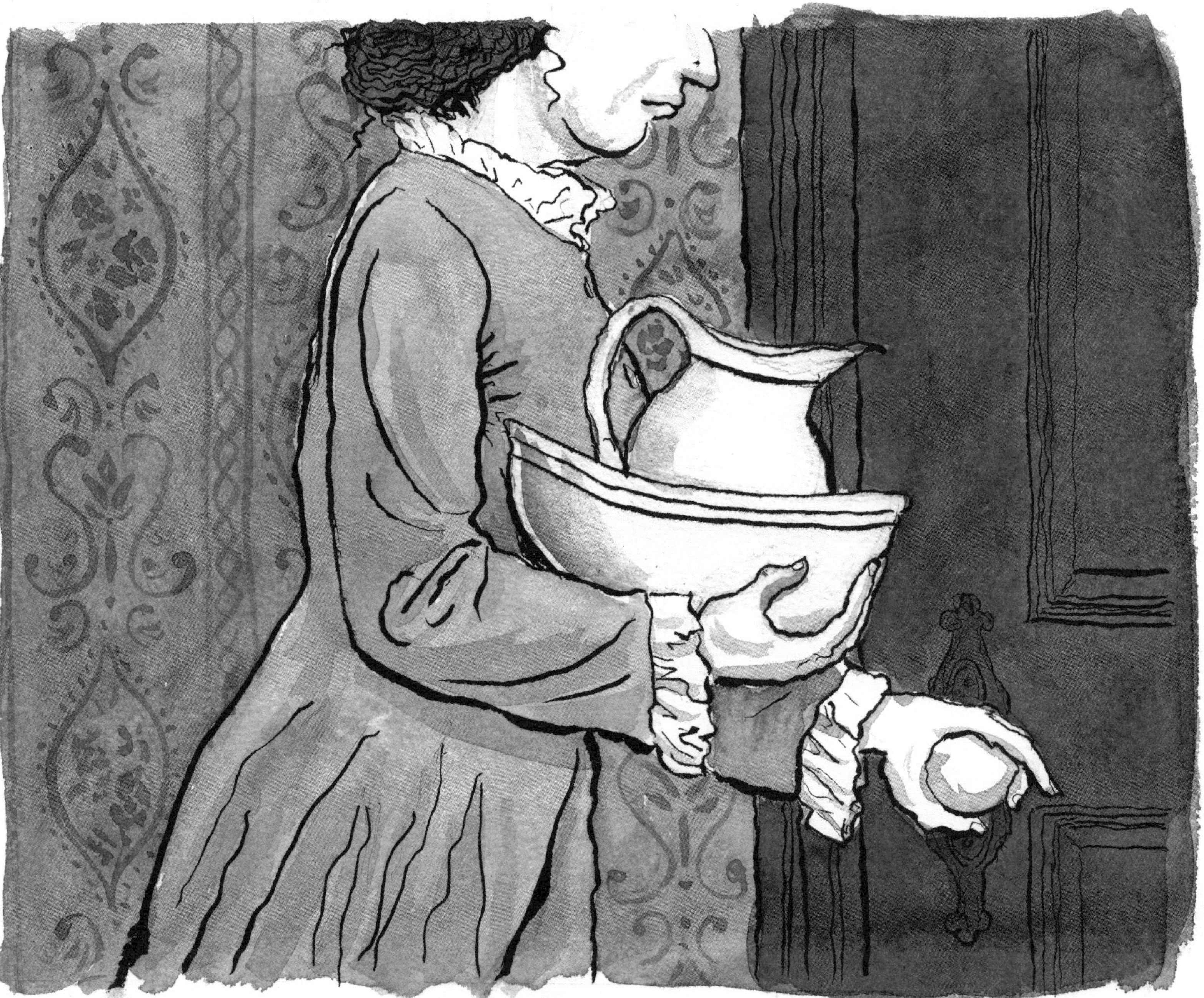

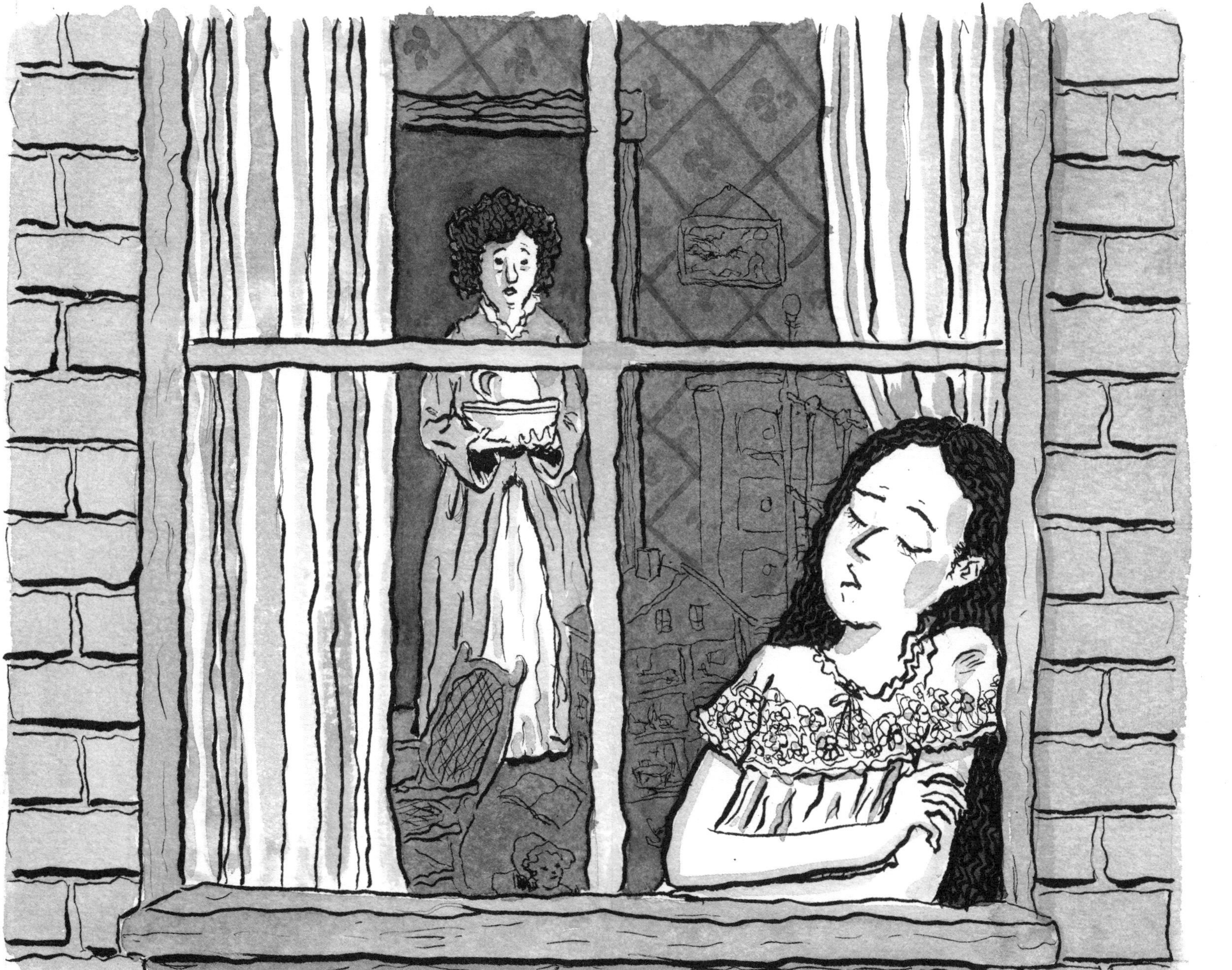

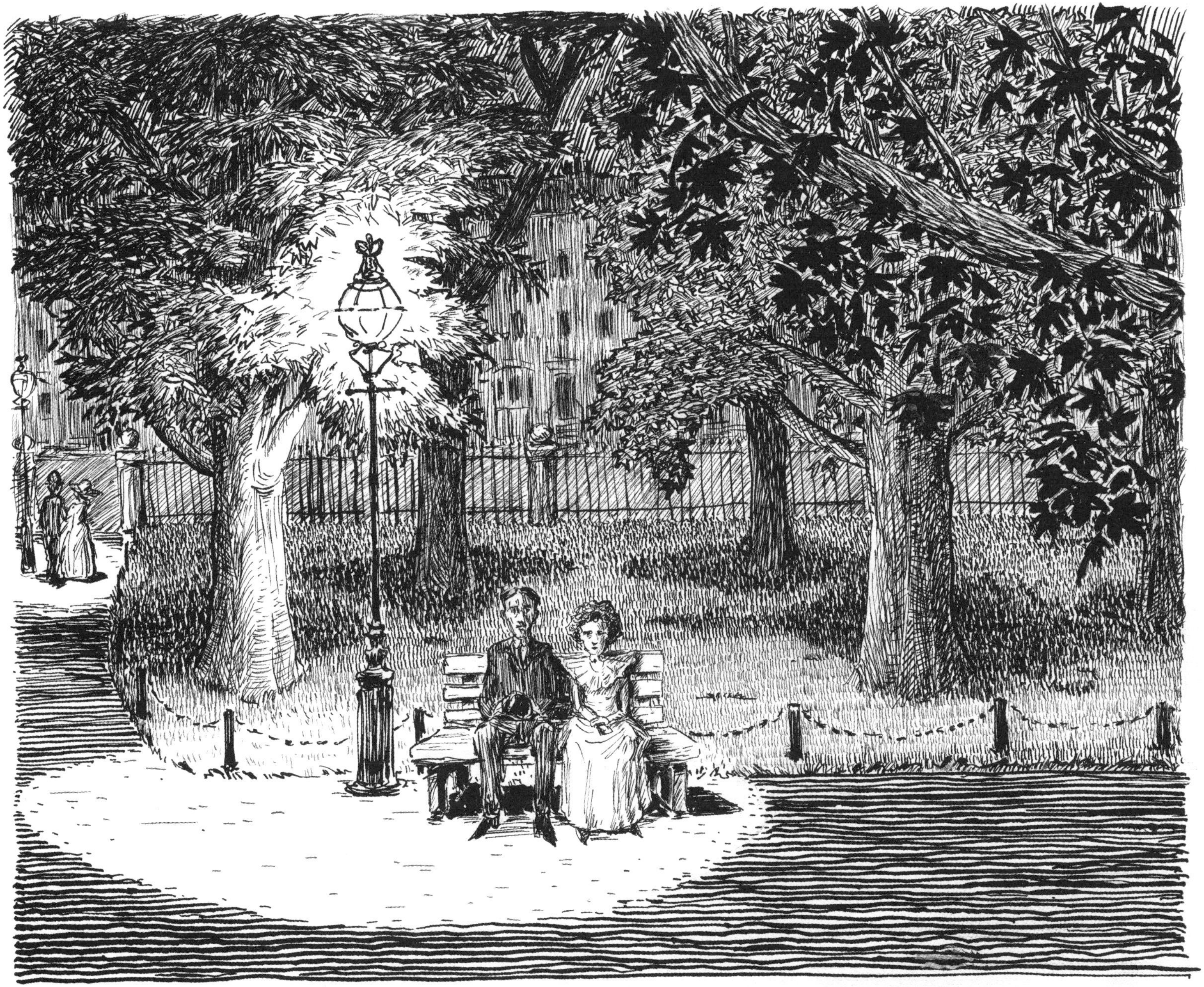

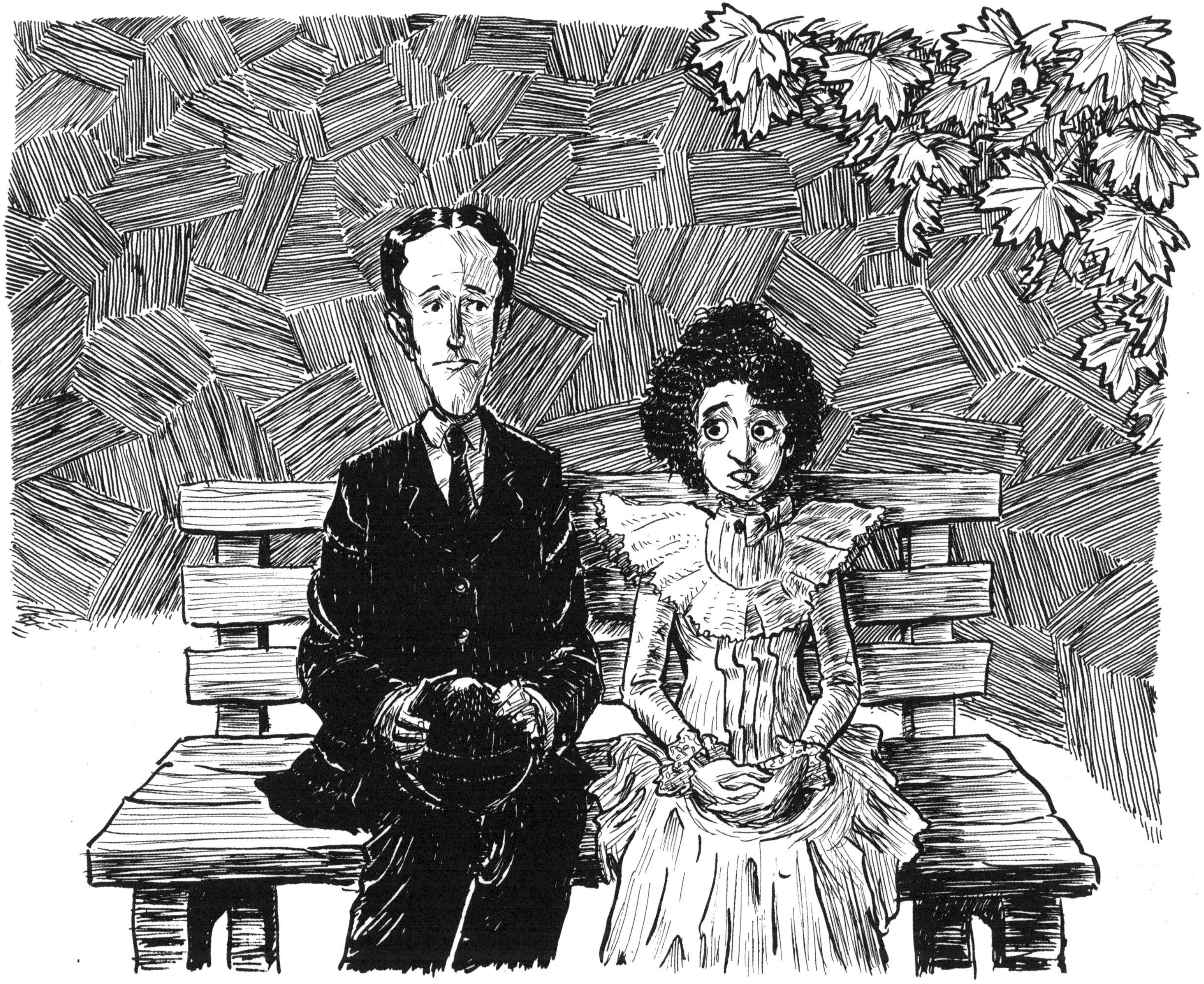

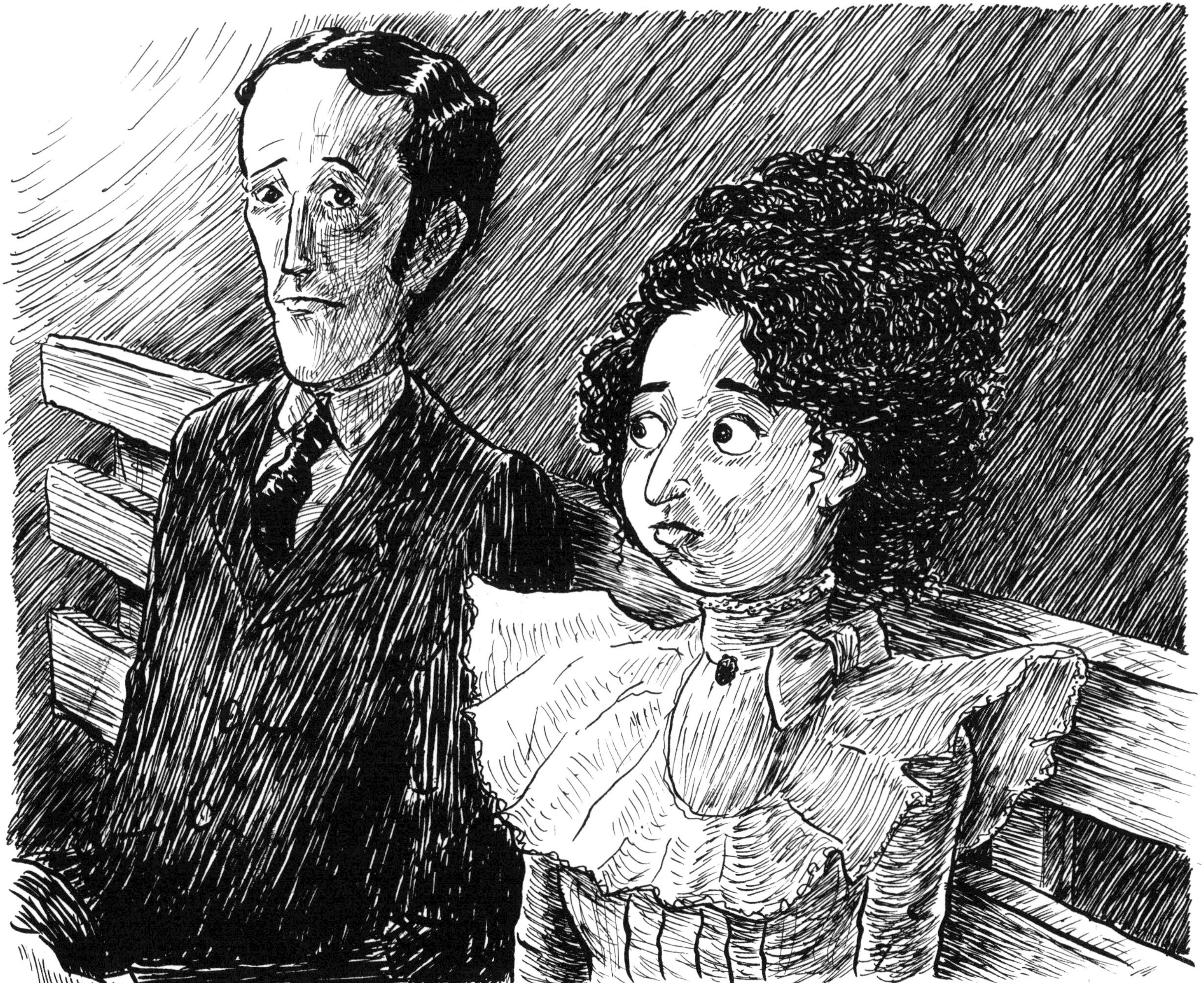

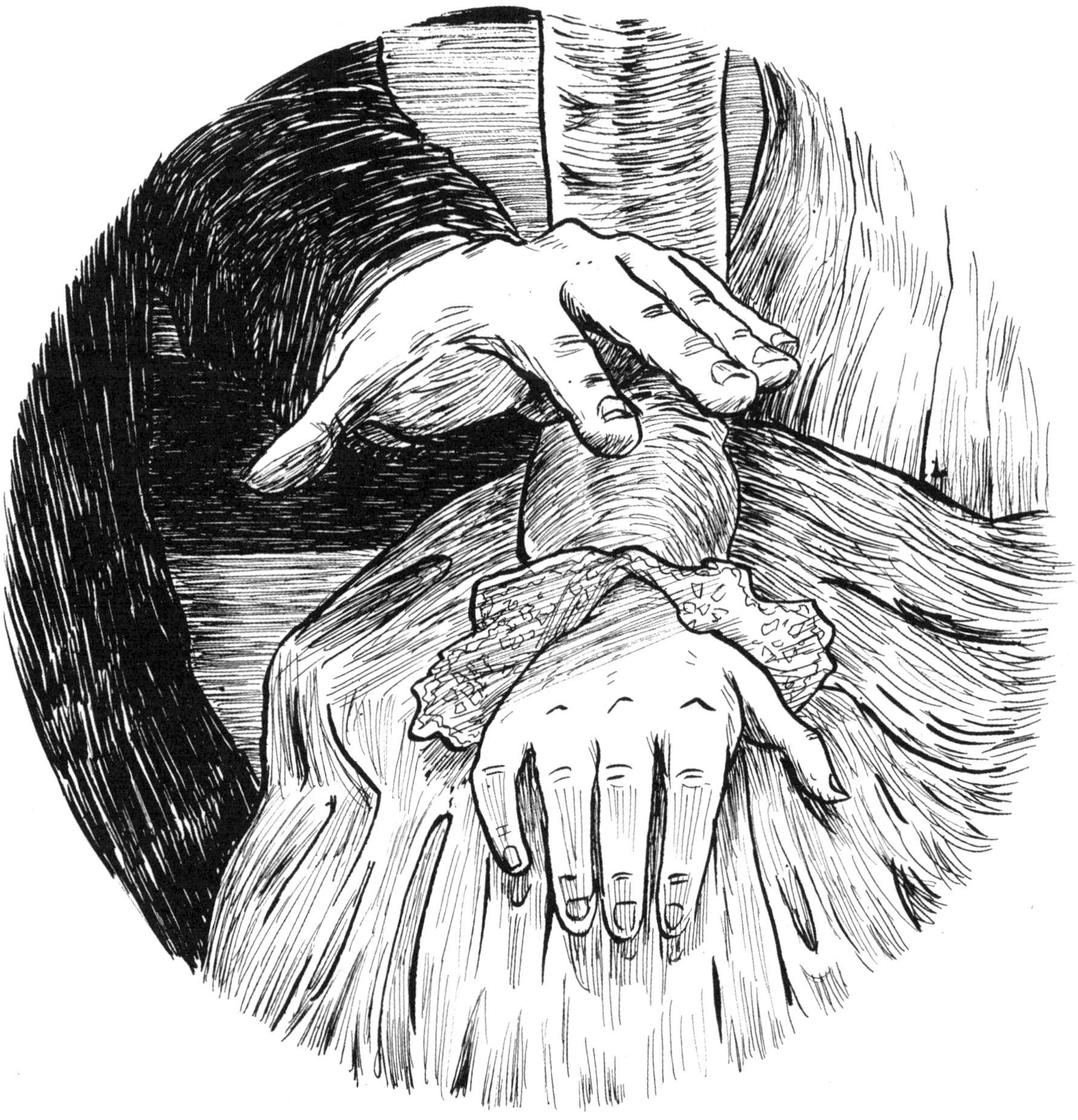

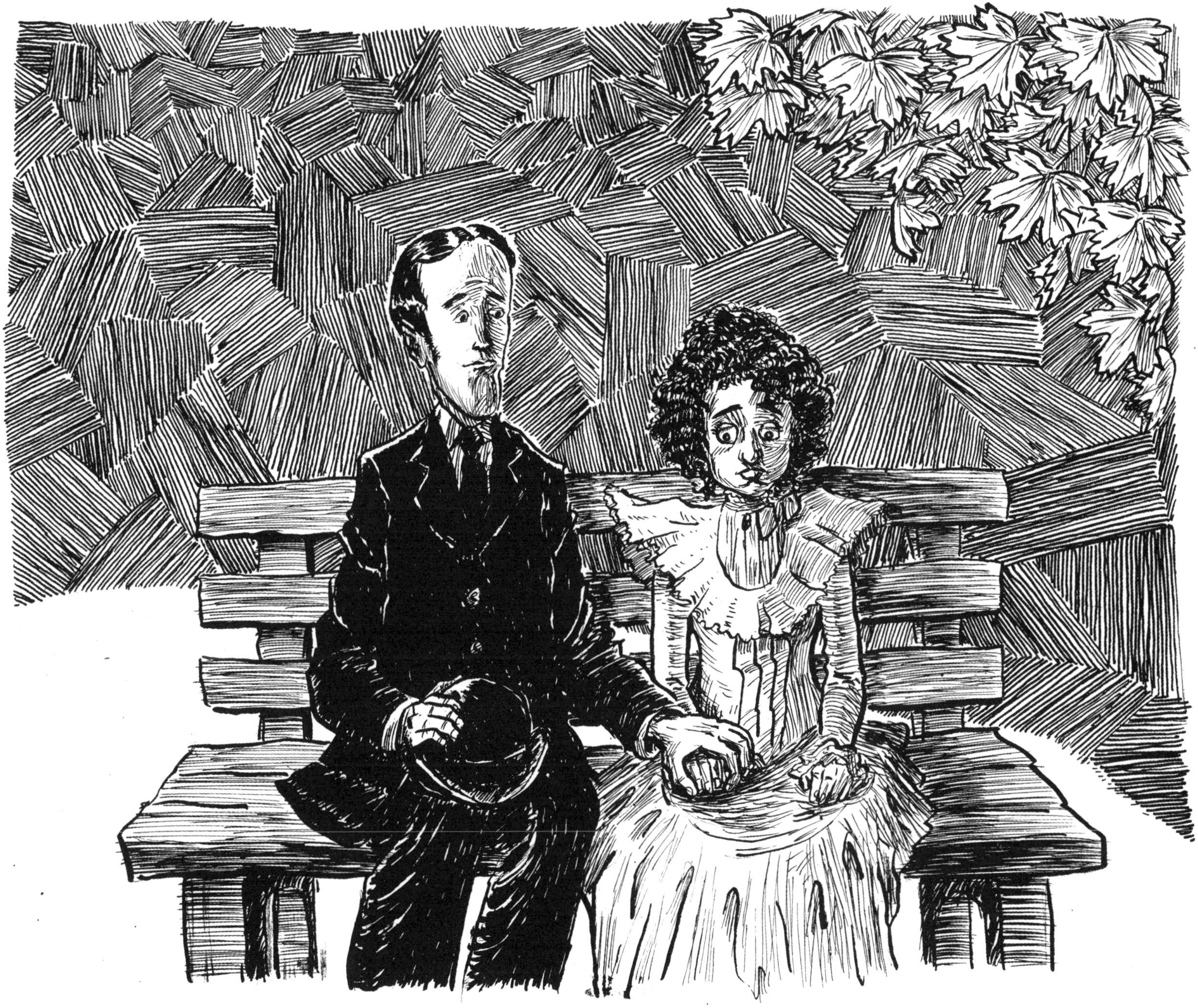

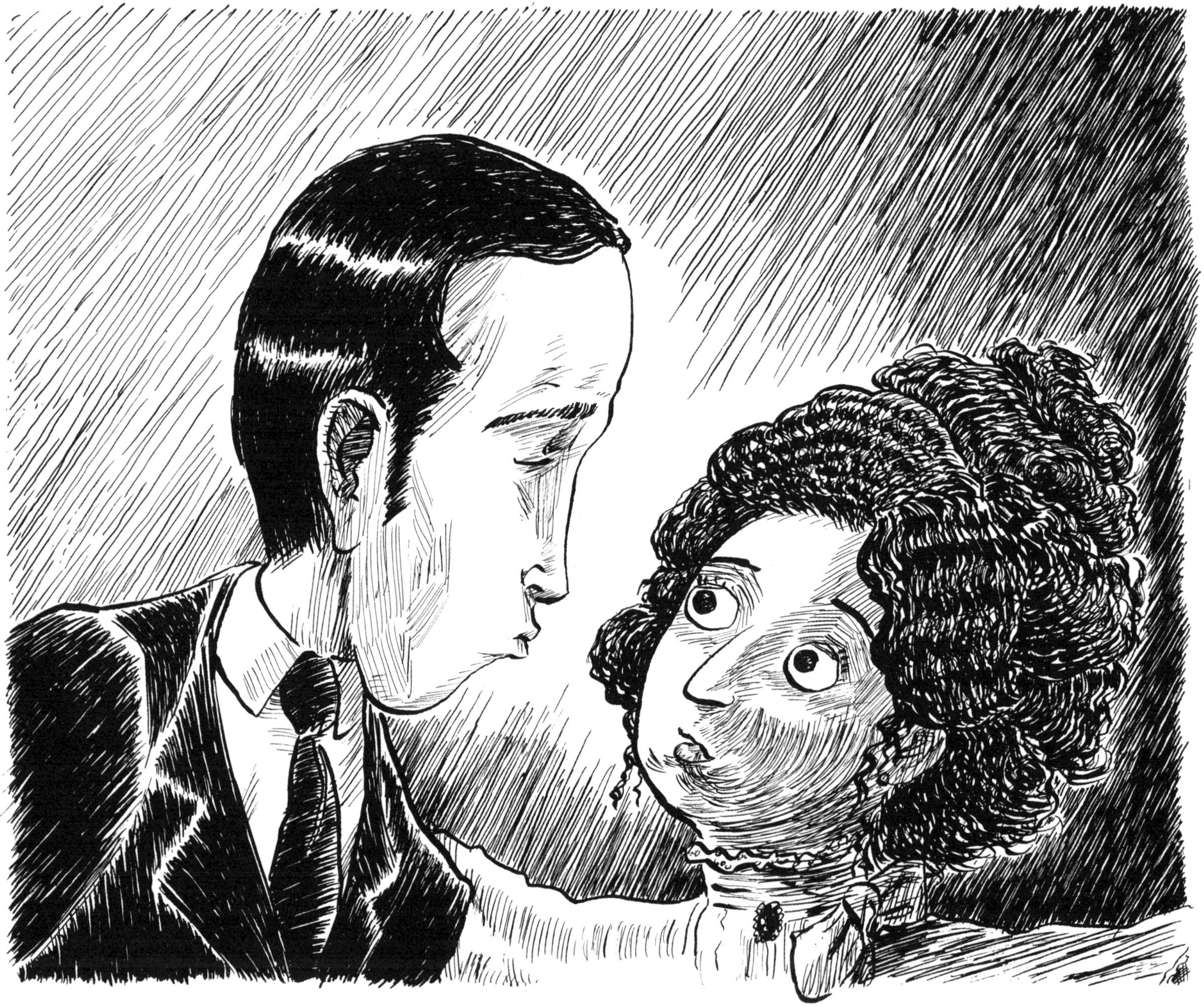

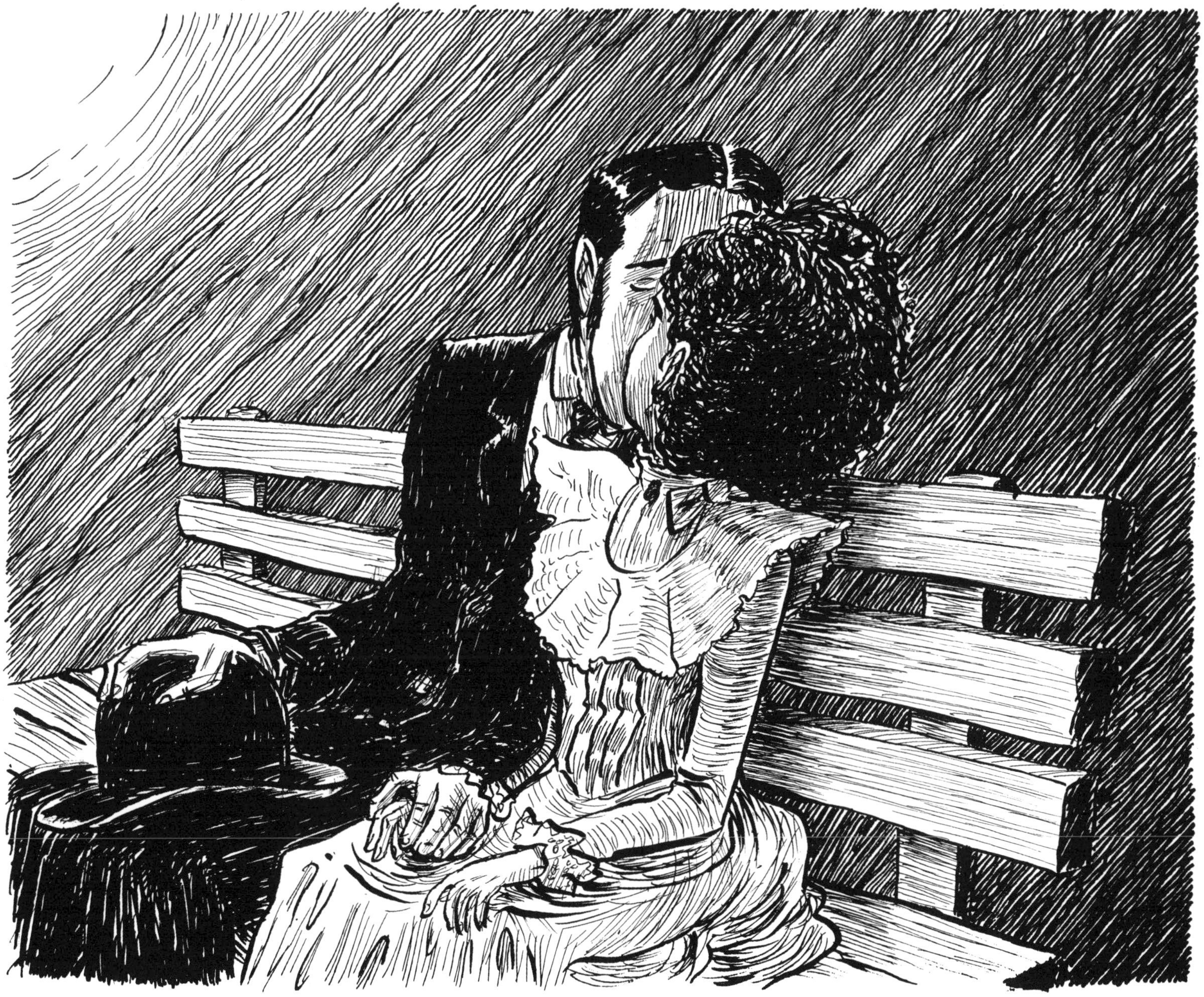

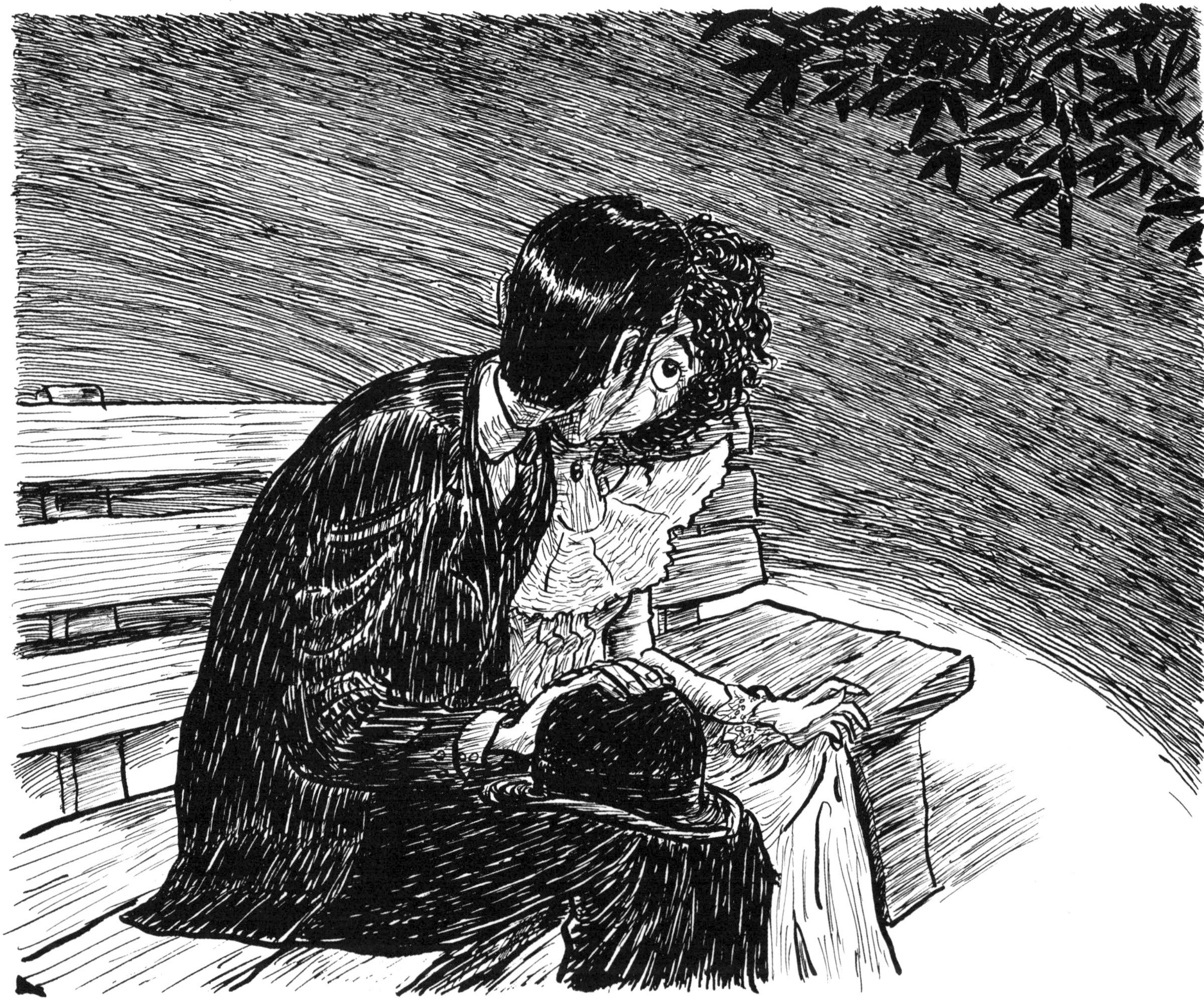

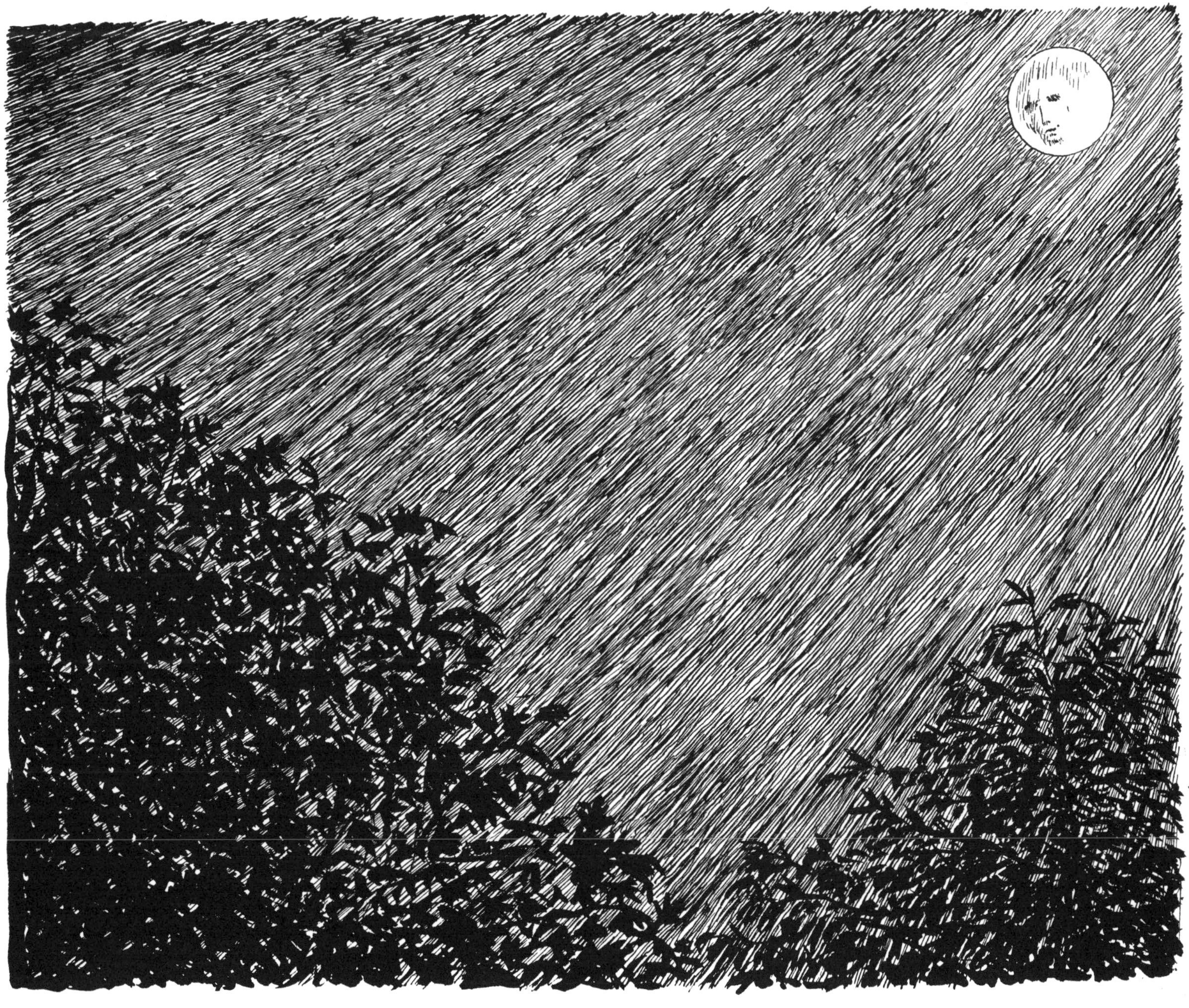

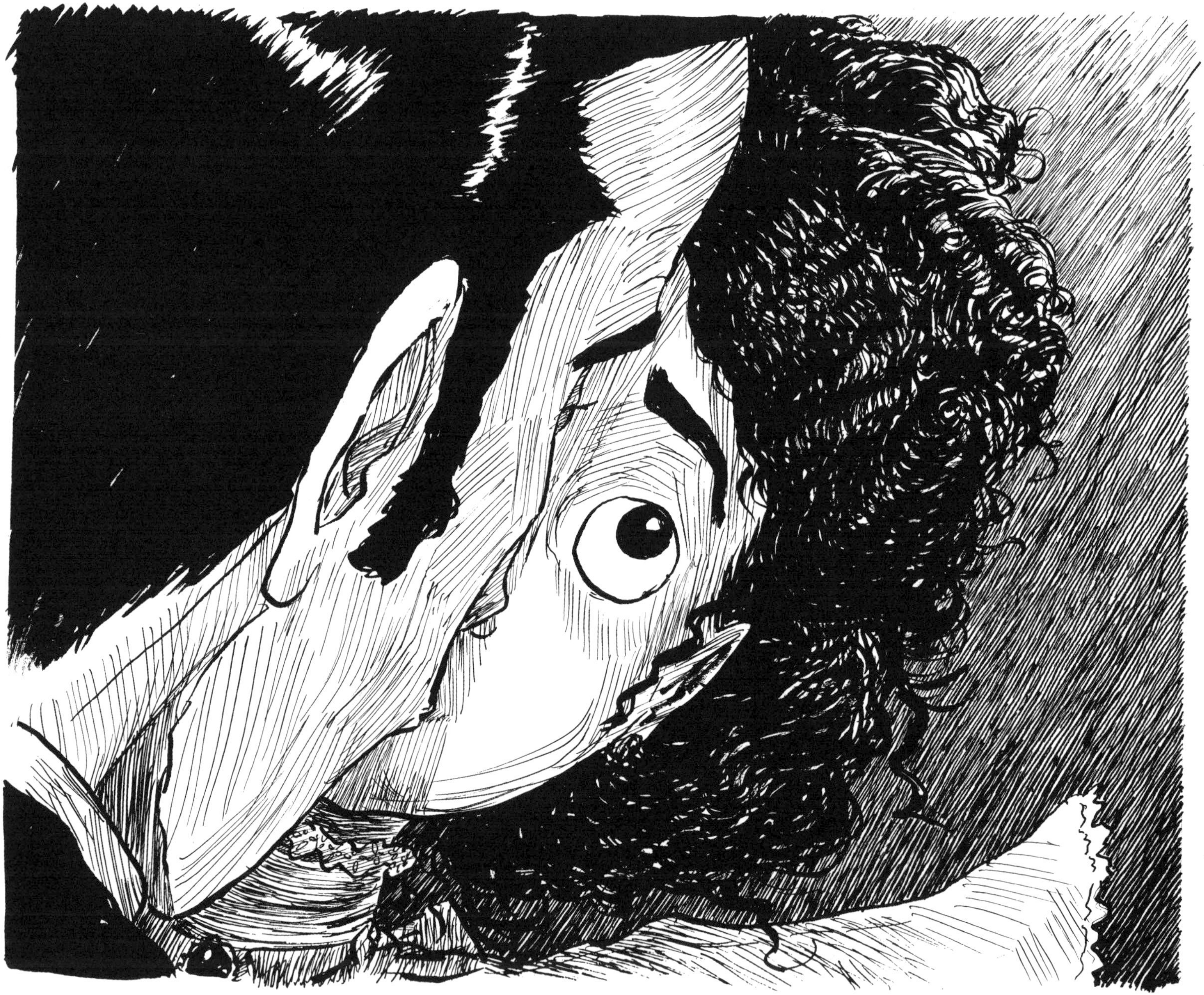

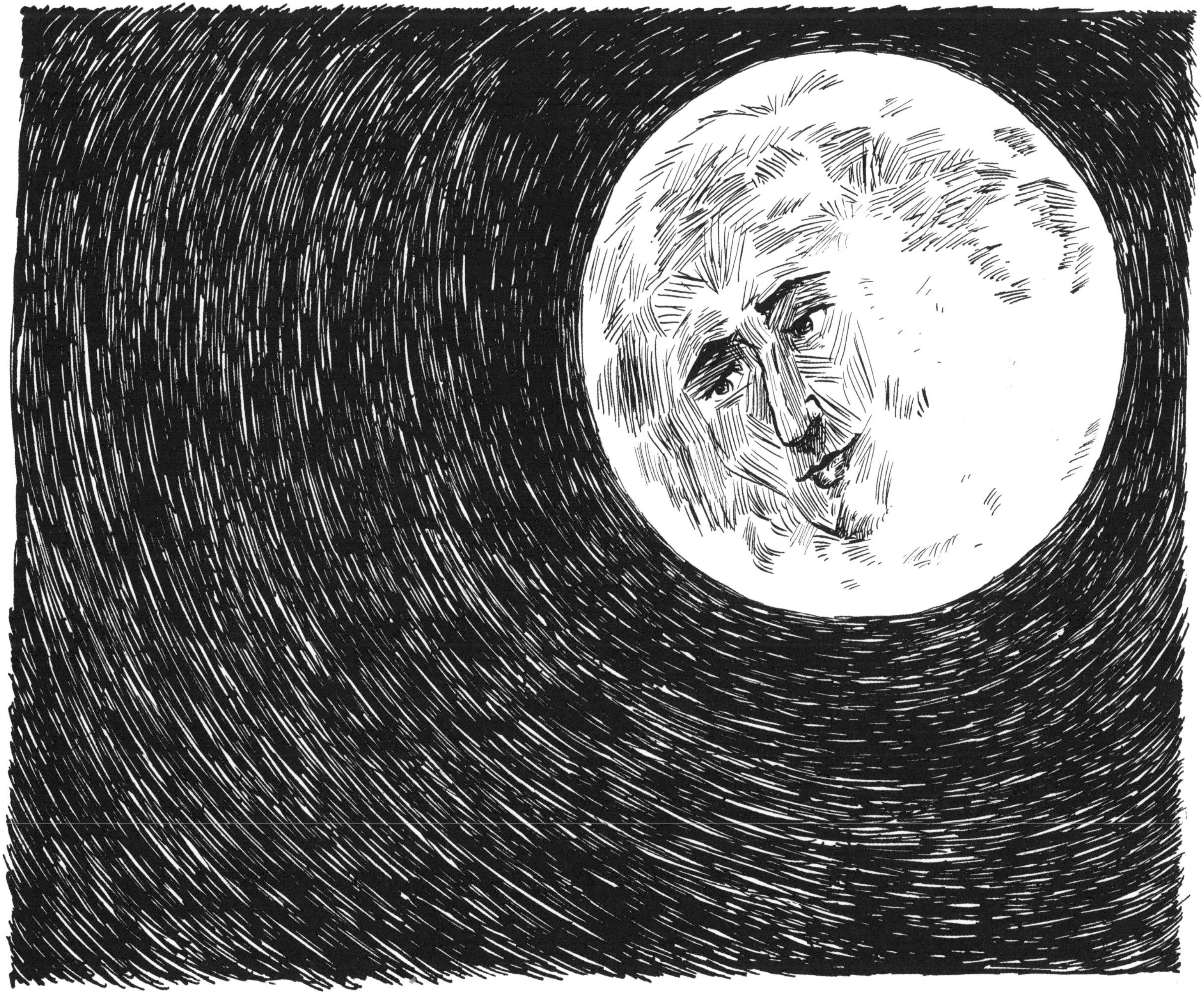

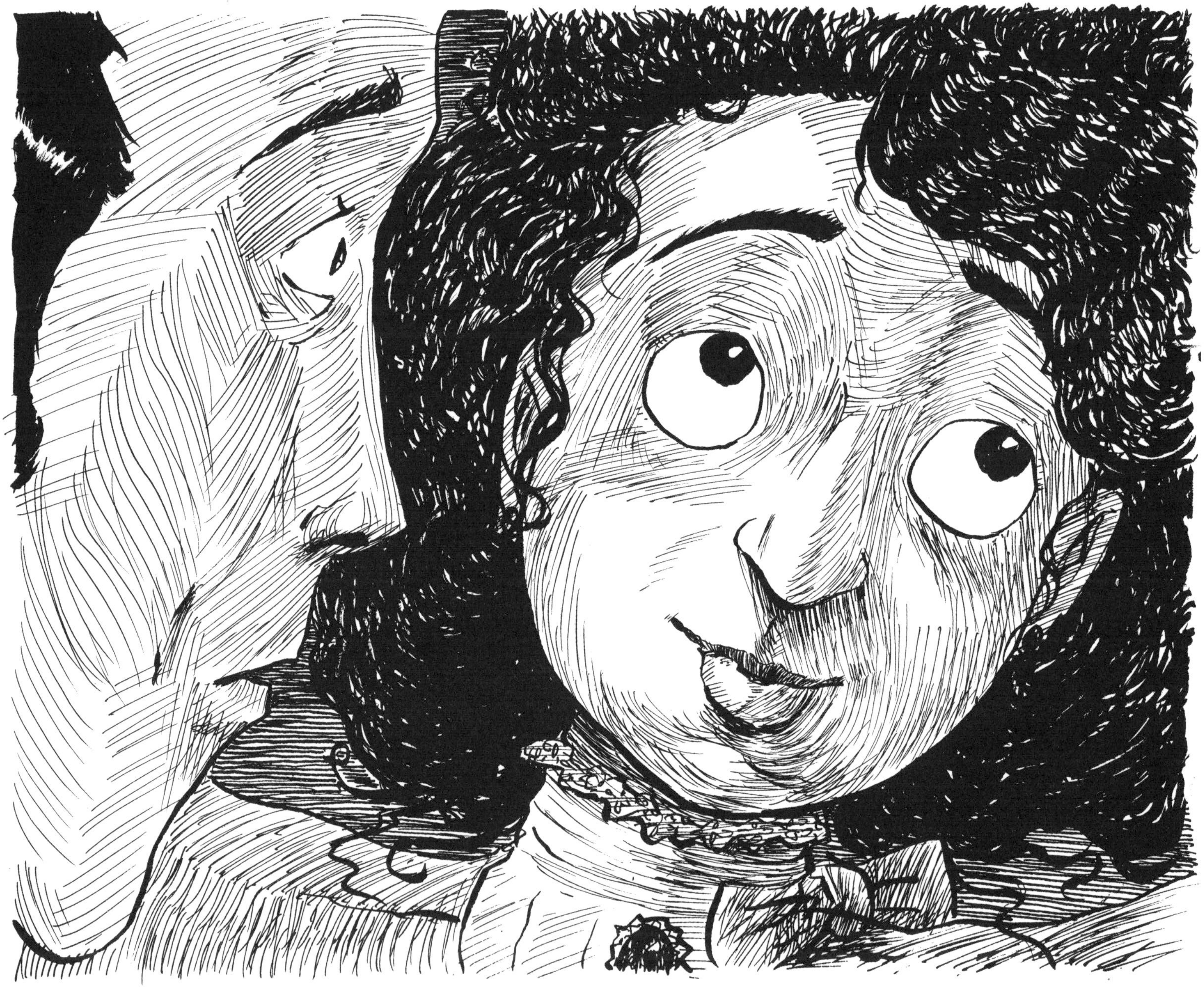

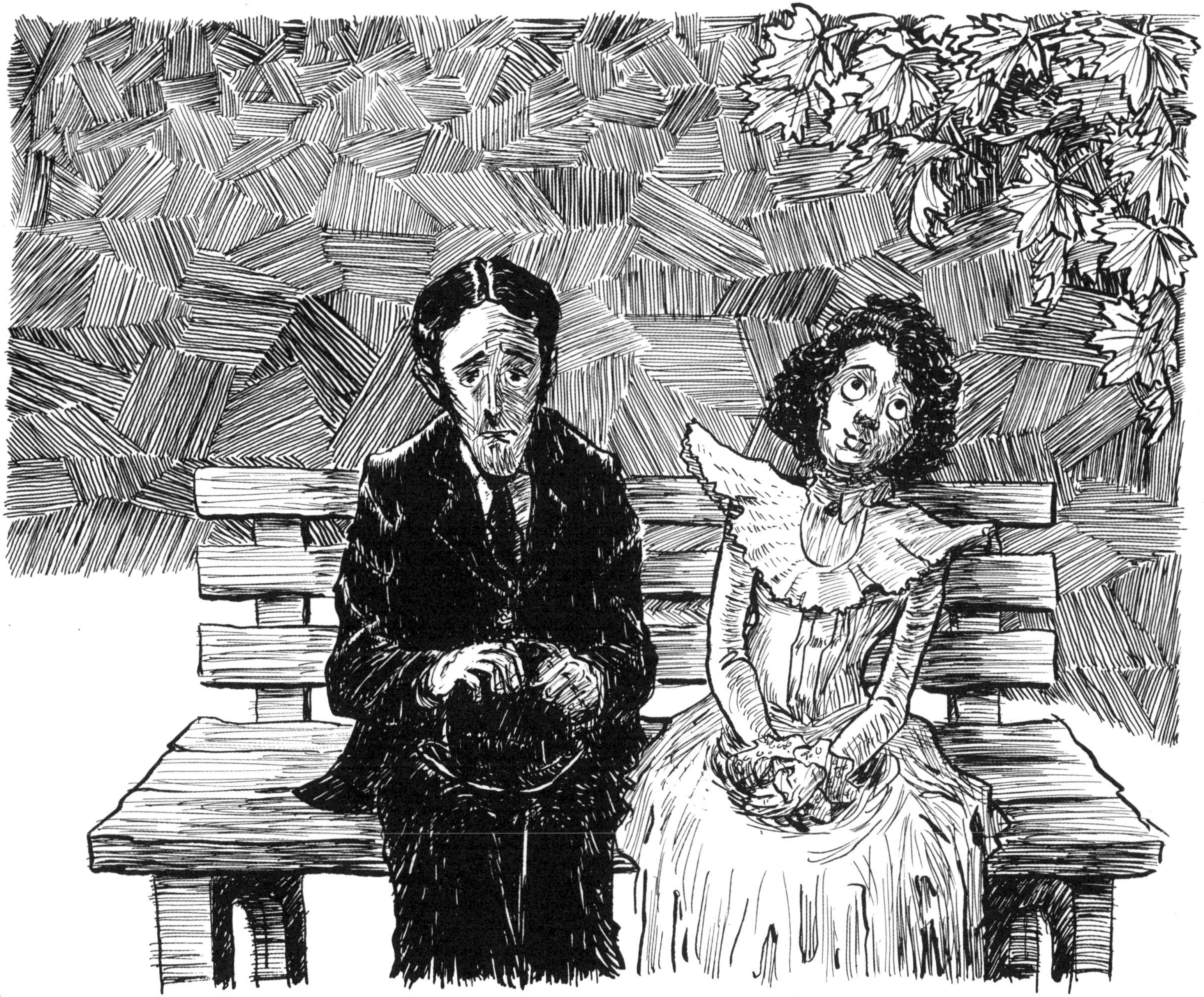

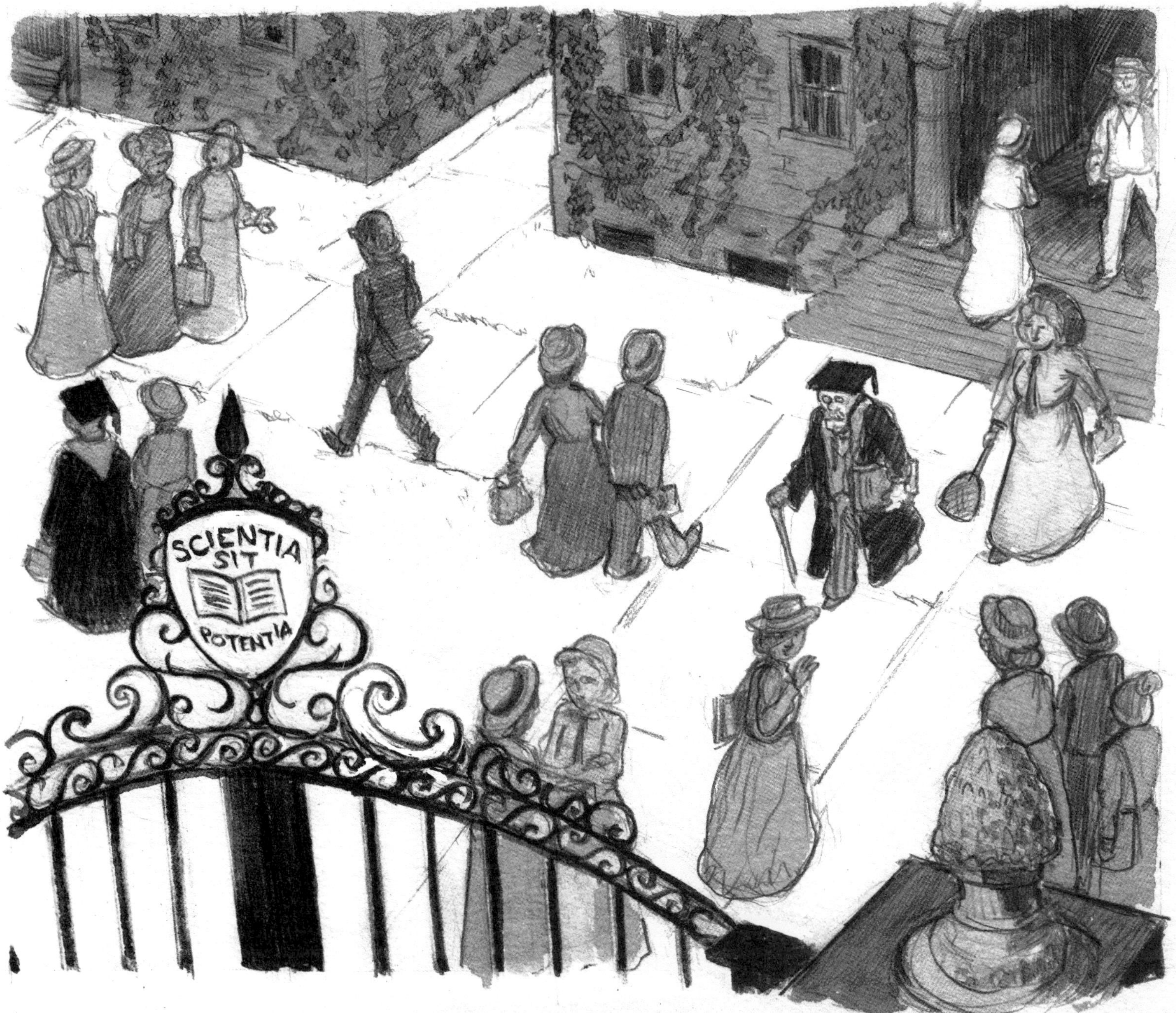
SCIENTIA SIT POTENTIA

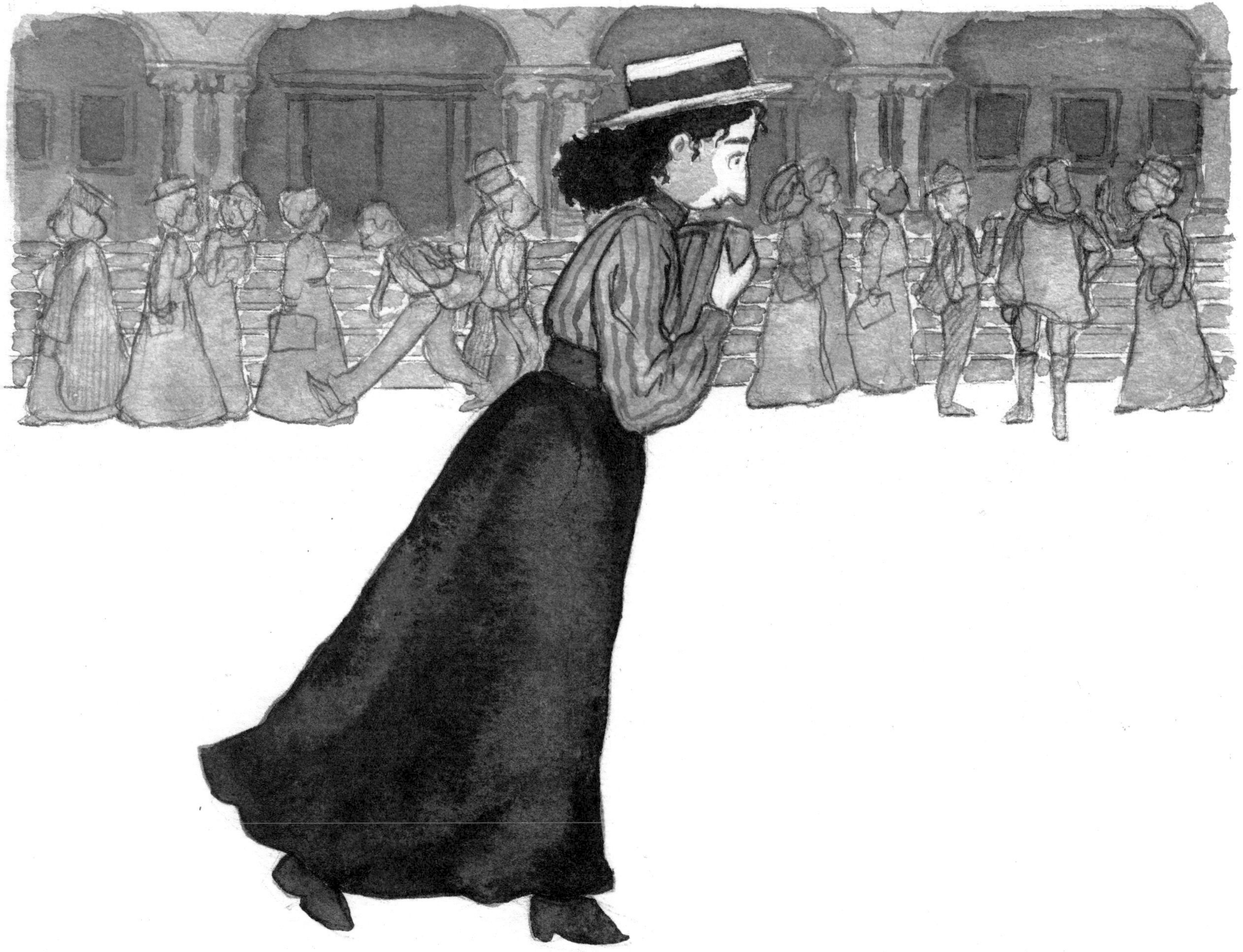

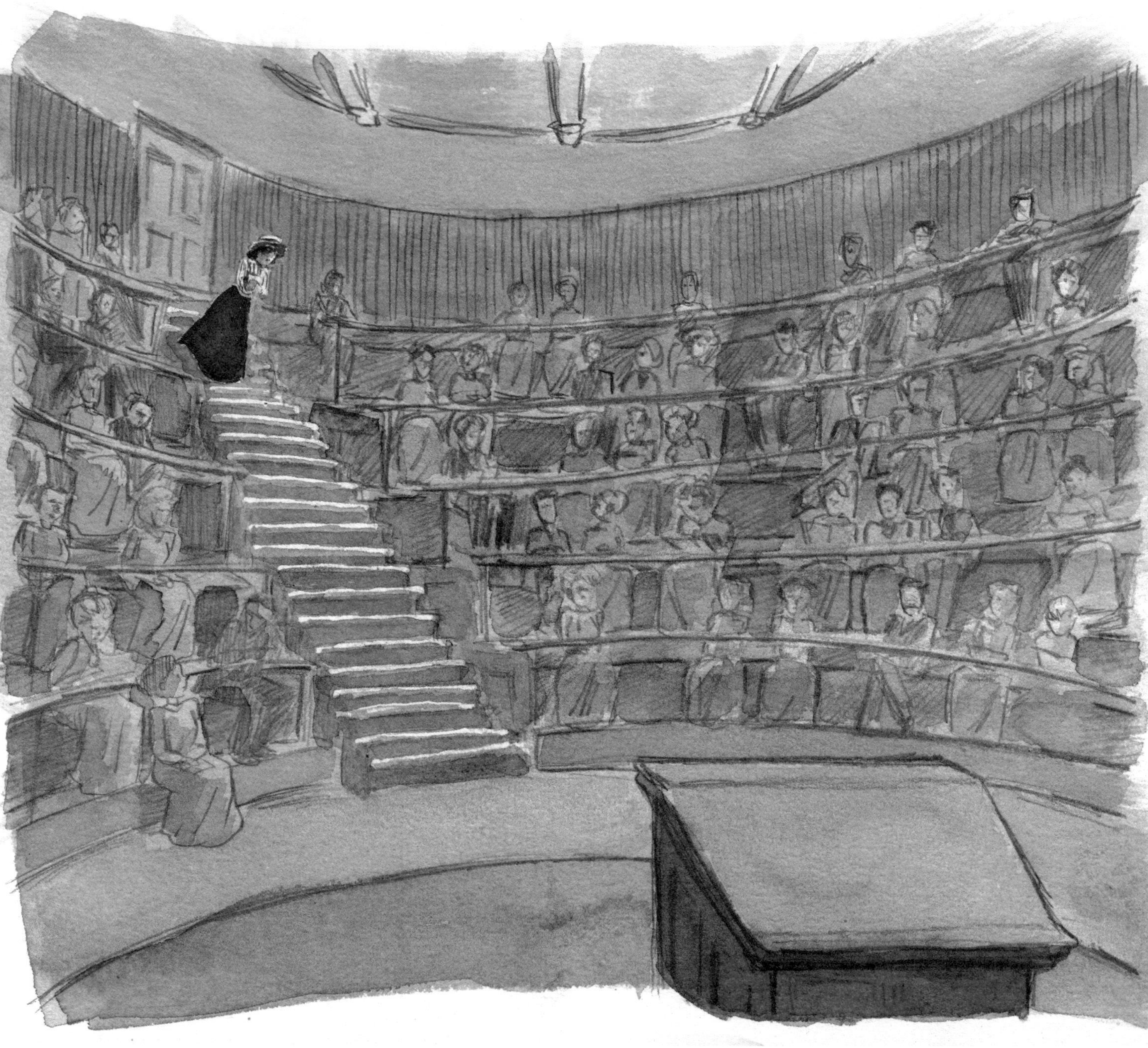

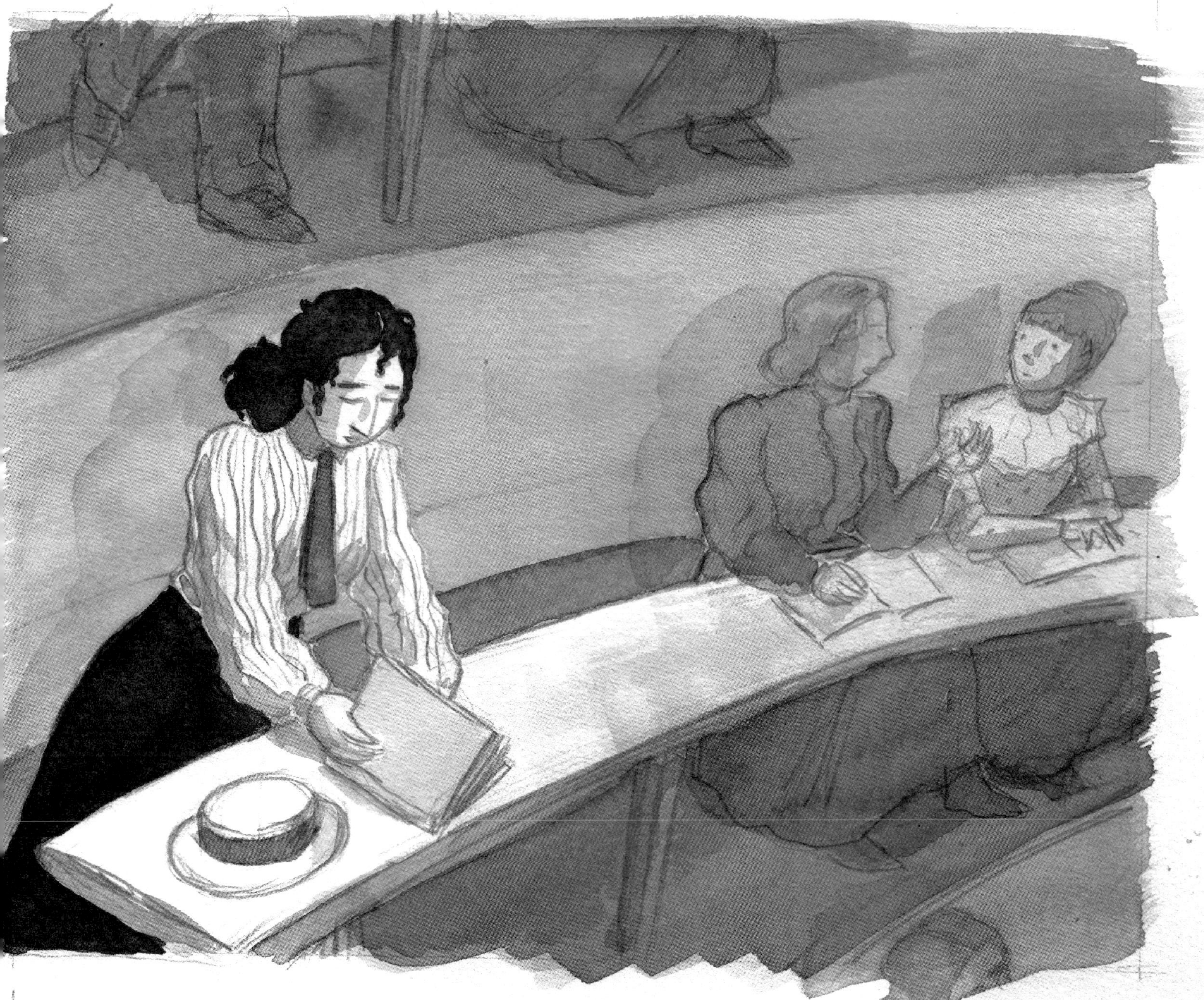

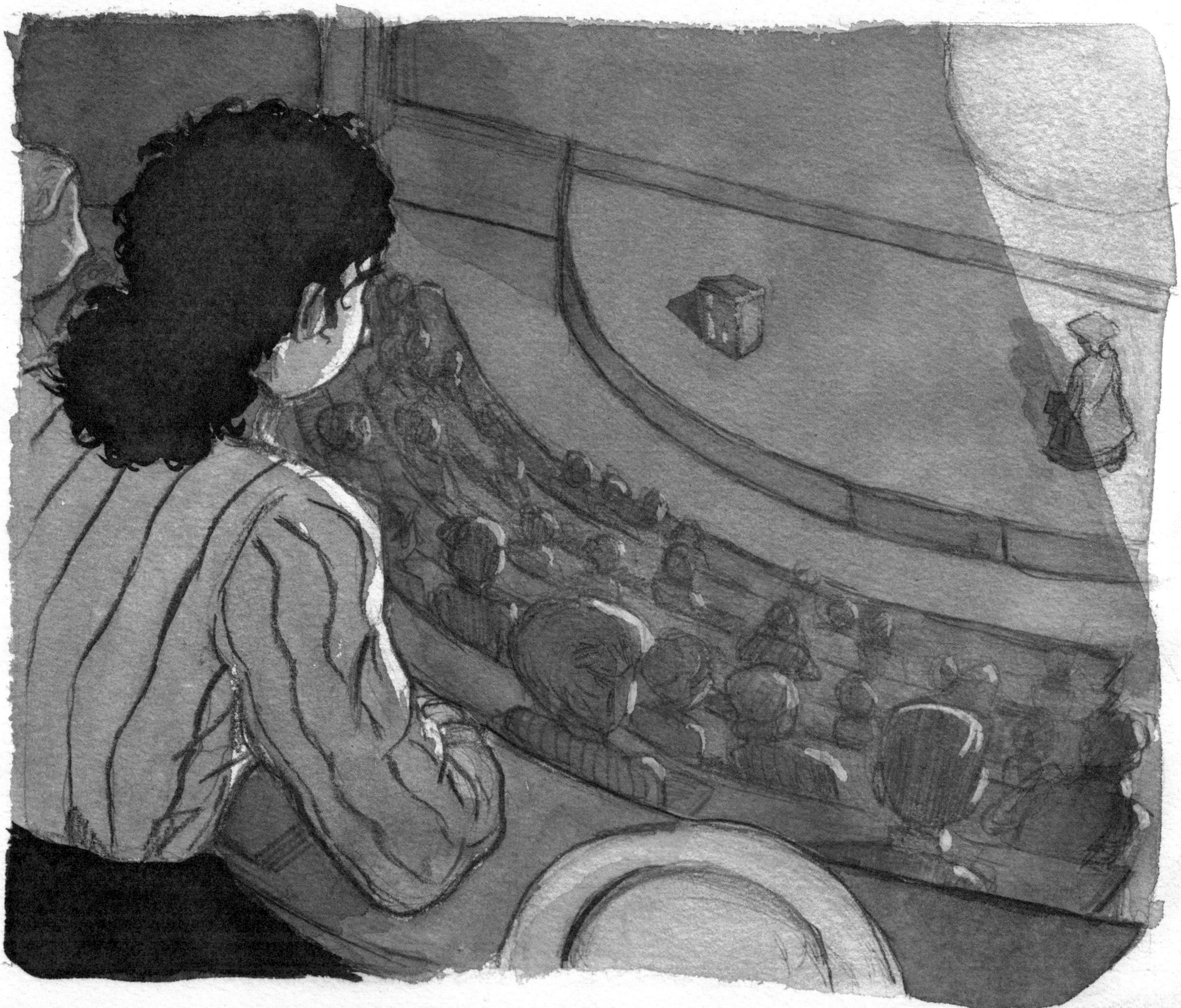

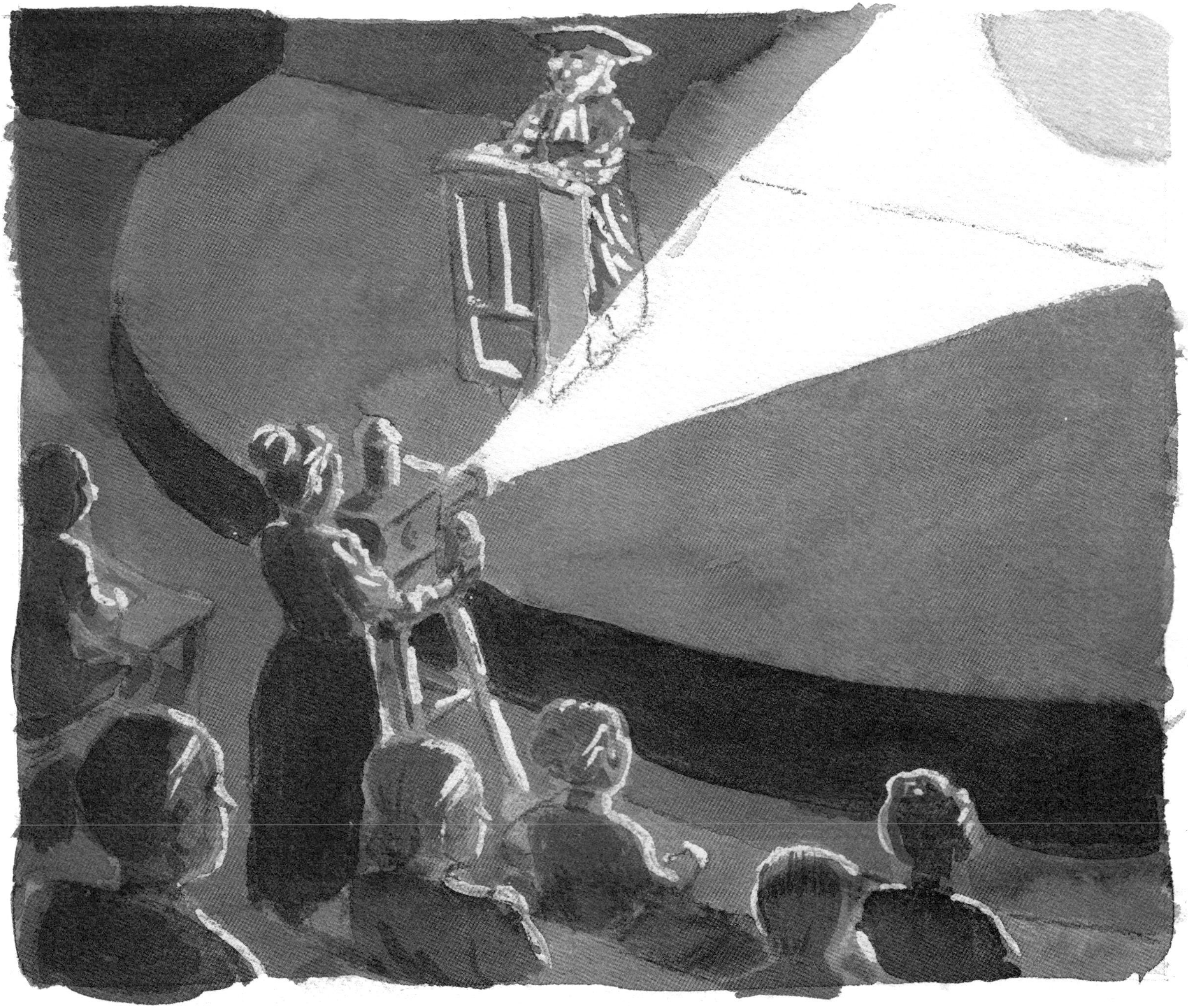

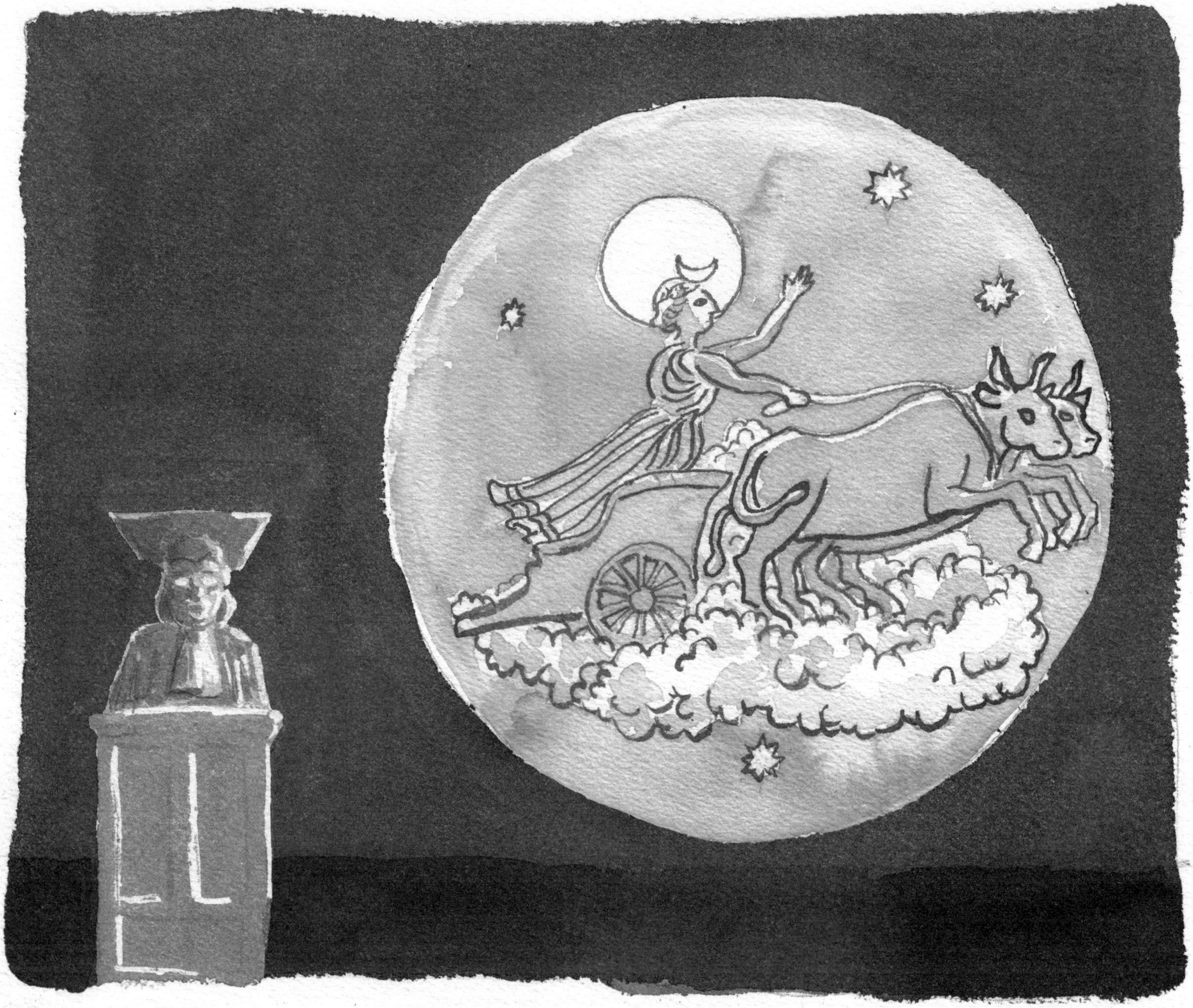

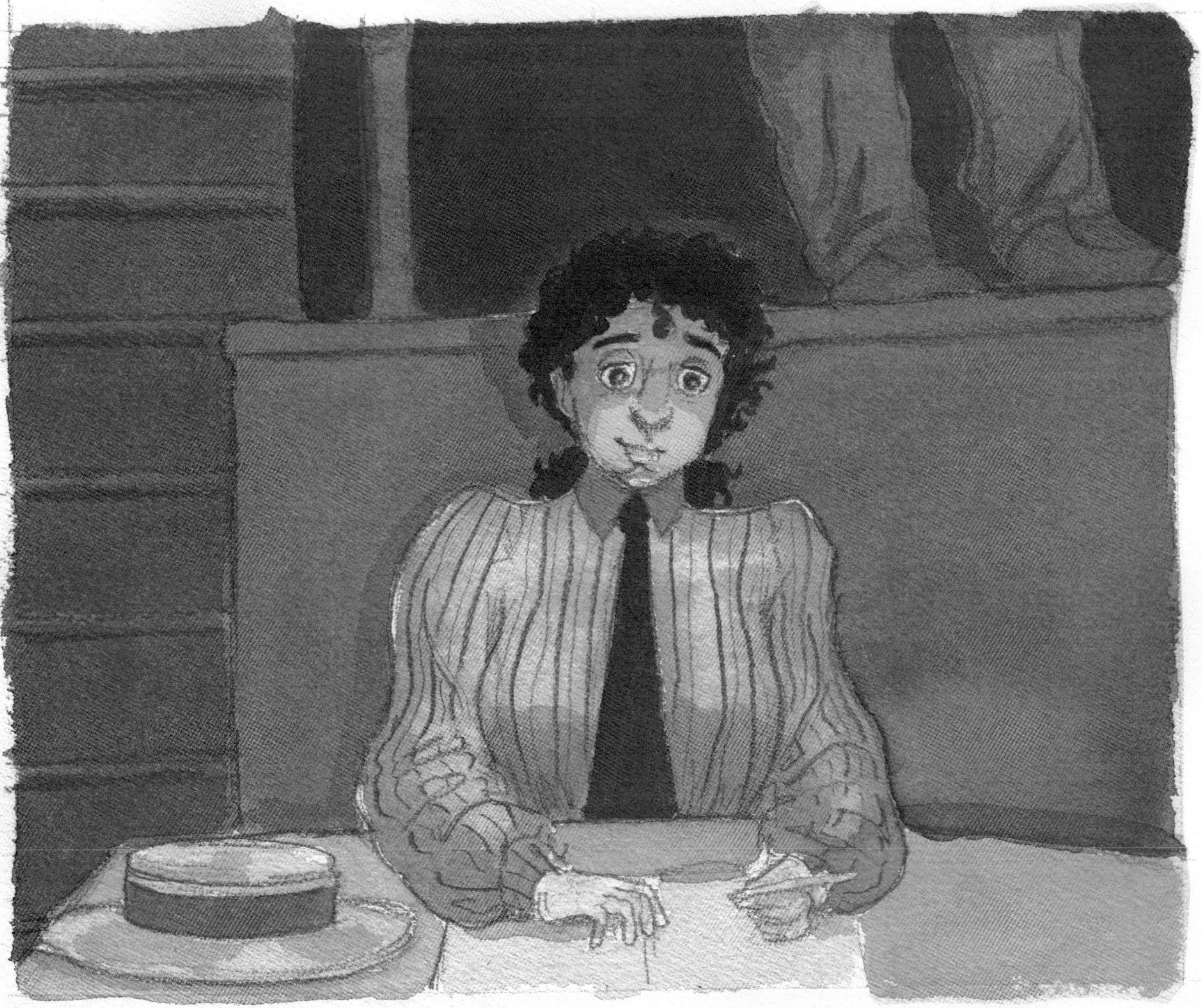

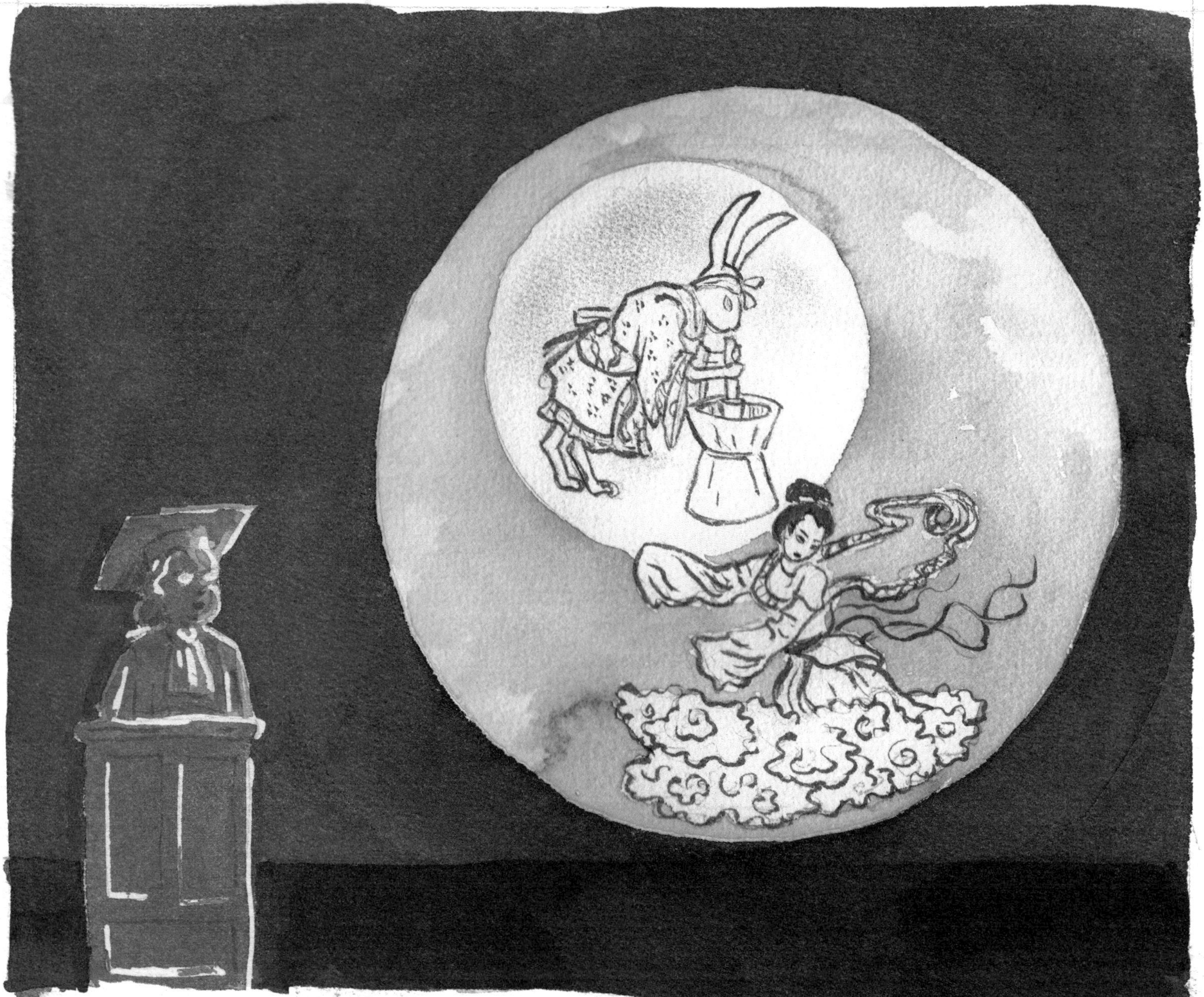

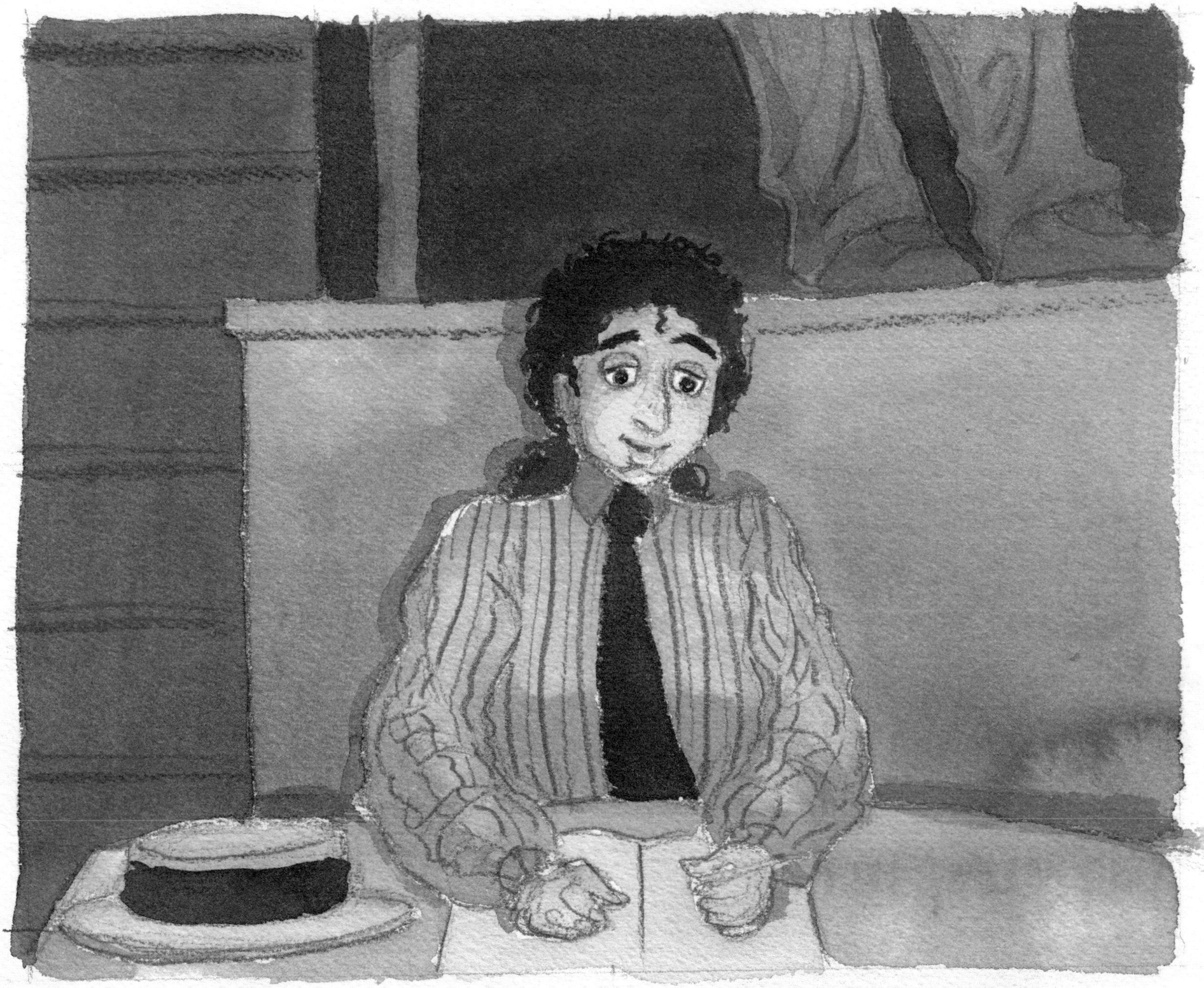

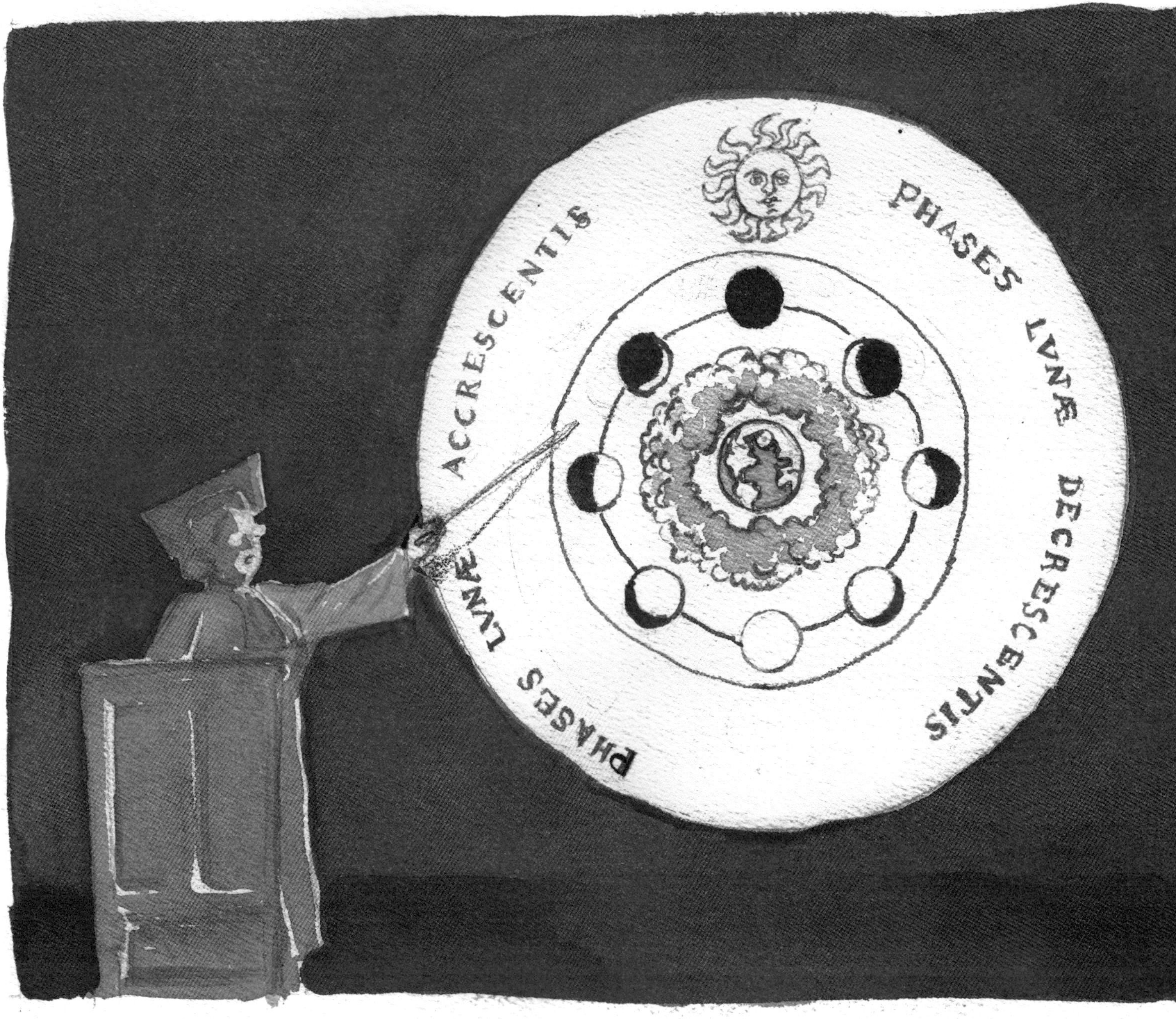
PHASES LVNÆ DECRESCENTIS
PHASES LVNÆ ACCRESCENTIS

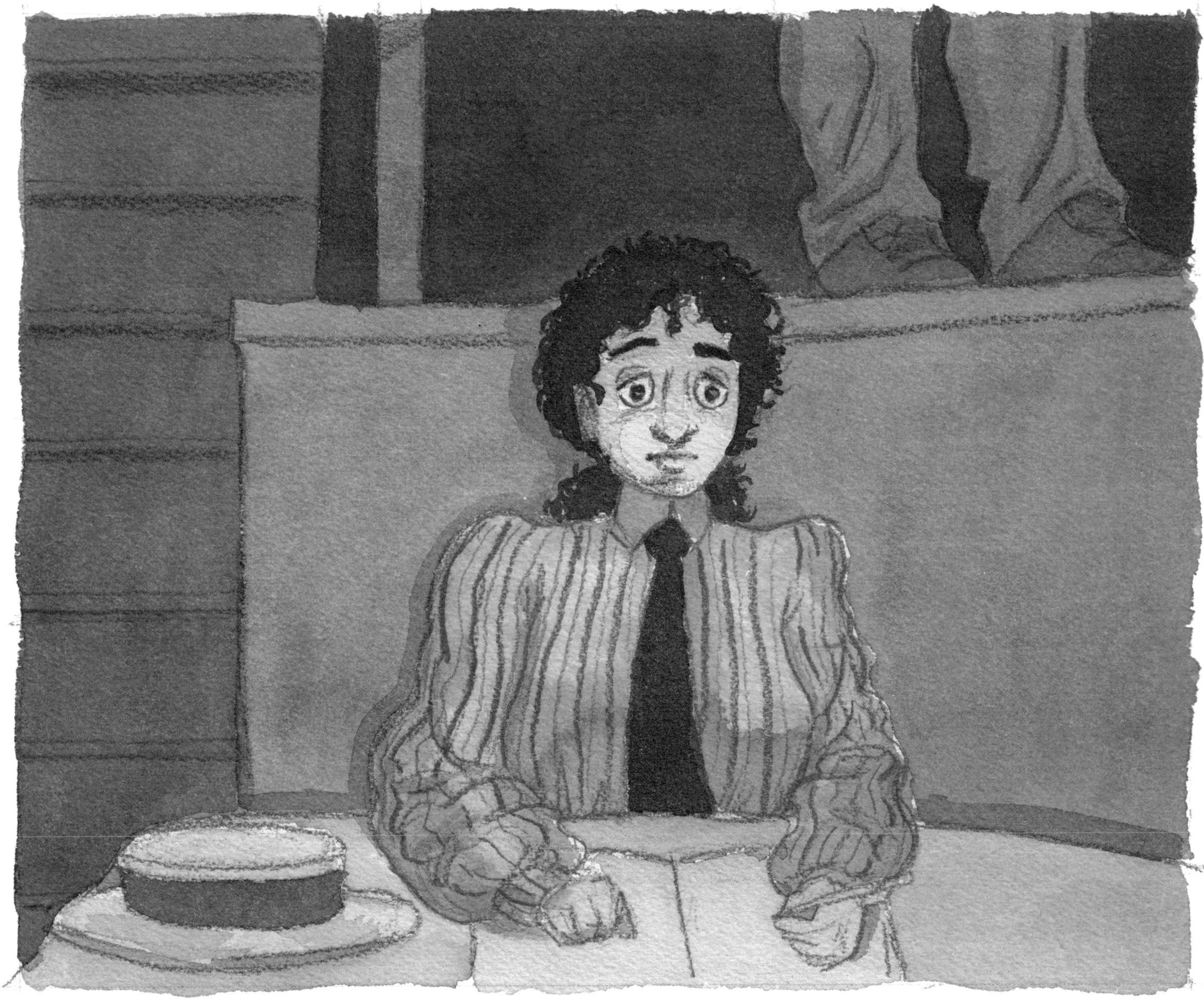

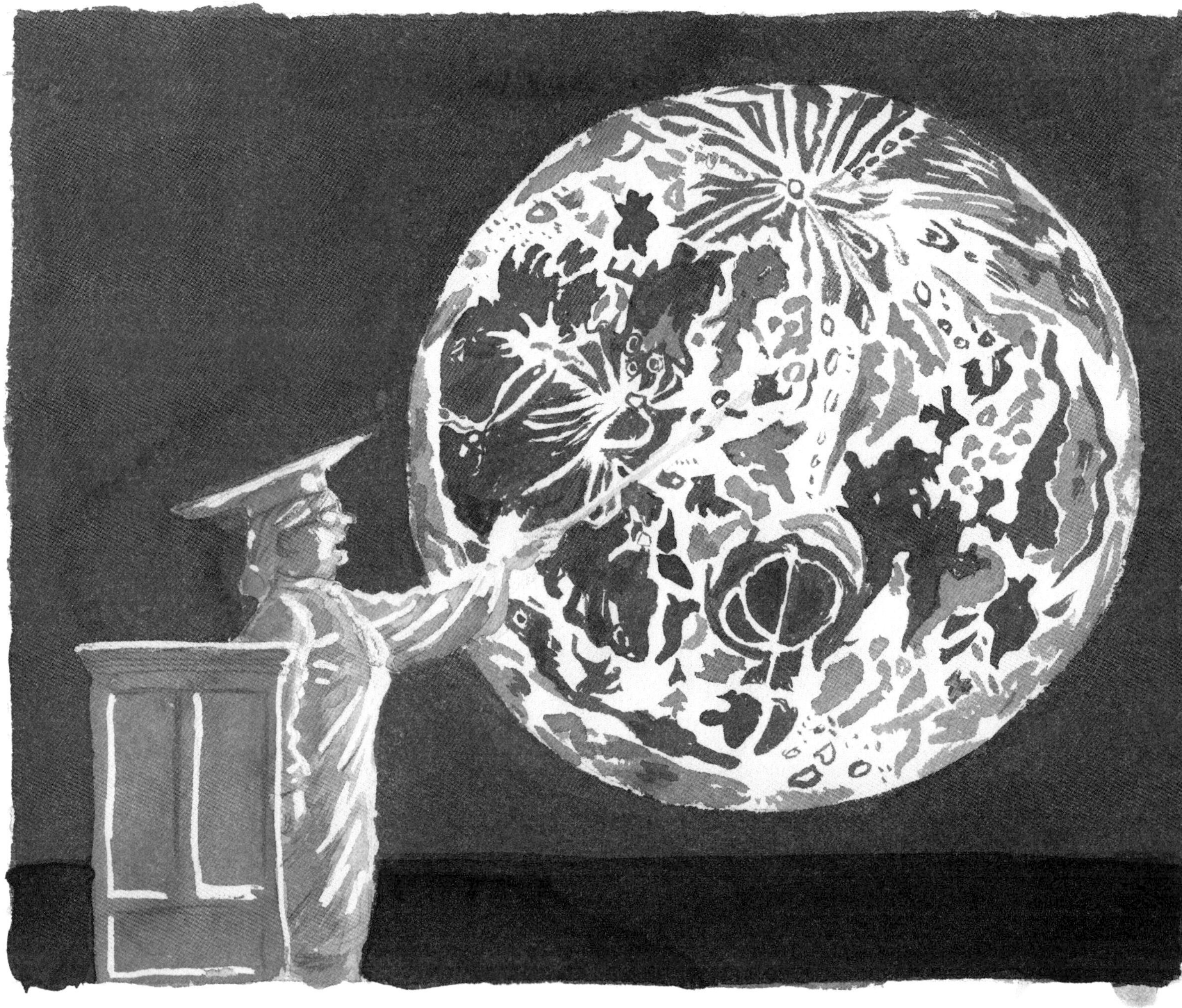

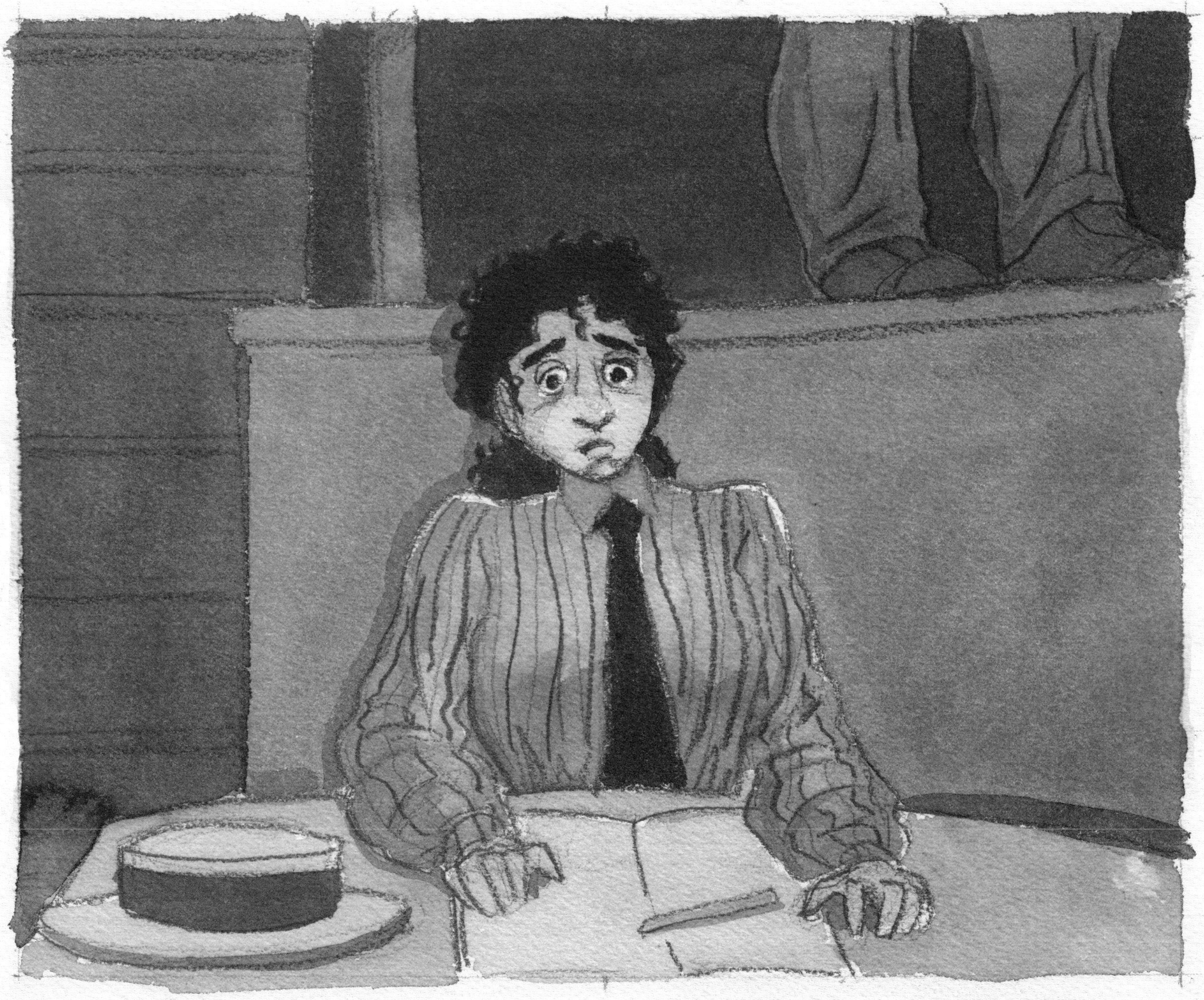

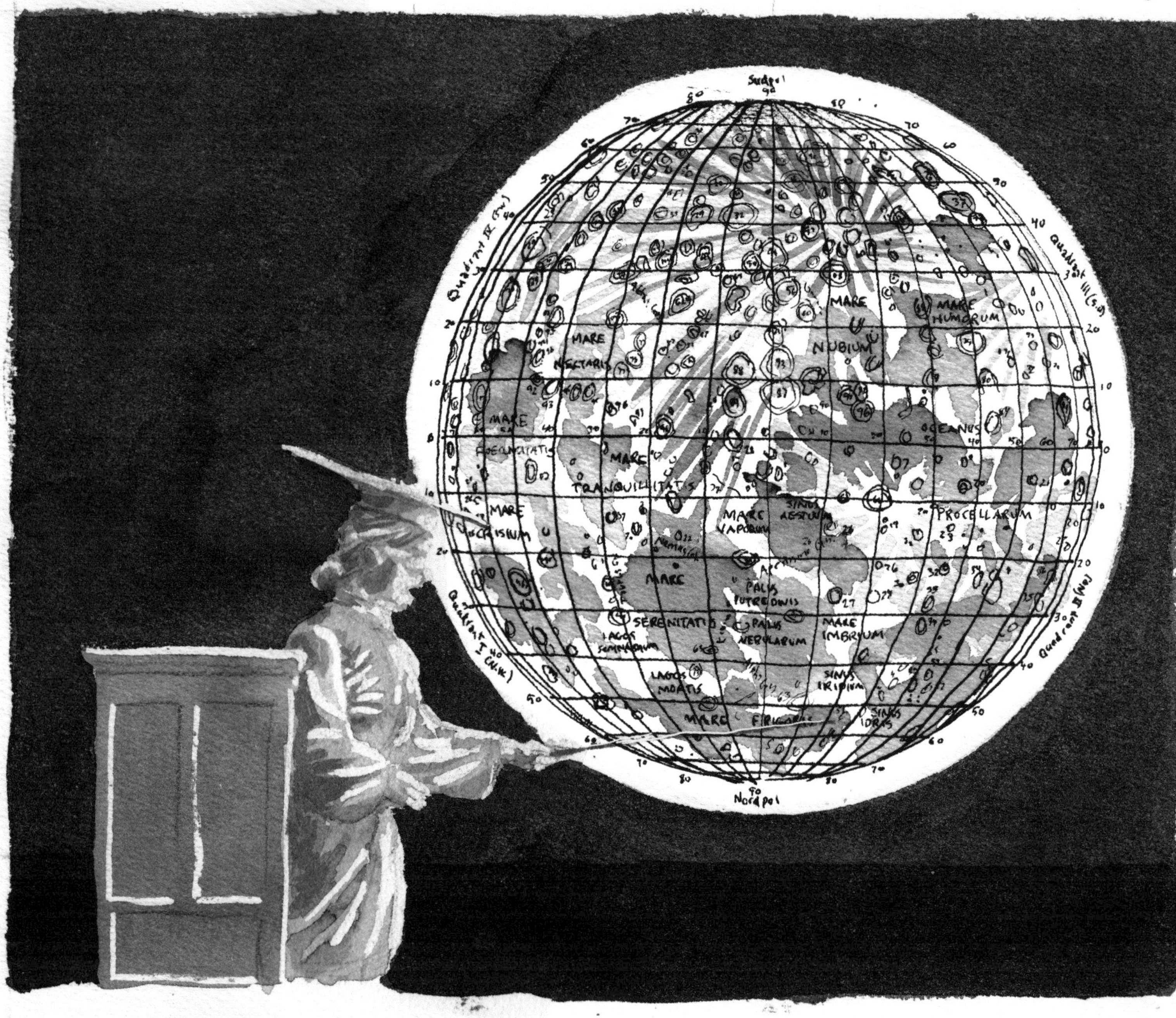
Sudpol
MARE NECTARIS
MARE NUBIUM
MARE HUMORUM
MARE TRANQUILLITATIS
OCEANUS PROCELLARUM
MARE CRISIUM
MARE VAPORUM
SINUS AESTUUM
PALUS PUTREDINIS
MARE SERENITATIS
PALUS NEBULARUM
MARE IMBRIUM
SINUS IRIDUM
MARE FRIGORIS
Nordpol

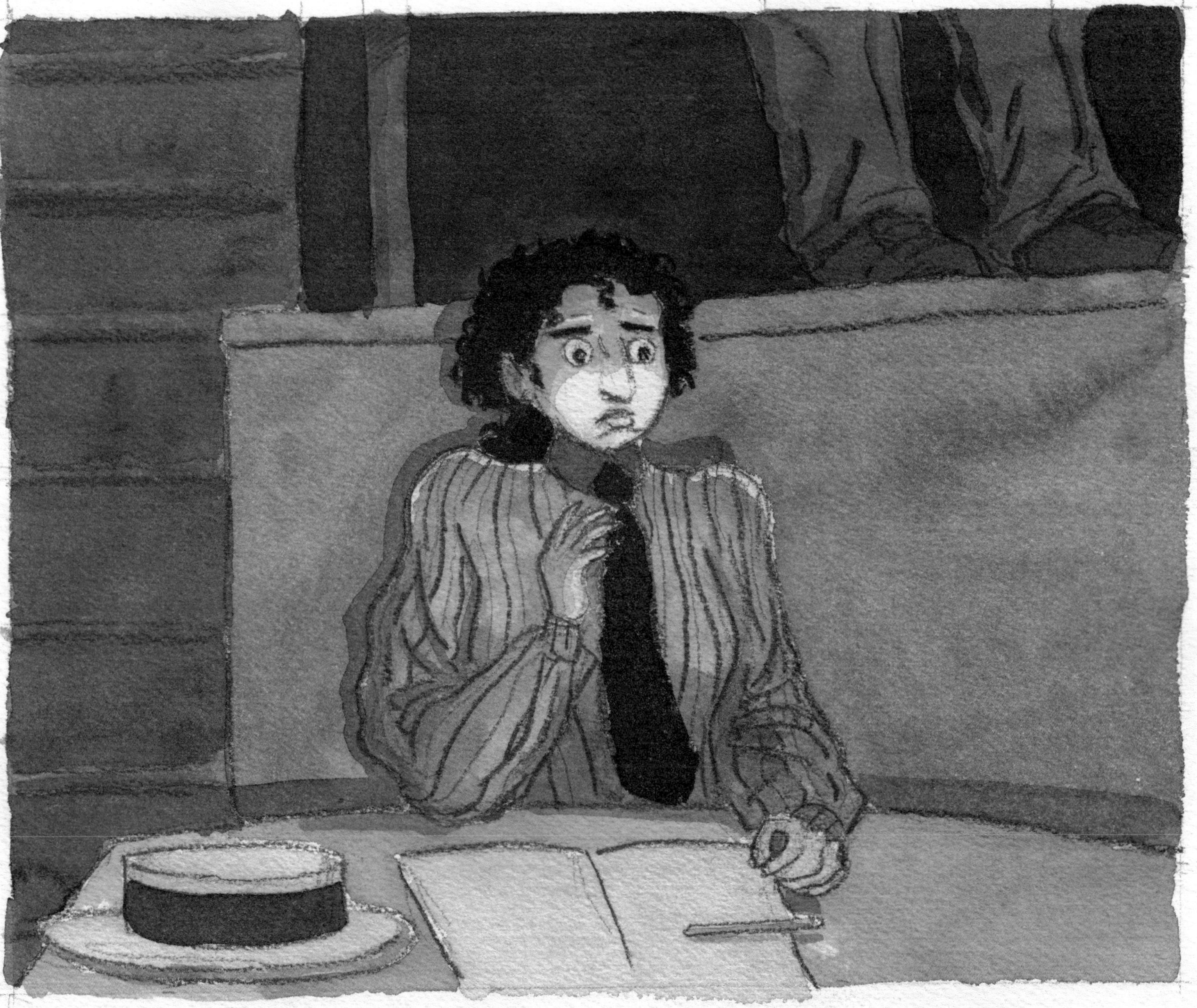

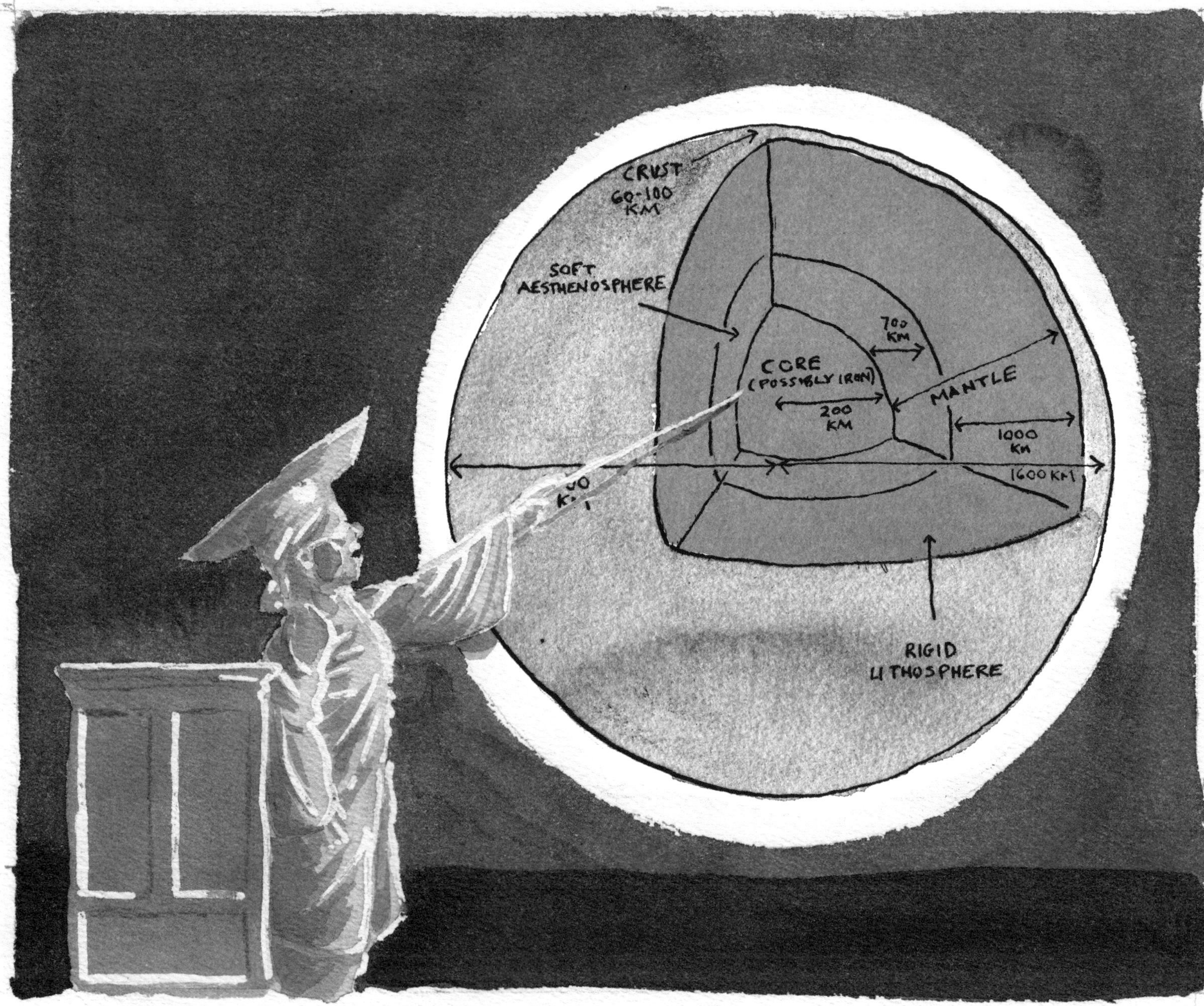
CRUST
60-100
KM
SOFT
AESTHENOSPHERE
700
KM
CORE
(POSSIBLY IRON)
200
KM
MANTLE
1000
KM
1600 KM
RIGID
LITHOSPHERE

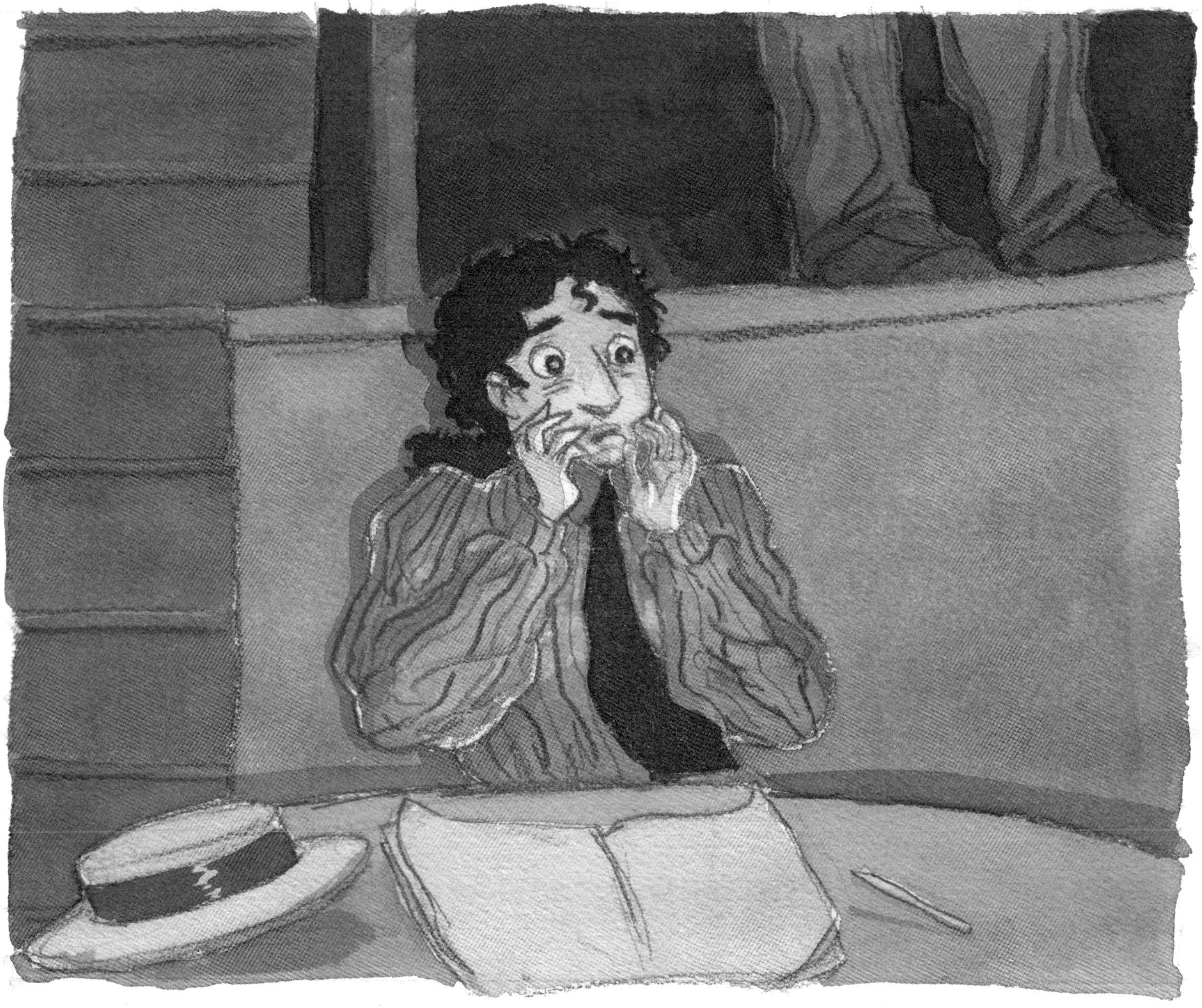

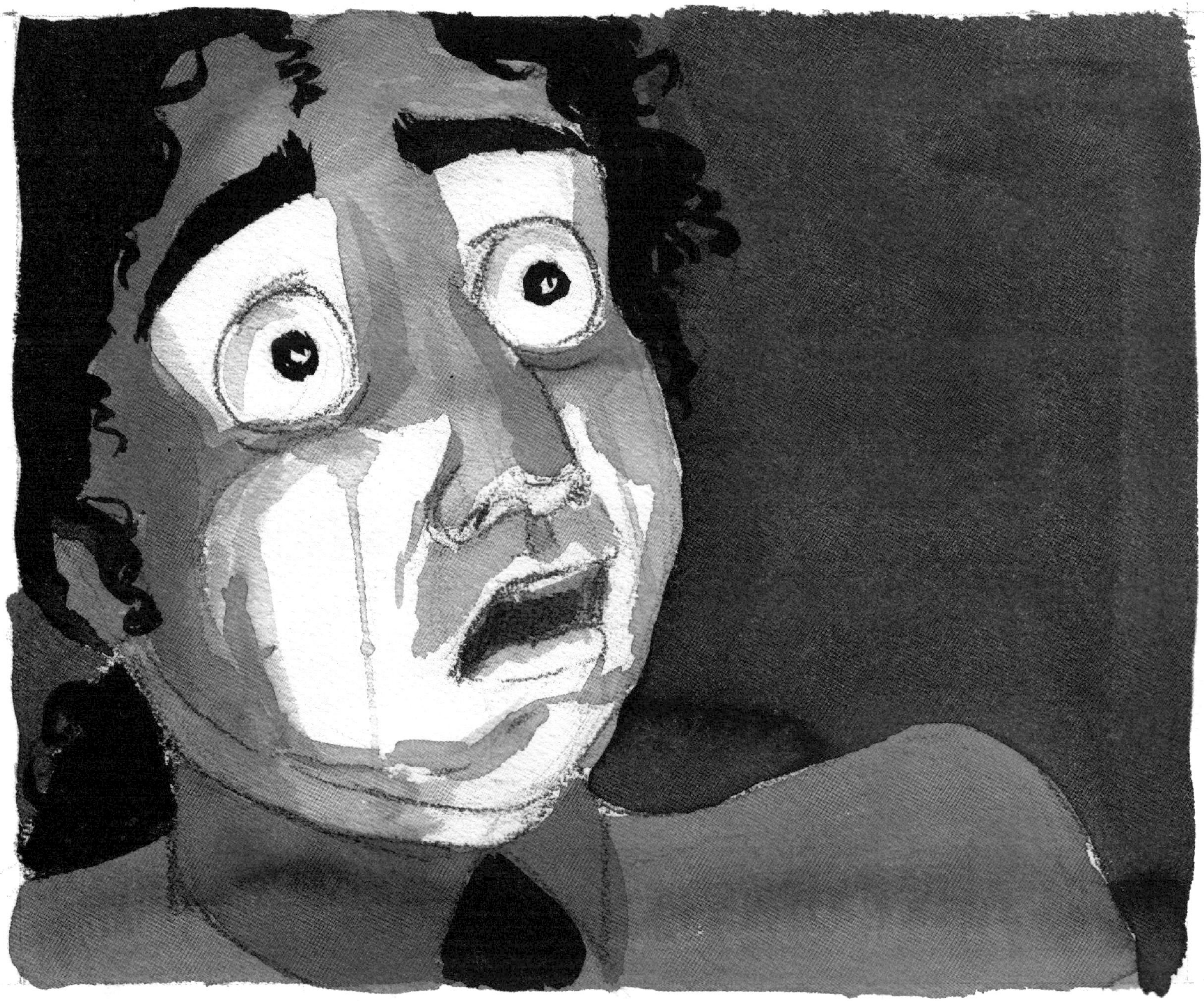

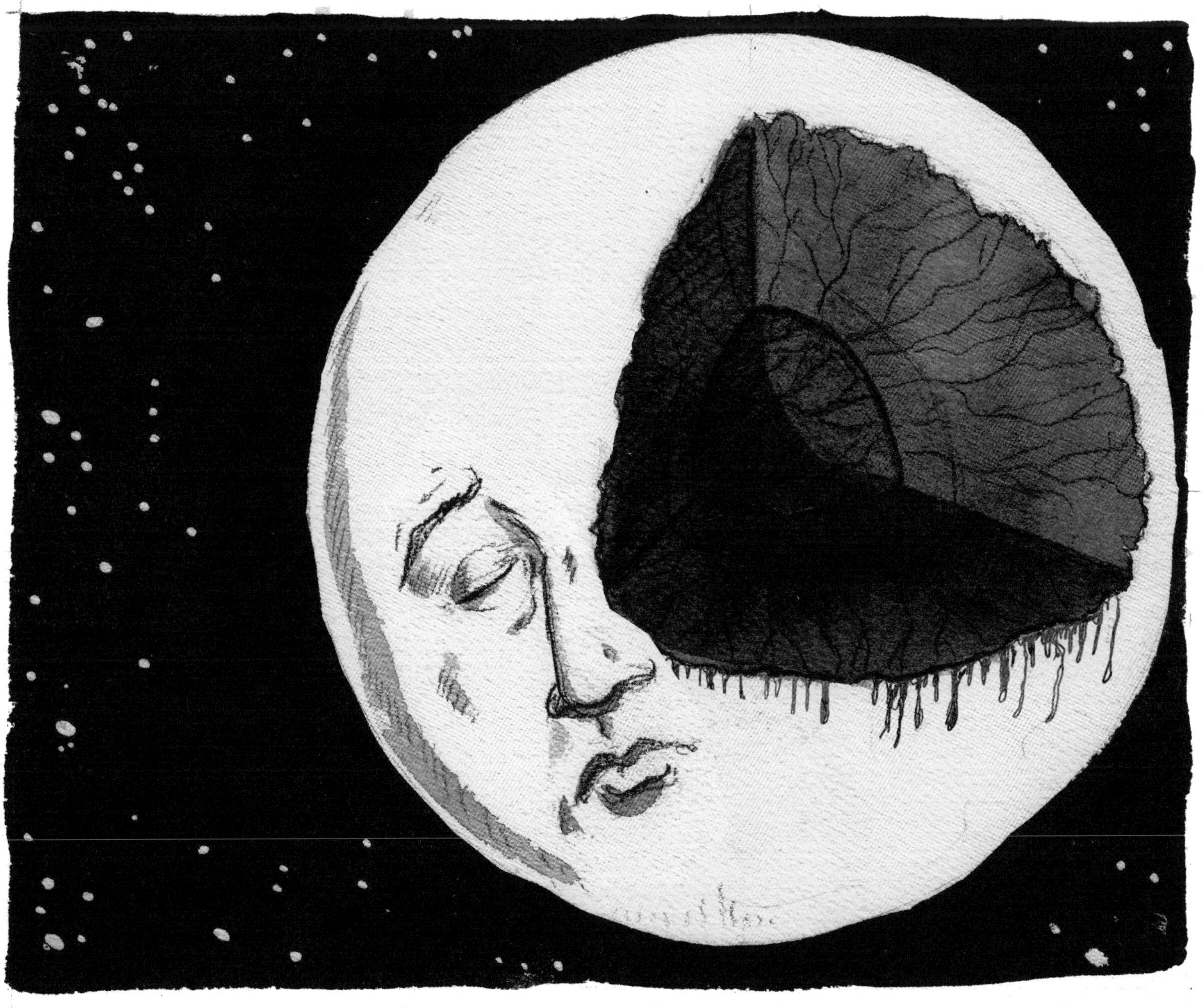

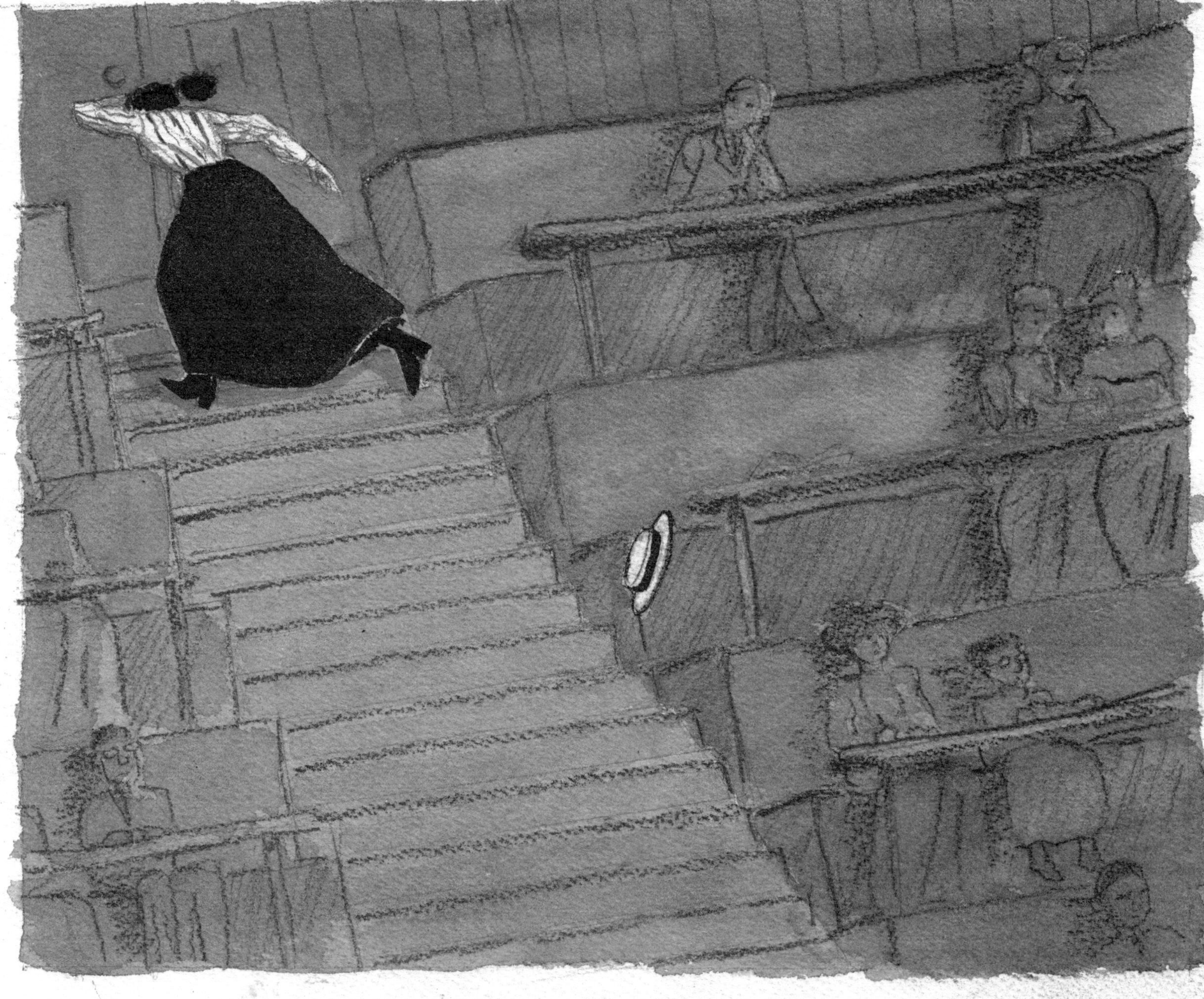

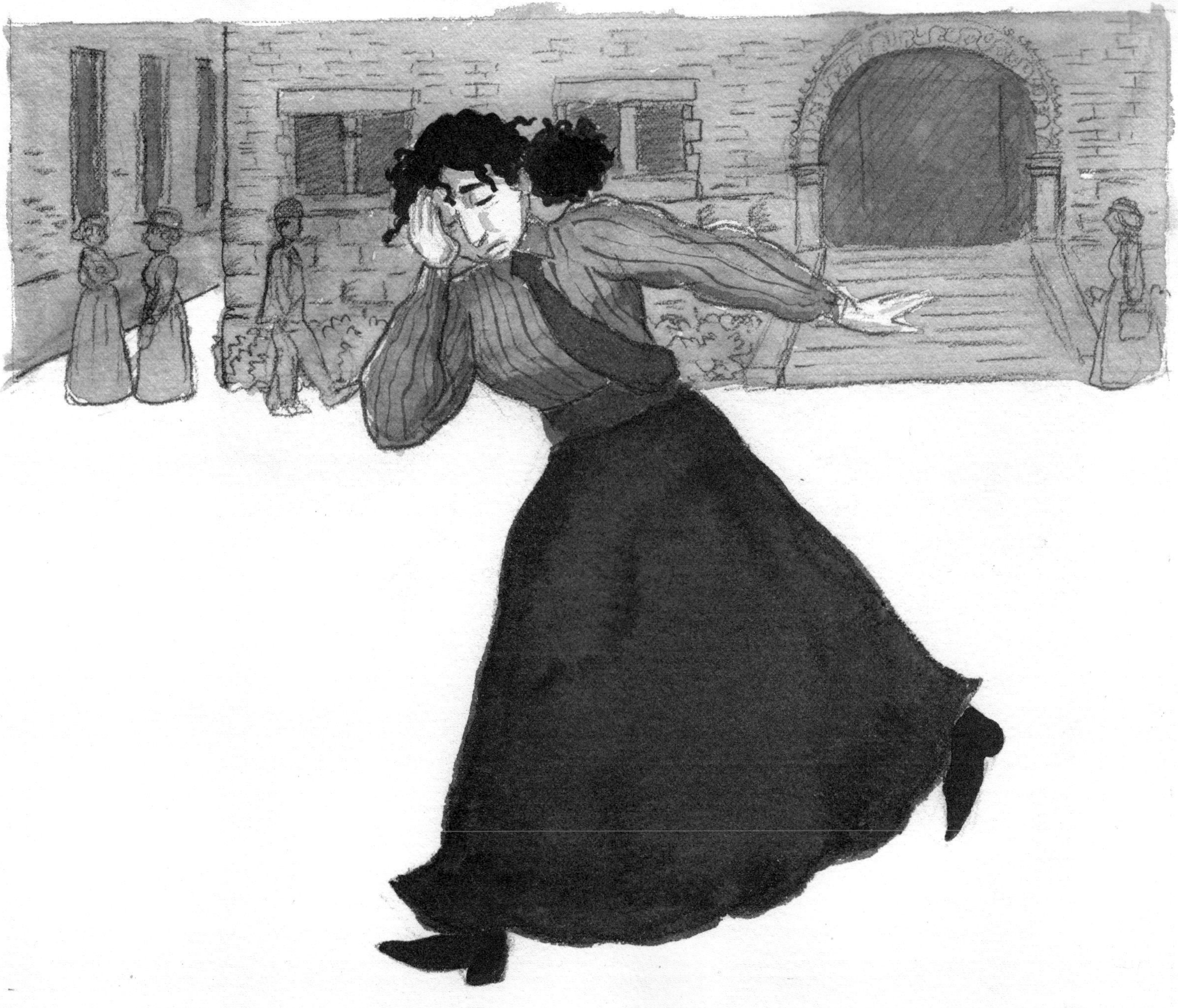

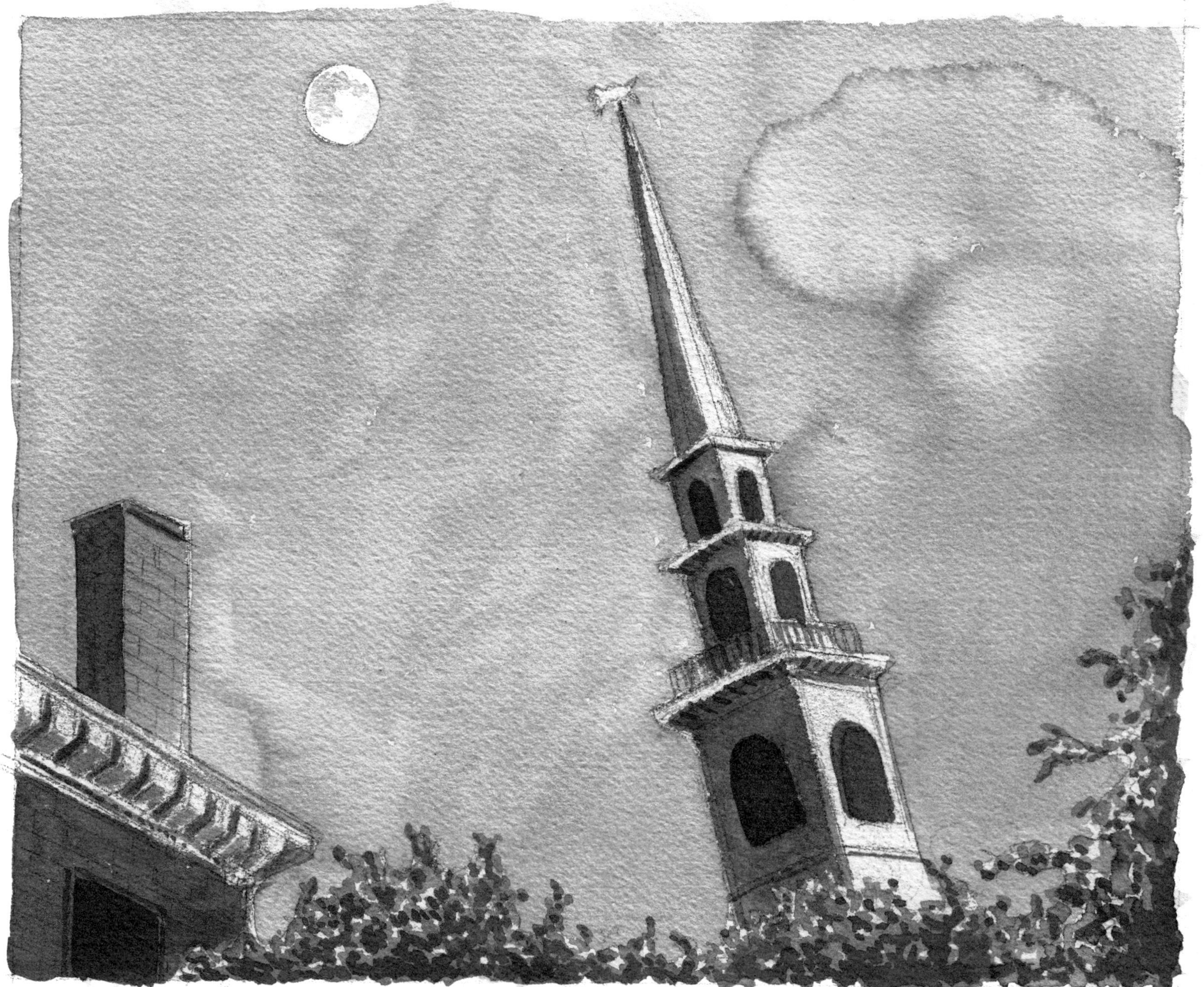

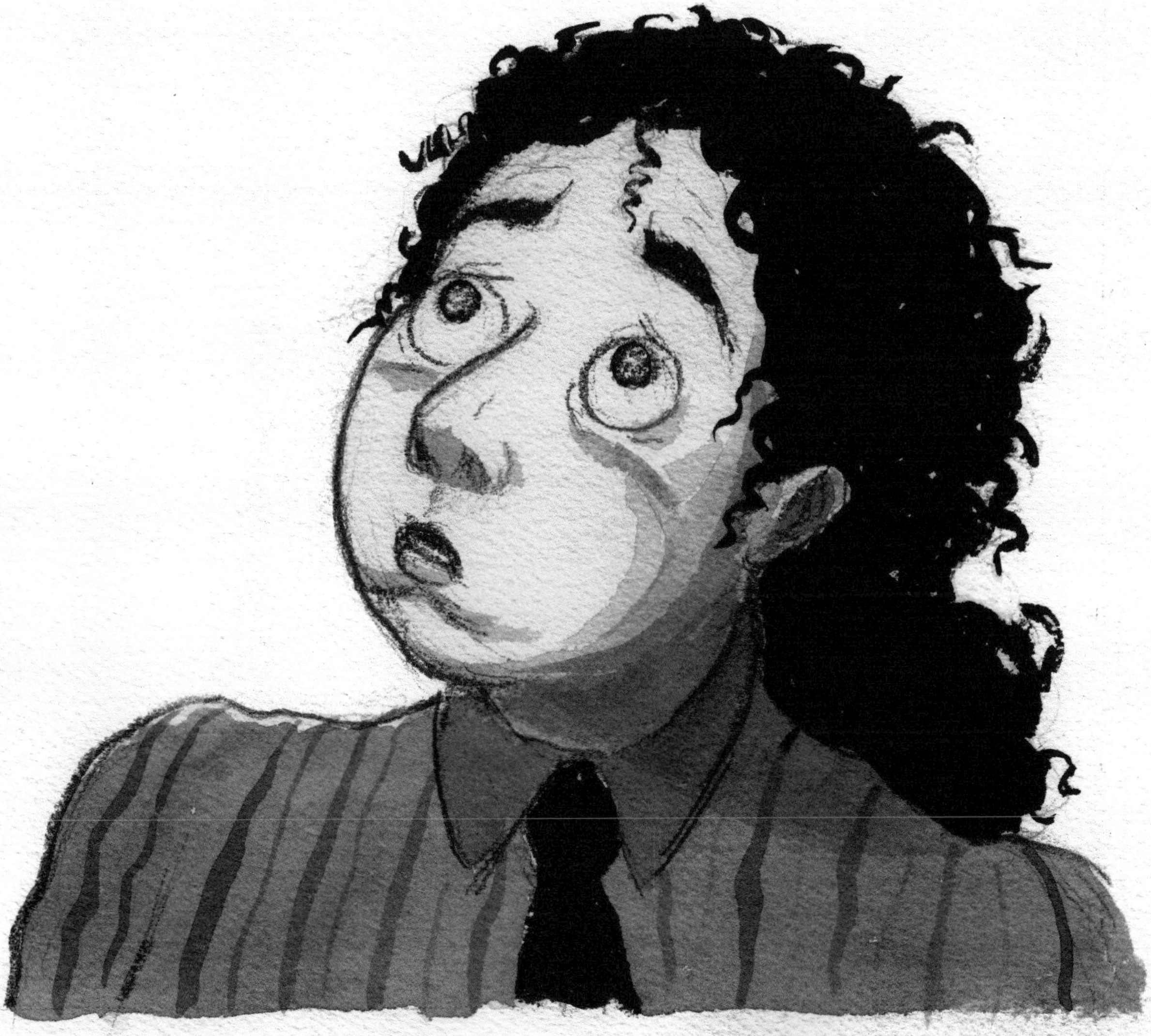

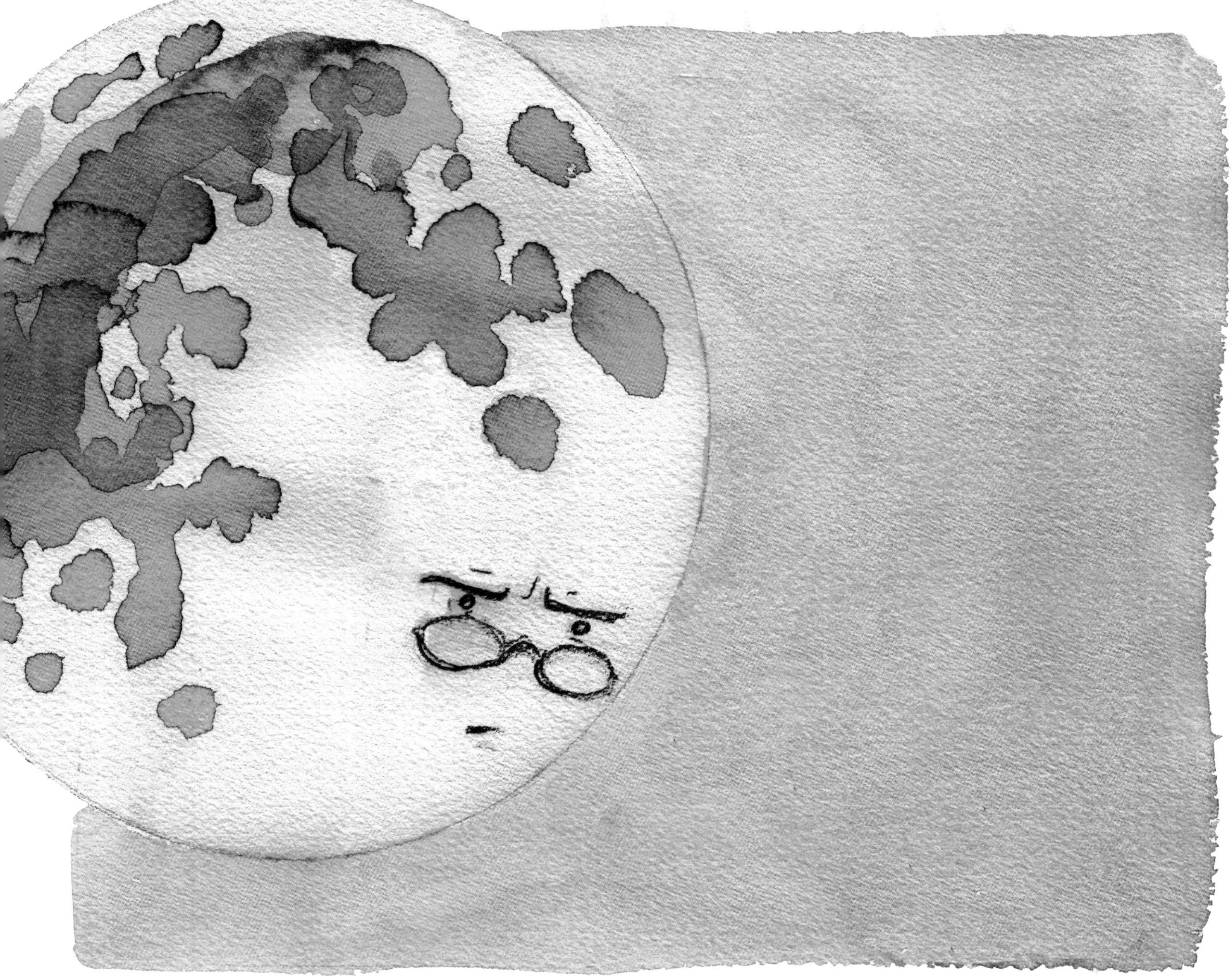

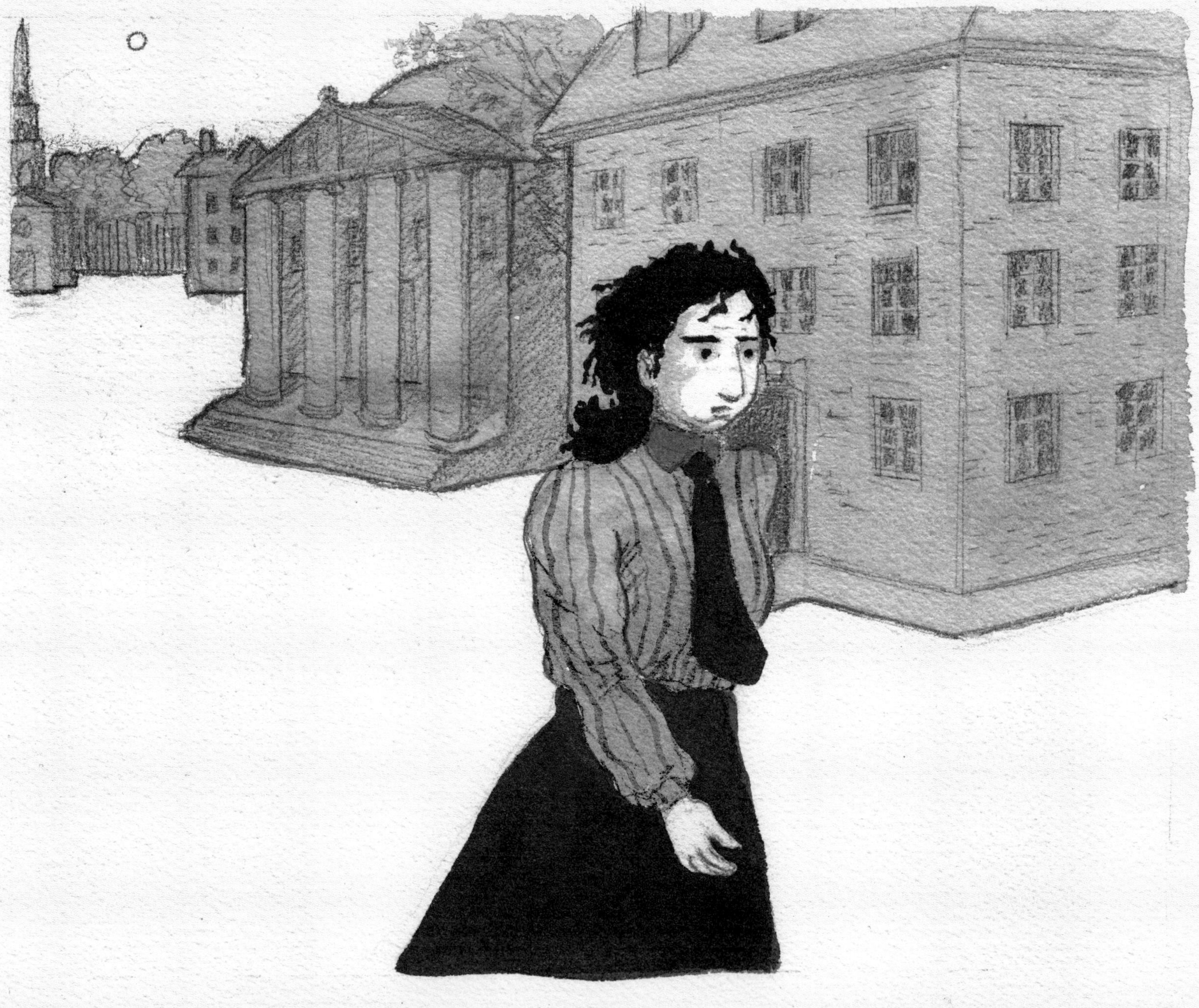

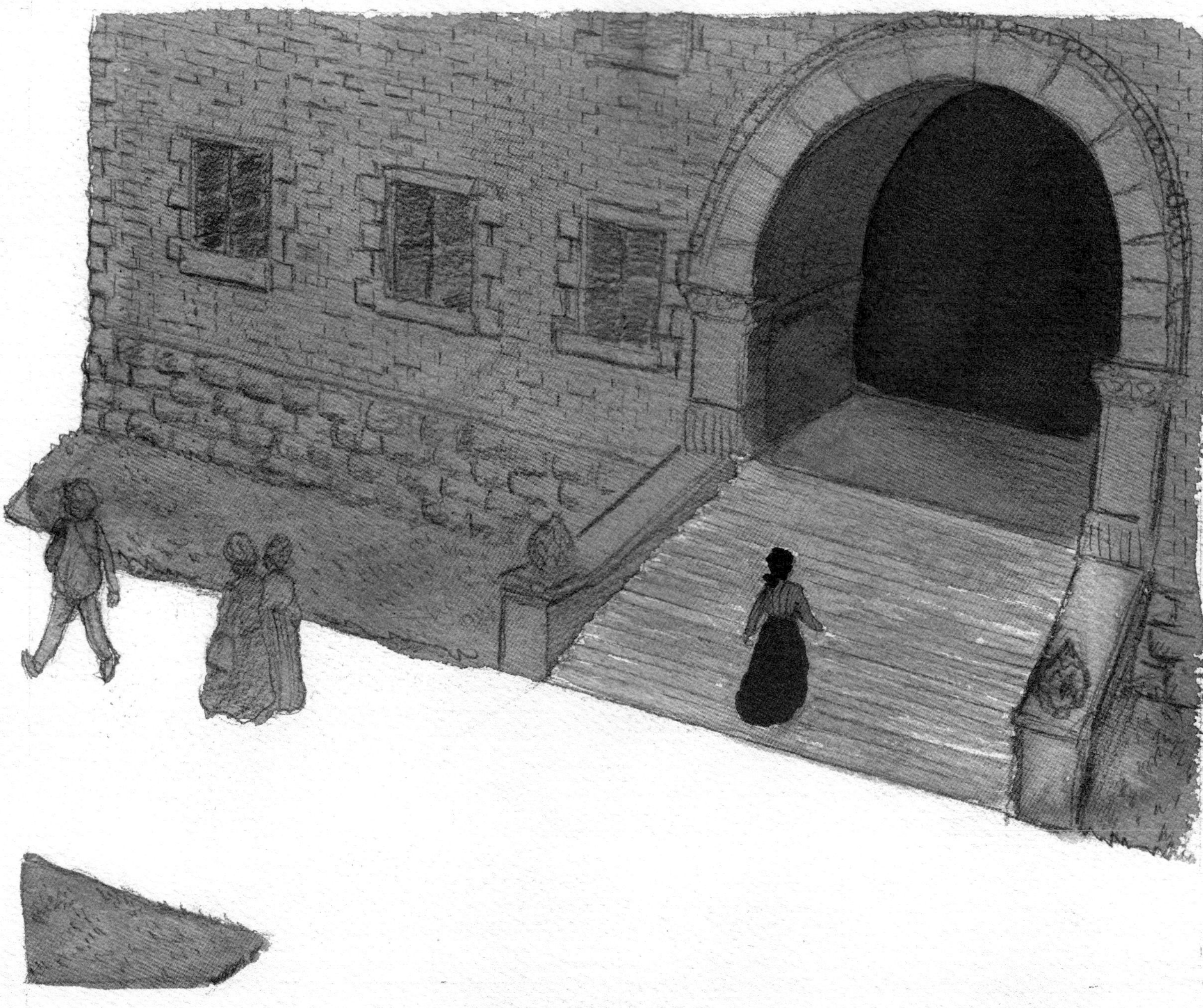

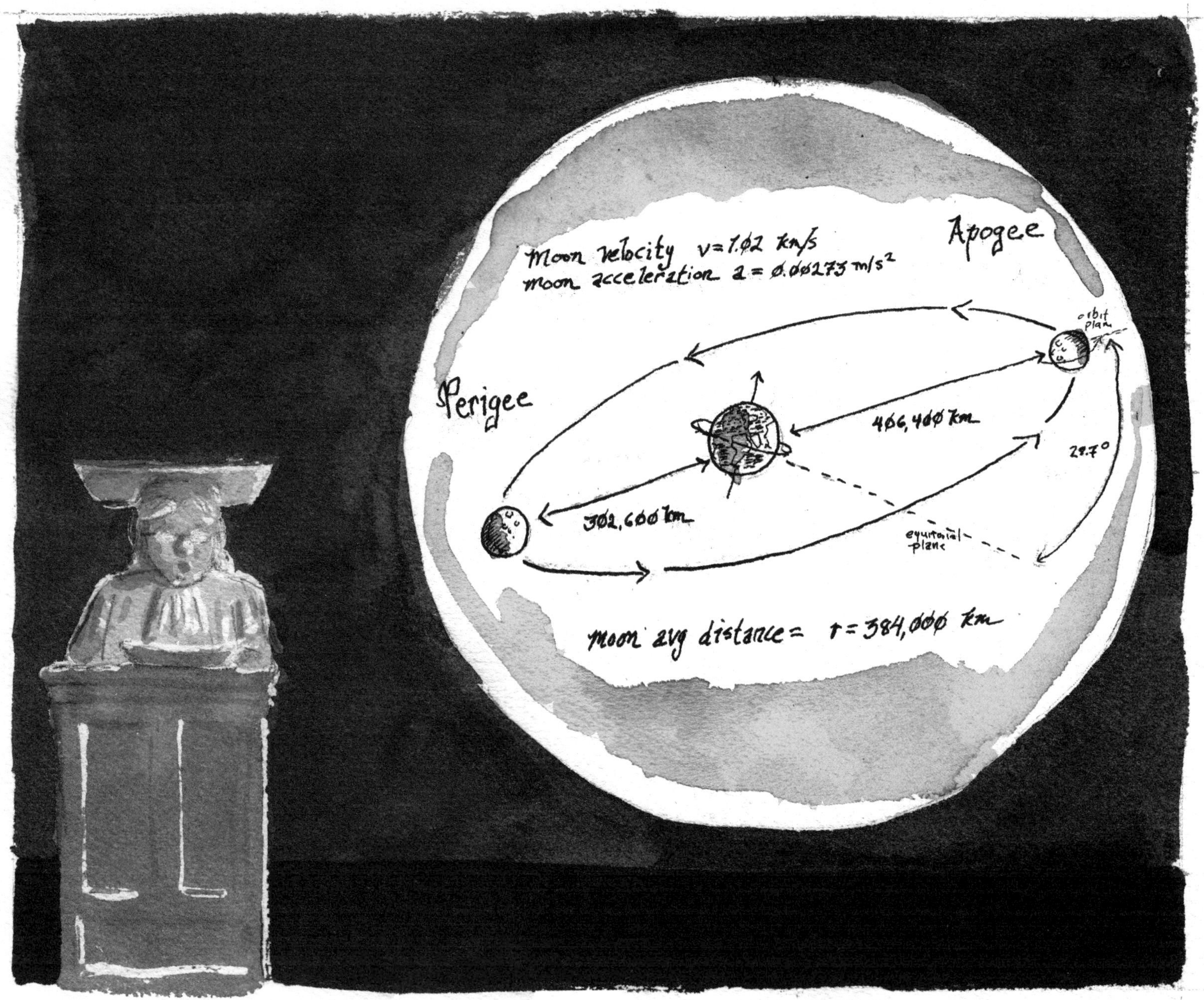

Moon velocity v=1.02 km/s
moon acceleration a = 0.00273 m/s²
Apogee
Perigee
orbit plan
406,400 km
302,600 km
equitorial plane
moon avg distance = r = 384,000 km

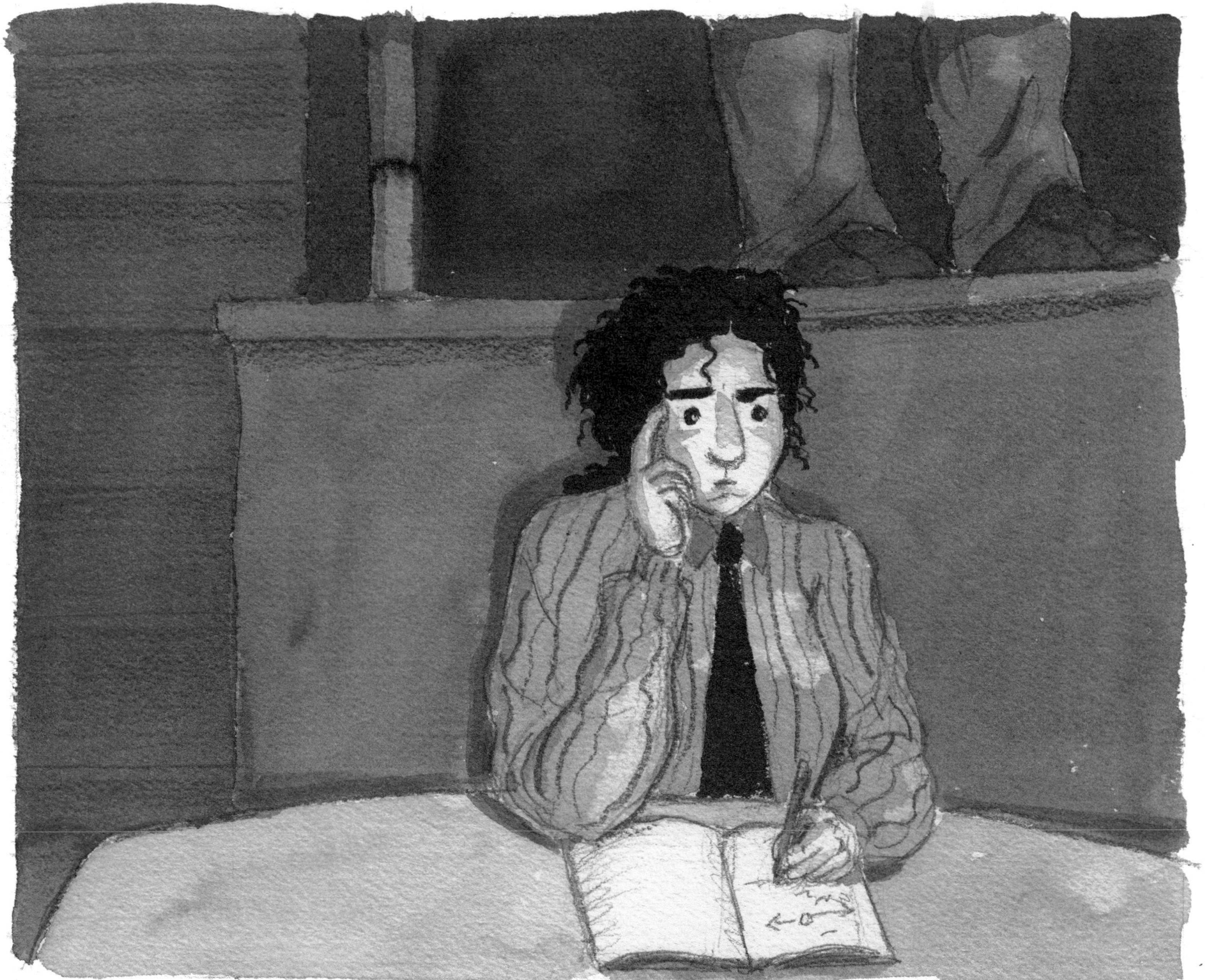

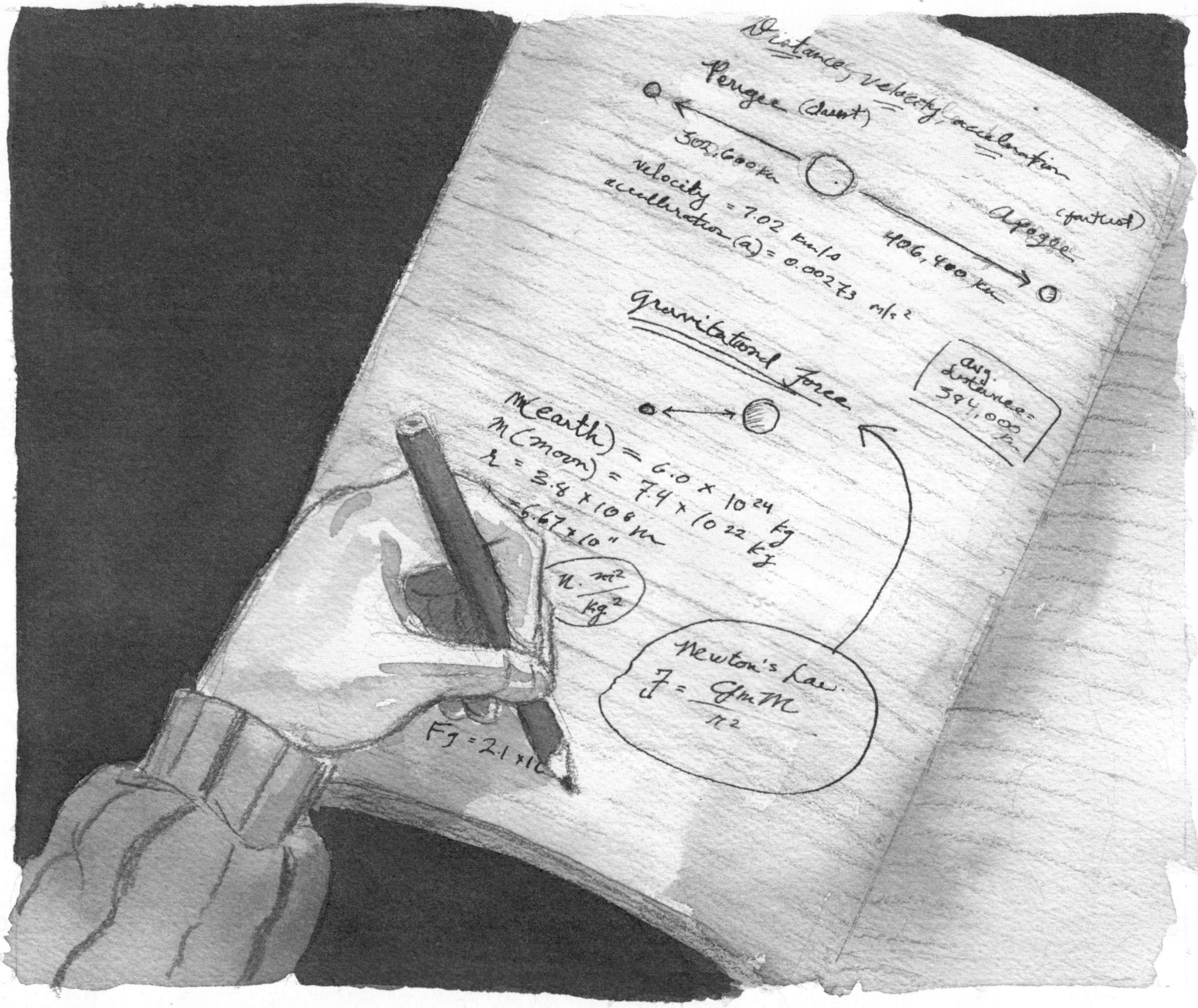
Distance, velocity, acceleration
Perigee (closest)
Apogee (farthest)
406,400 km
Gravitational Force
avg. distance = 384,000 km
Newton's Law
F = GmM/r²

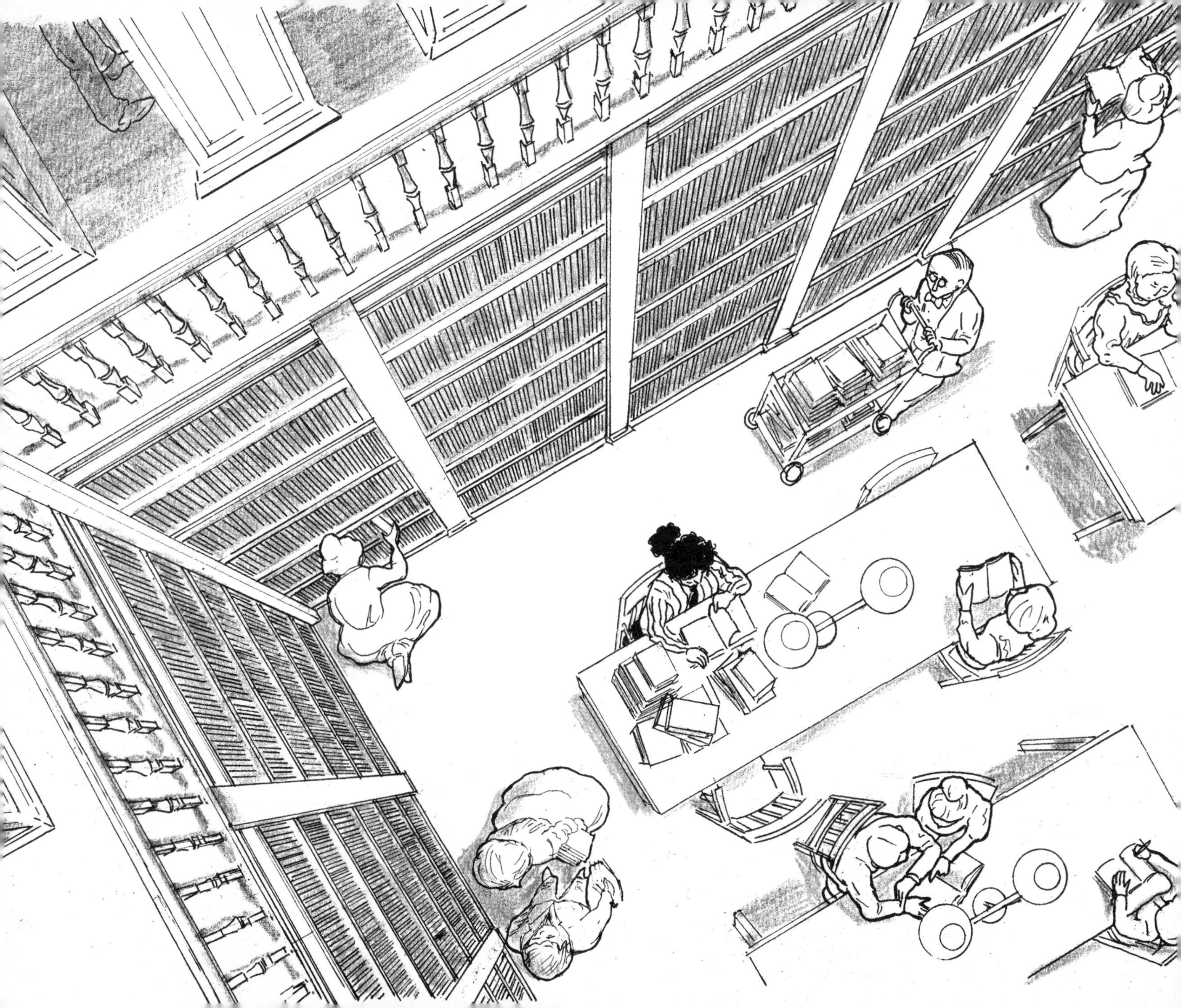

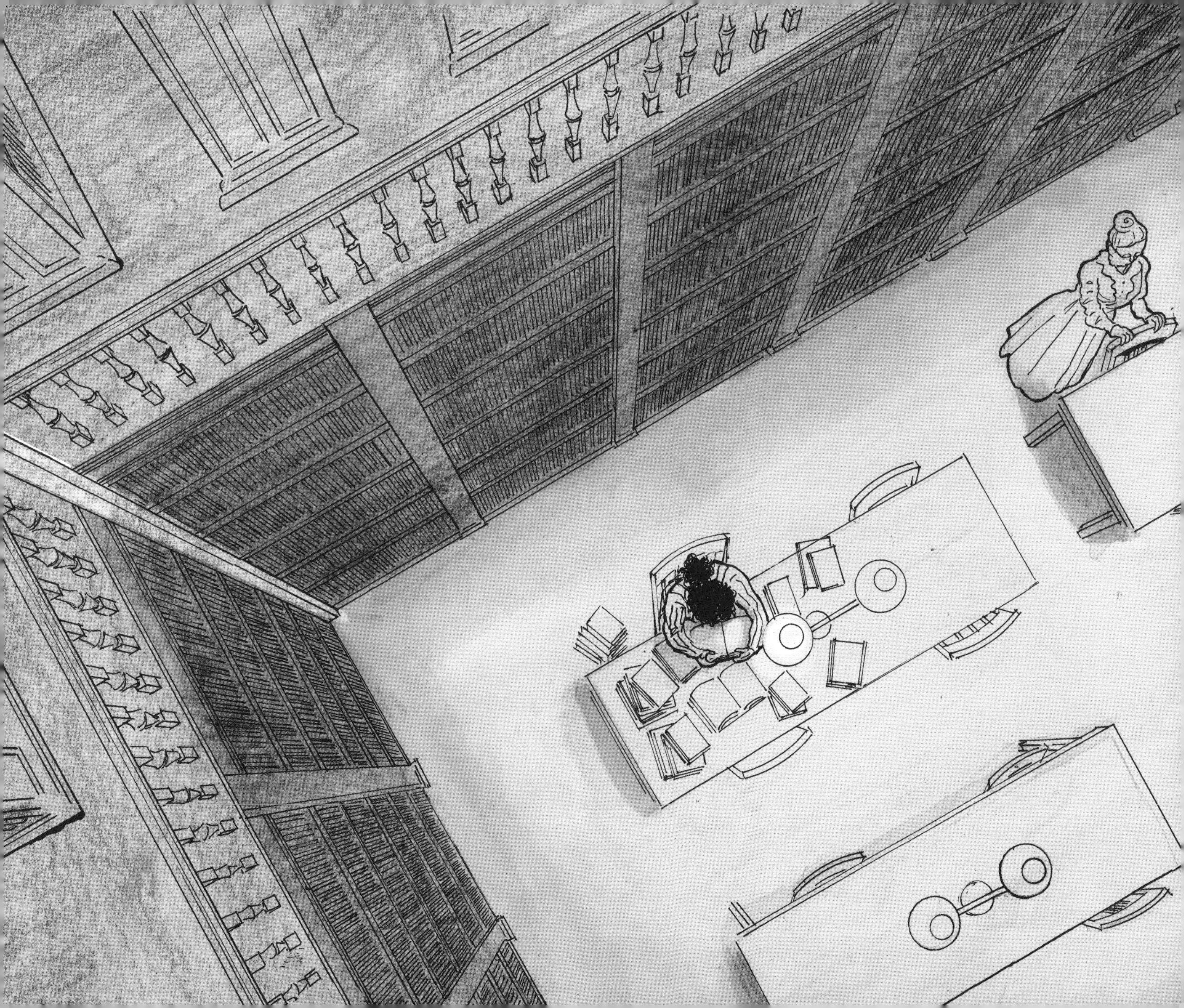

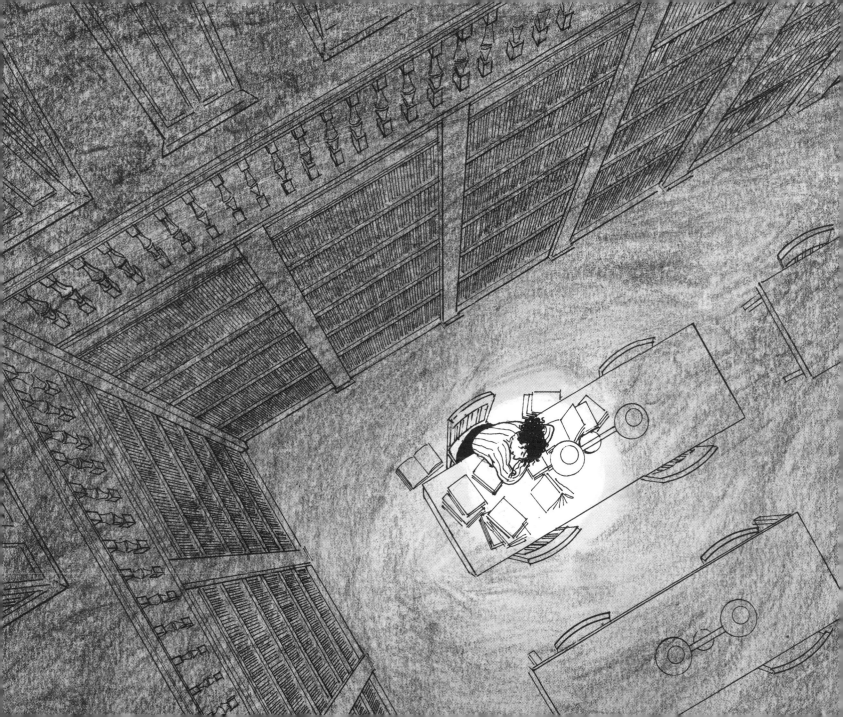

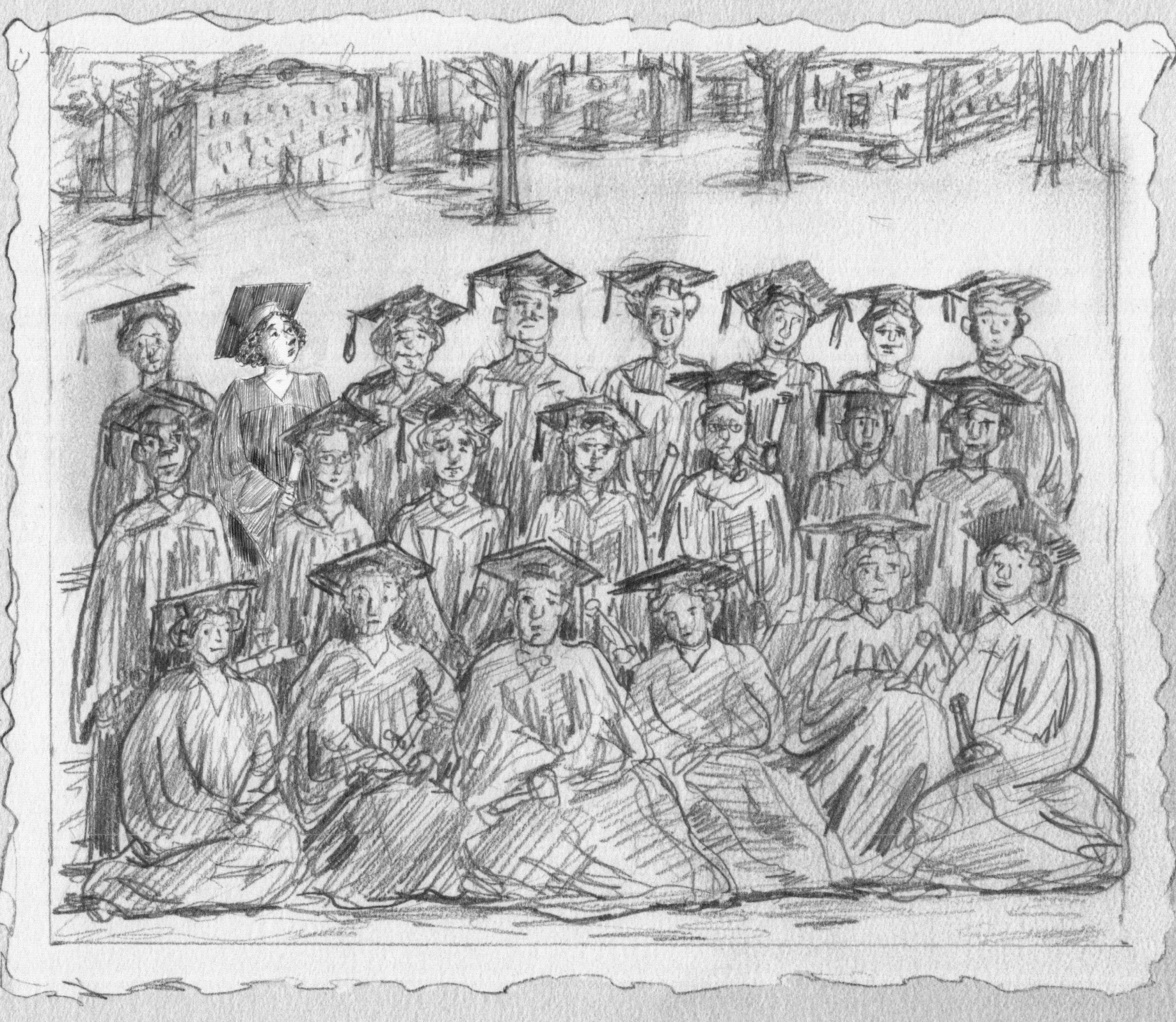

7

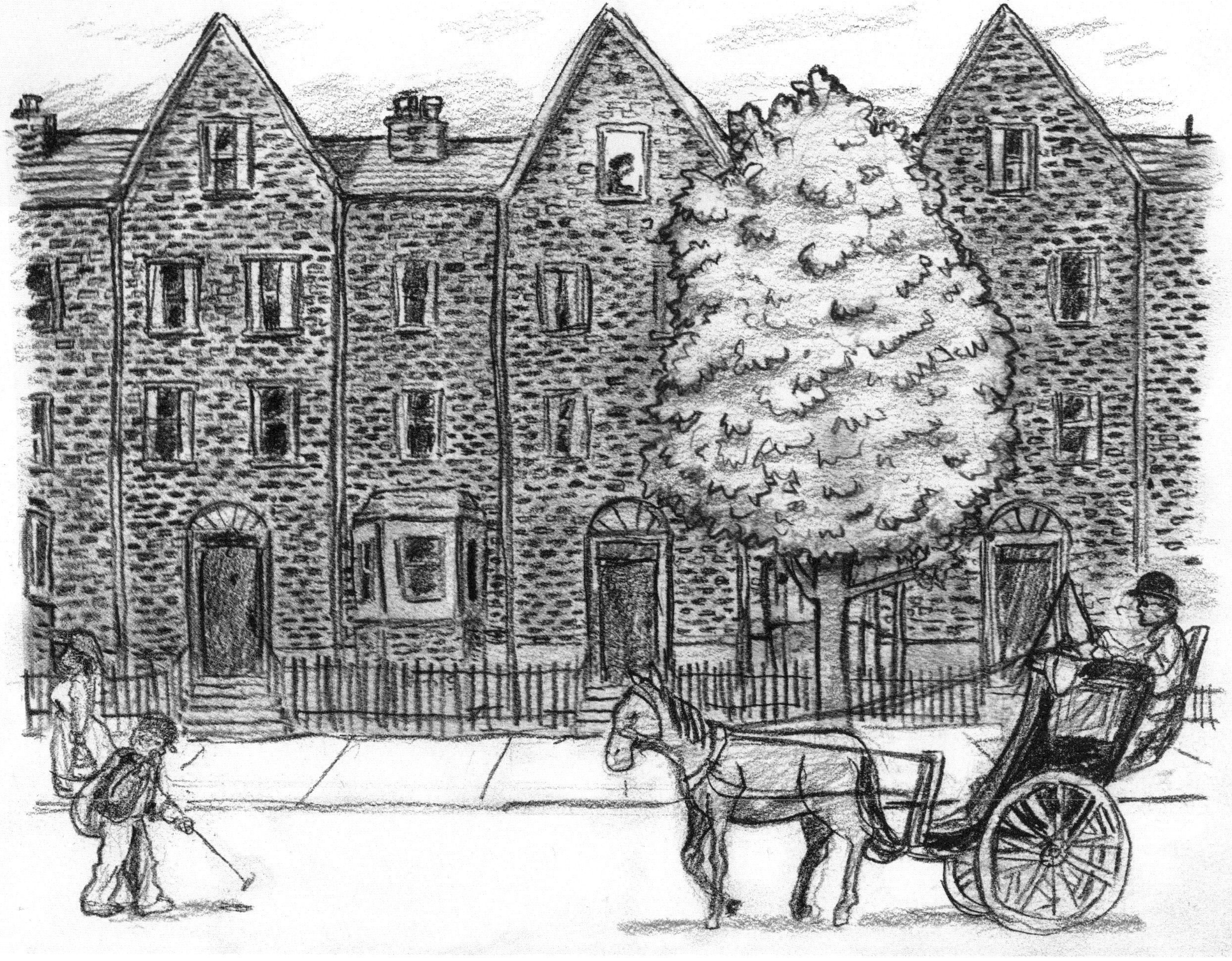

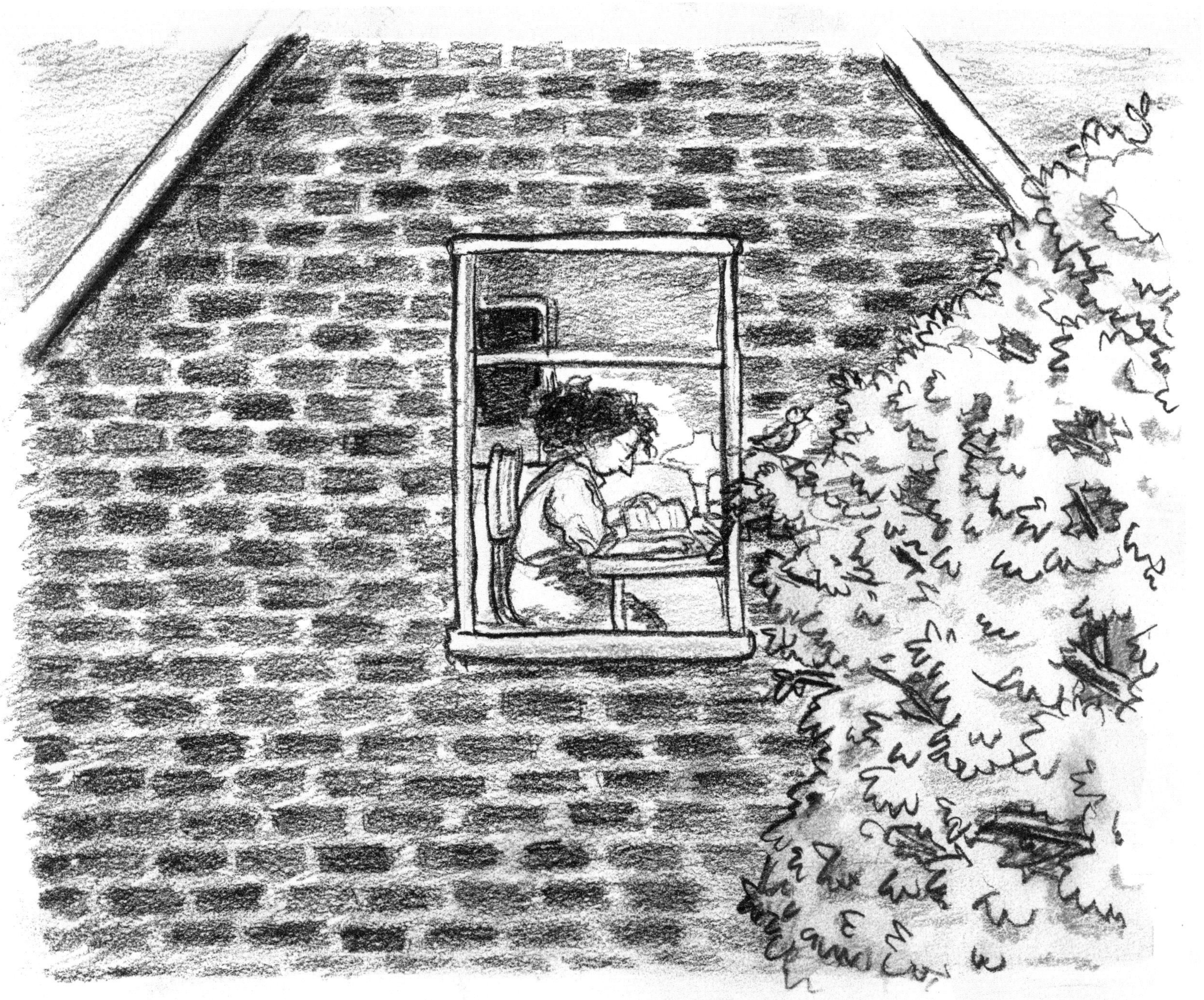

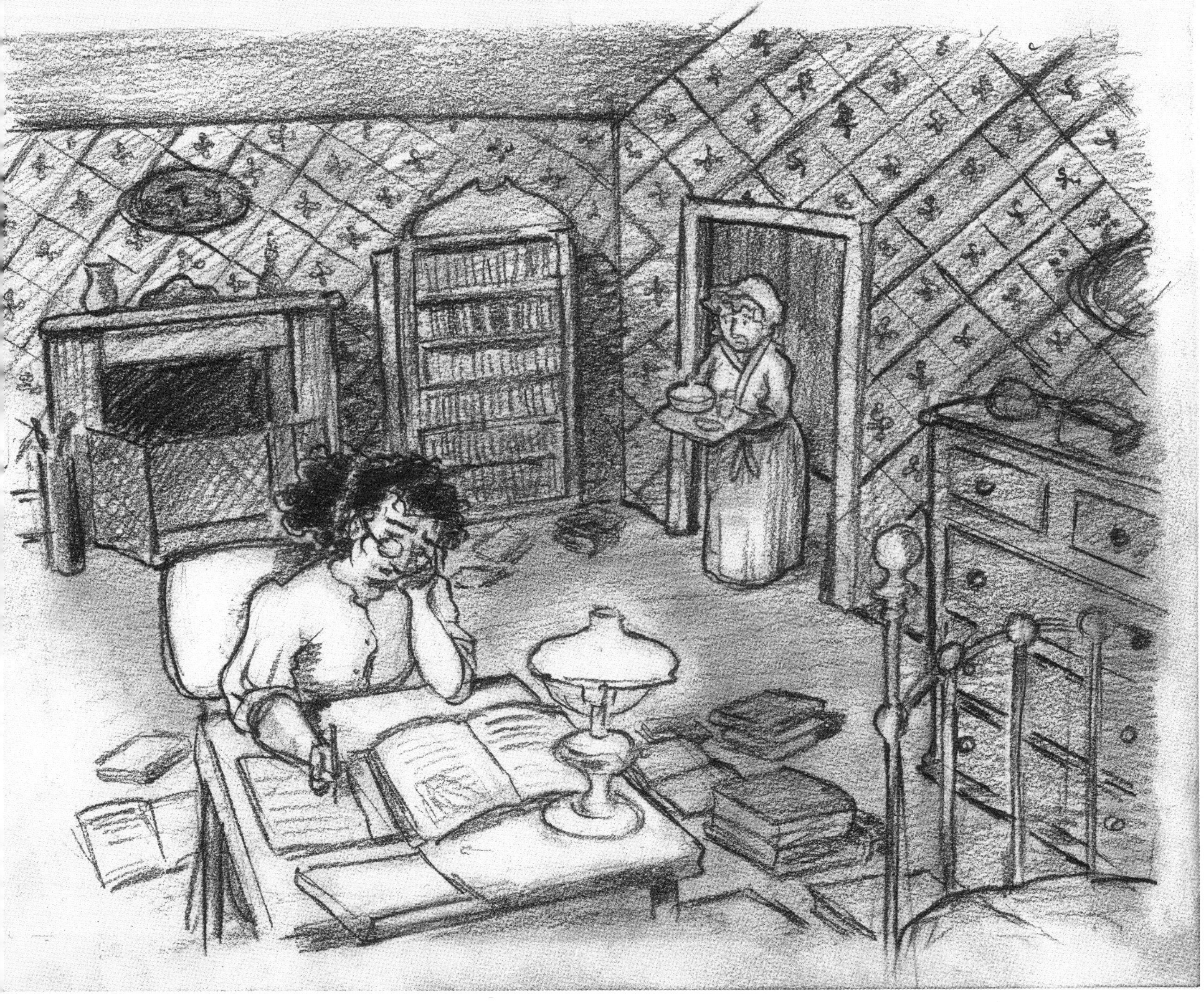

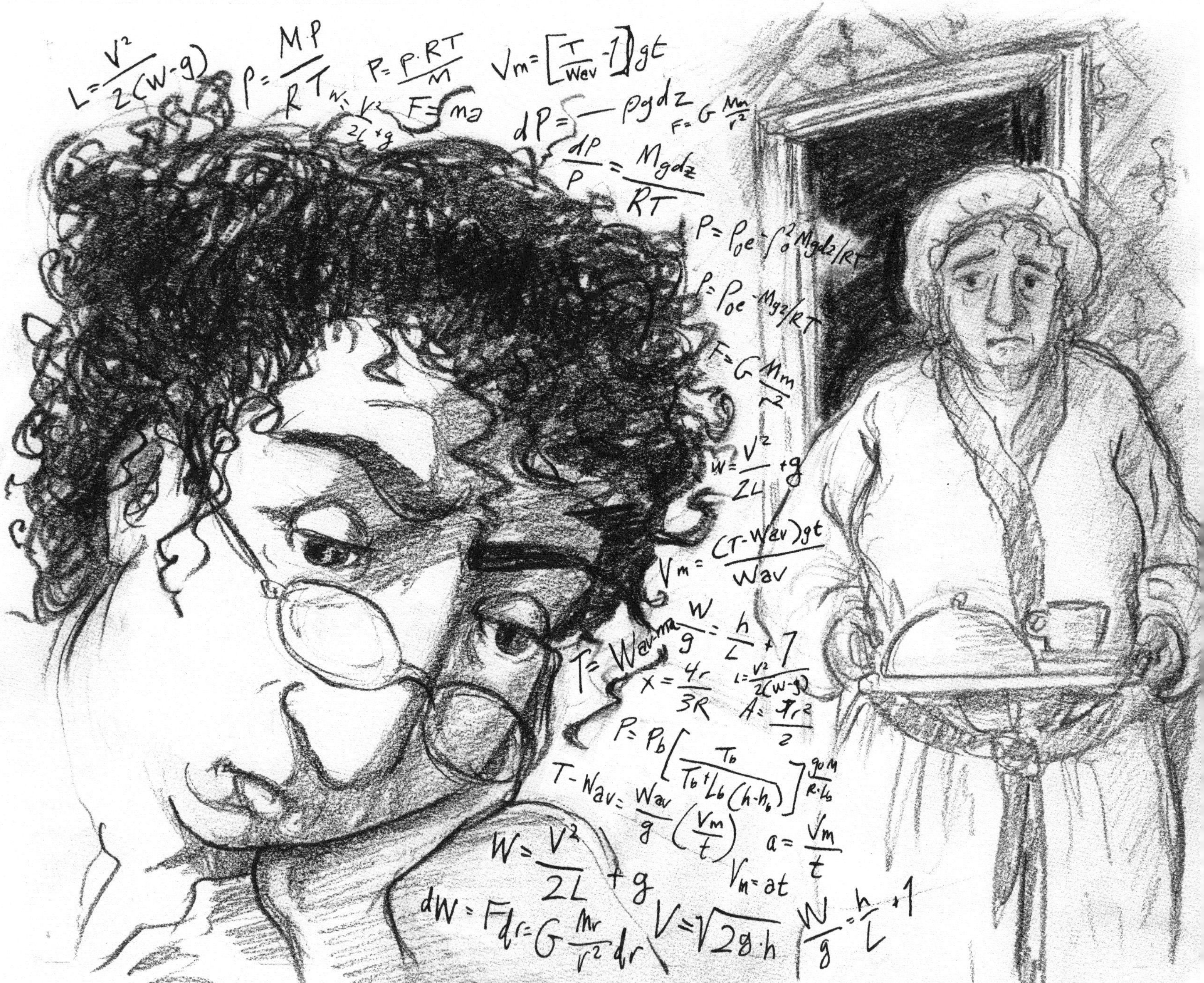
$L=\frac{V^2}{2(W-g)}$
$\rho=\frac{M\cdot P}{RT}$
$P=\frac{\rho\cdot RT}{M}$
$V_m=\left[\frac{T}{W_{av}}-1\right]gt$
$F=ma$
$F=G\frac{Mm}{r^2}$
$\frac{dP}{P}=\frac{Mg\,dz}{RT}$
$P=P_0e^{-Mgz/RT}$
$W=\frac{V^2}{2L}+g$
$V_m=\frac{(T-W_{av})gt}{W_{av}}$
$\frac{W}{g}=\frac{h}{L}+1$
$x=\frac{4r}{3R}$
$T-W_{av}=\frac{W_{av}}{g}\left(\frac{V_m}{t}\right)$
$a=\frac{V_m}{t}$
$V_m=at$
$V=\sqrt{2g\cdot h}$

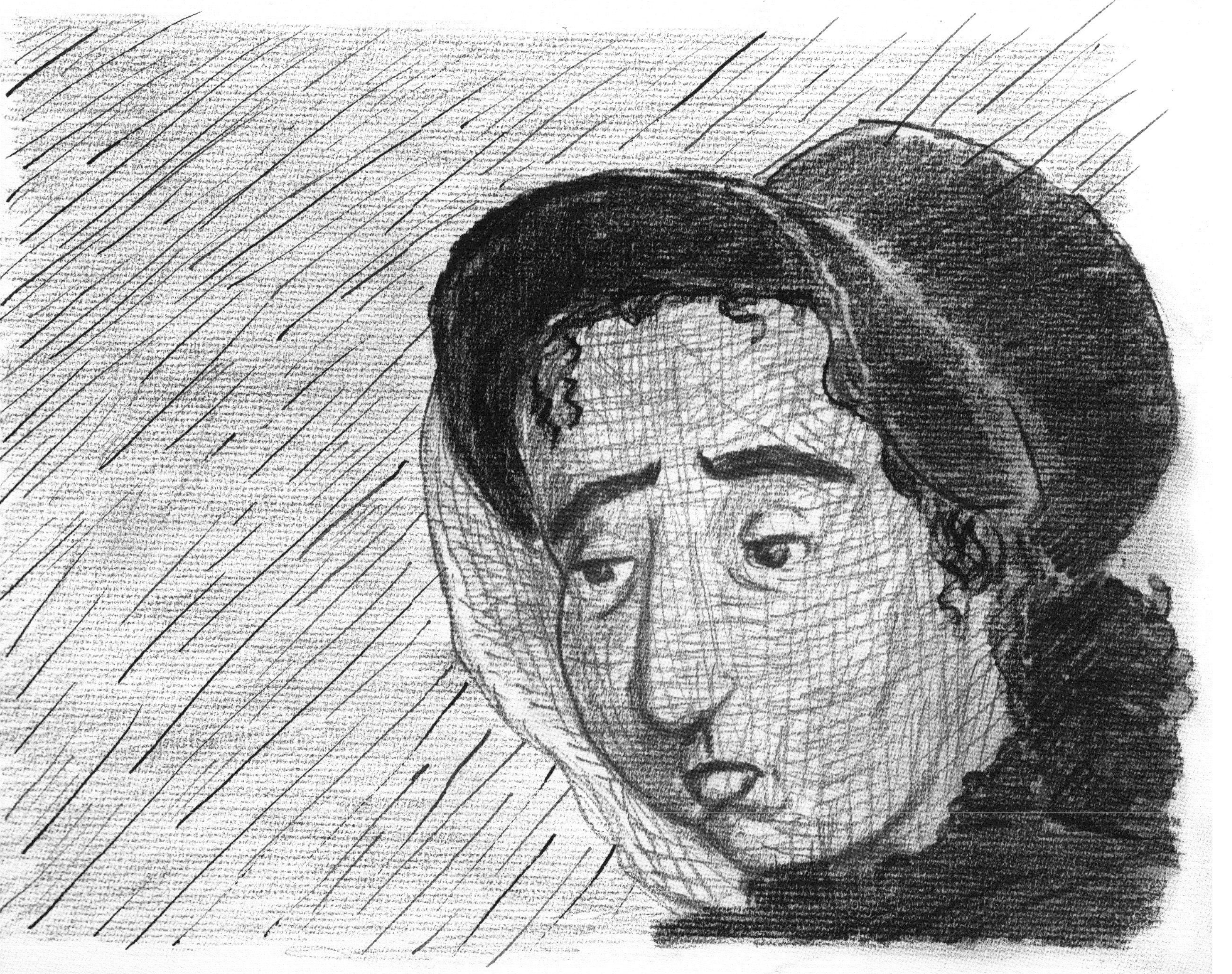

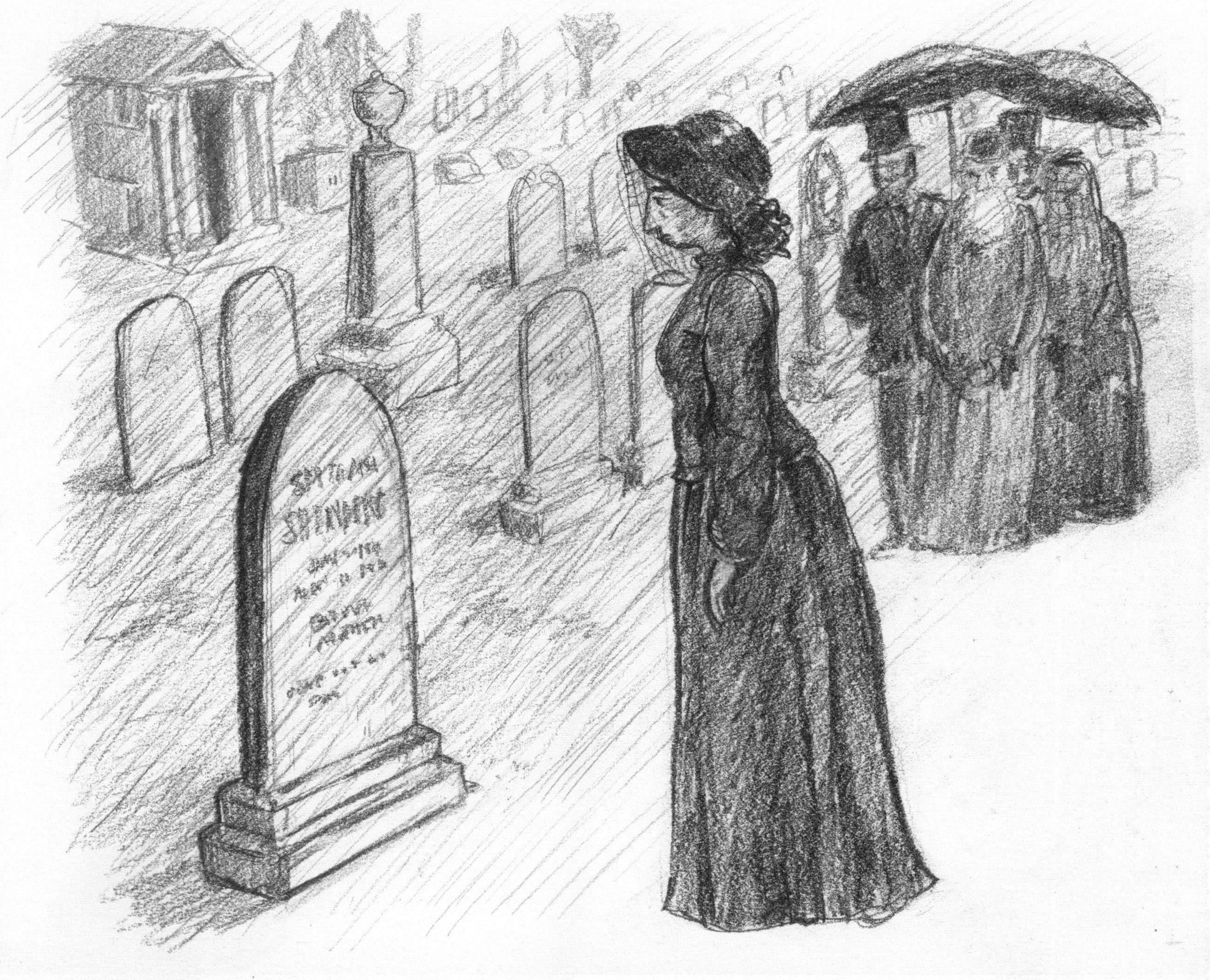

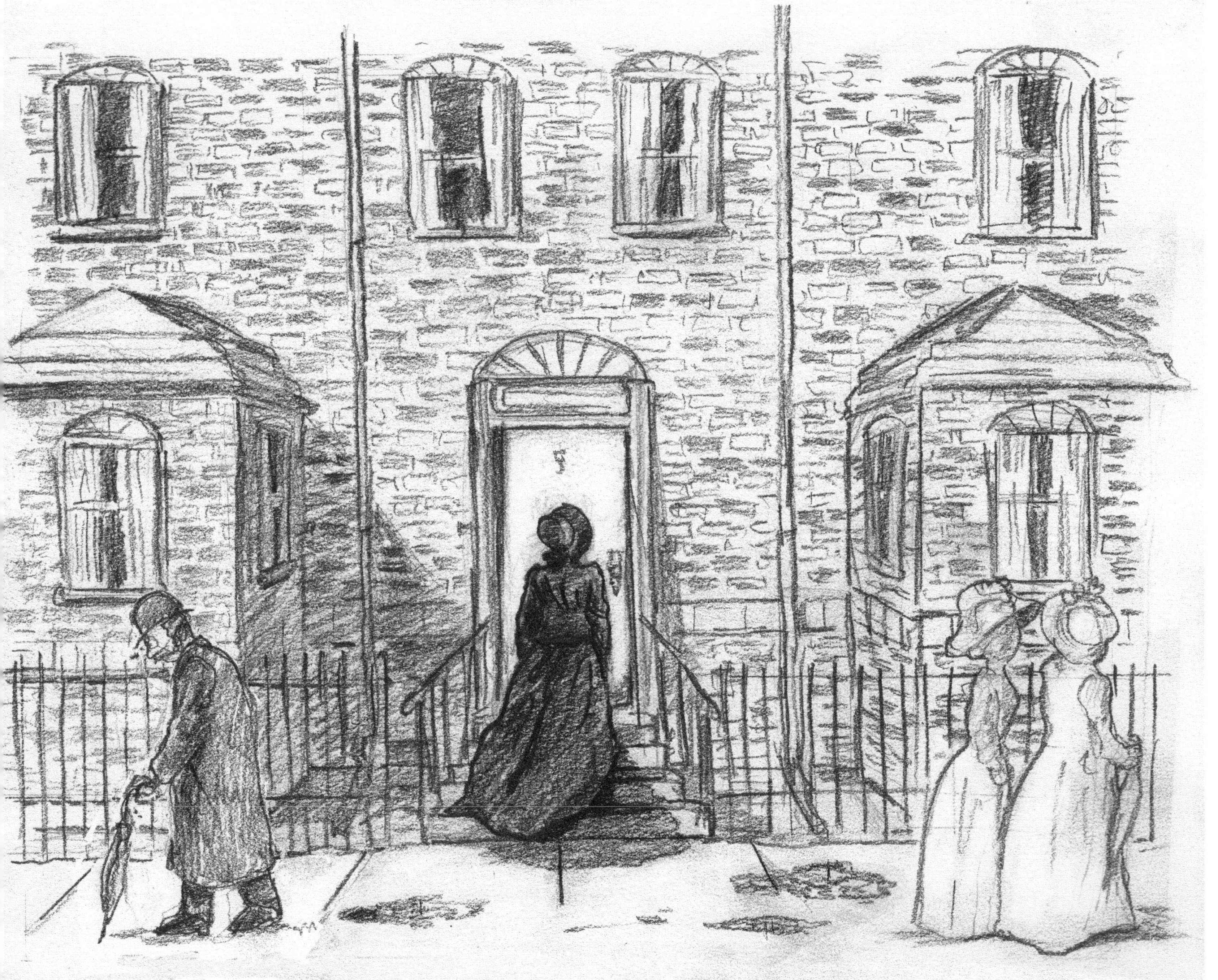

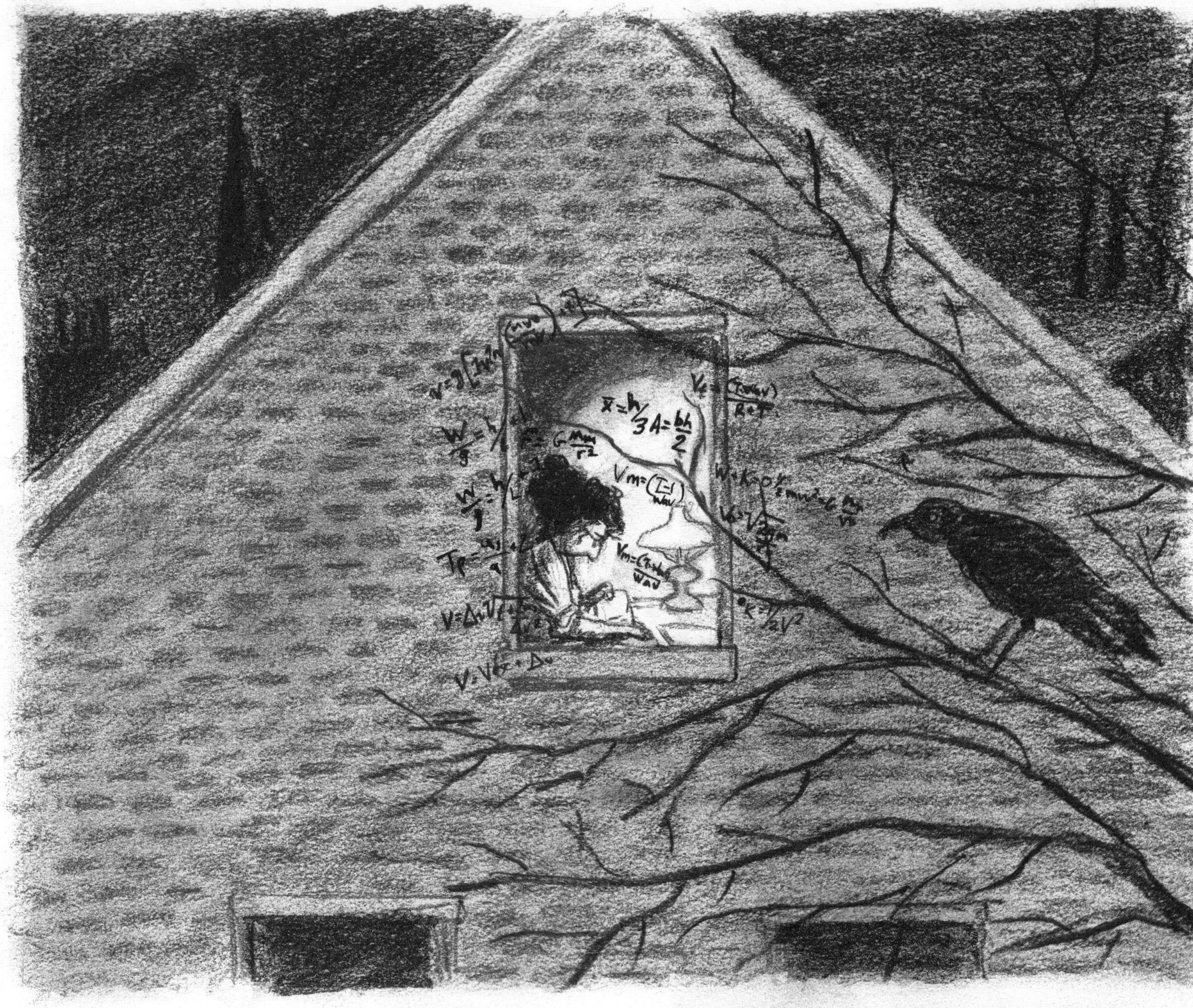

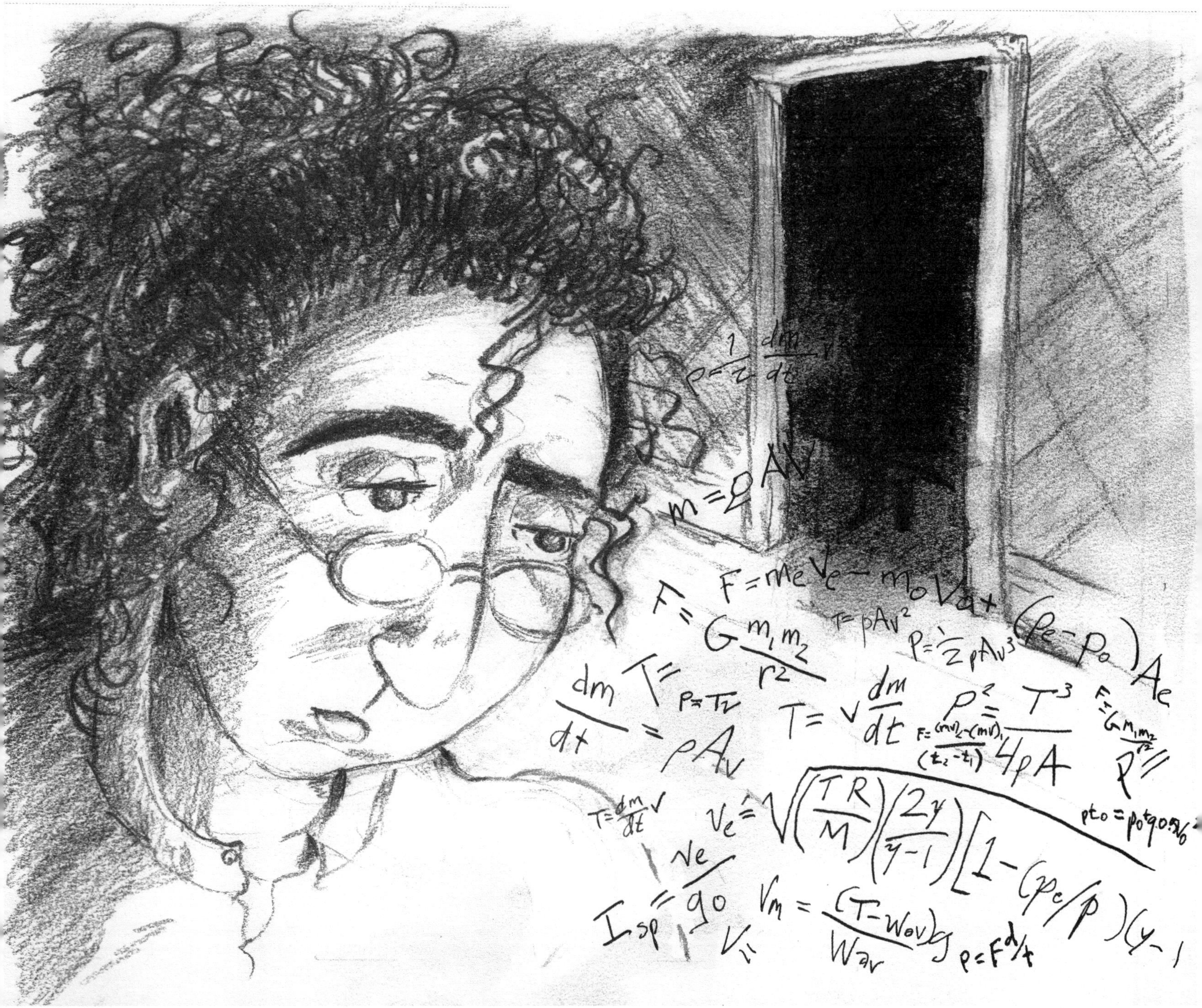

m=ρAV
F=meVe − moVa + (Pe − Po) Ae
F=G m1m2/r2
T=ρAv2
P=1/2 ρAv3
T=v dm/dt
Isp = Ve/g0
Vm = (T−Wov)g/War

ΔV = Ve ln m0/m1
dm/dt
m dV/dt = −Ve
∫ F dt = J
P2 − P1 = mΔV − V ΔM
+ ΔmVe
Σ Fi = m dV/dt + Ve
e = V − Ve
P2 = m(V + ΔV)
P1 = (m + Δm)V
Σ Fi = lim Δt→0 (P2 − P1)/Δt
Σ Fi = 0
Δv = Ve ln m0/mf
= Isp g0 ln m0/mf
Ve = Isp g0

8

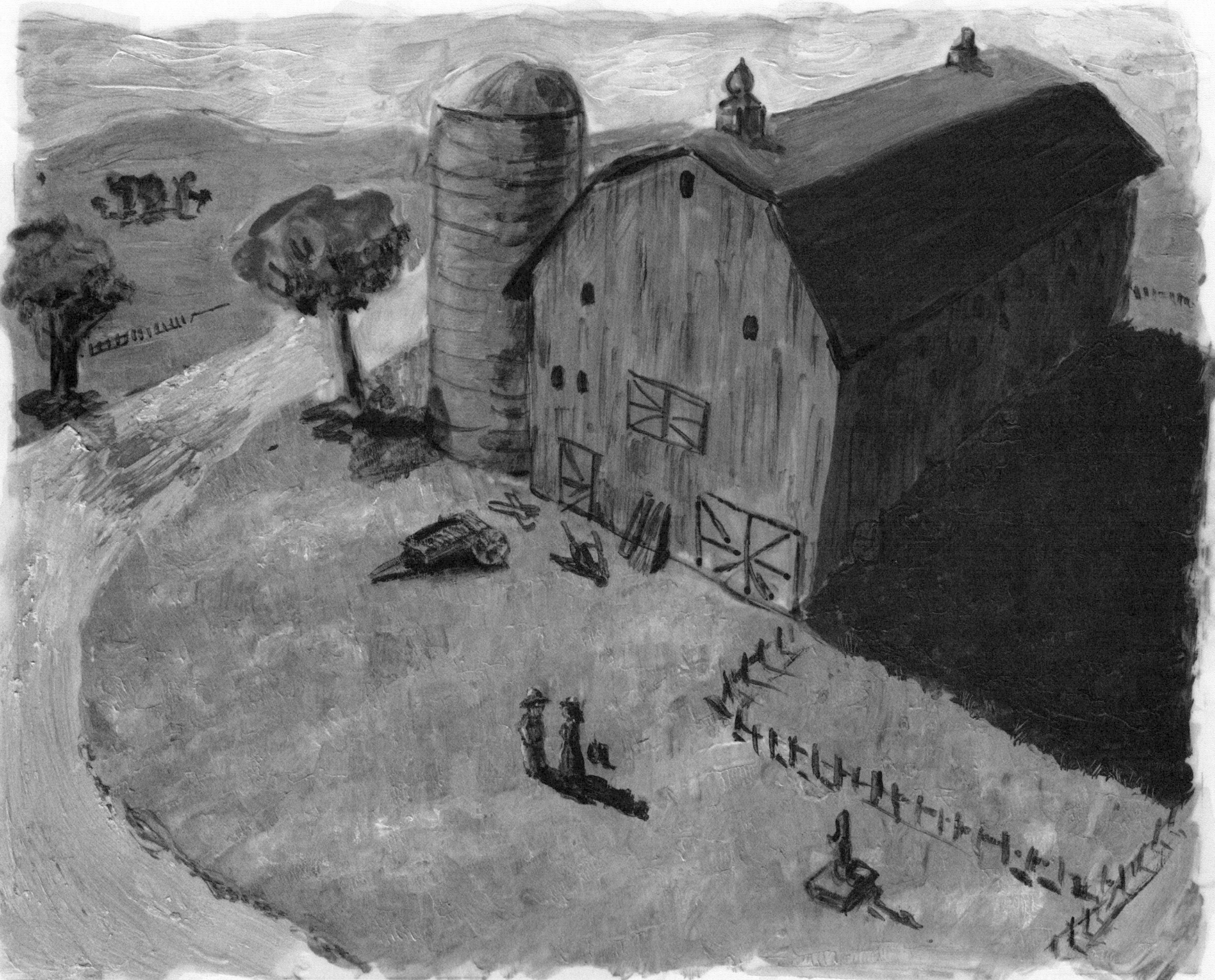

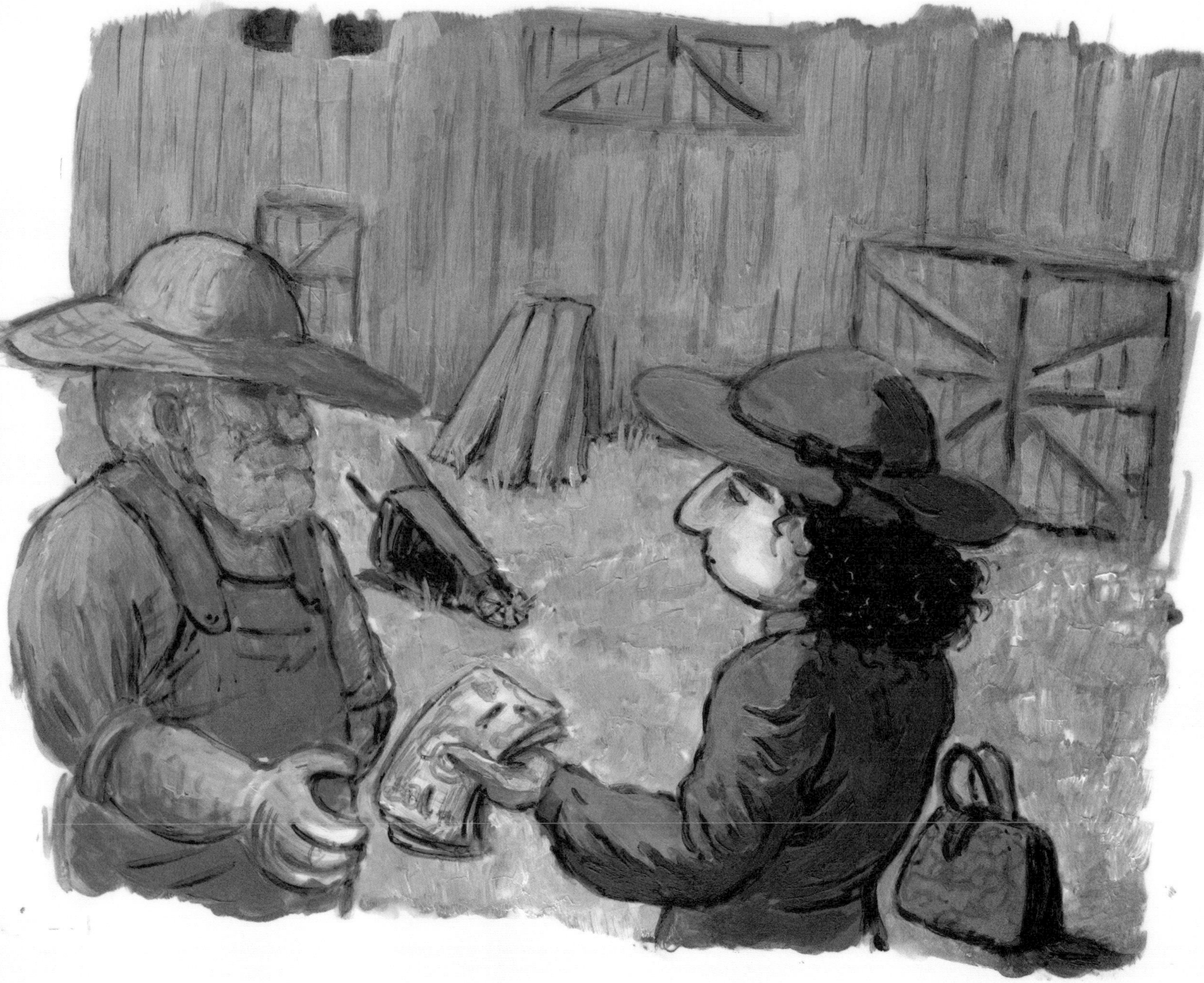

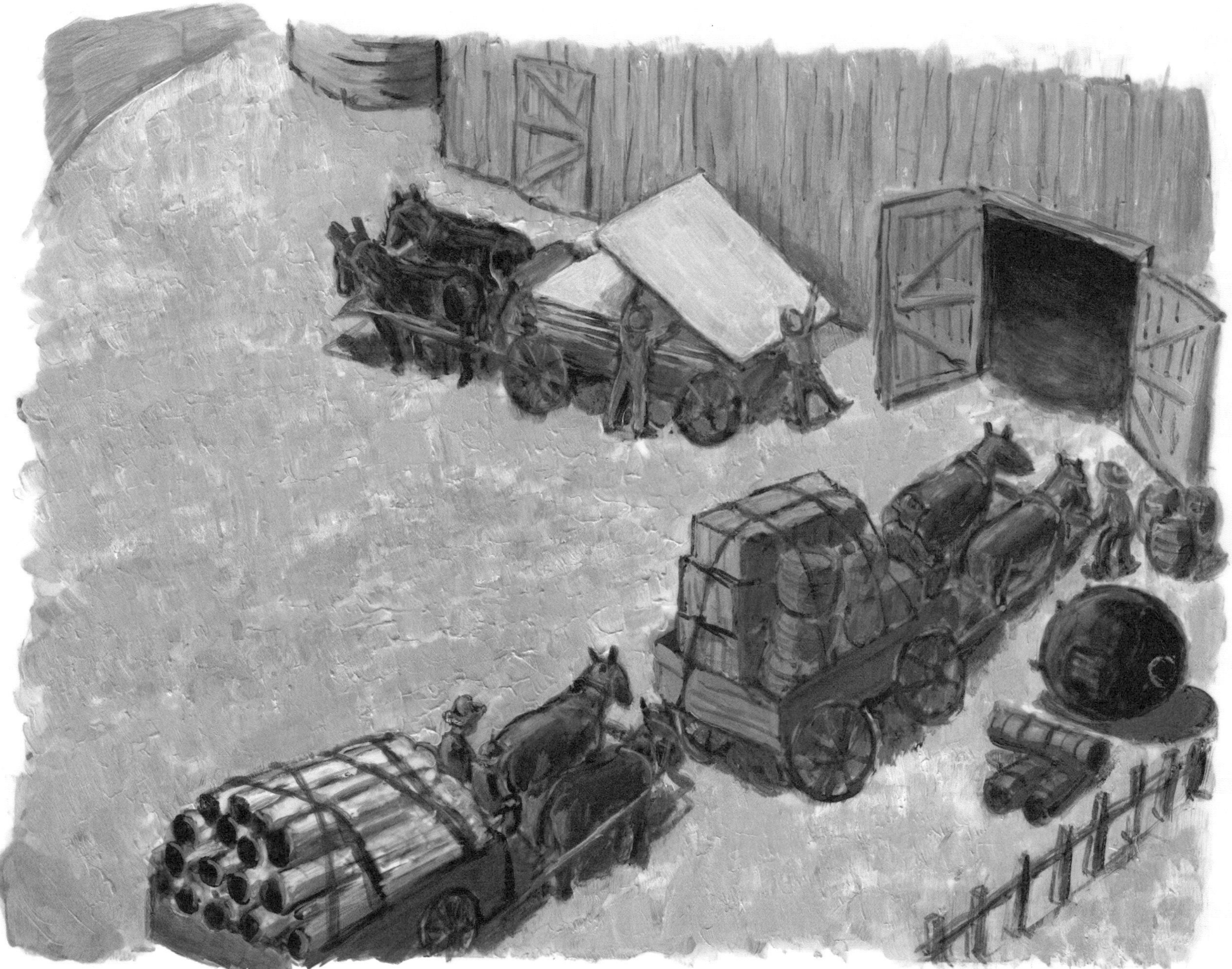

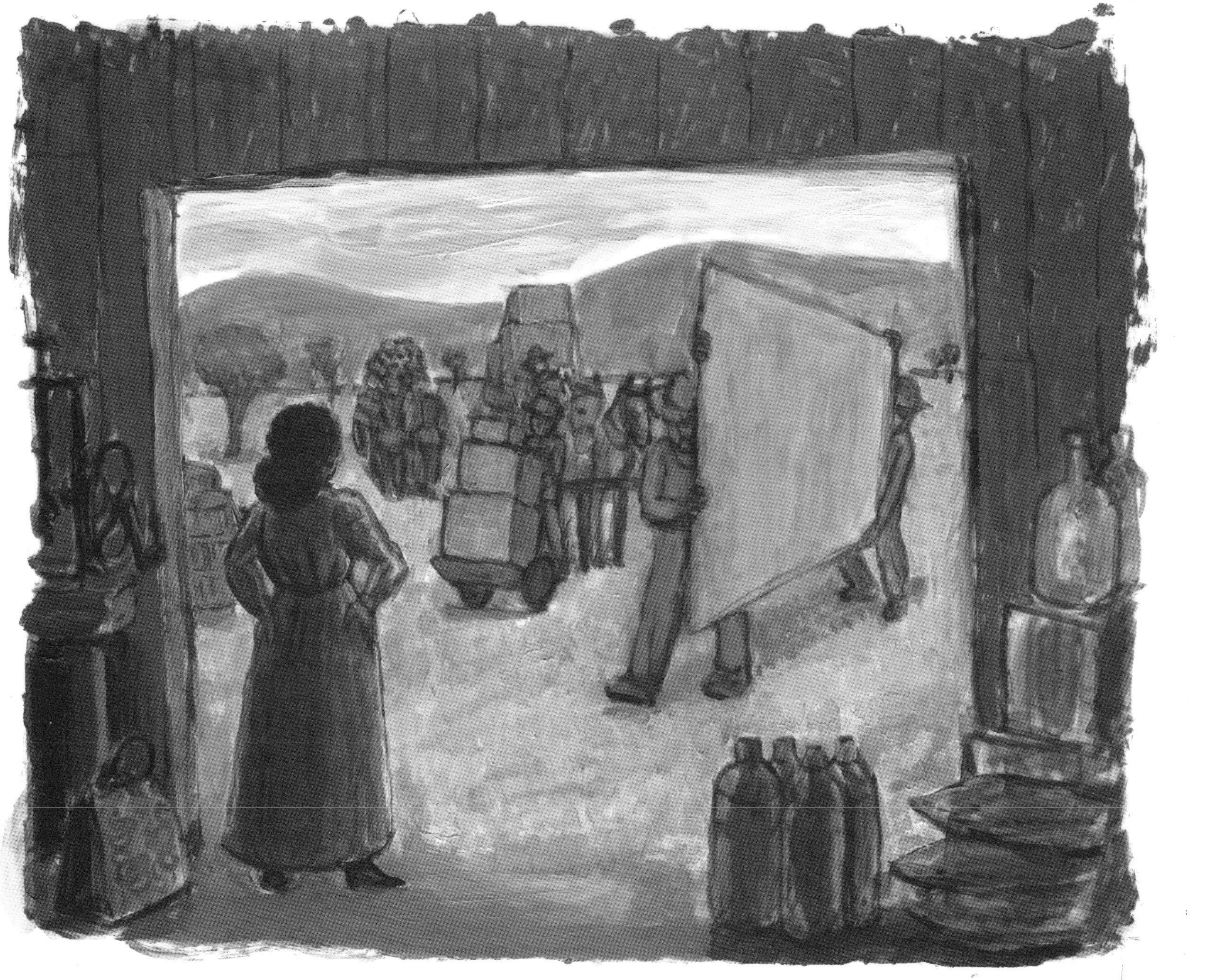

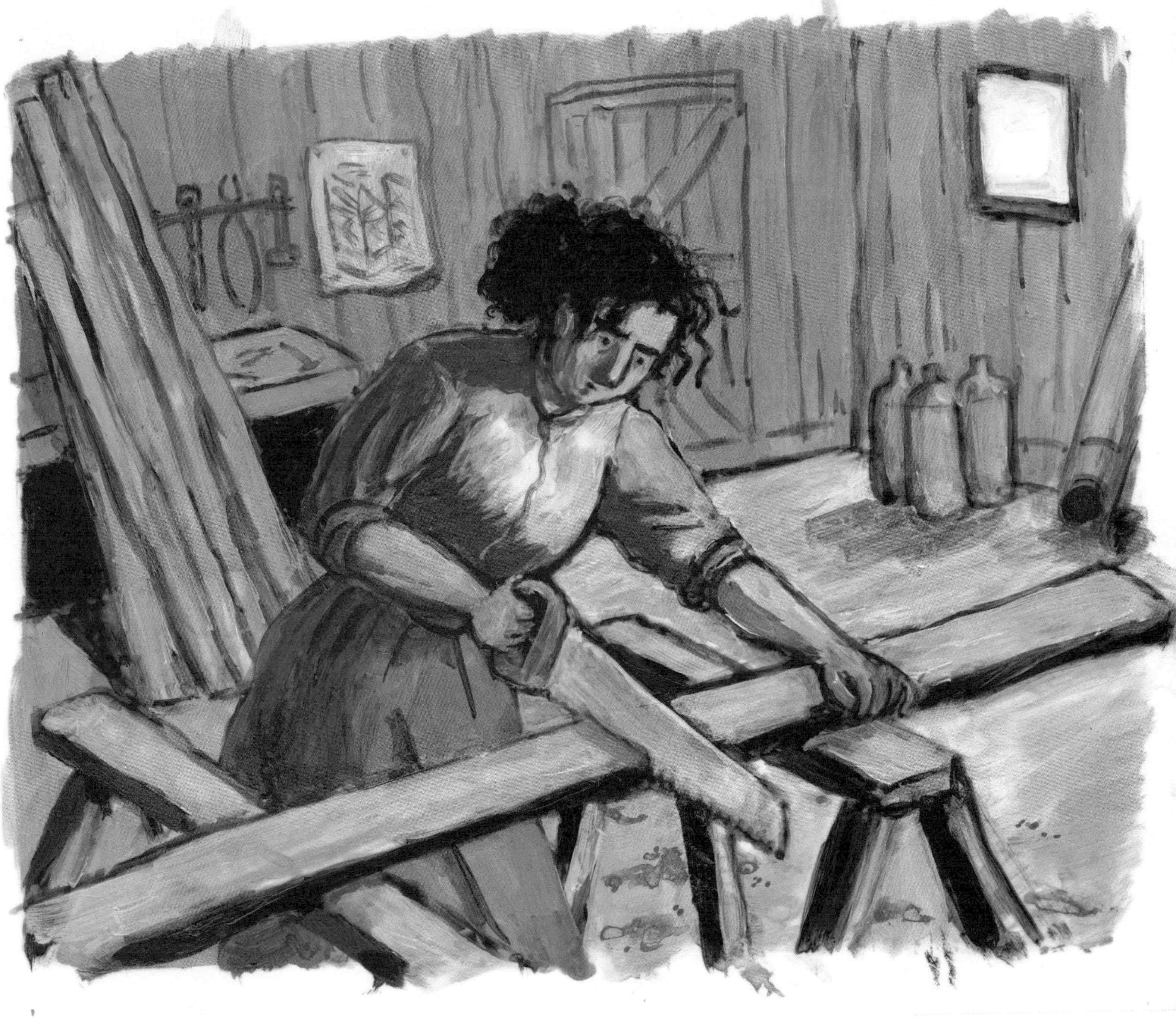

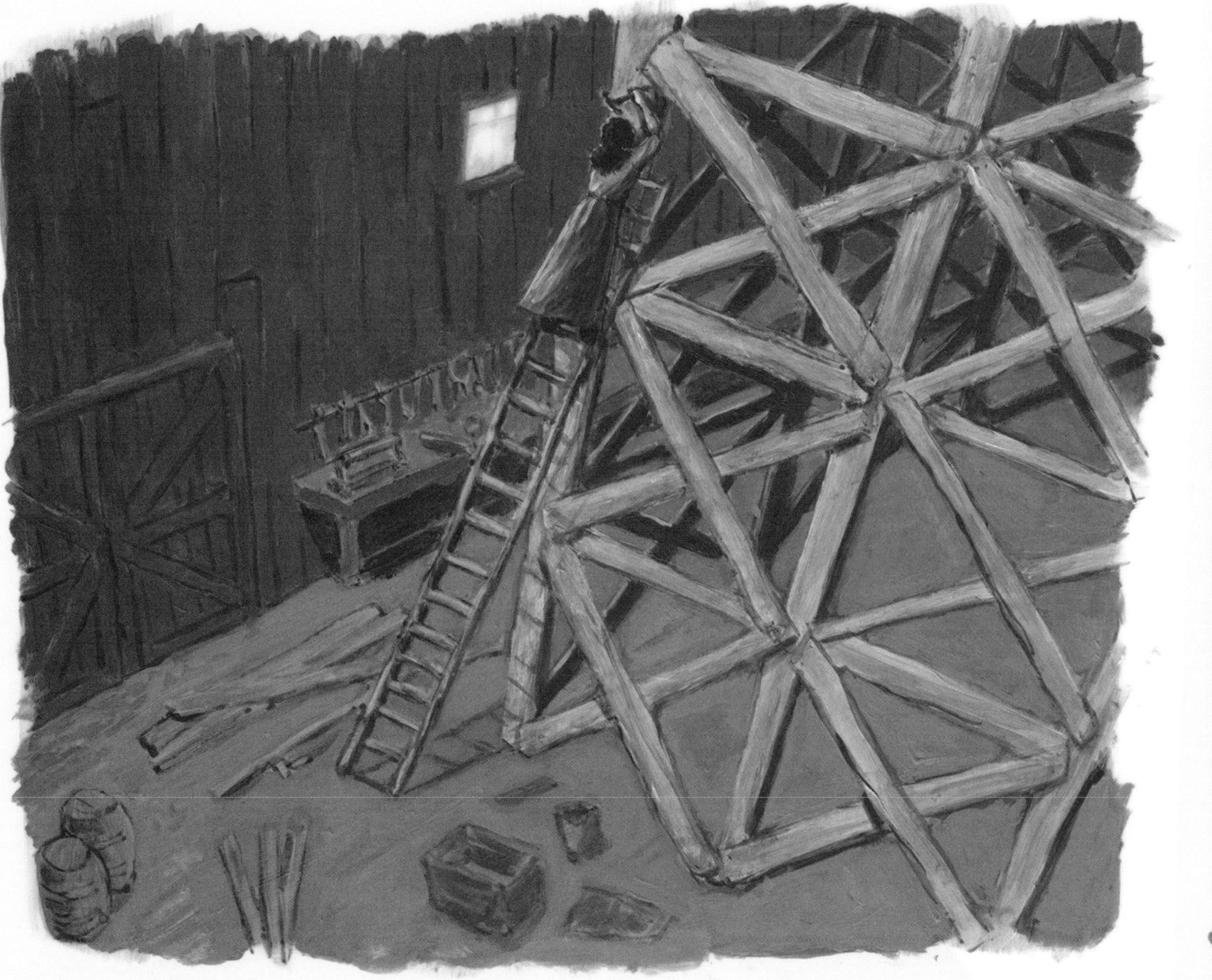

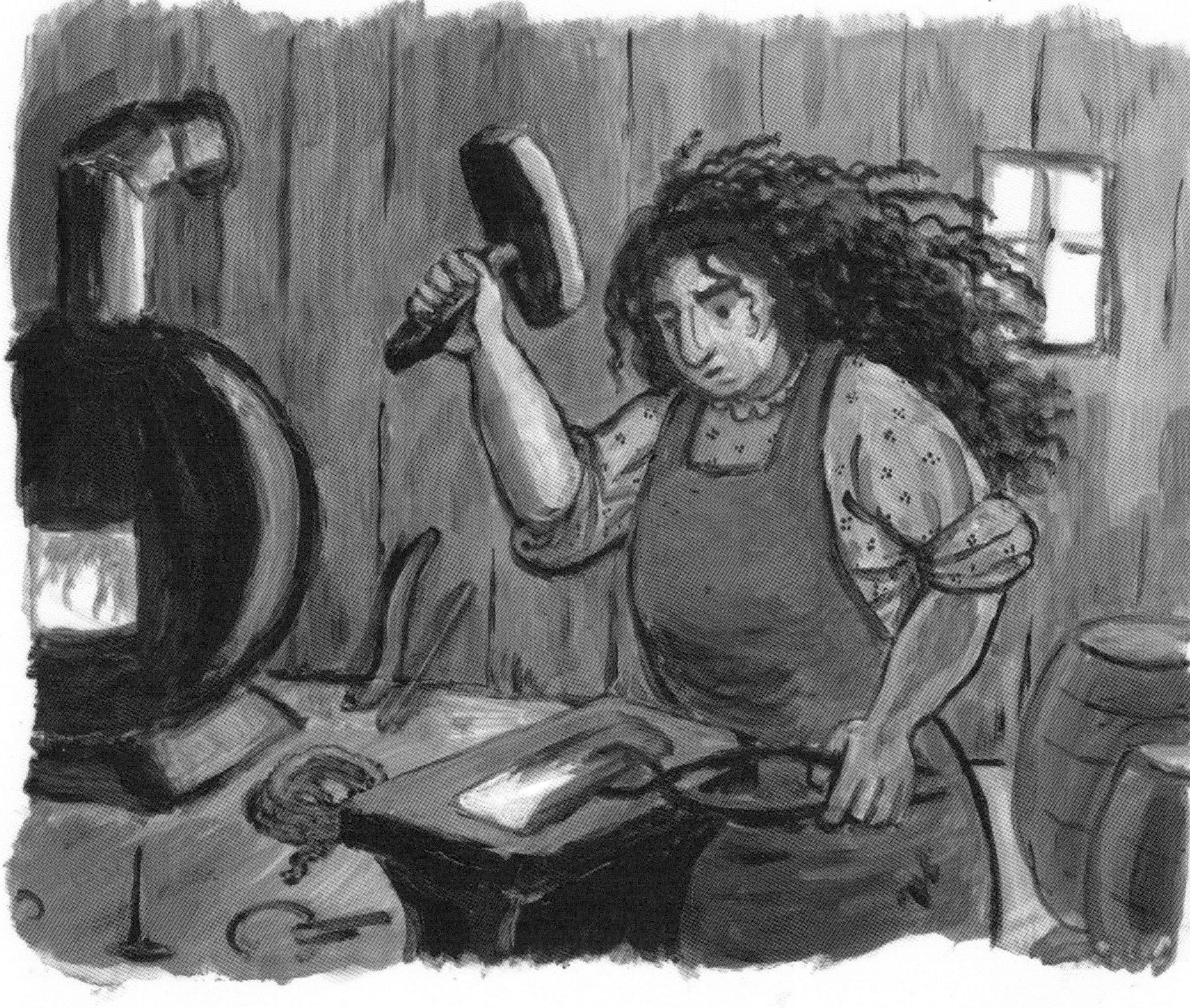

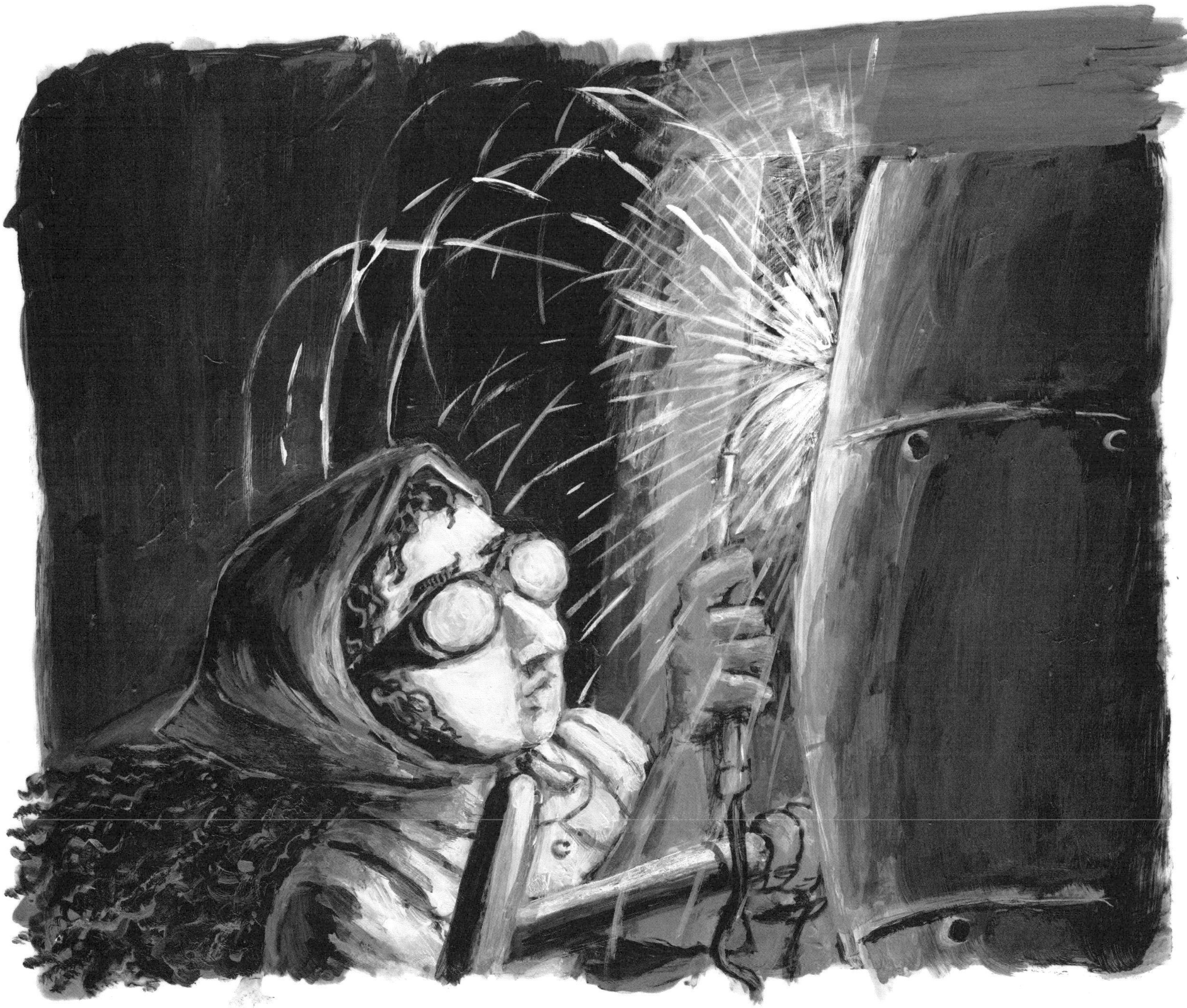

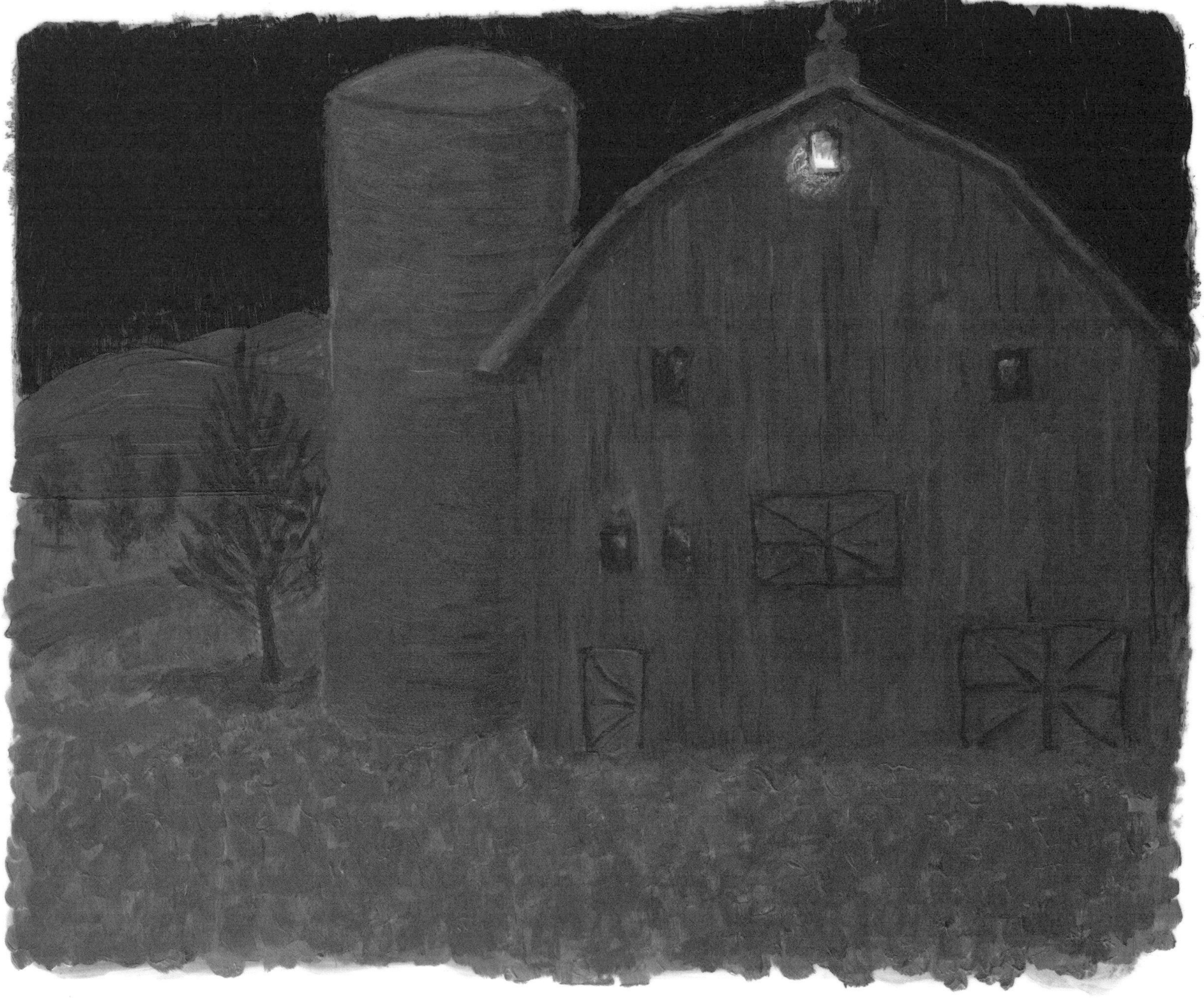

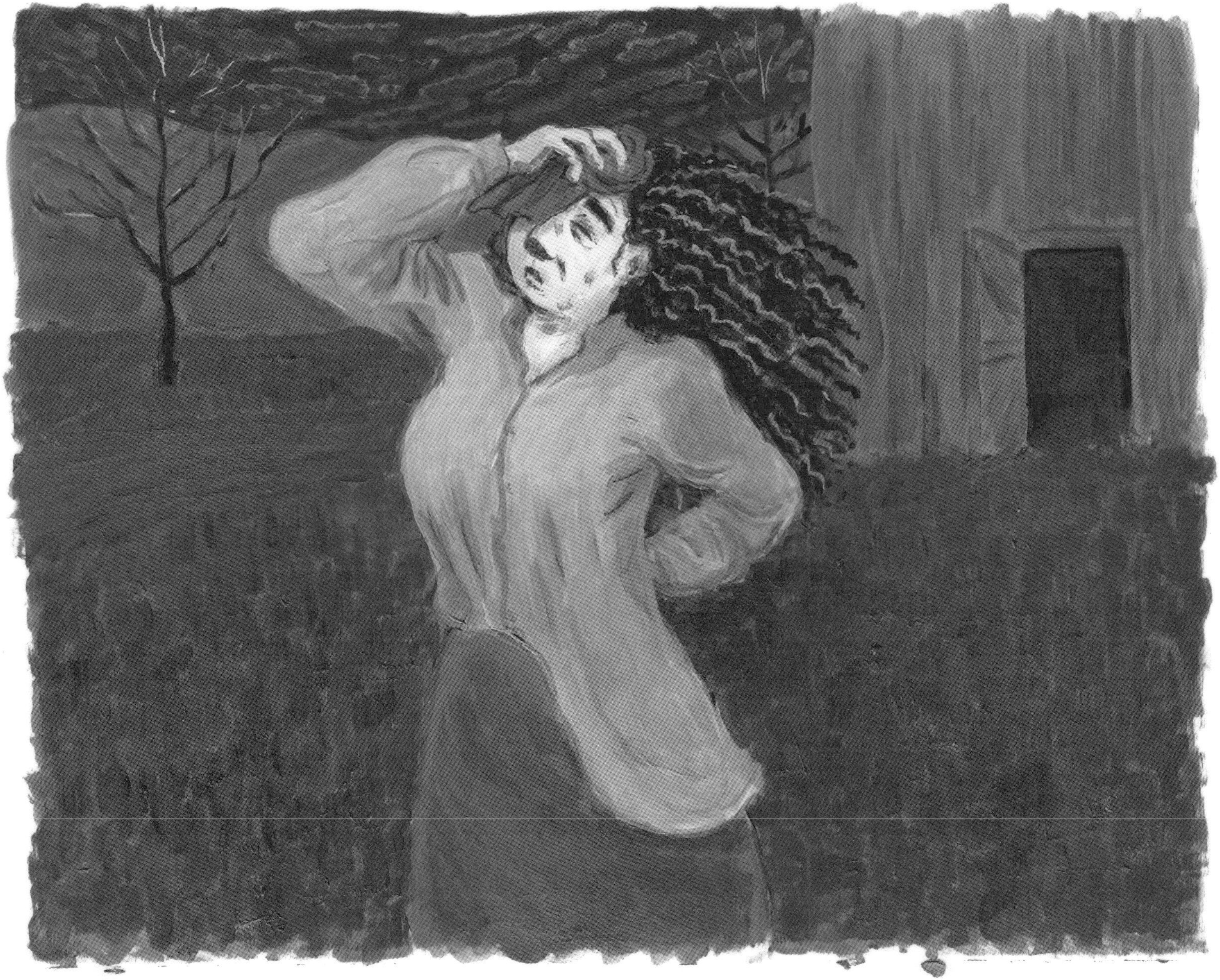

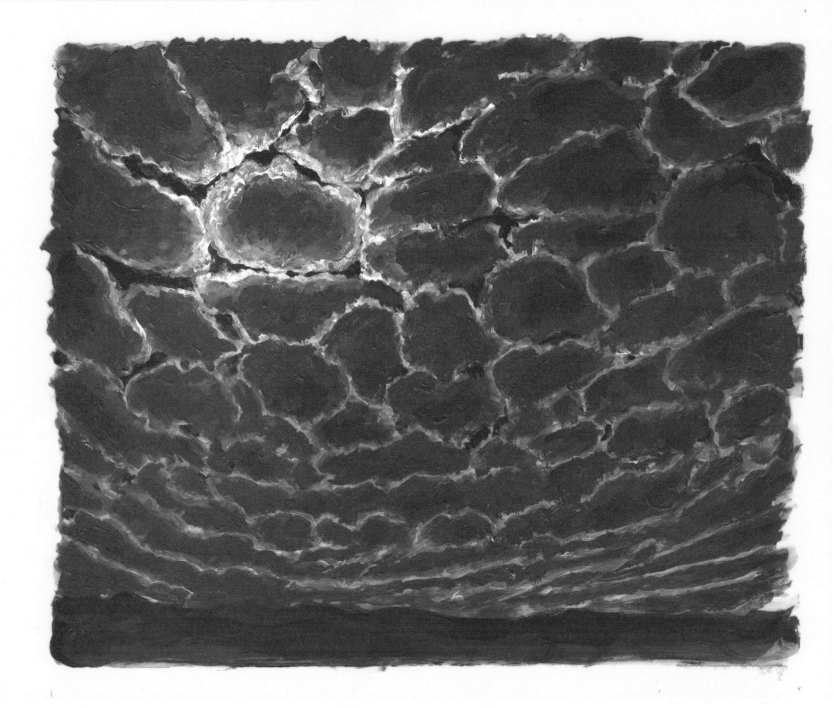

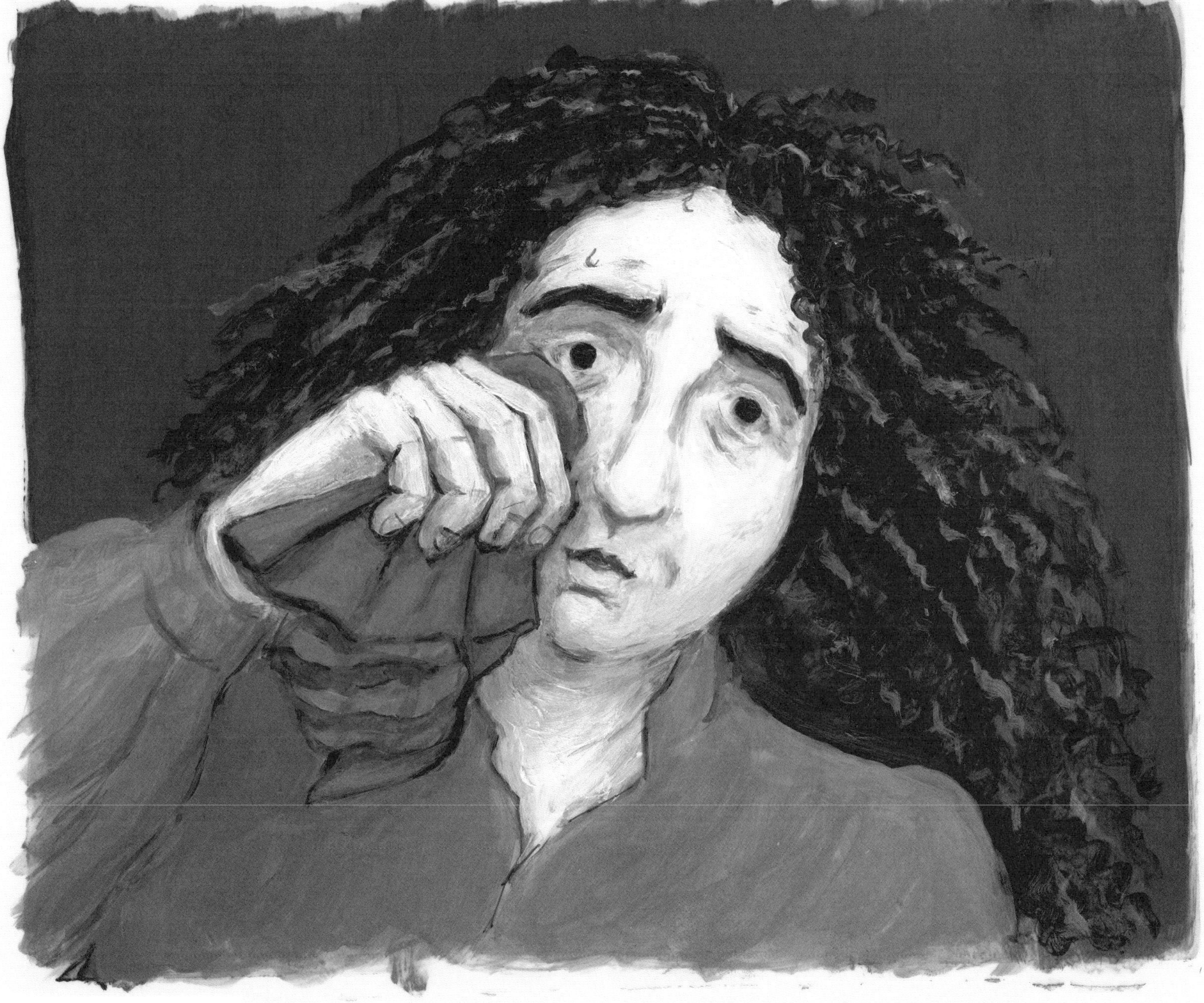

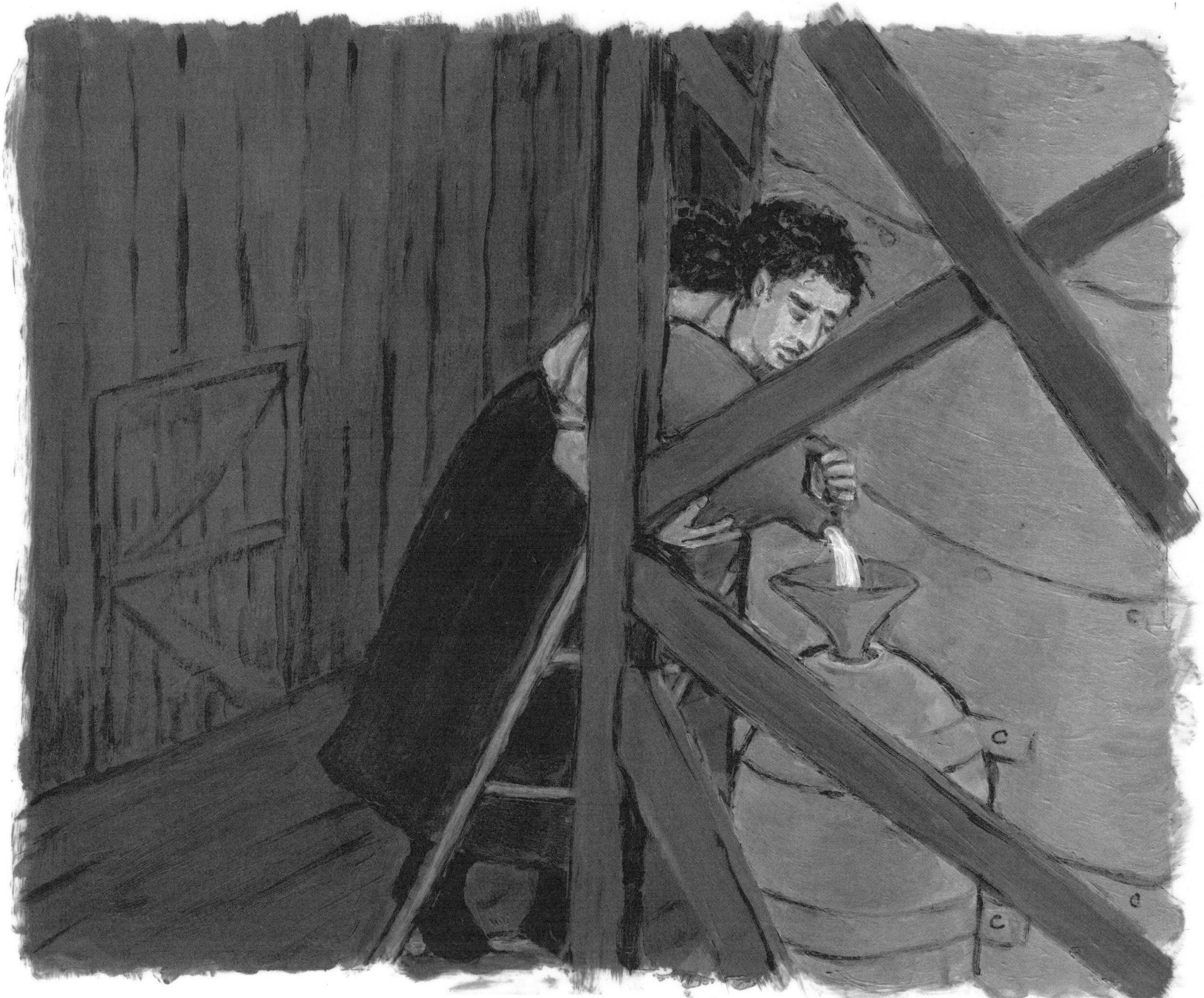

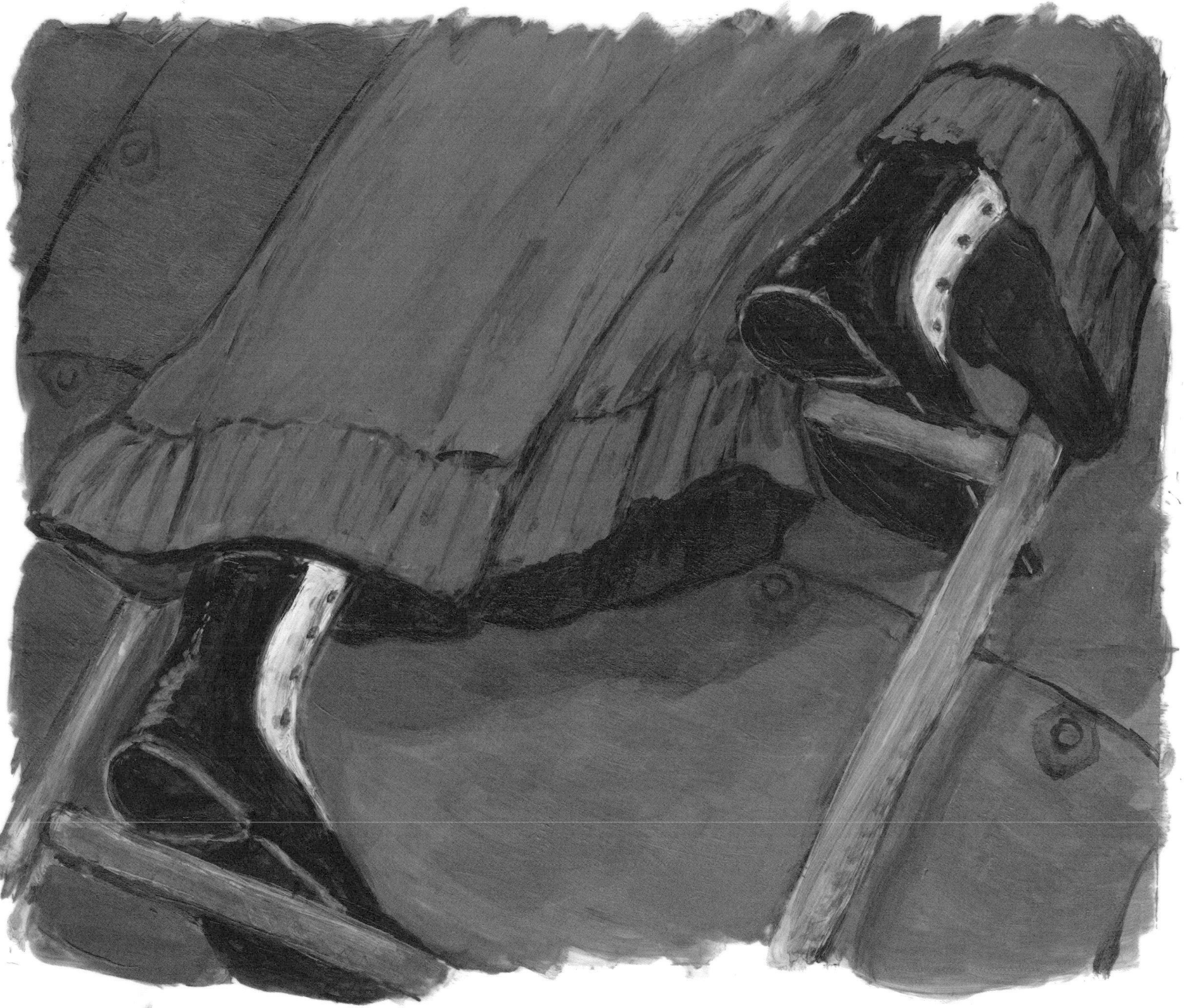

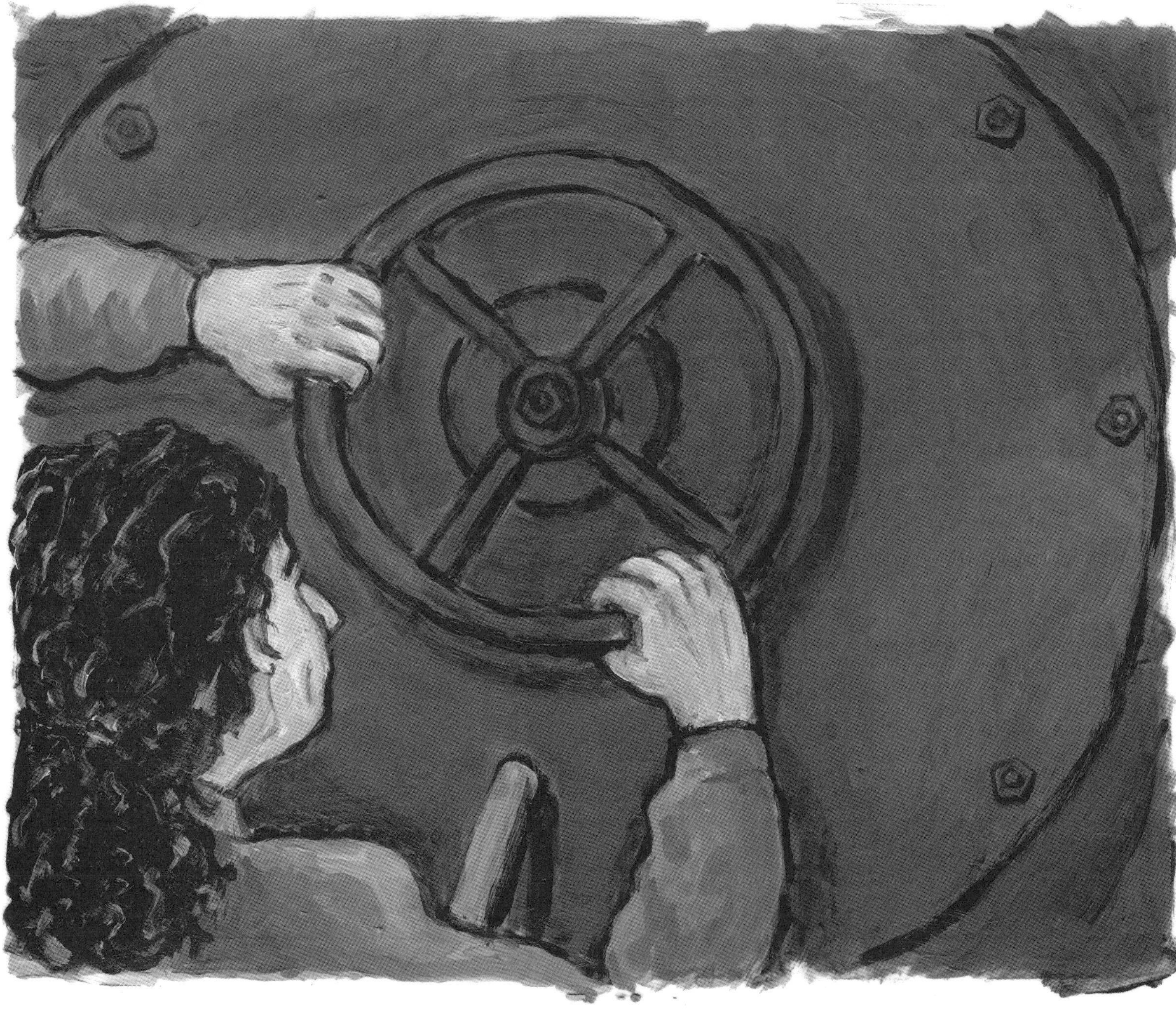

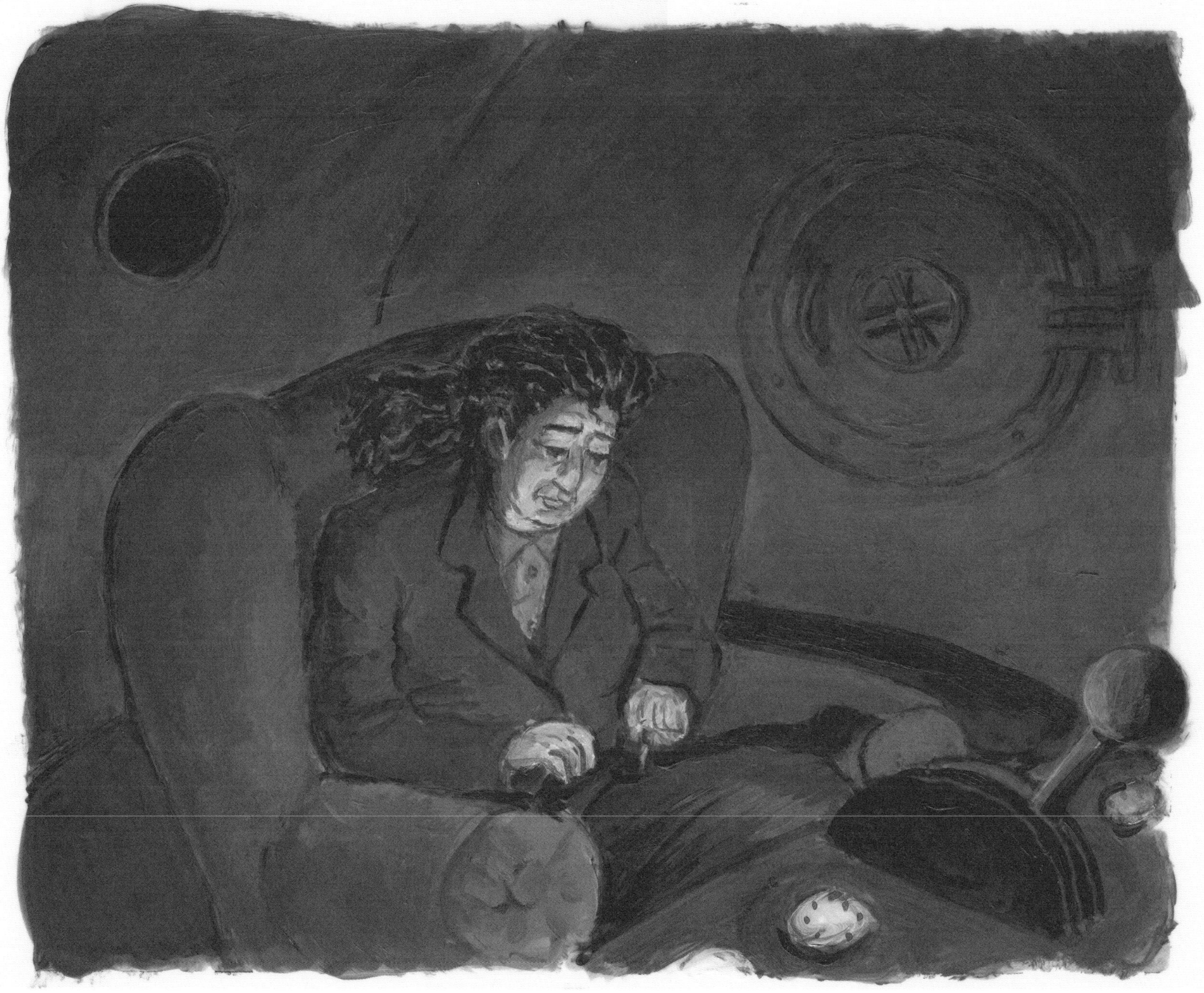

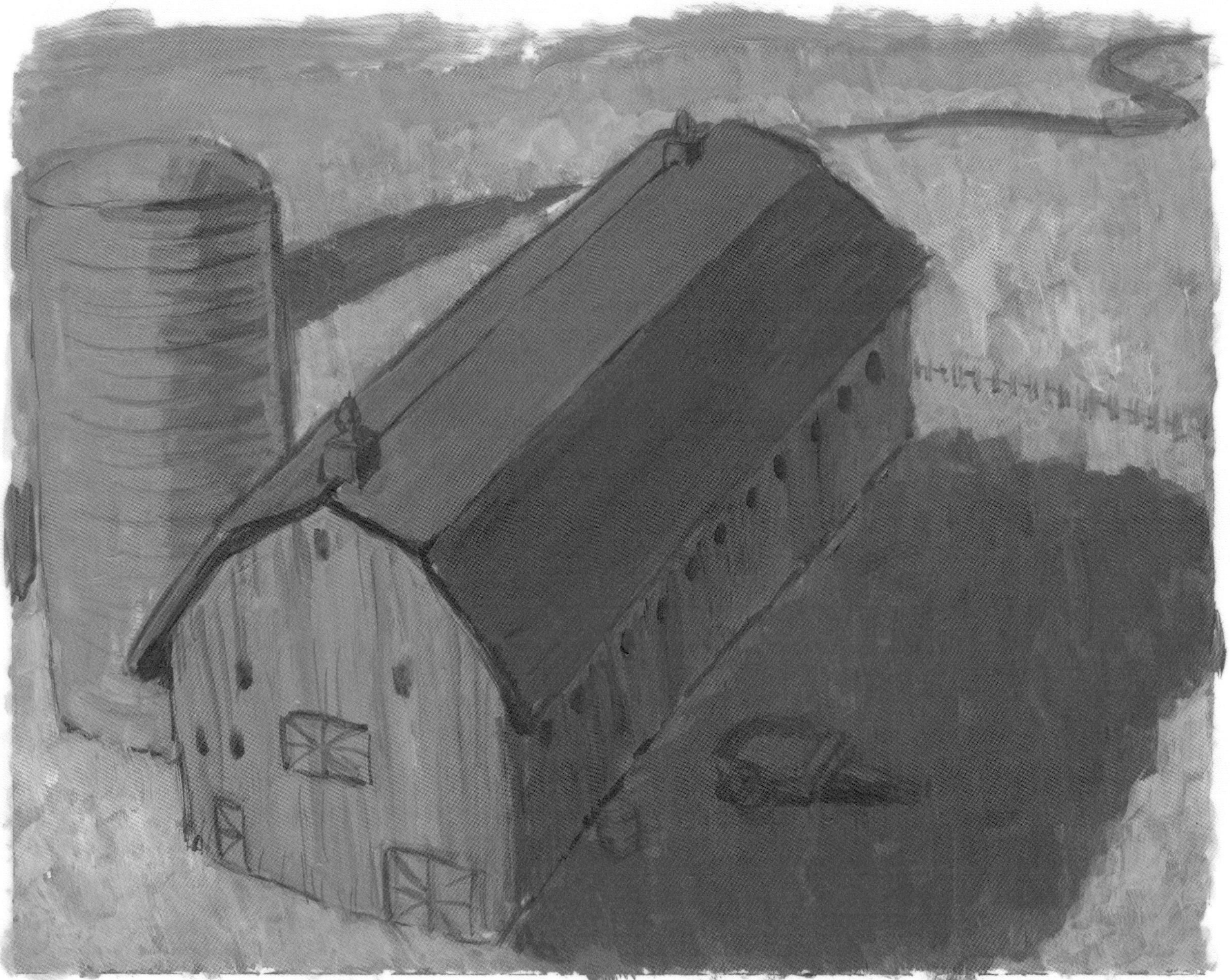

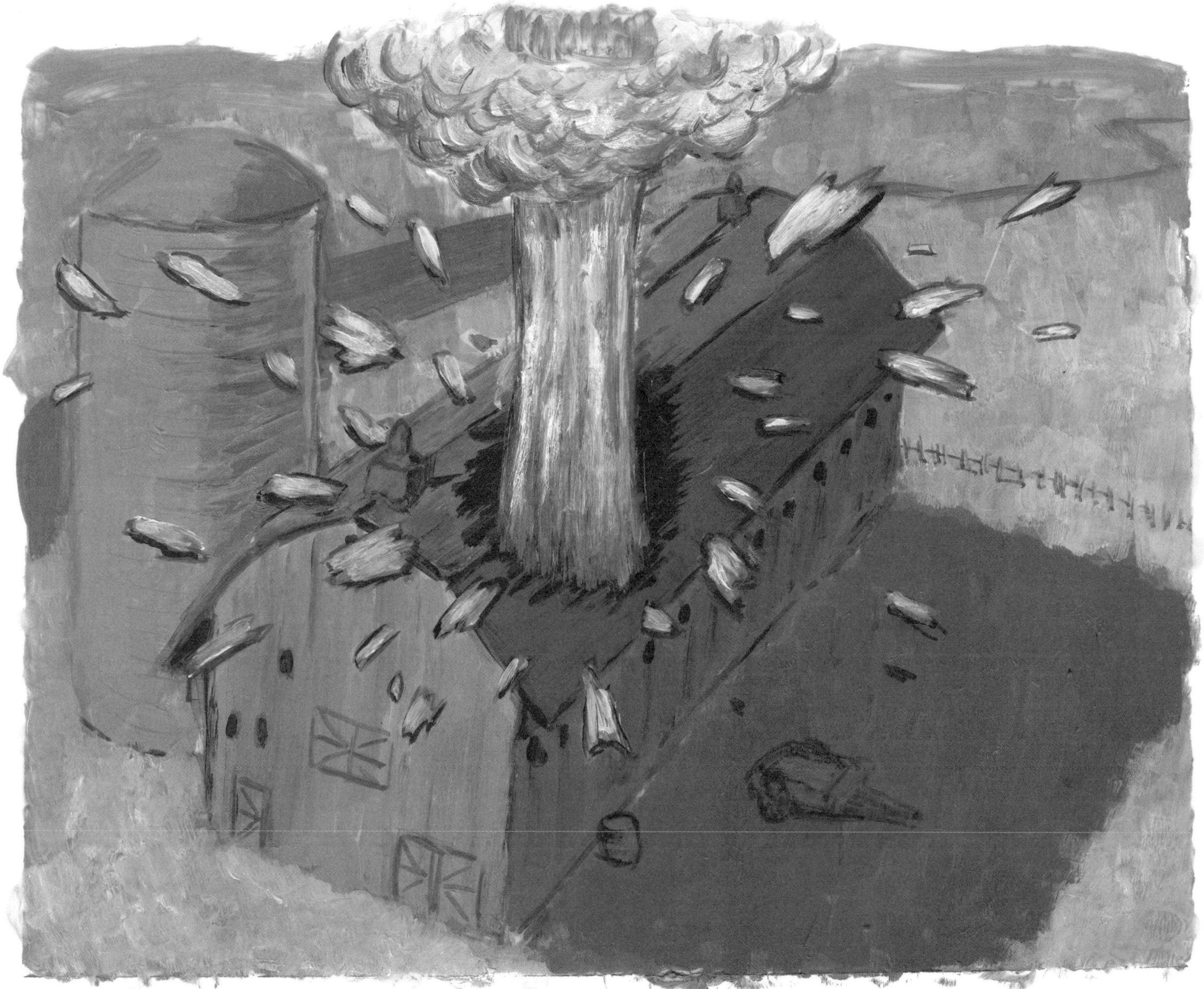

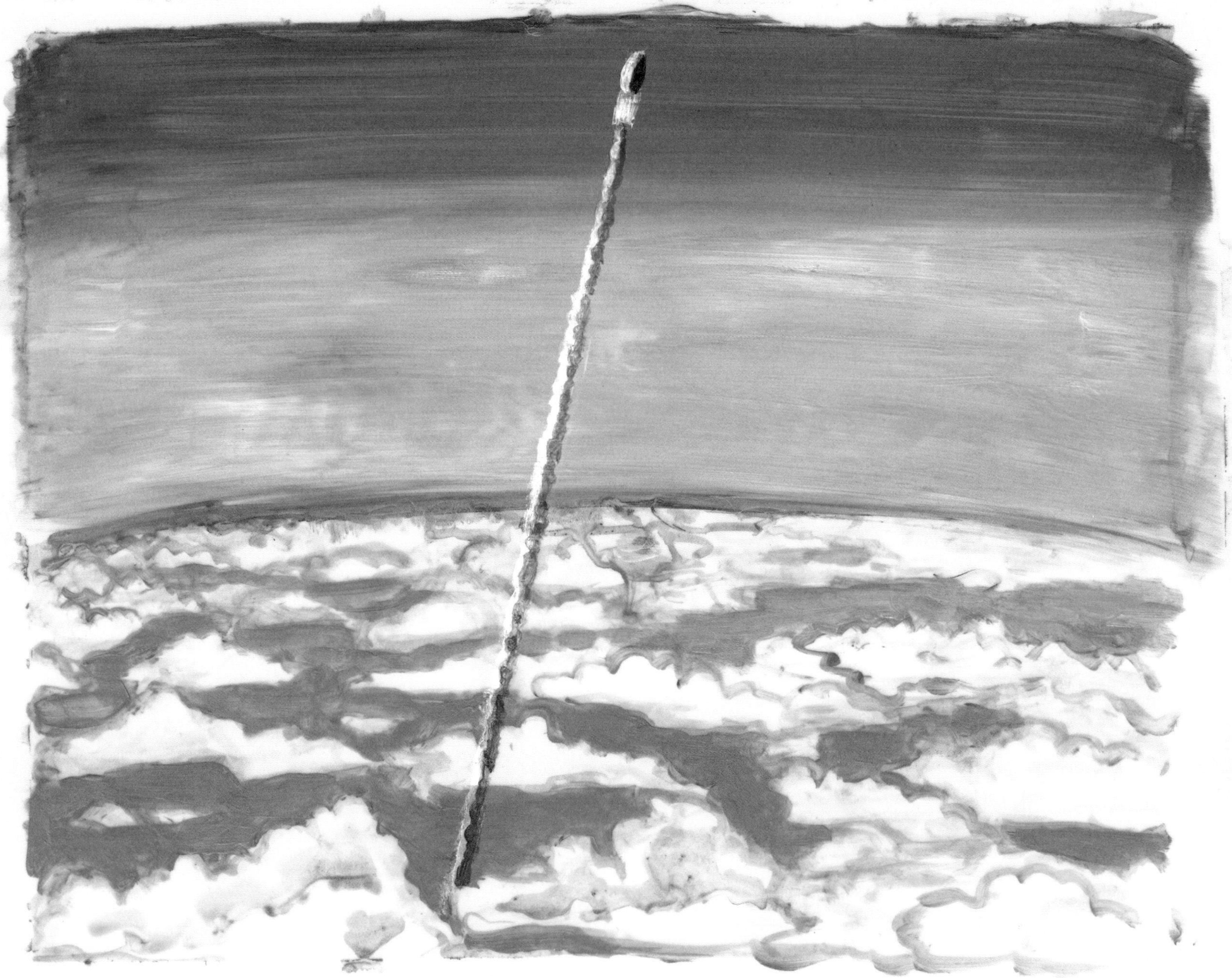

9

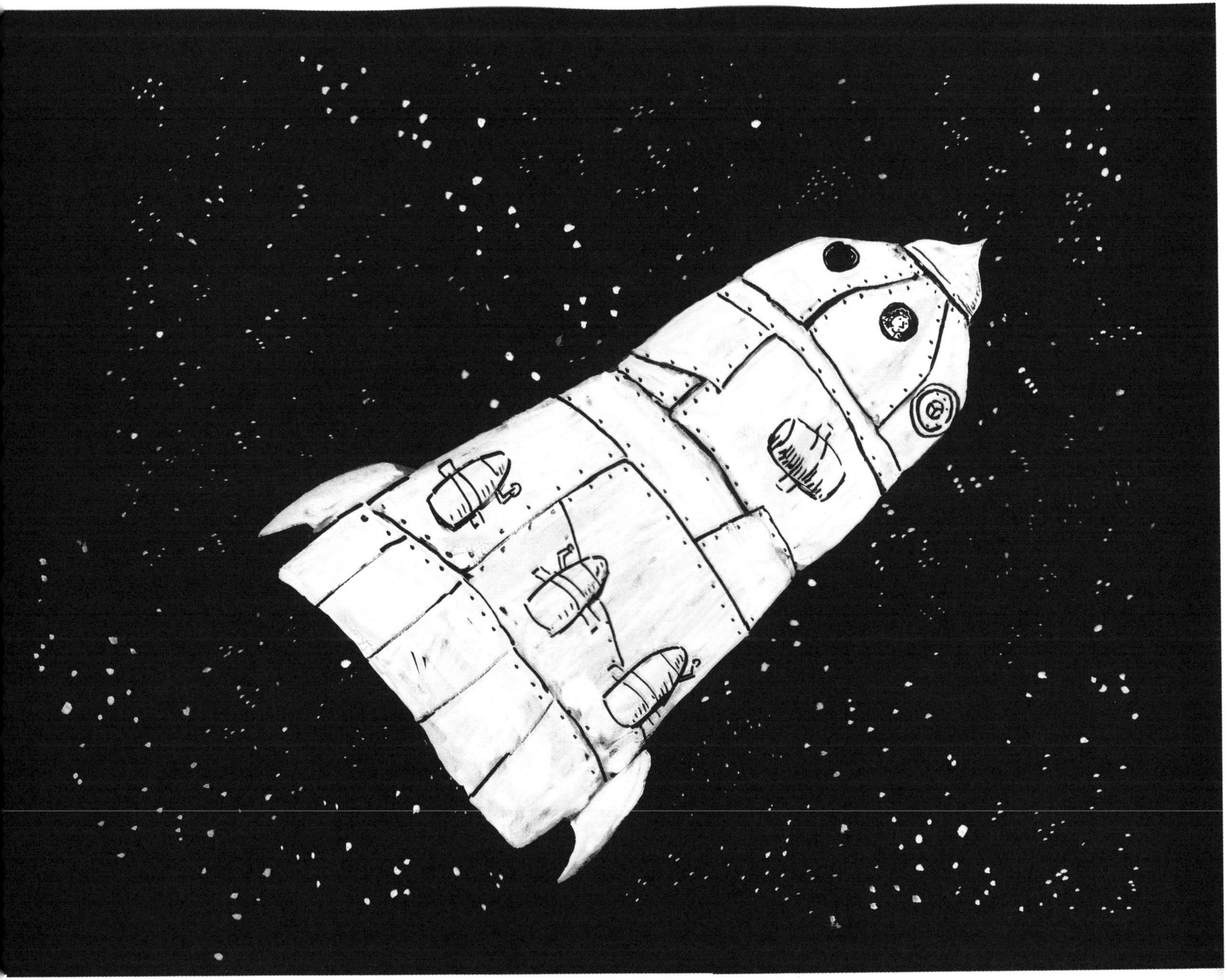

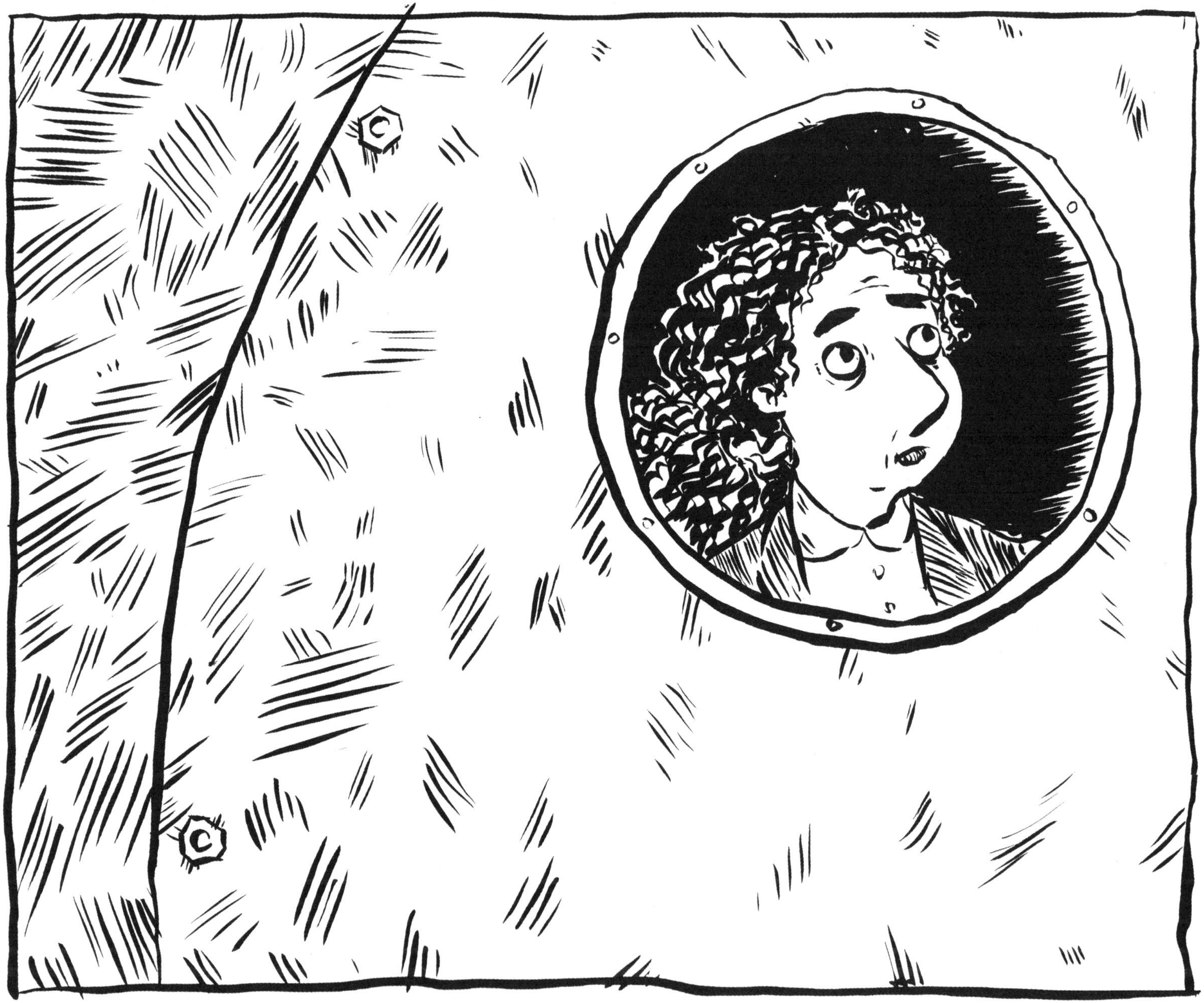

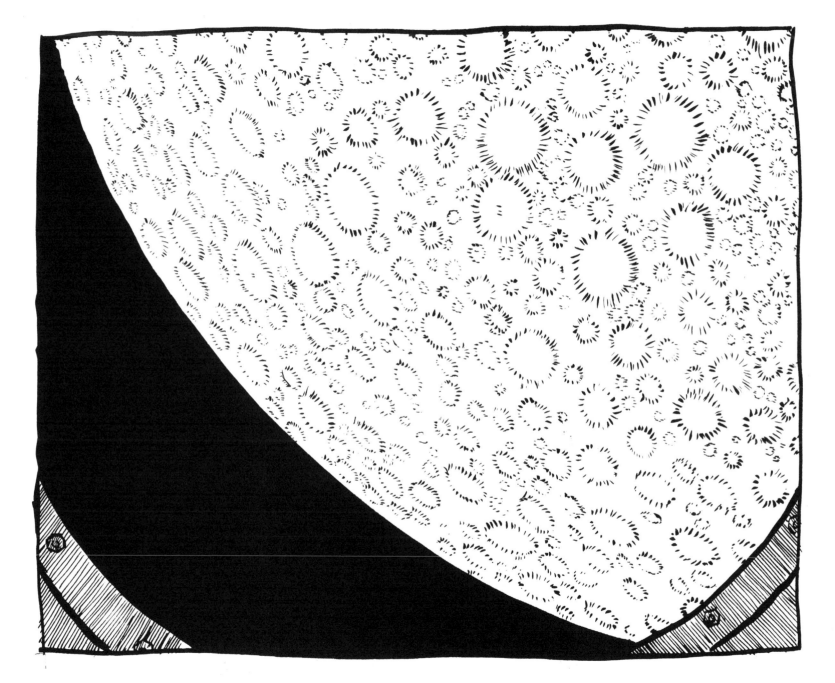

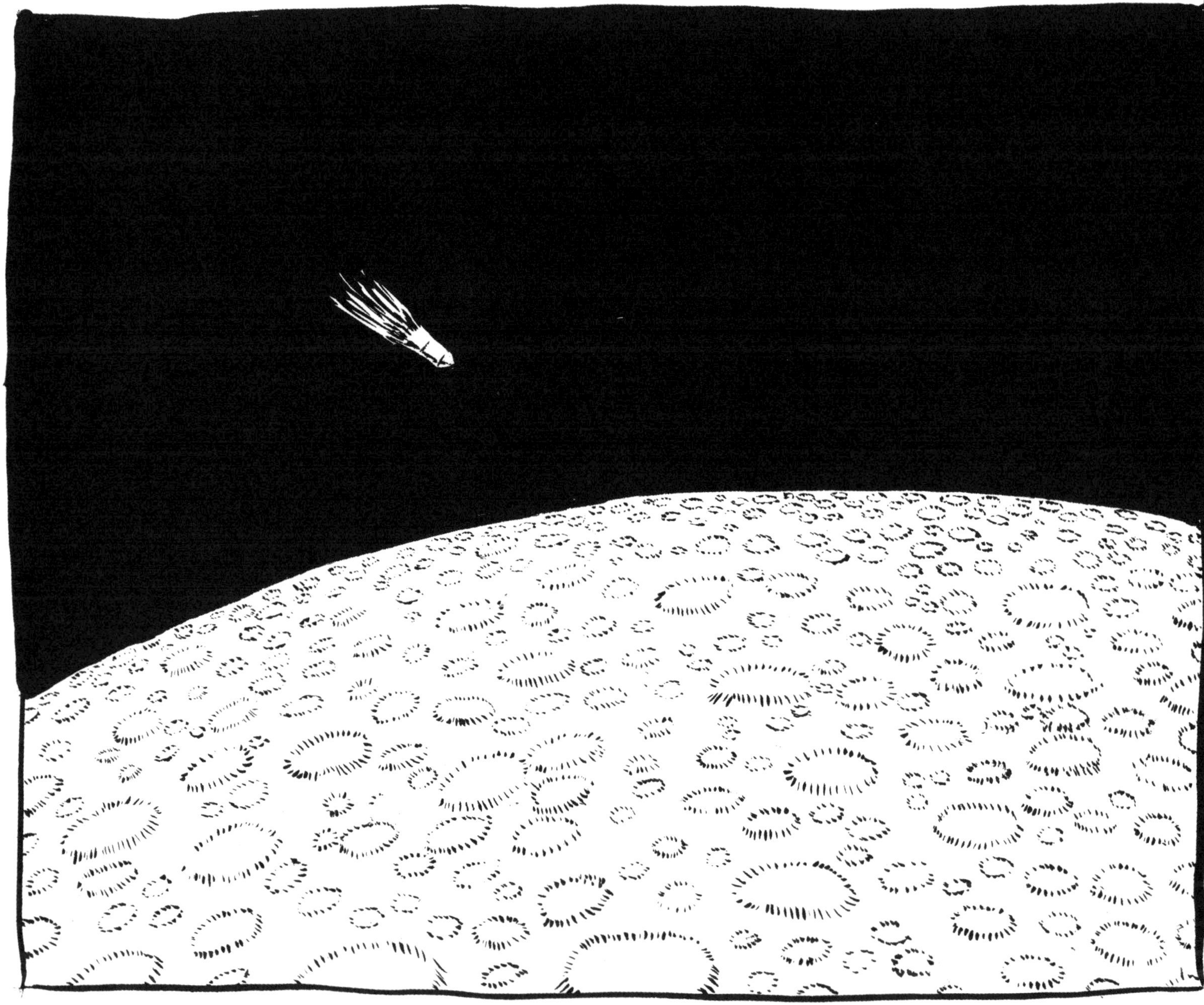

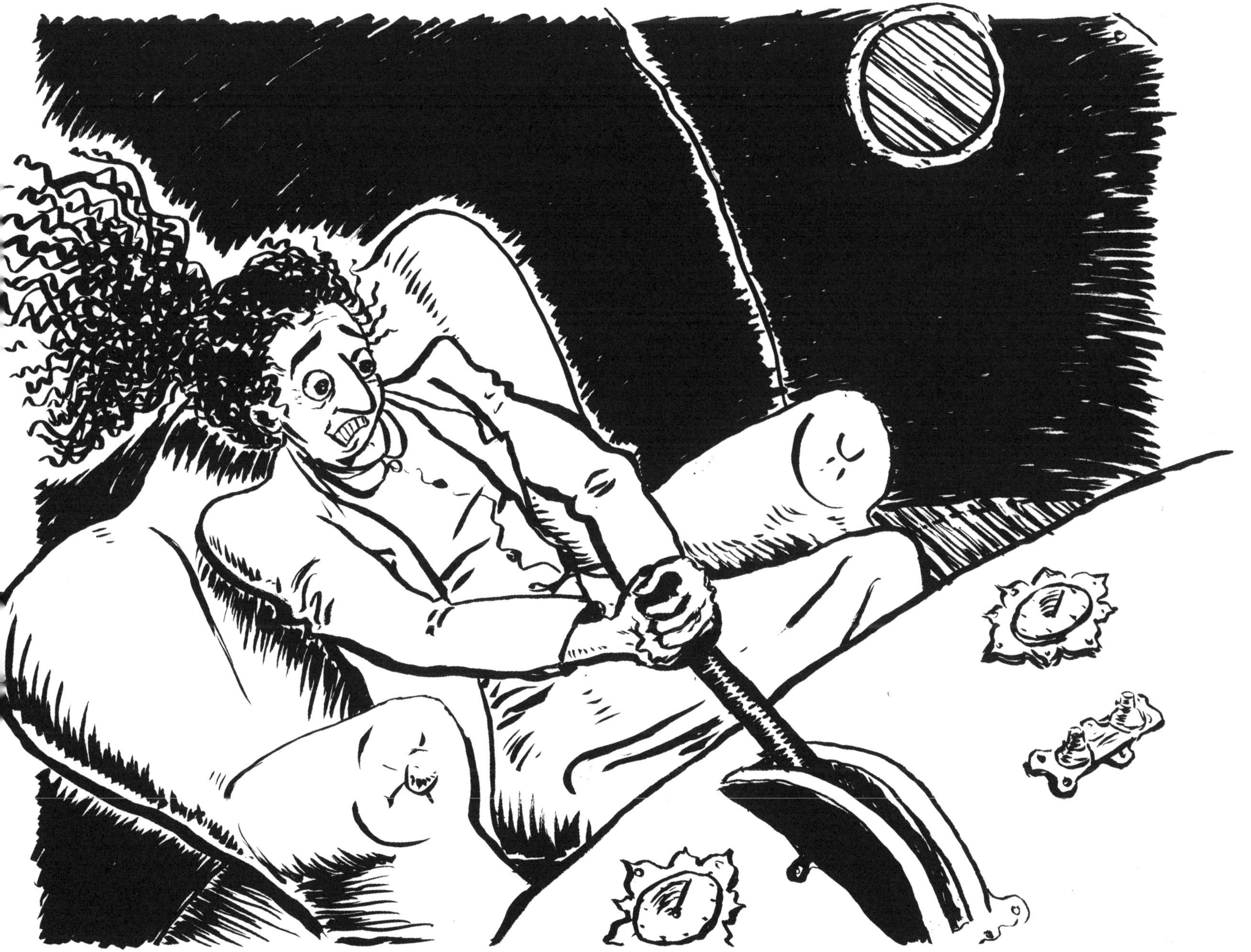

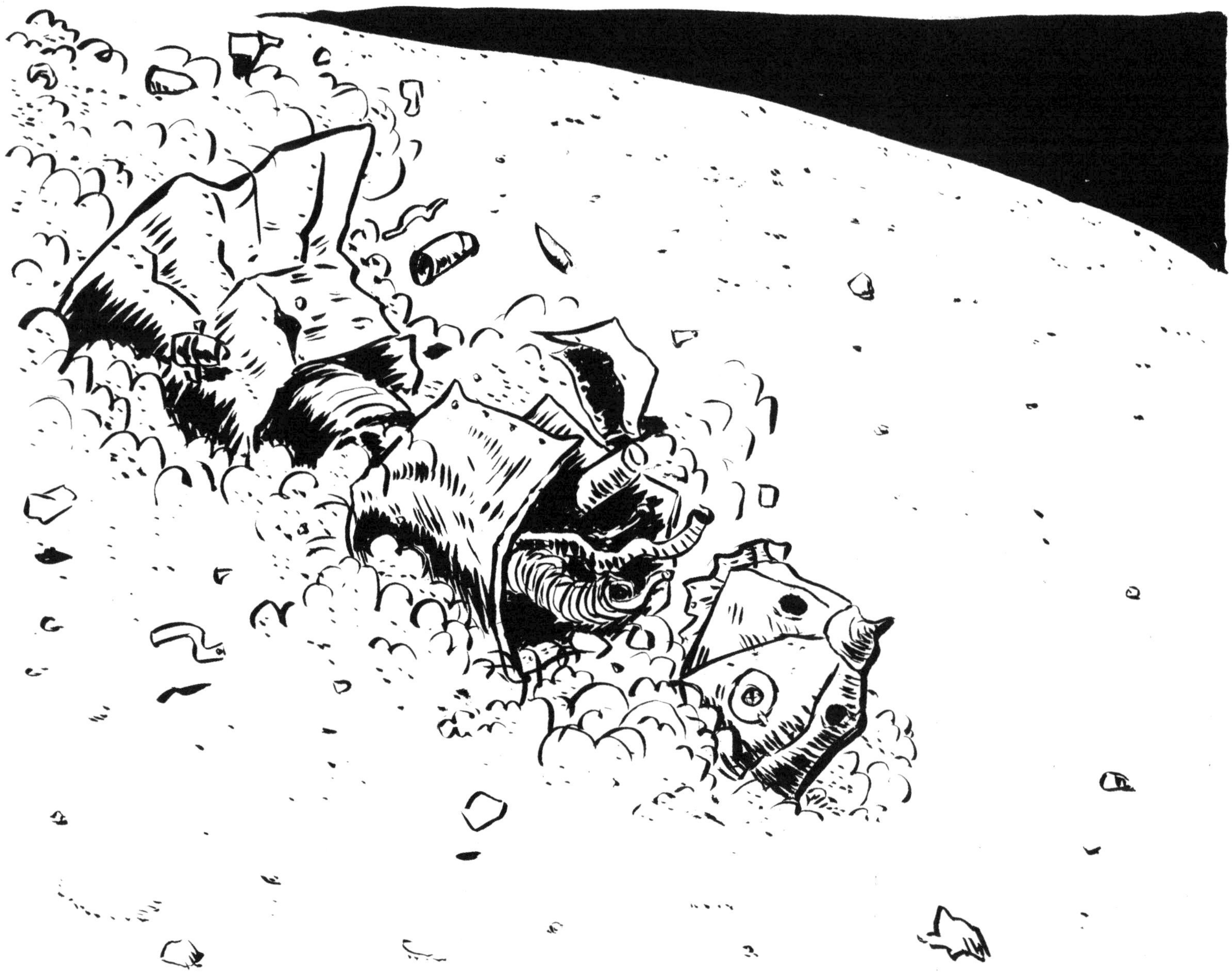

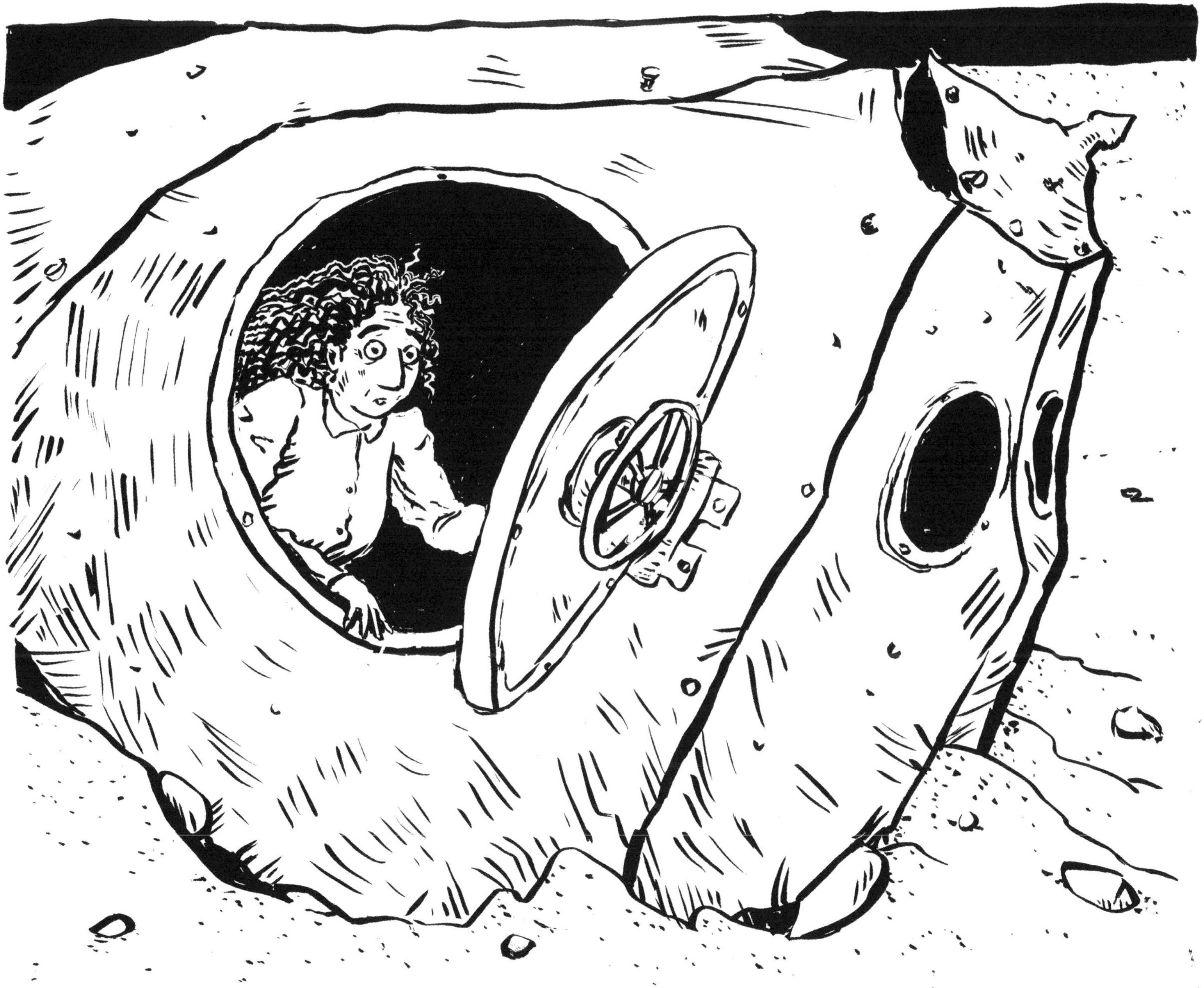

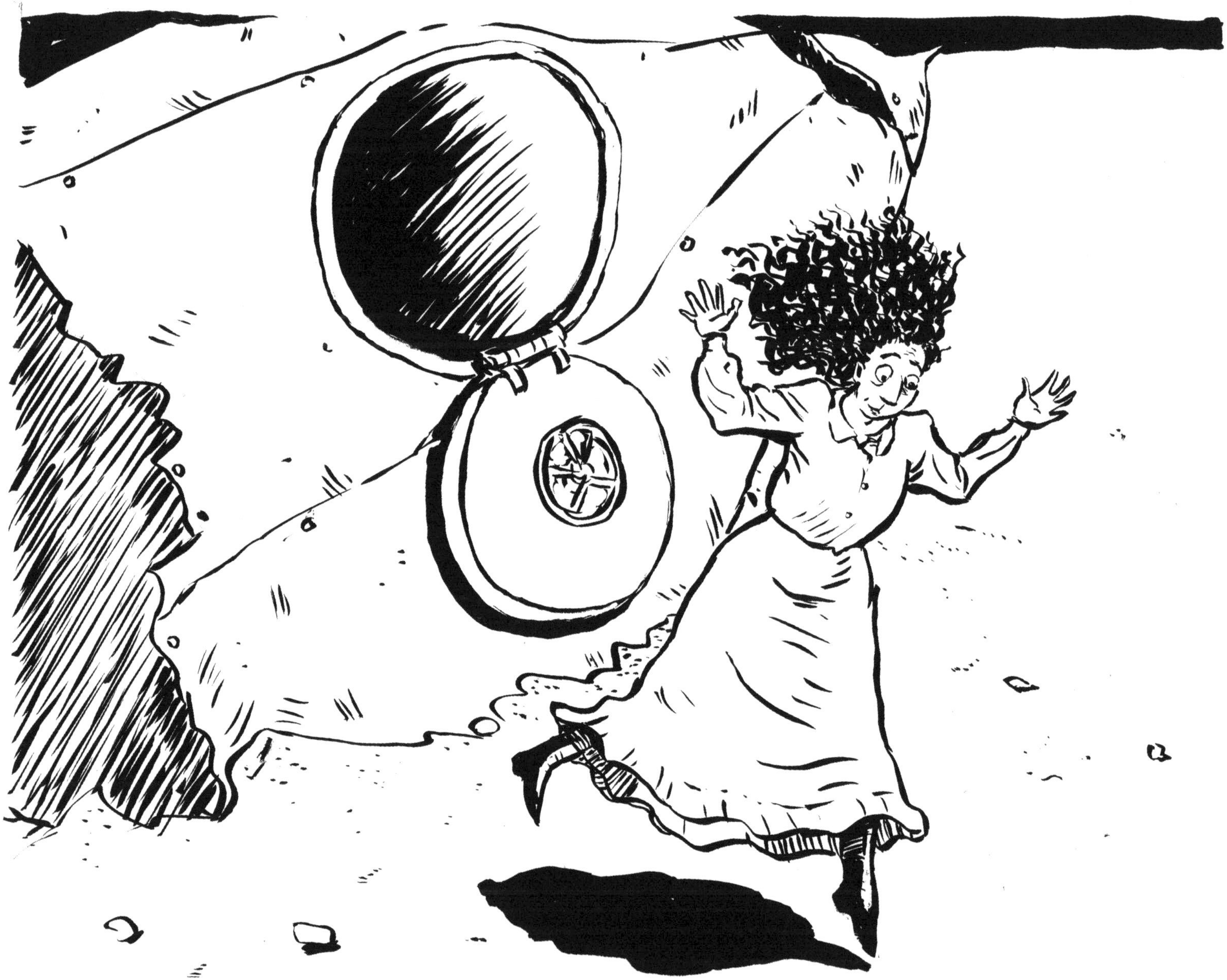

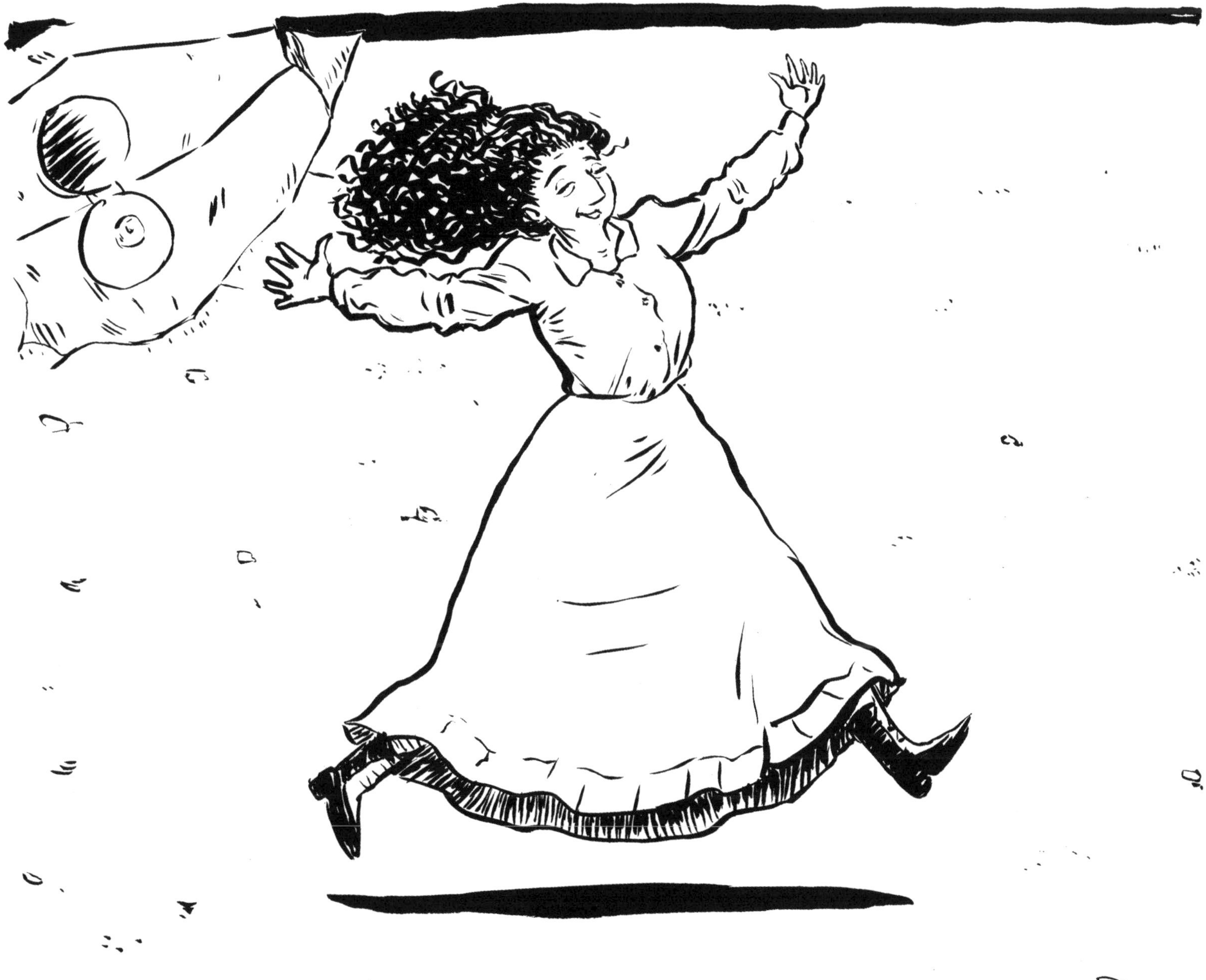

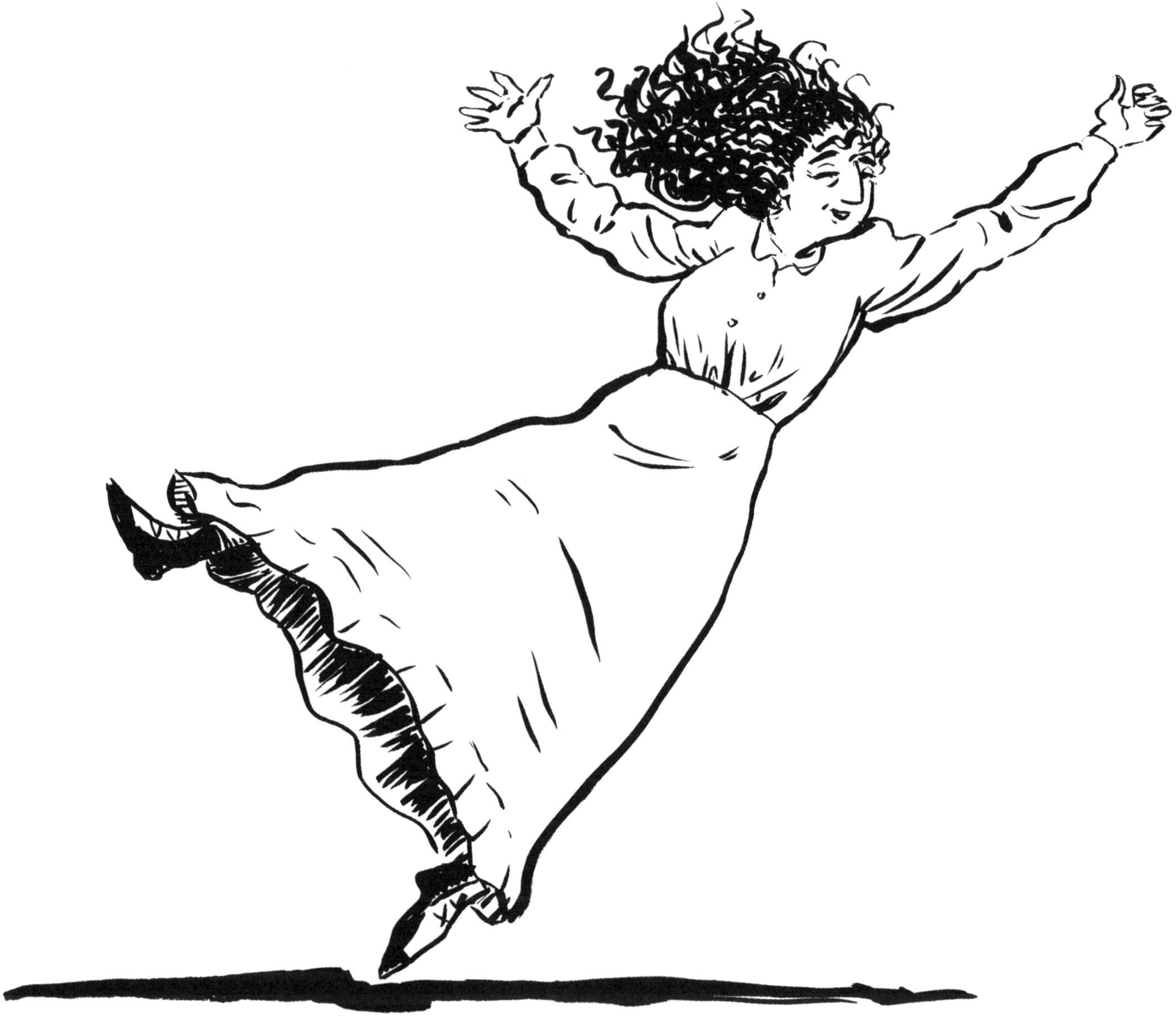

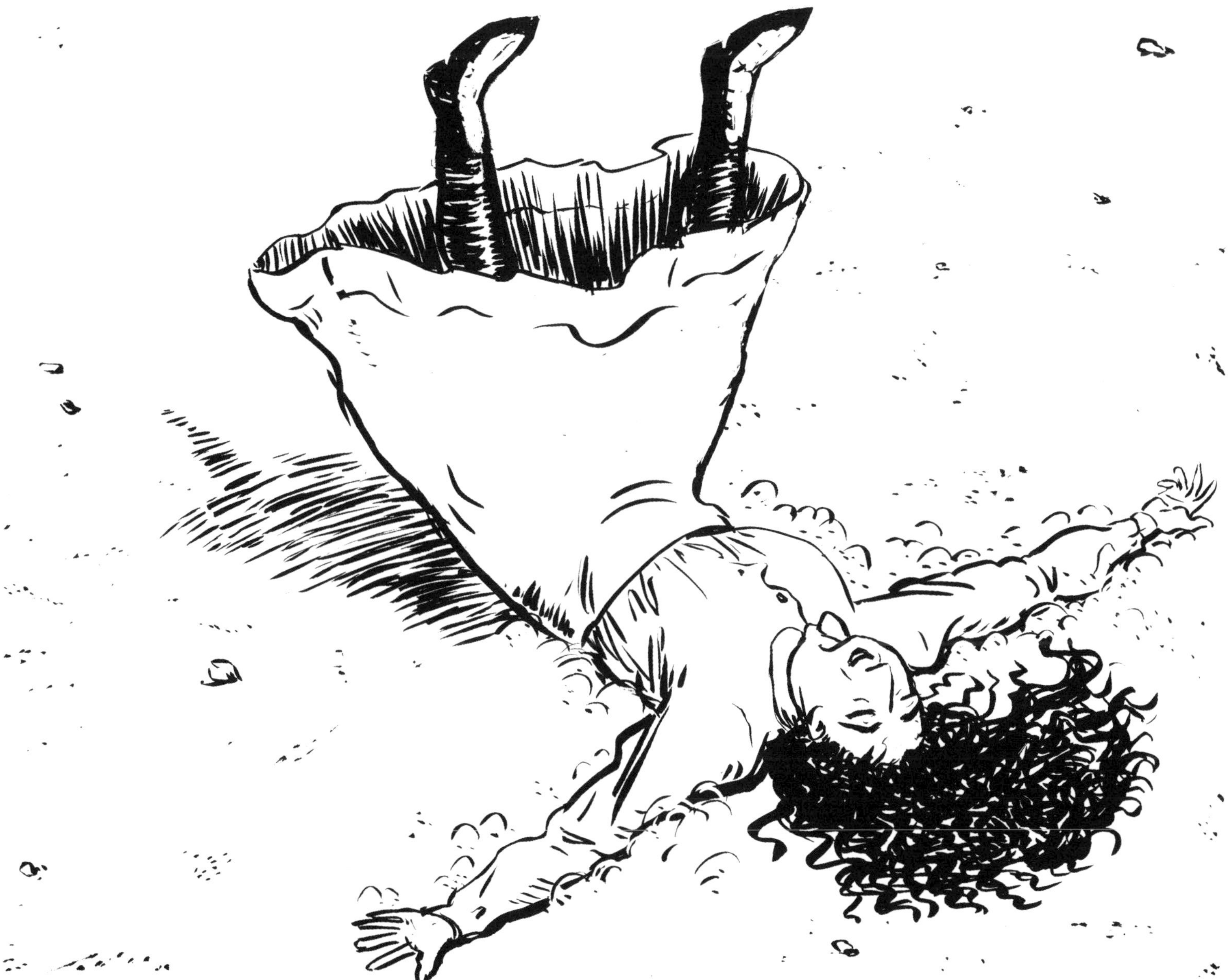

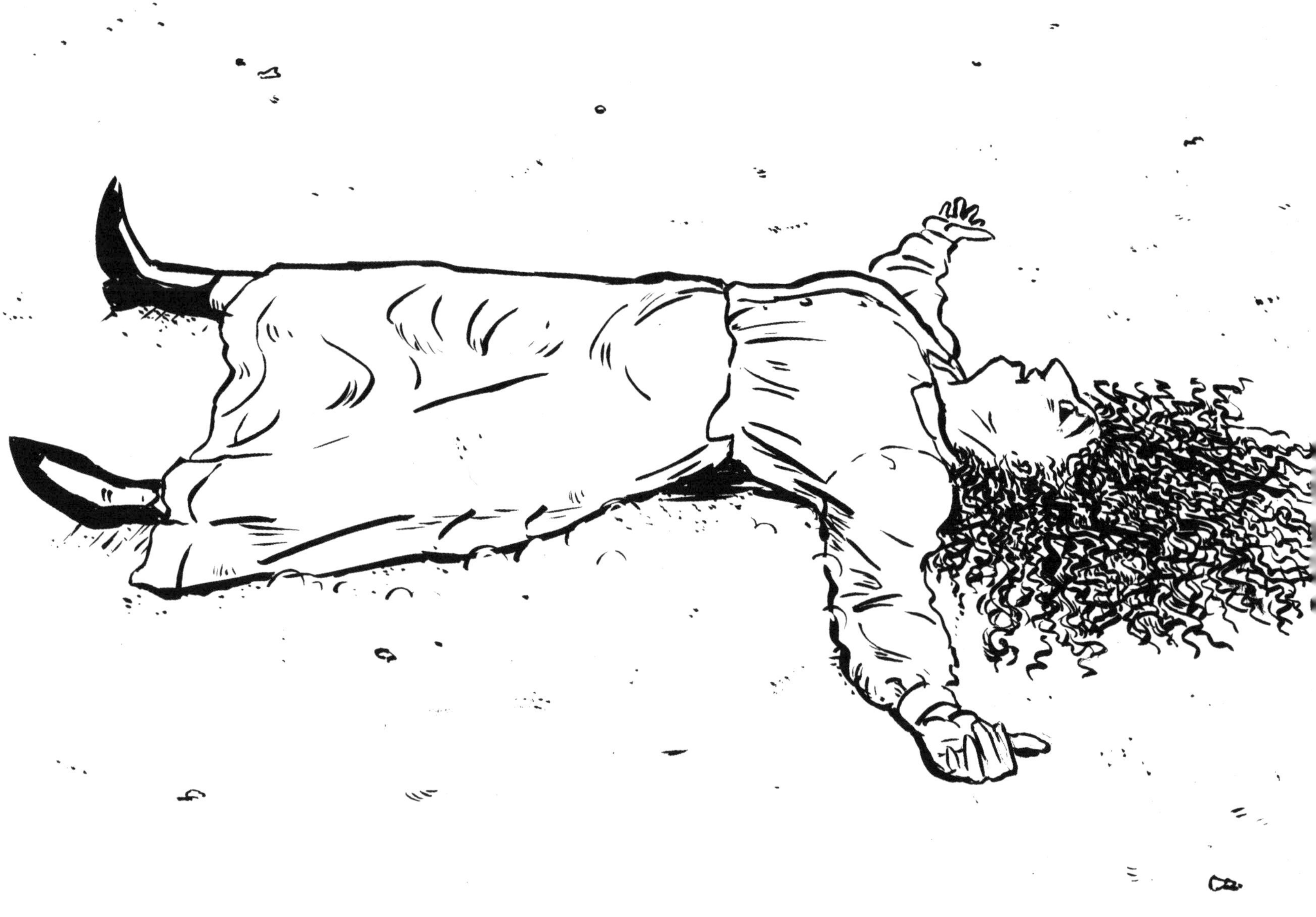

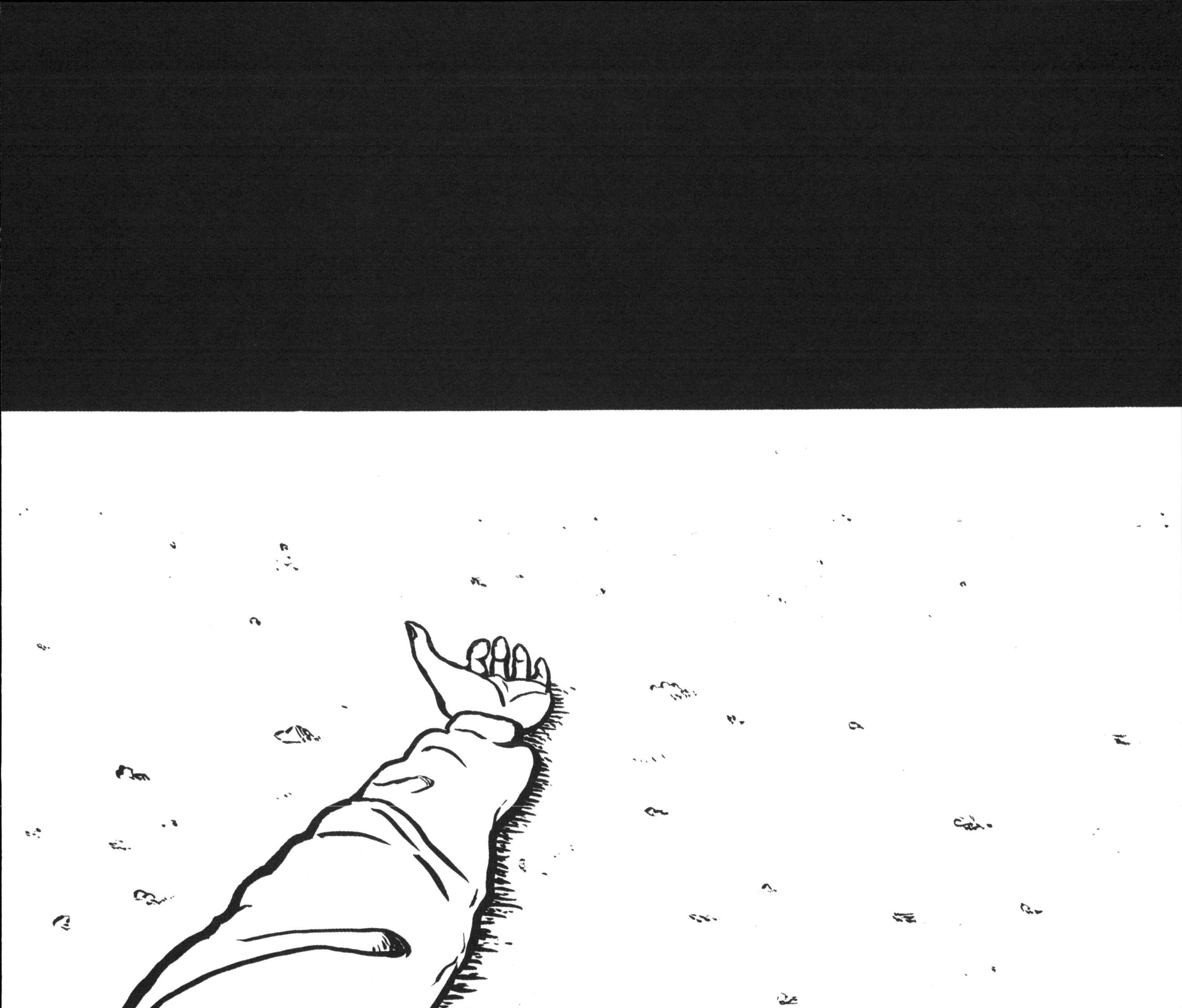

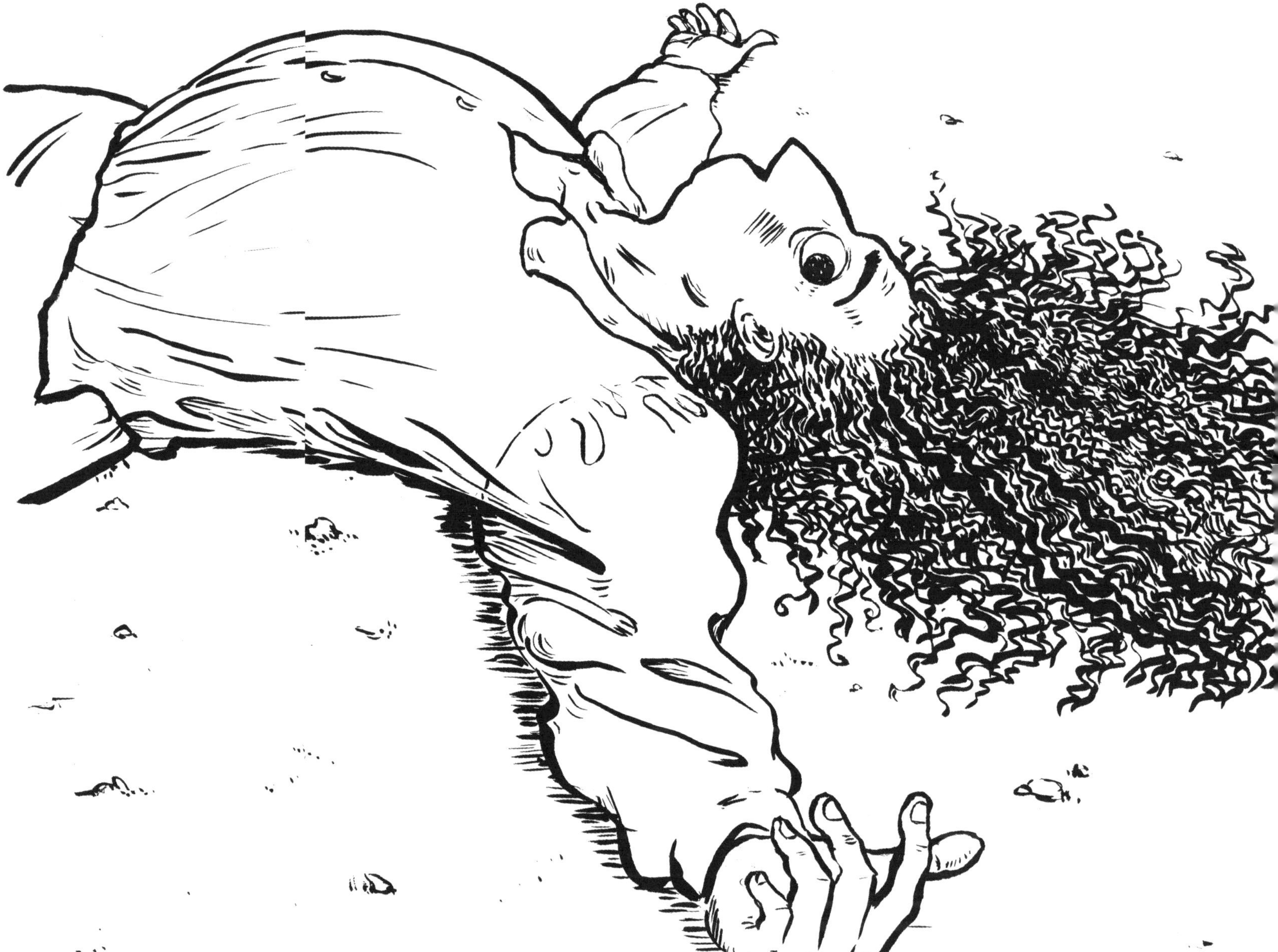

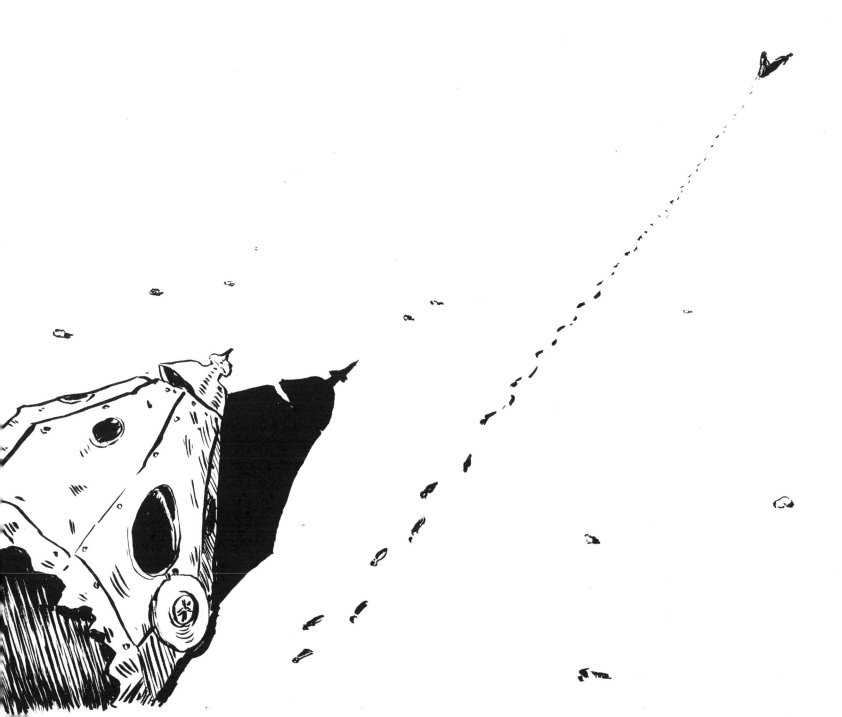

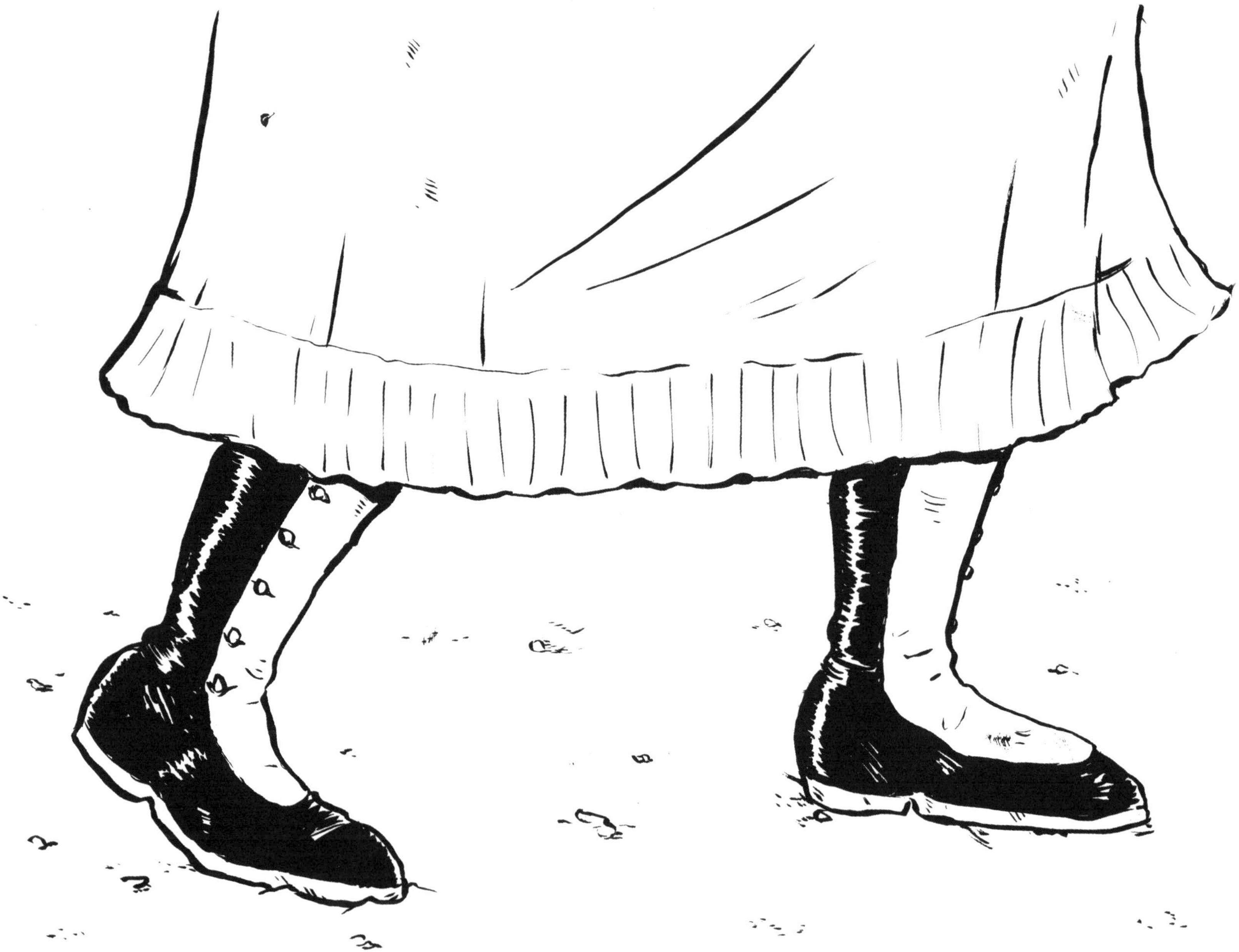

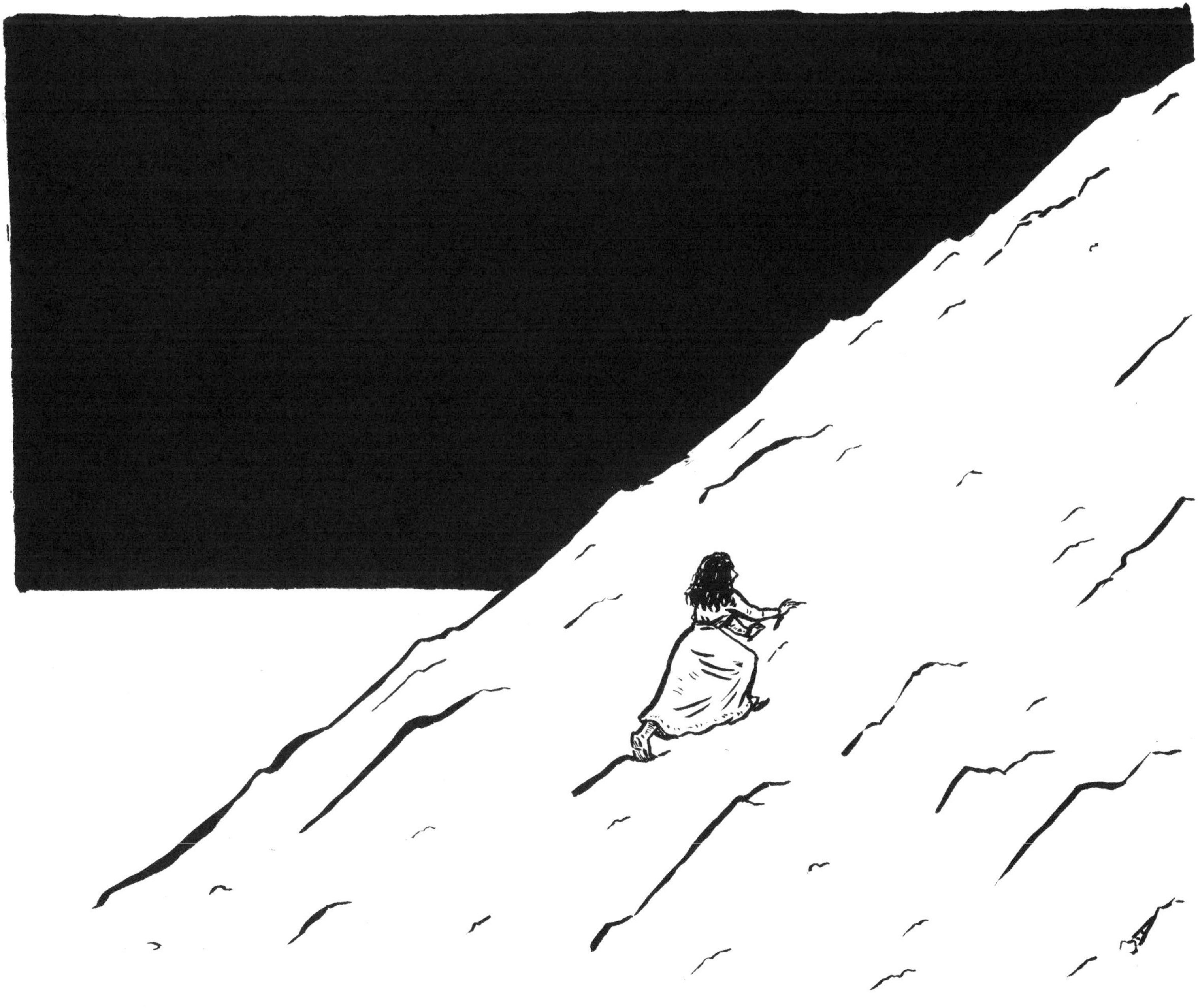

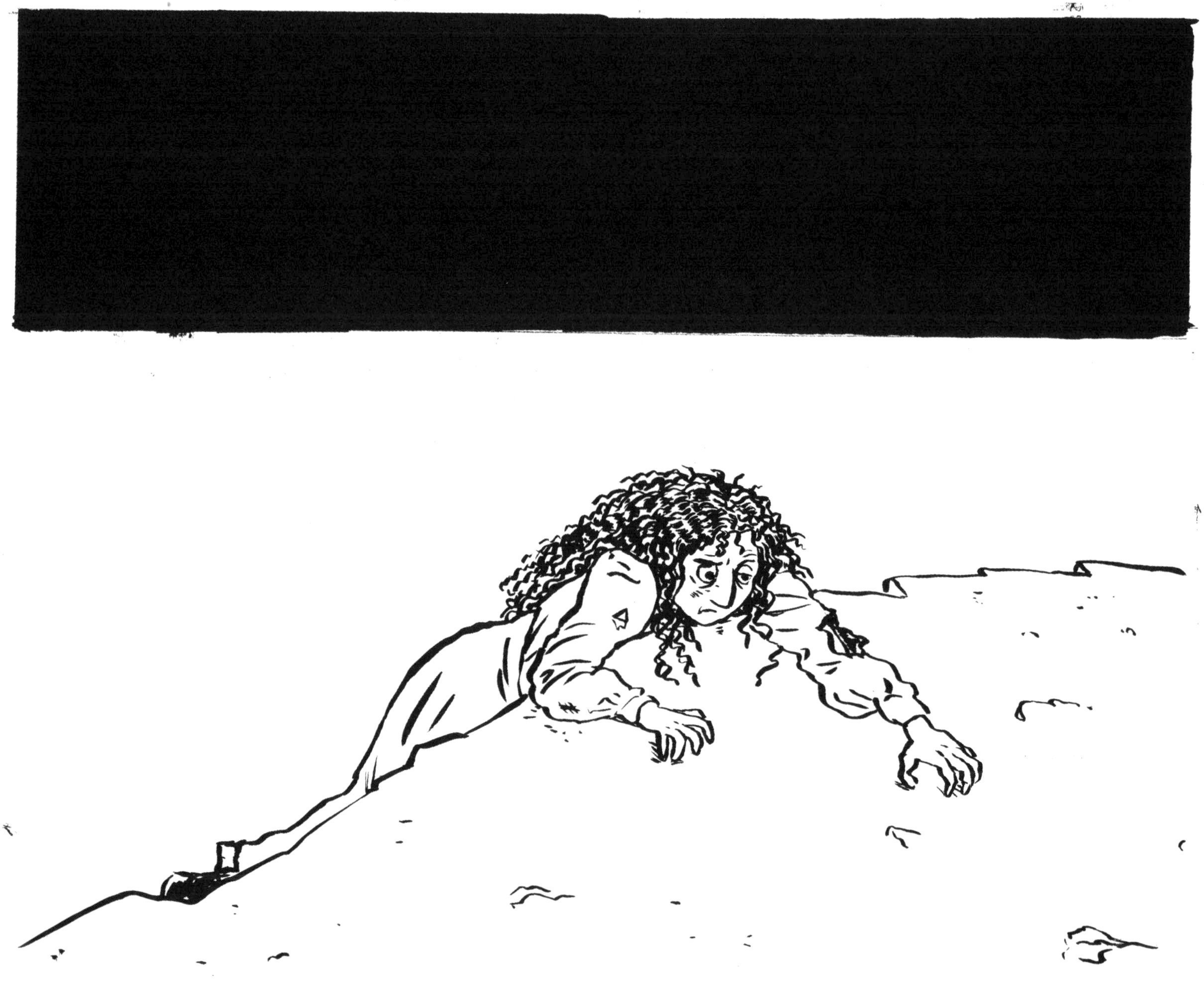

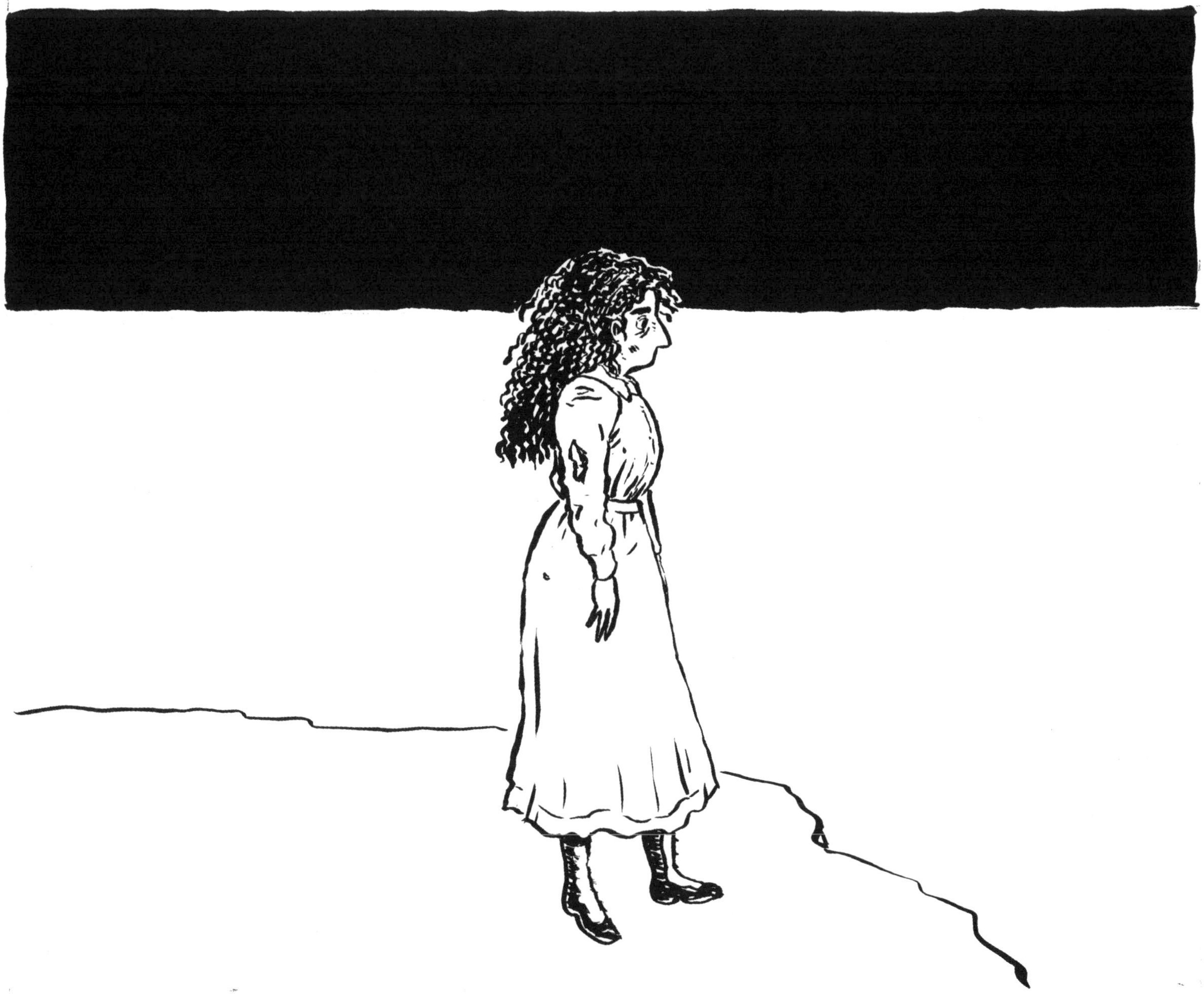

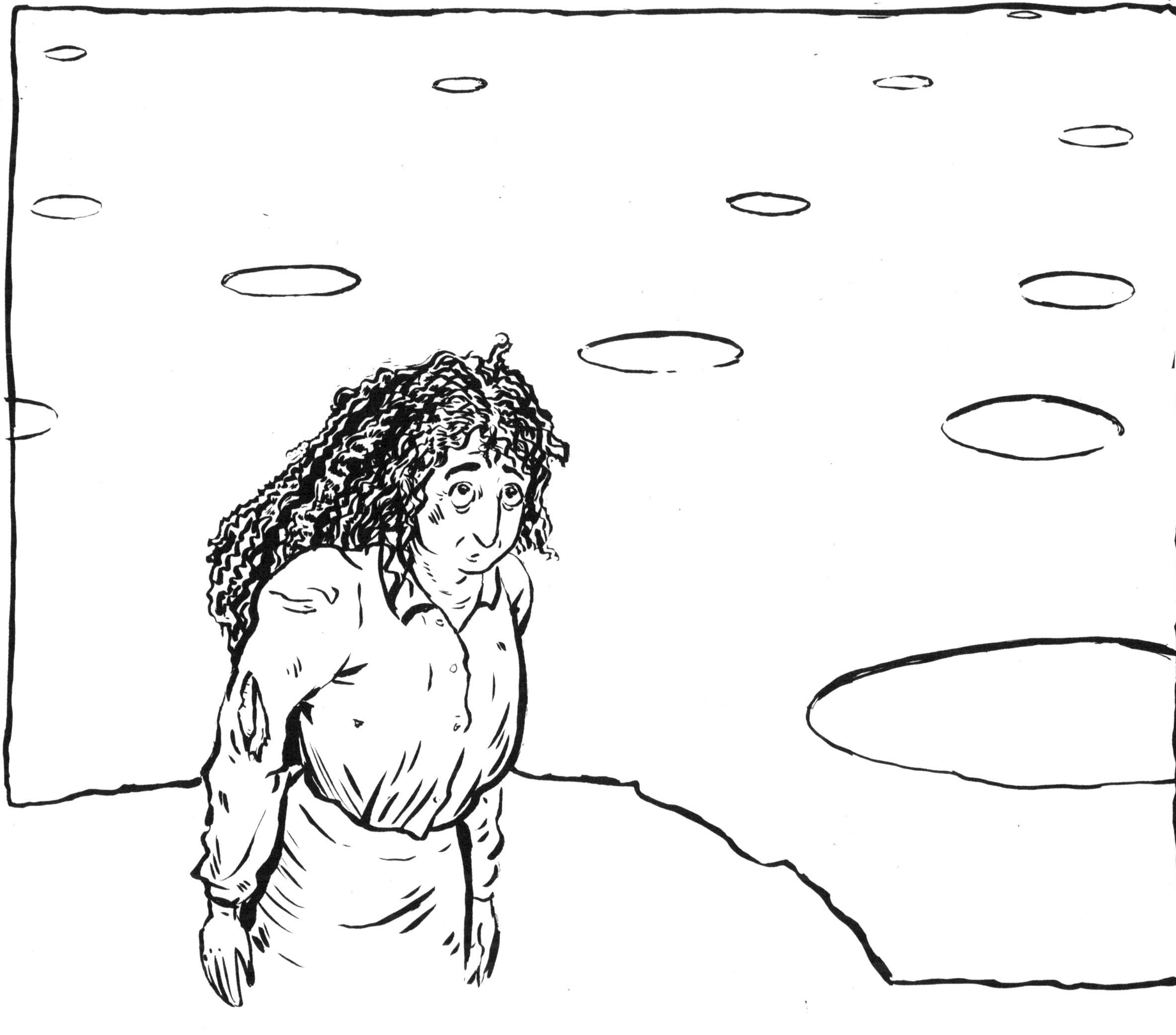

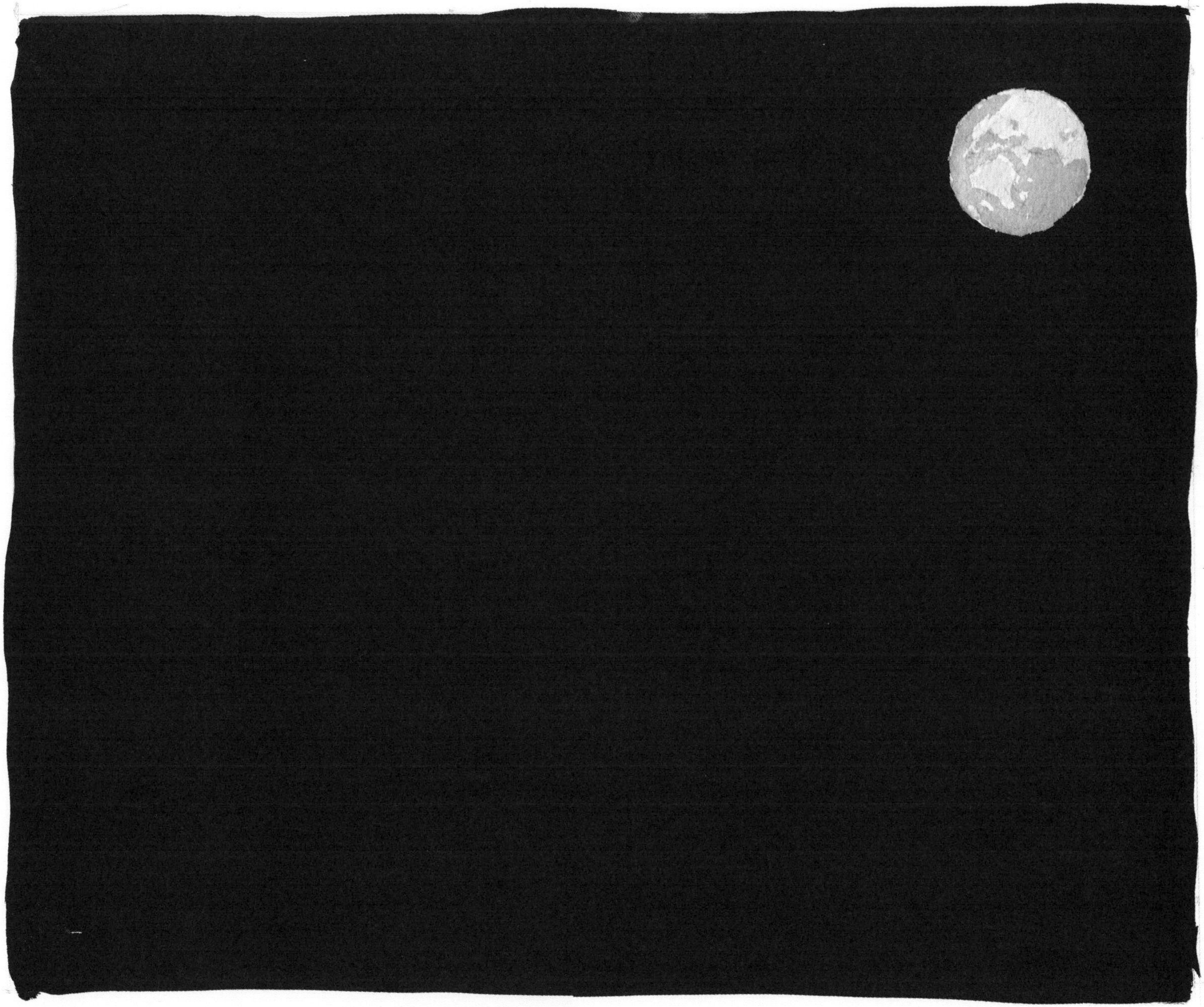

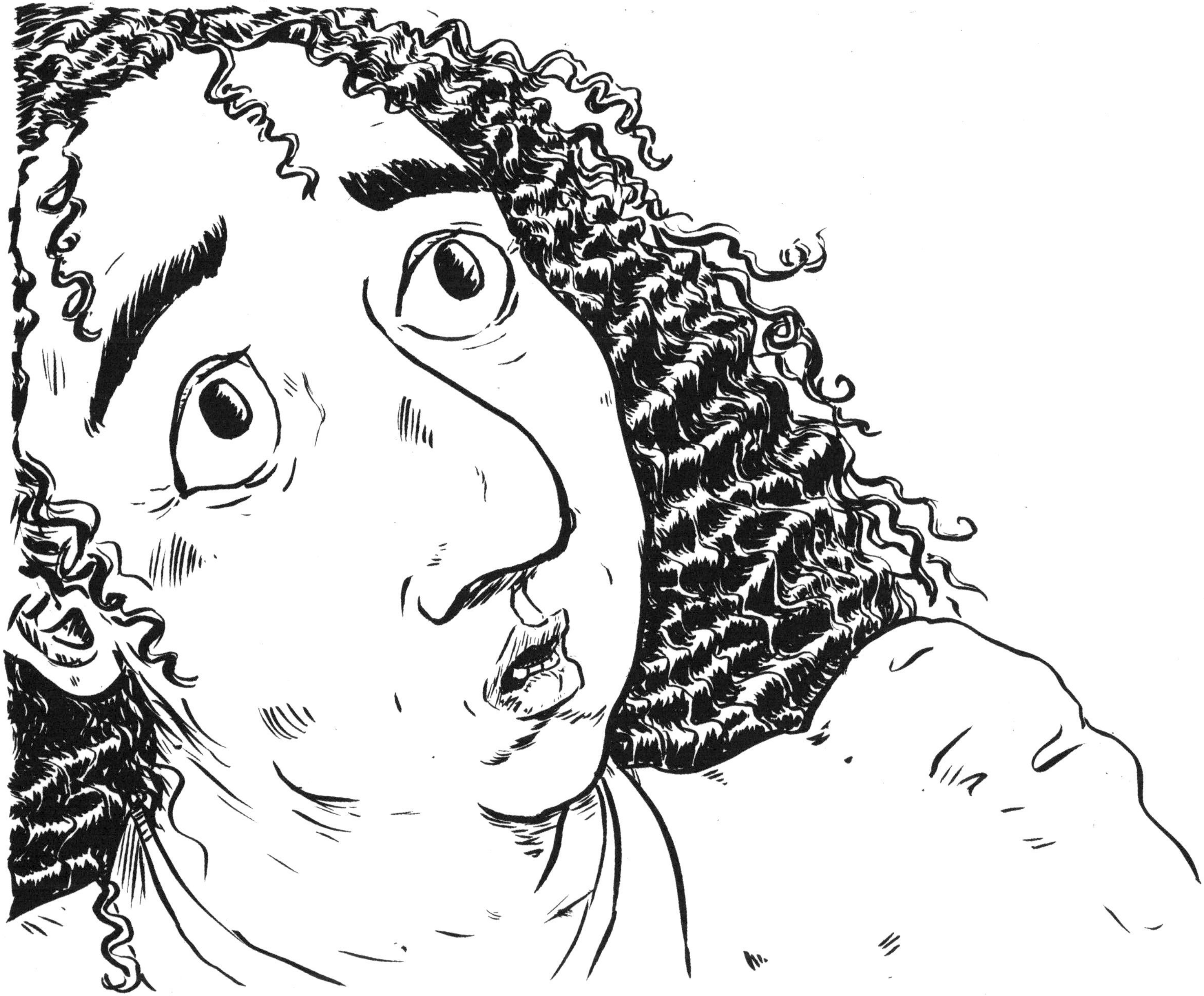

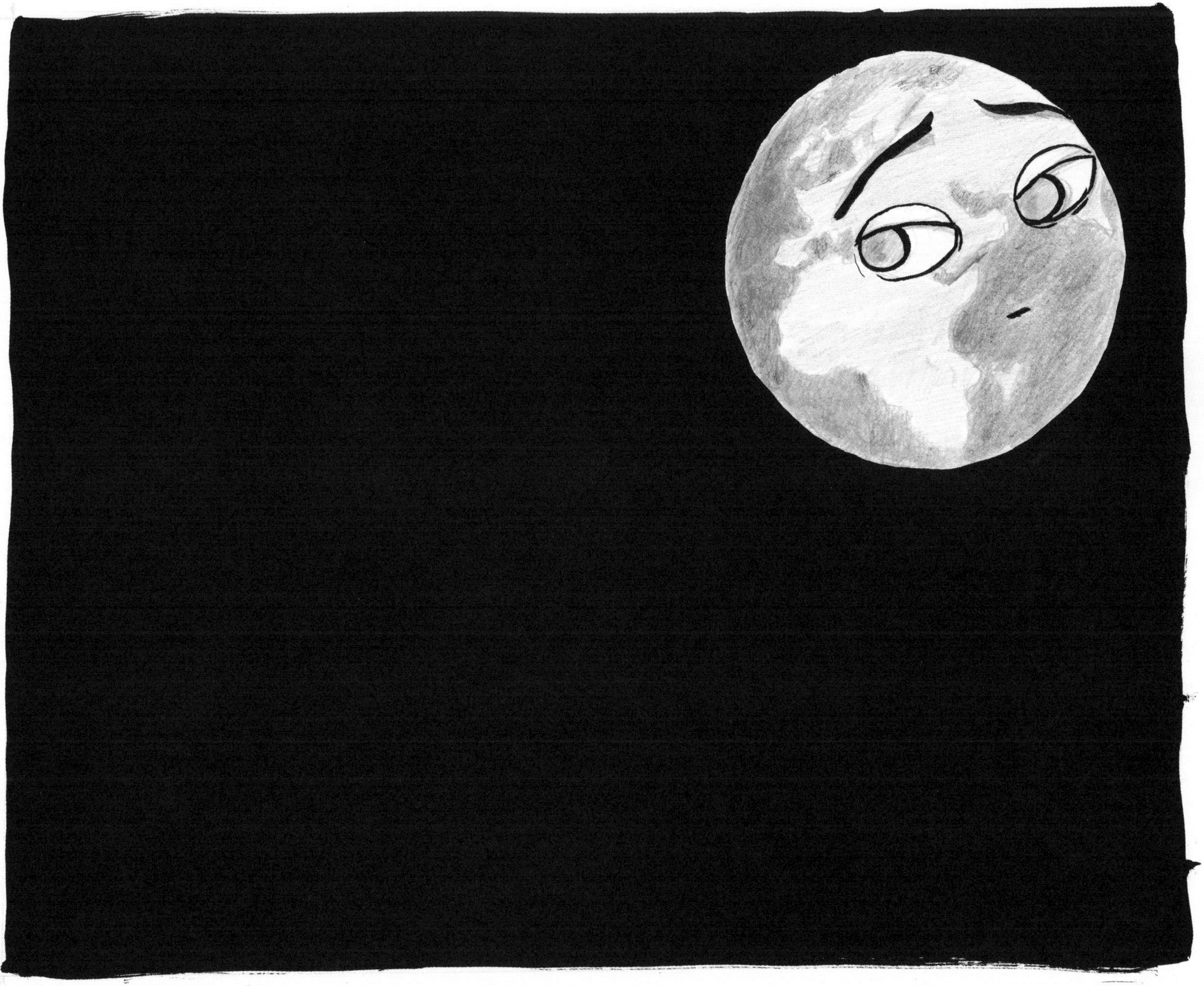

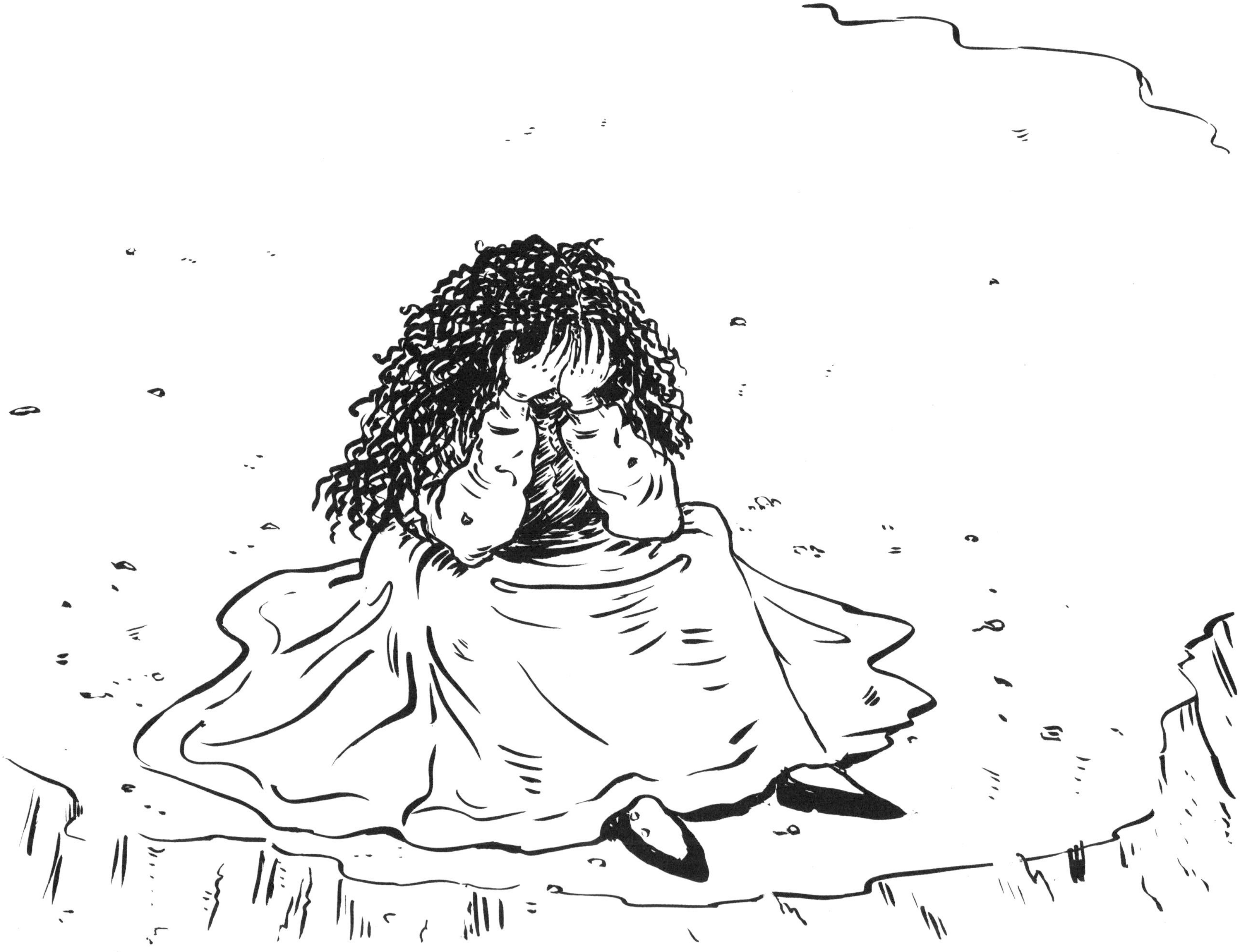

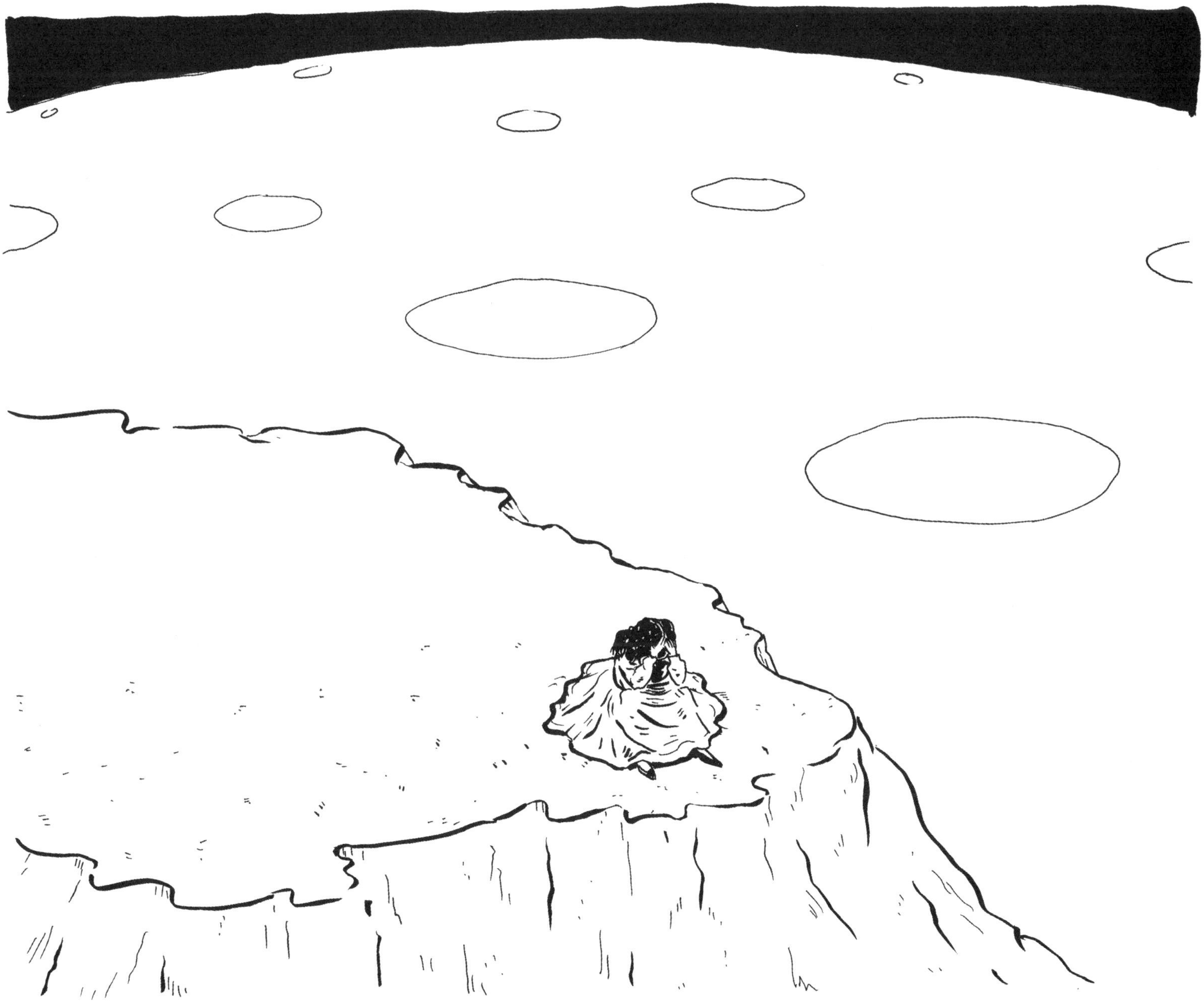

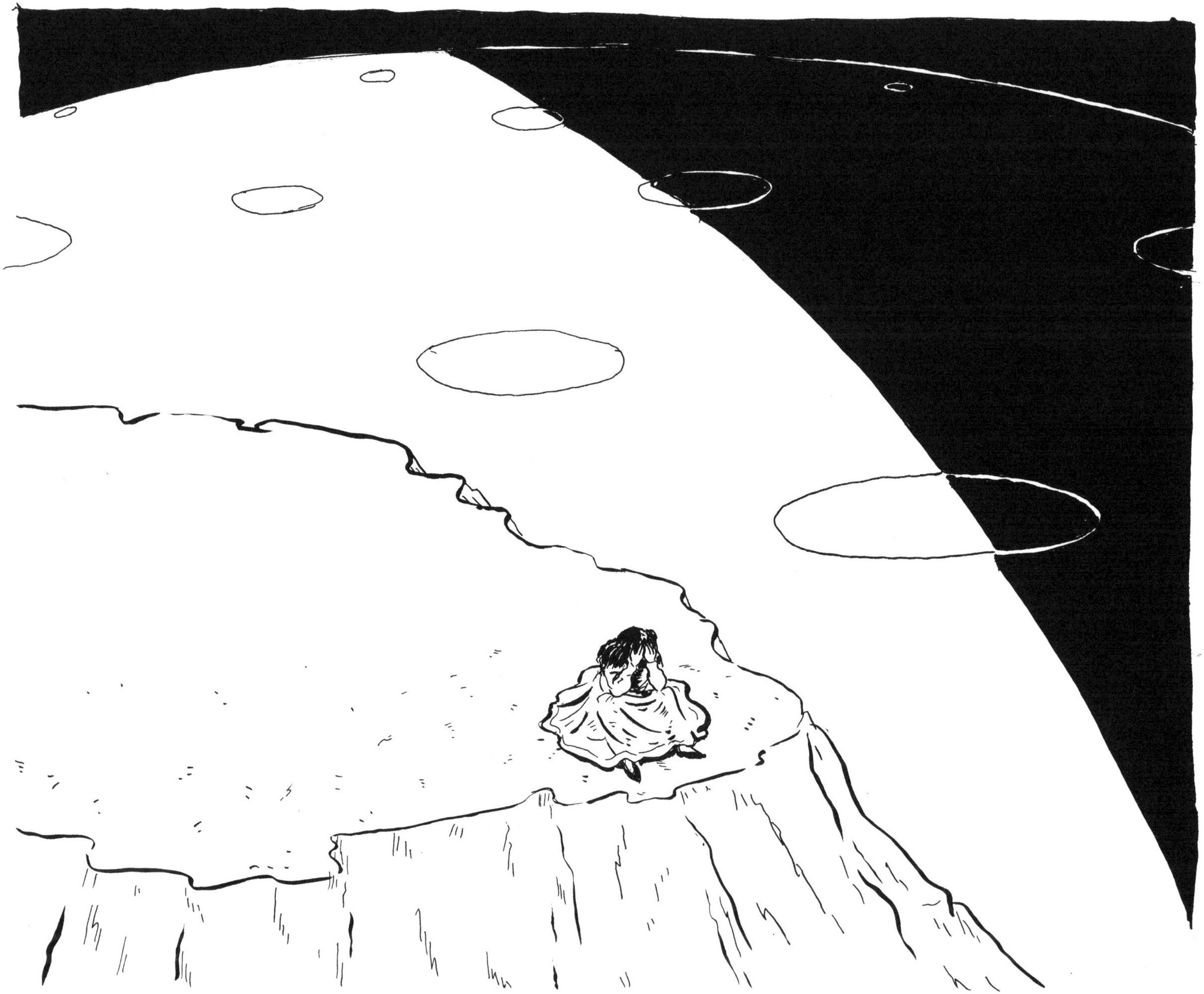

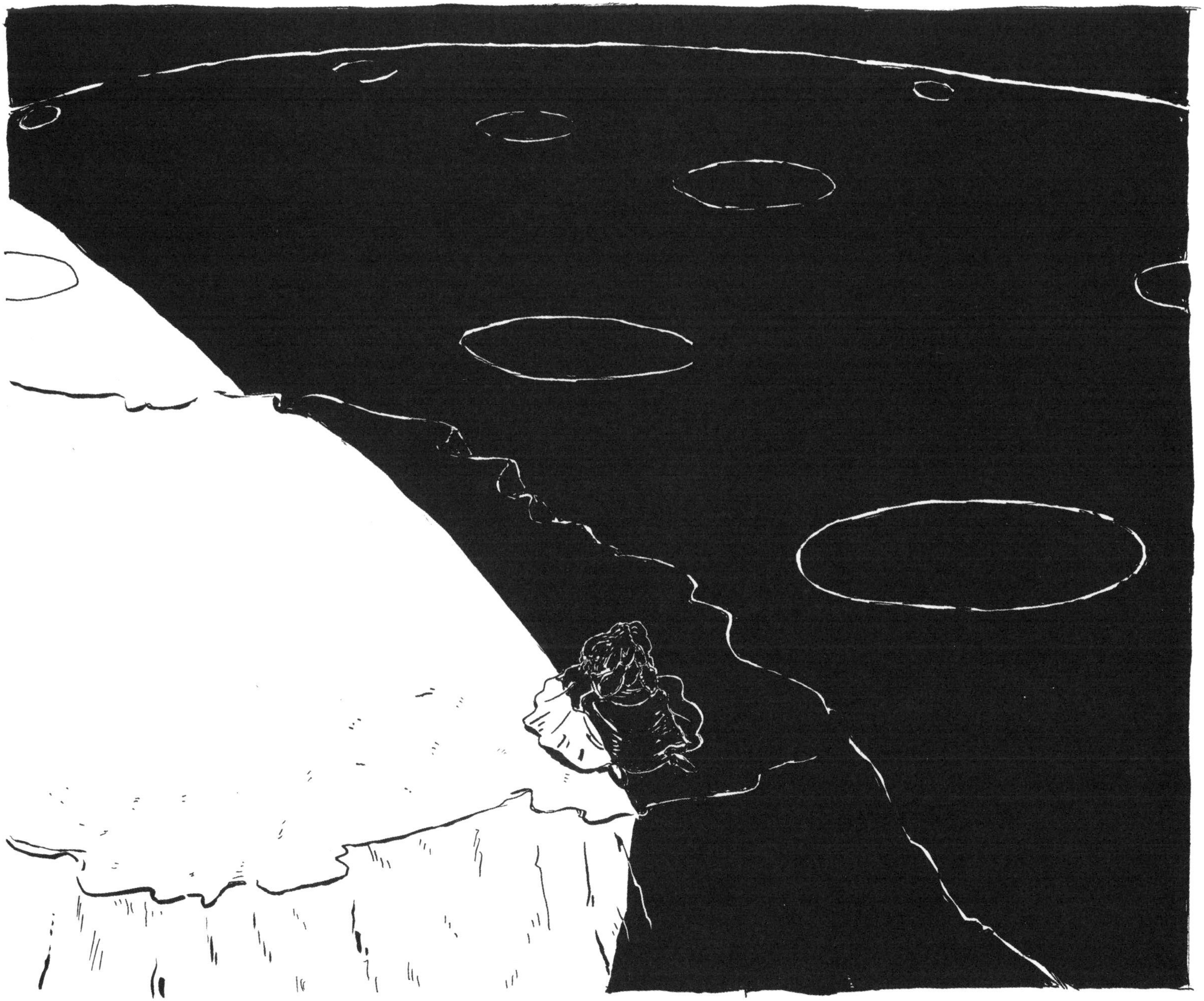

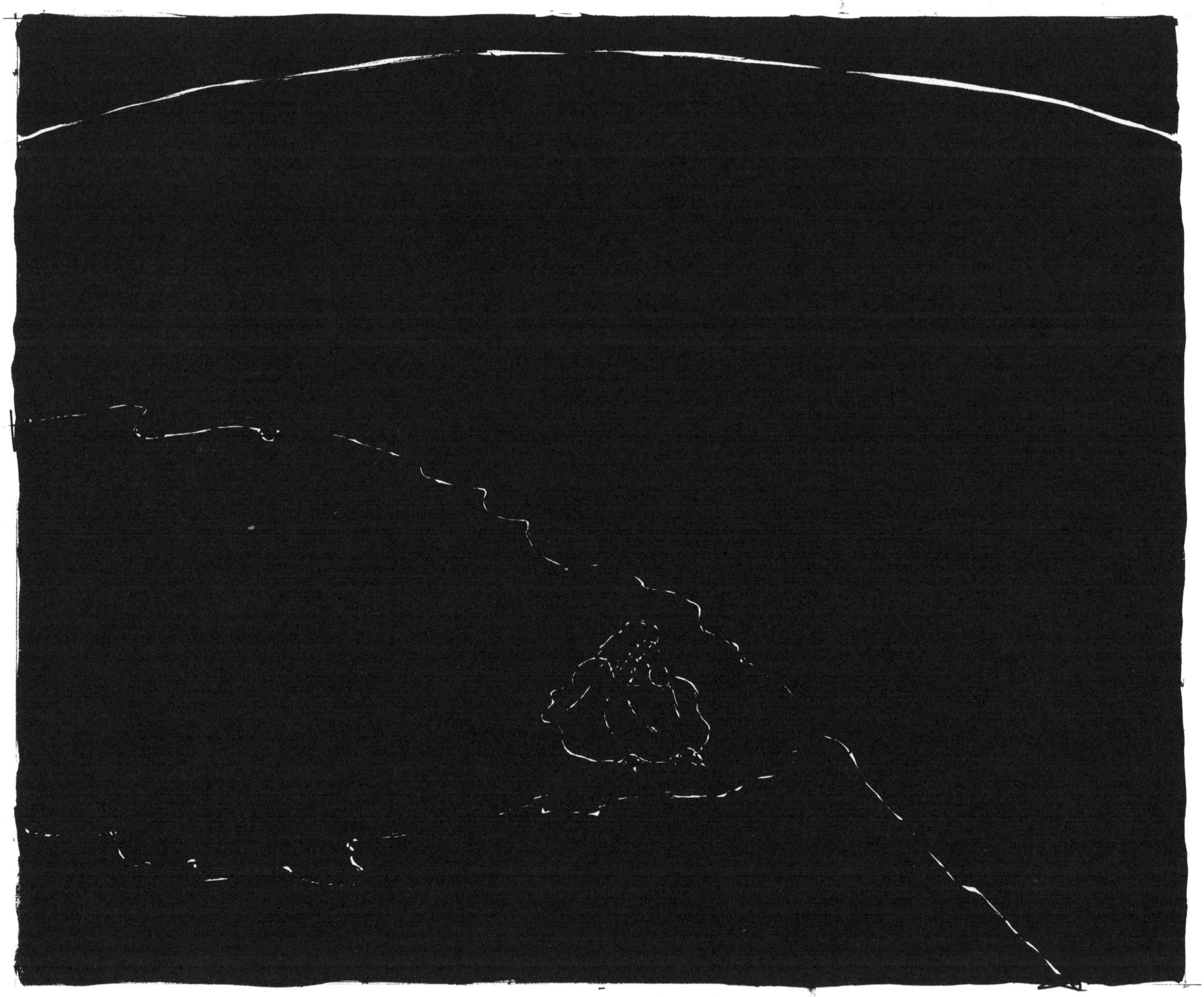

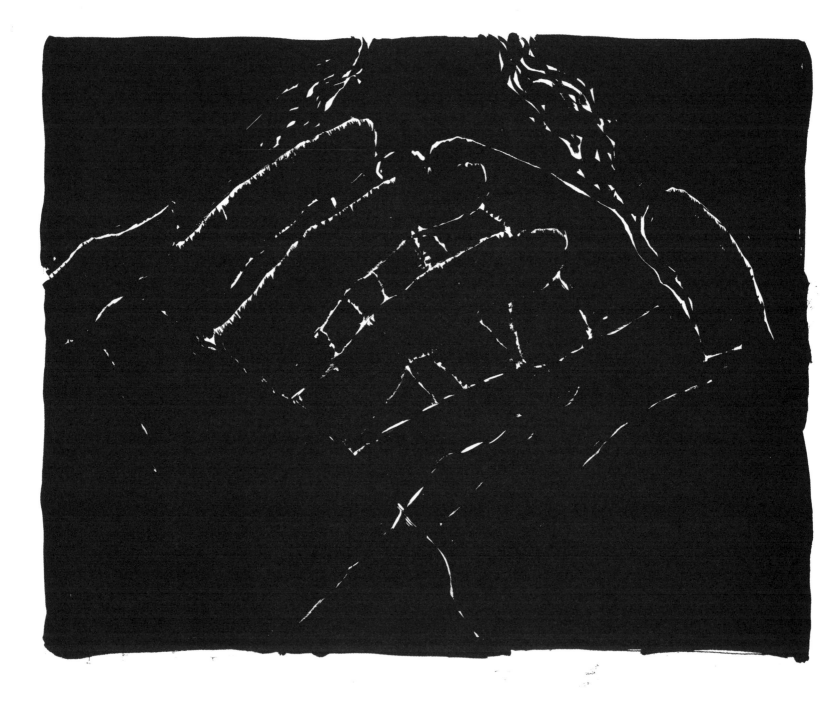

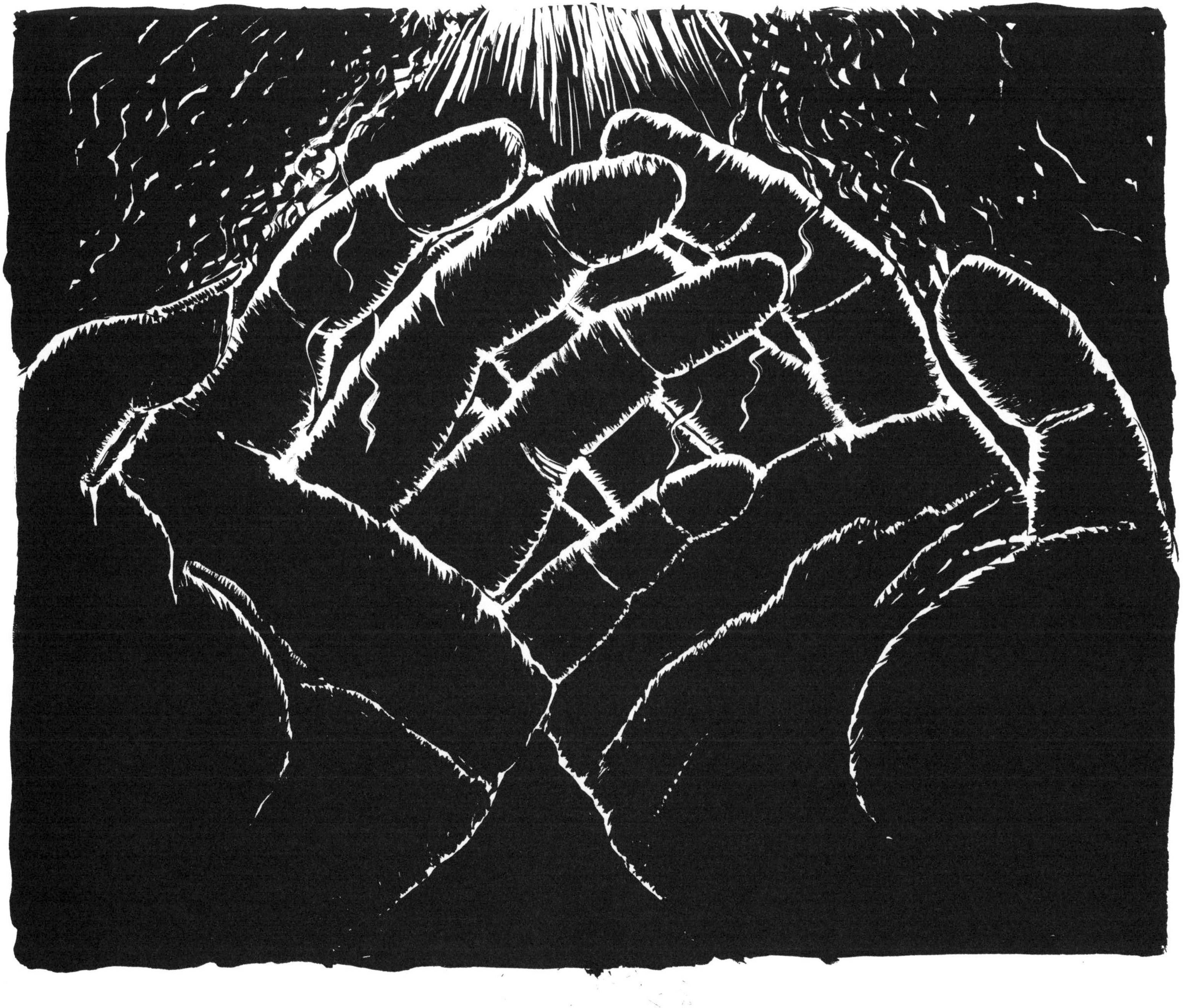

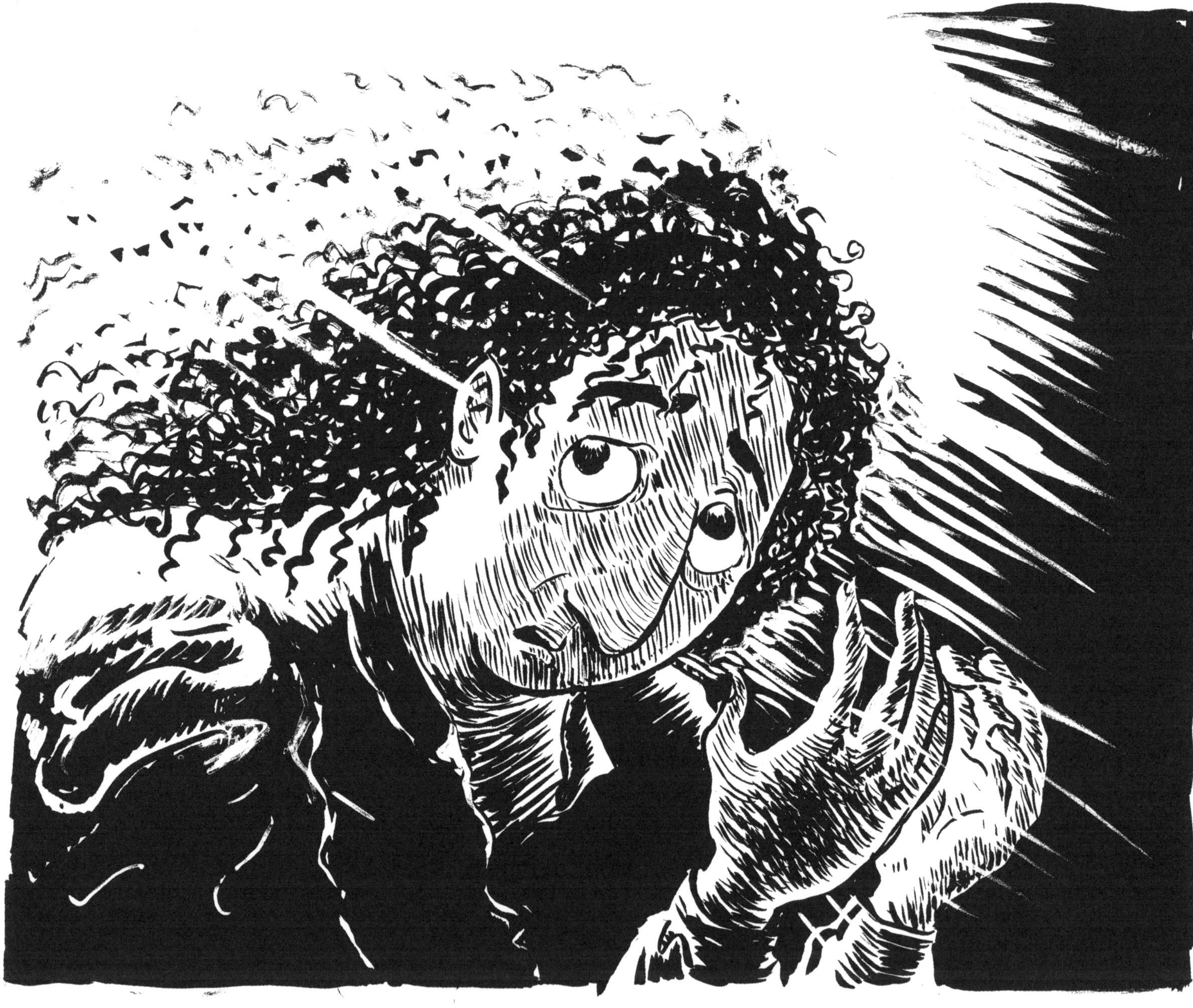

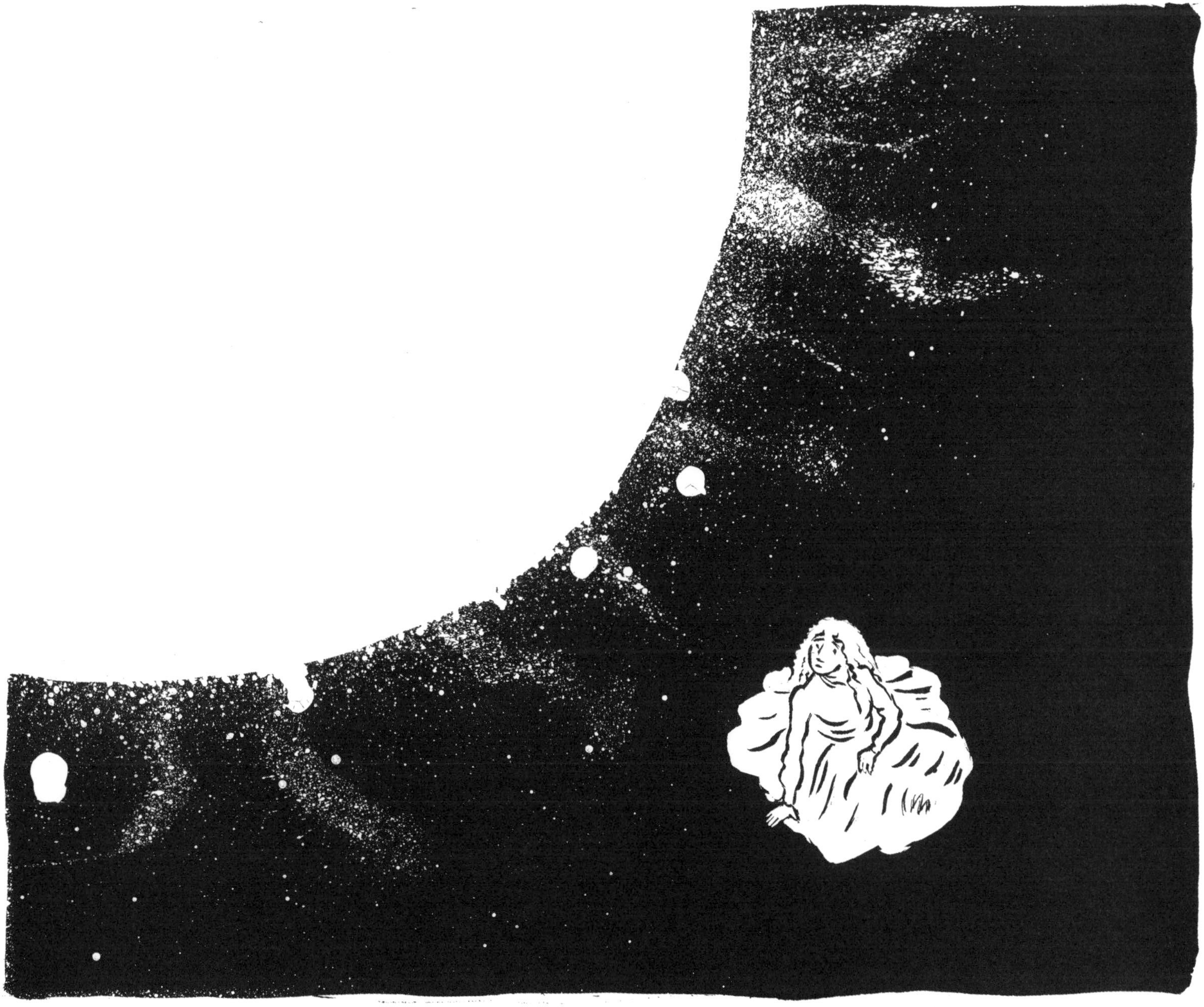

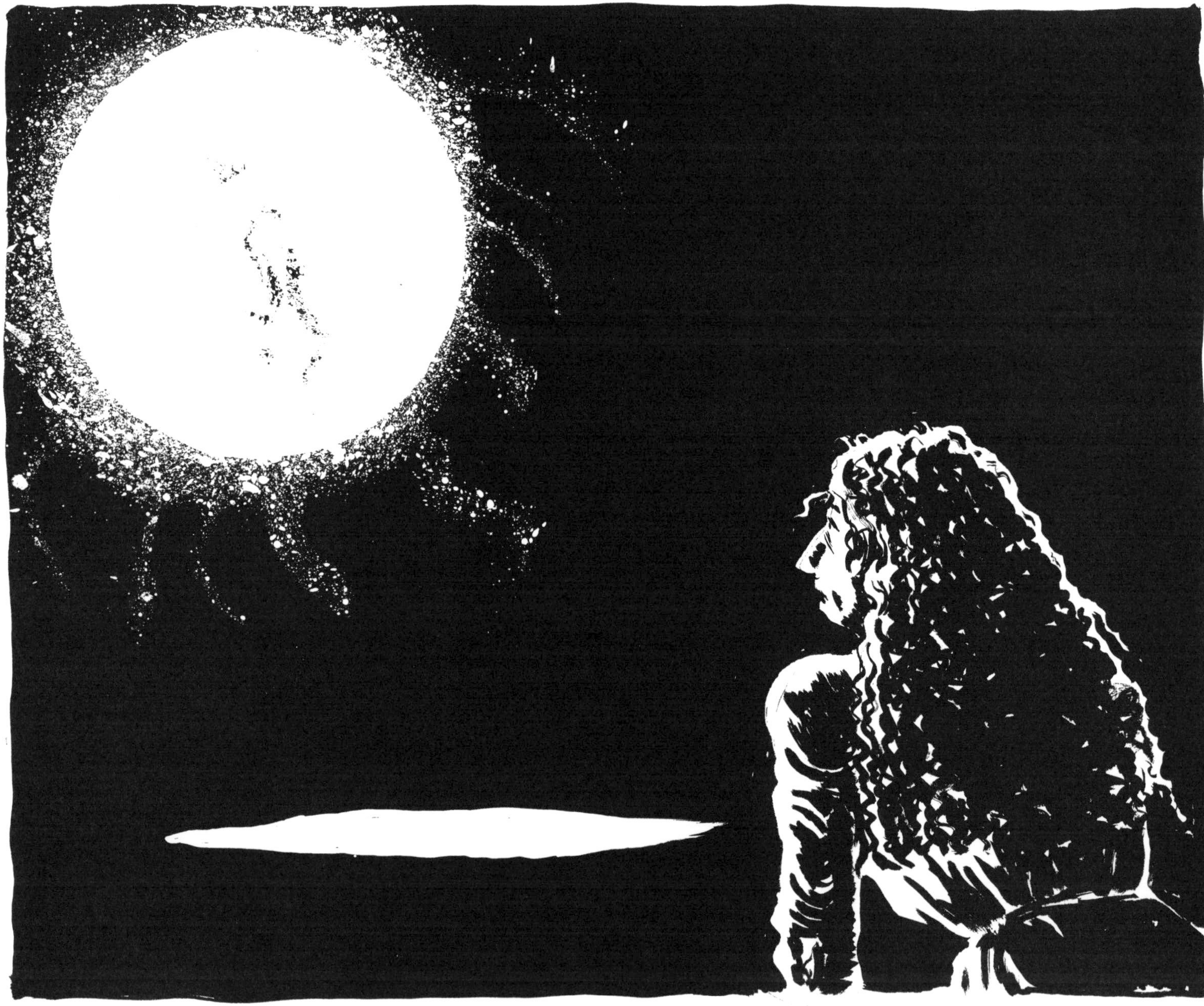

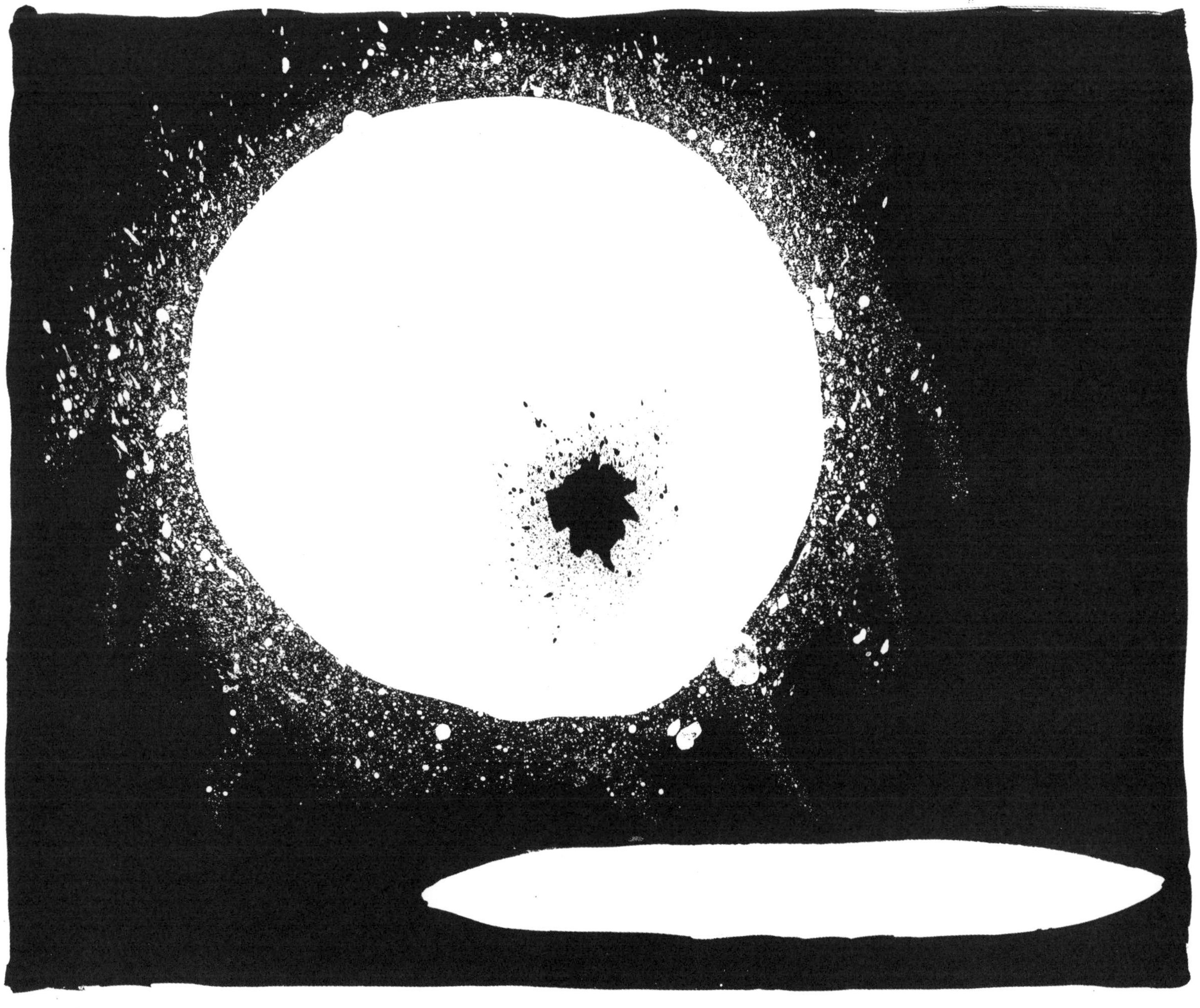

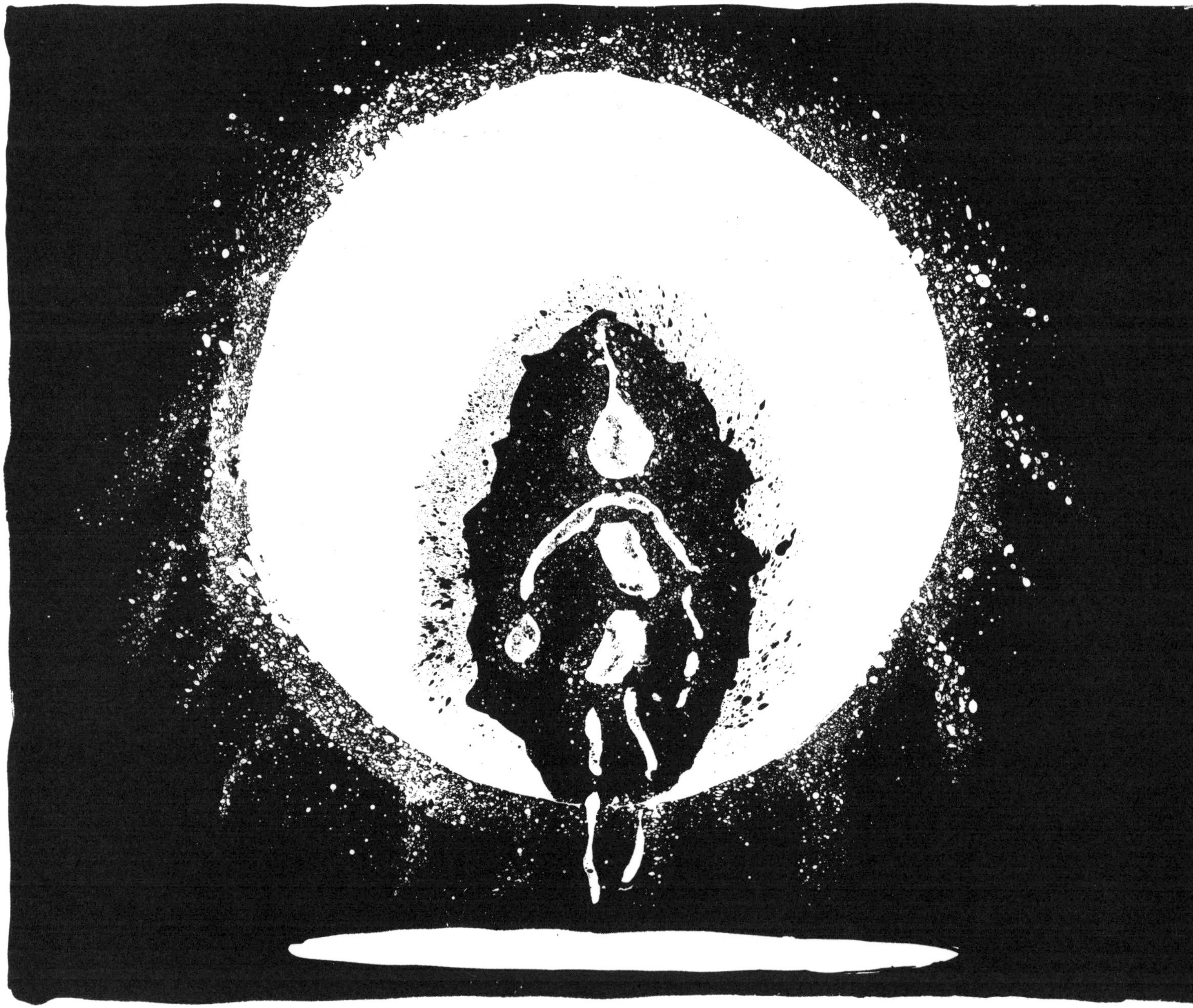

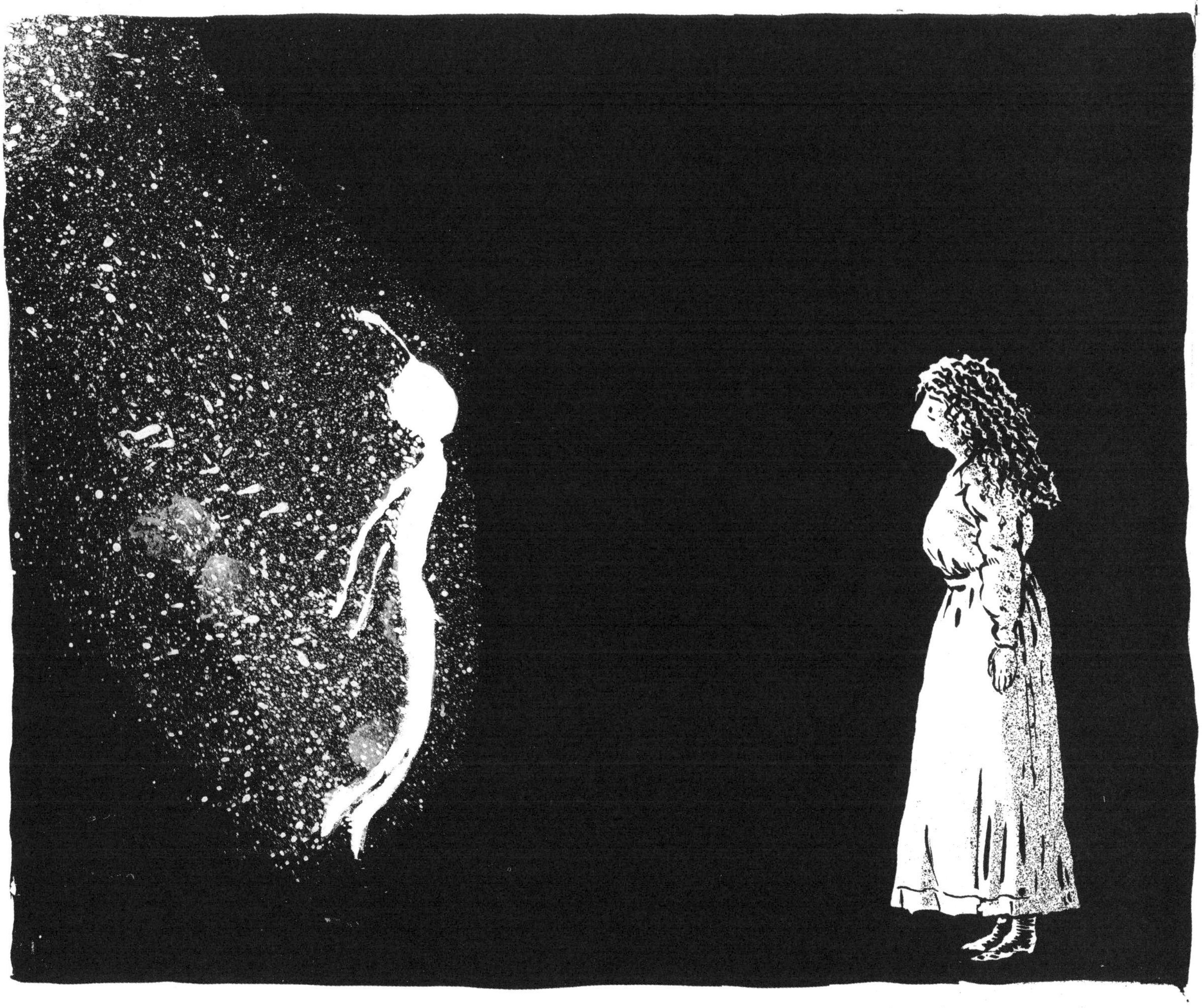

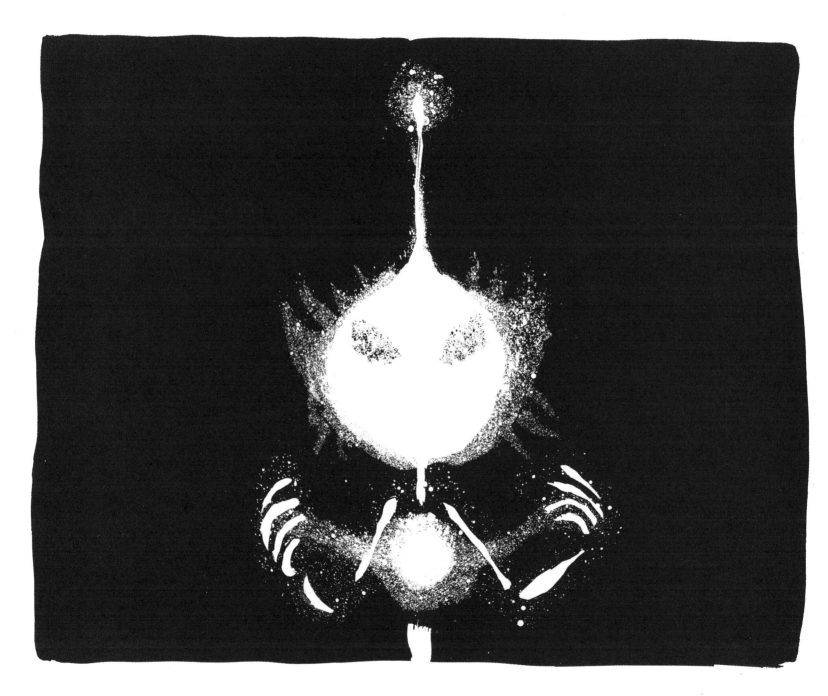

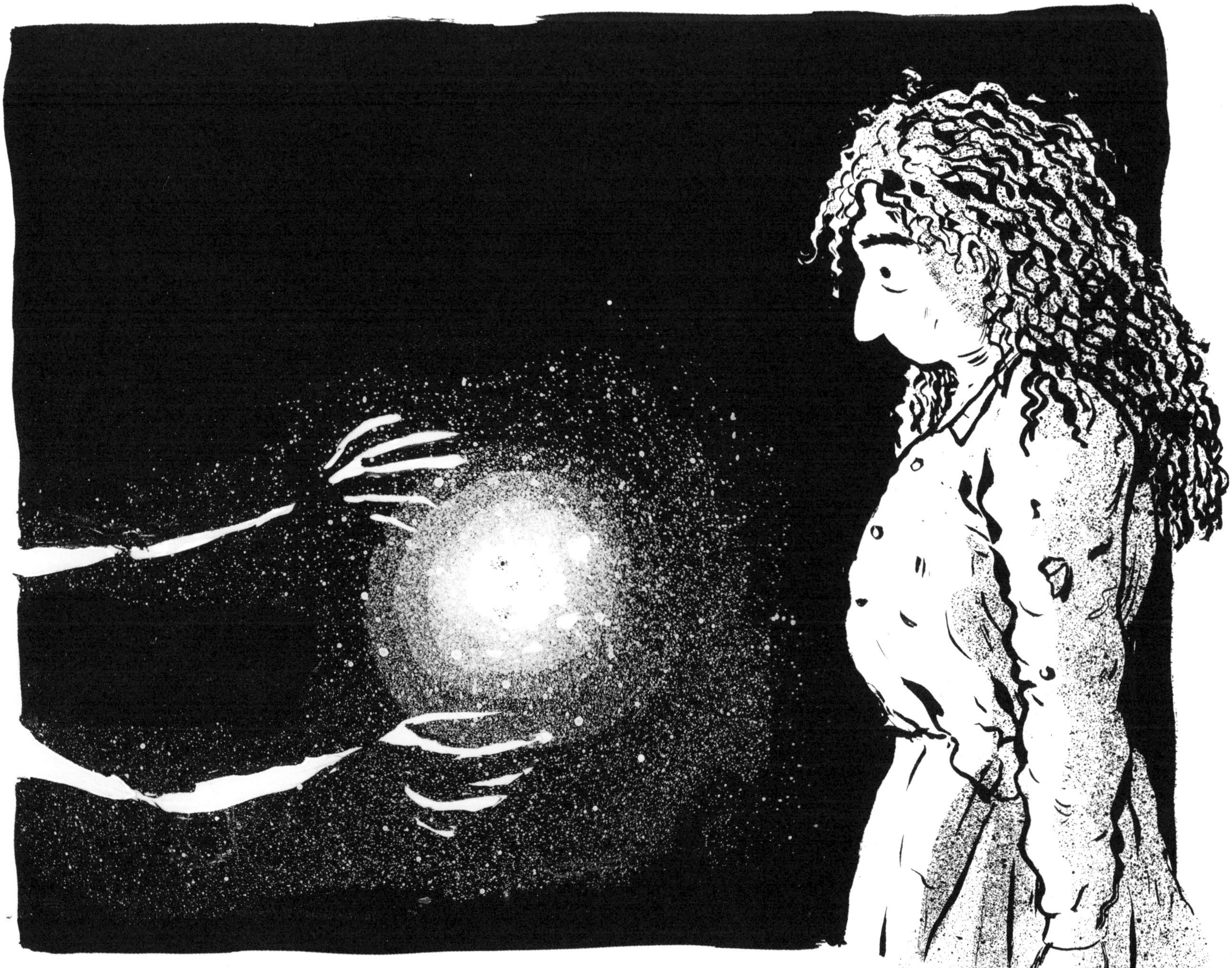

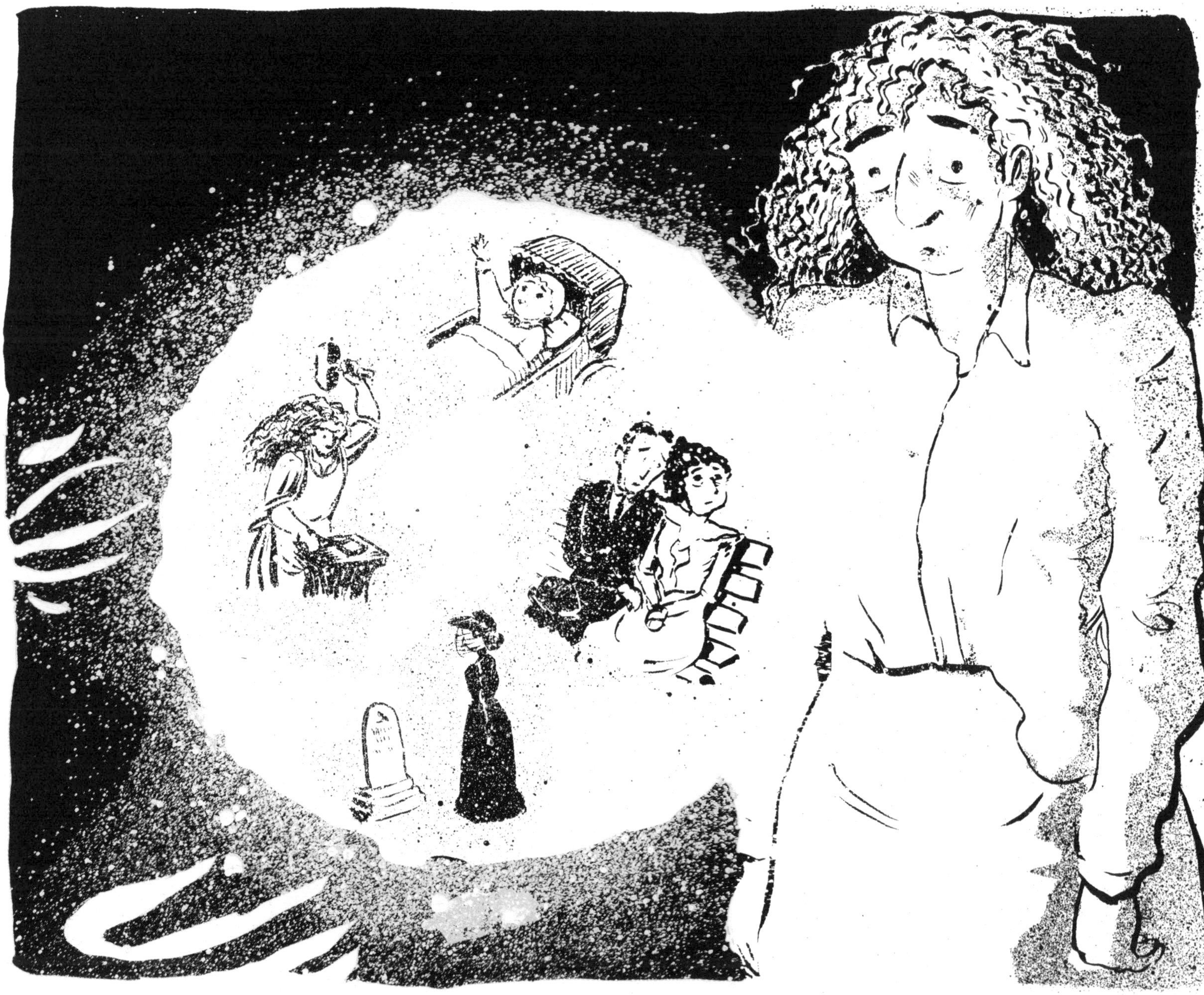

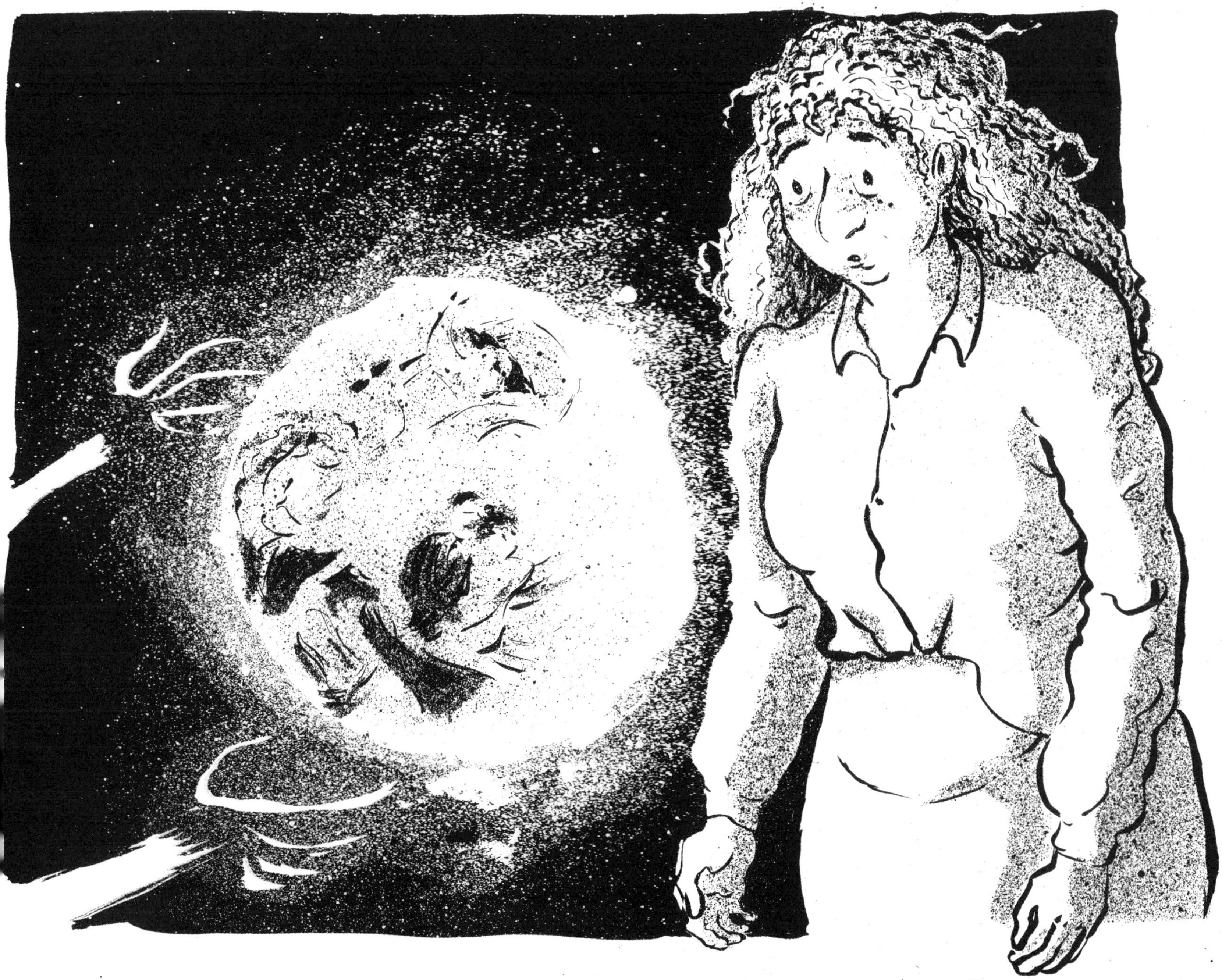

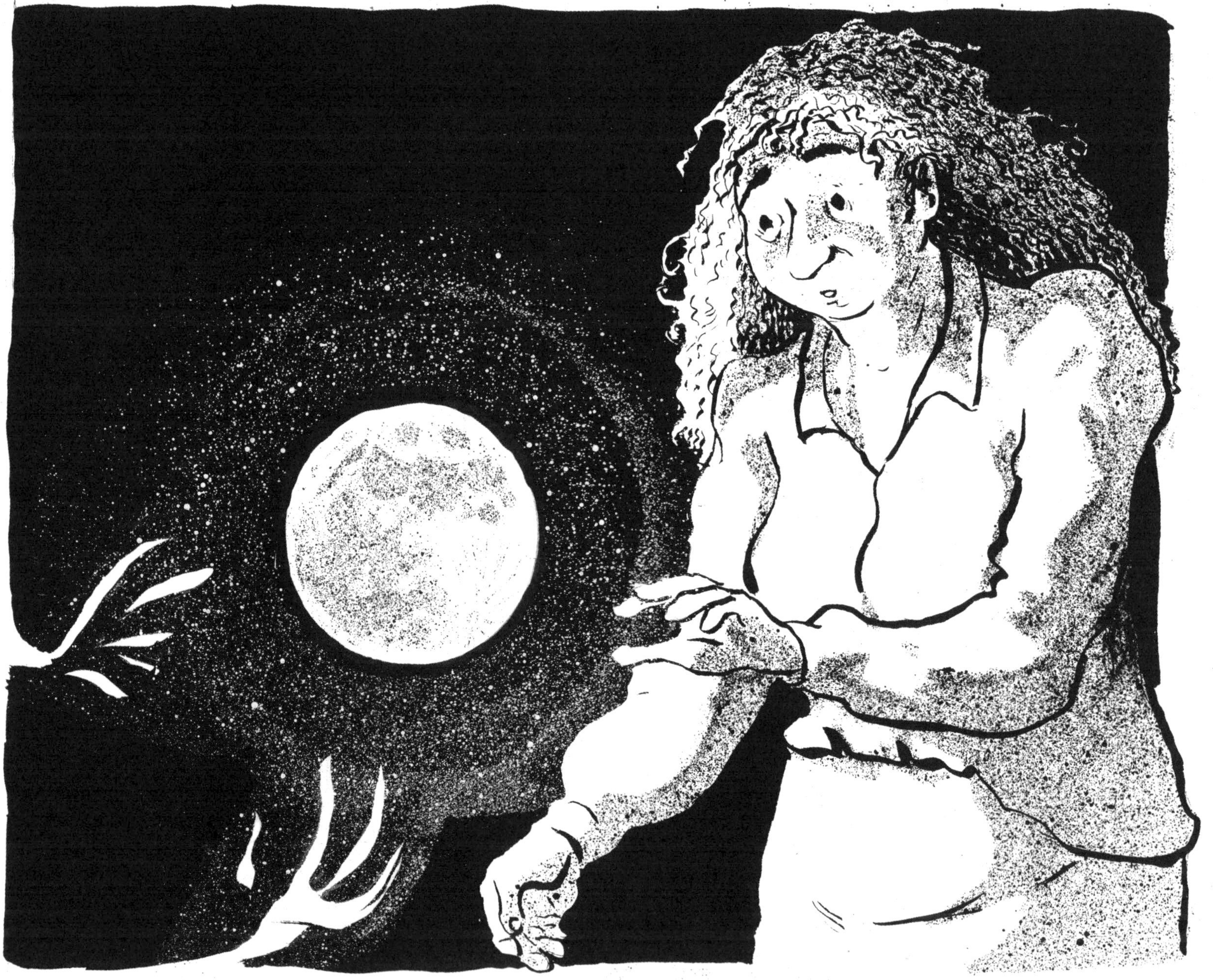

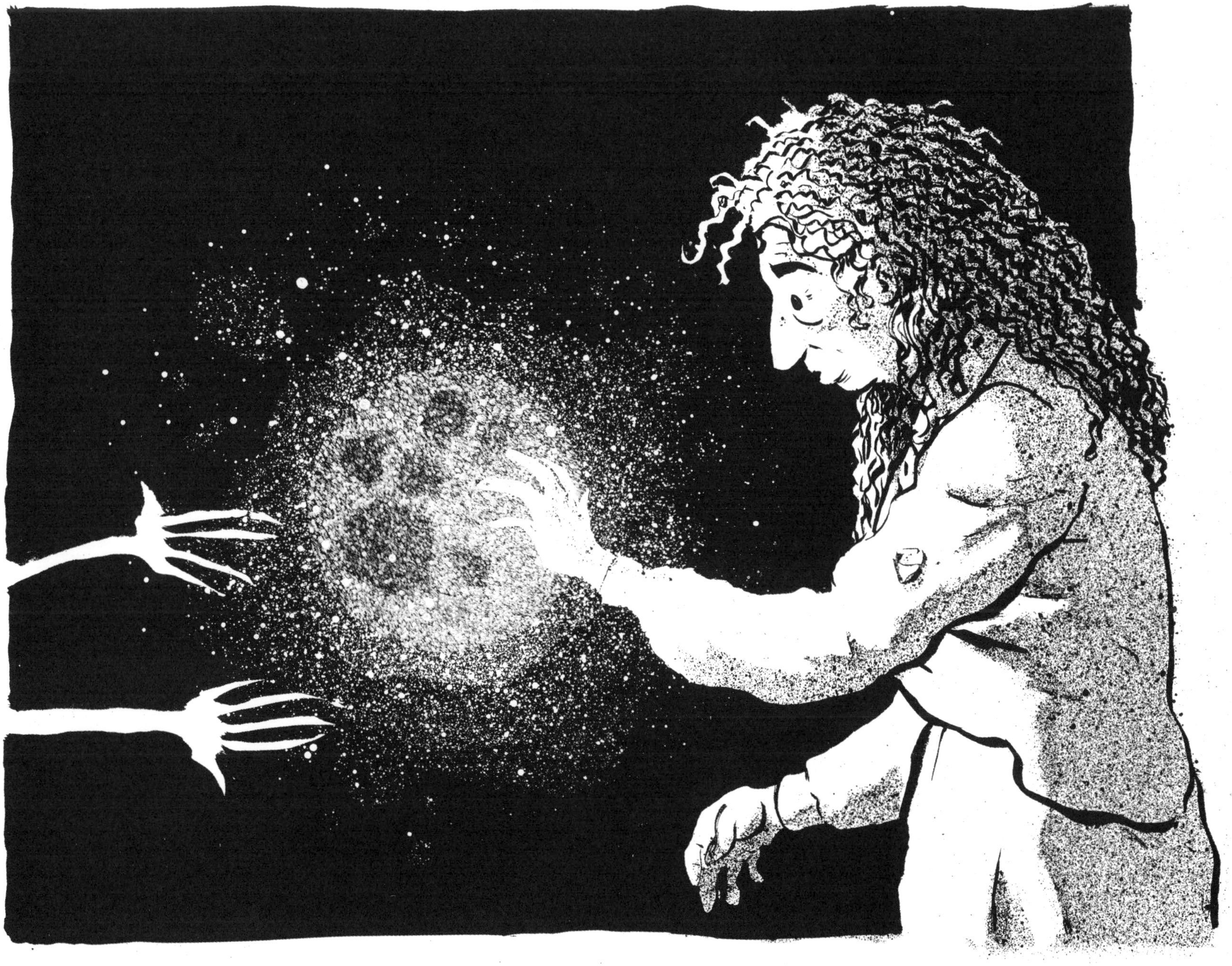

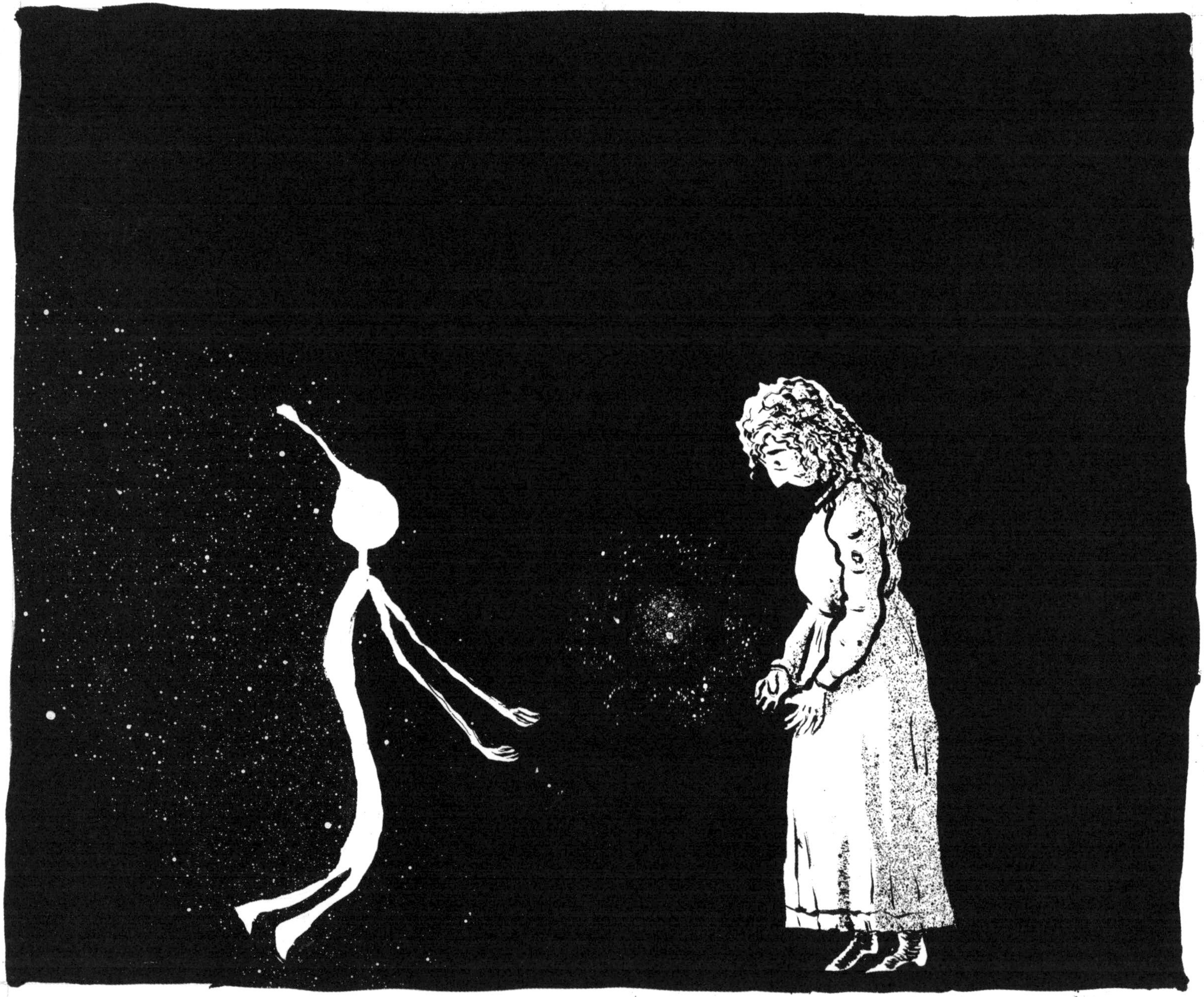

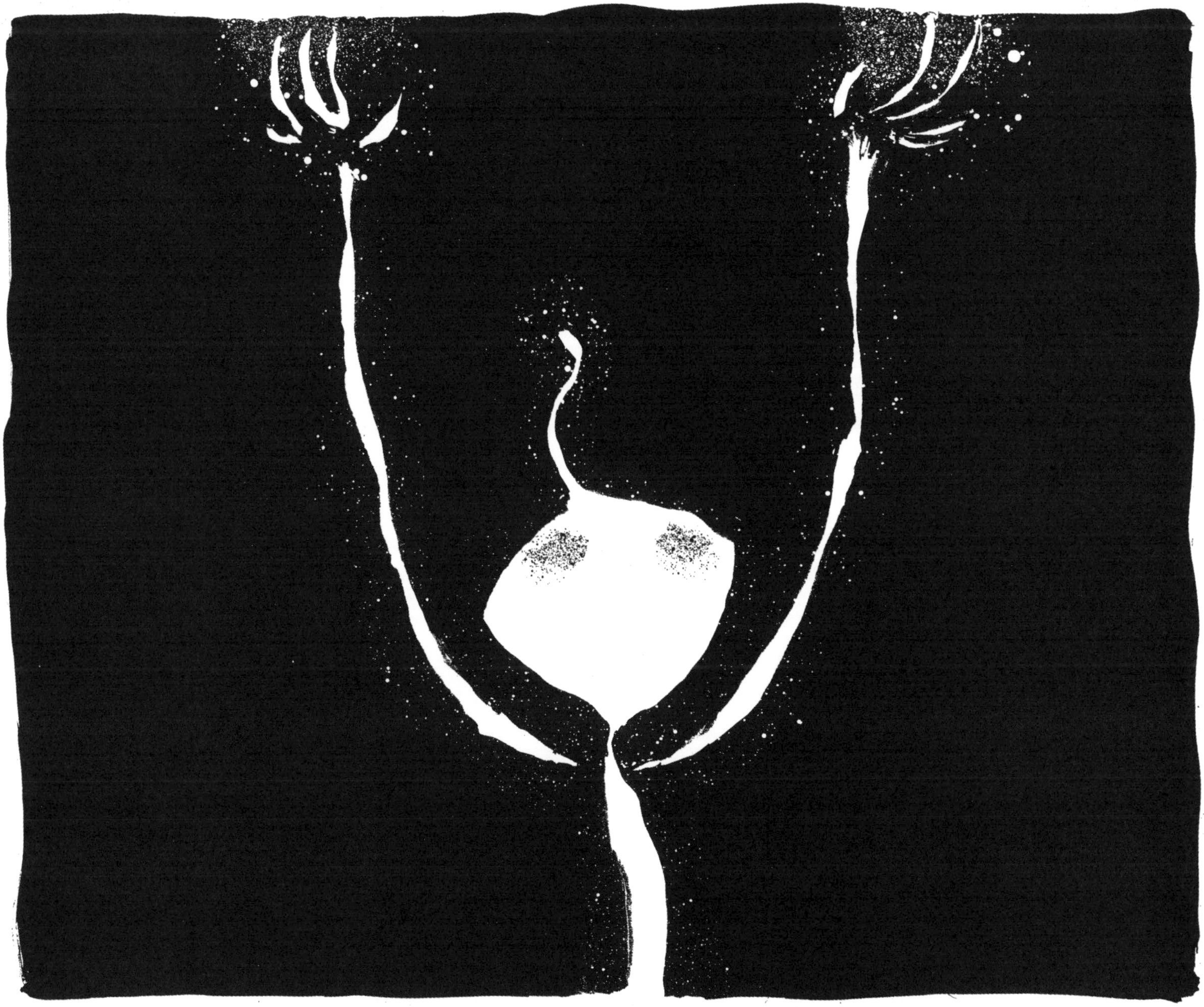

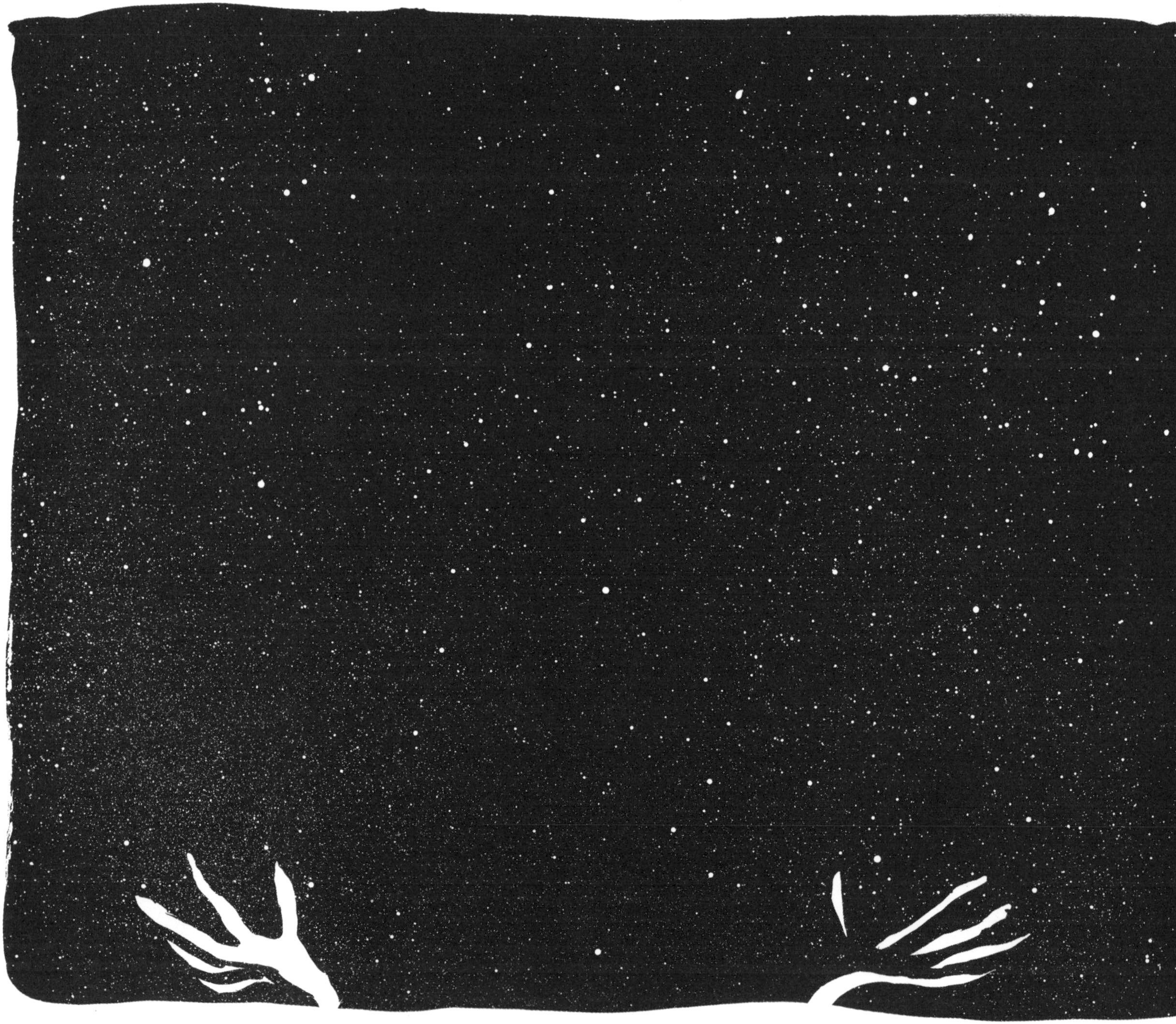

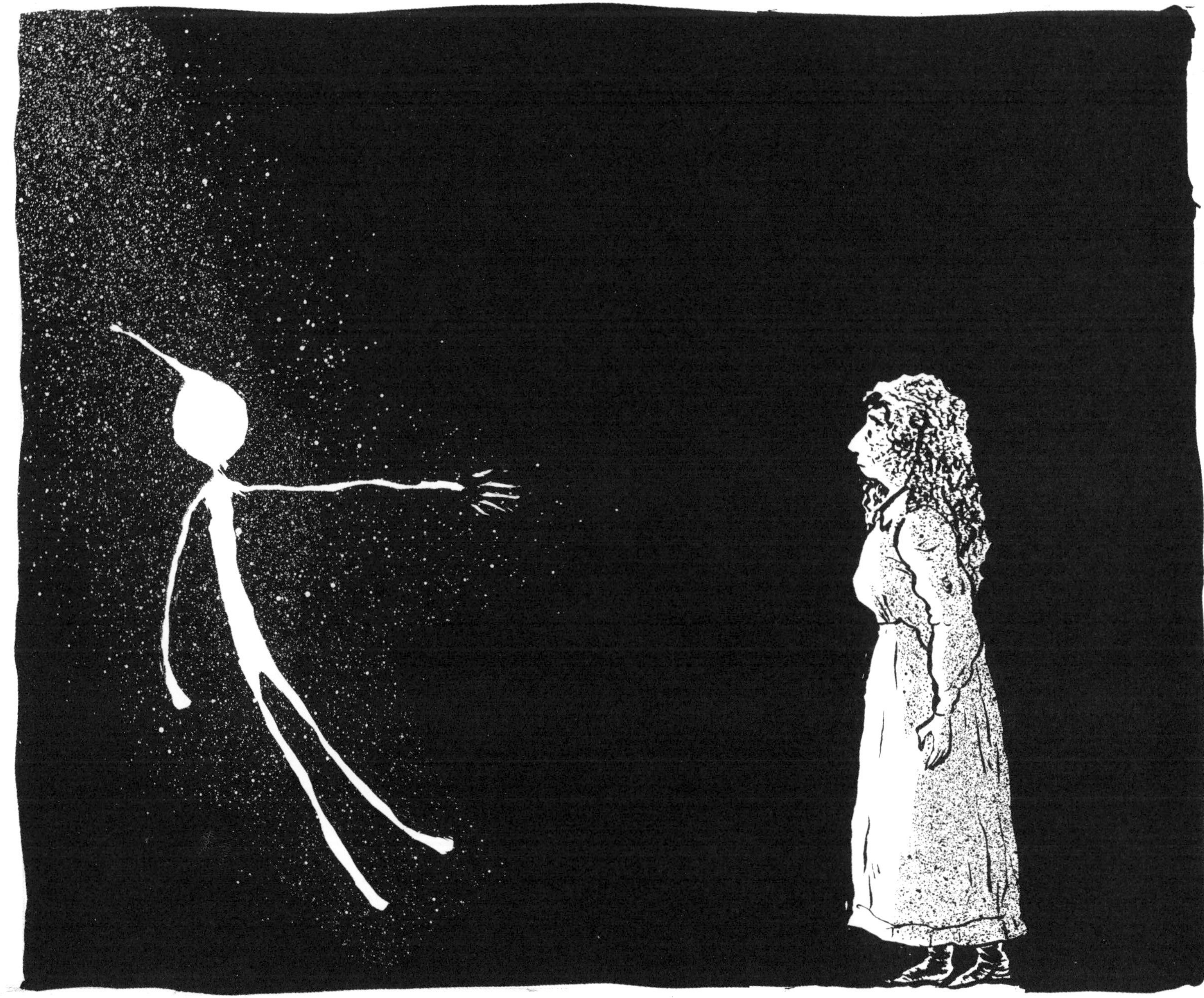

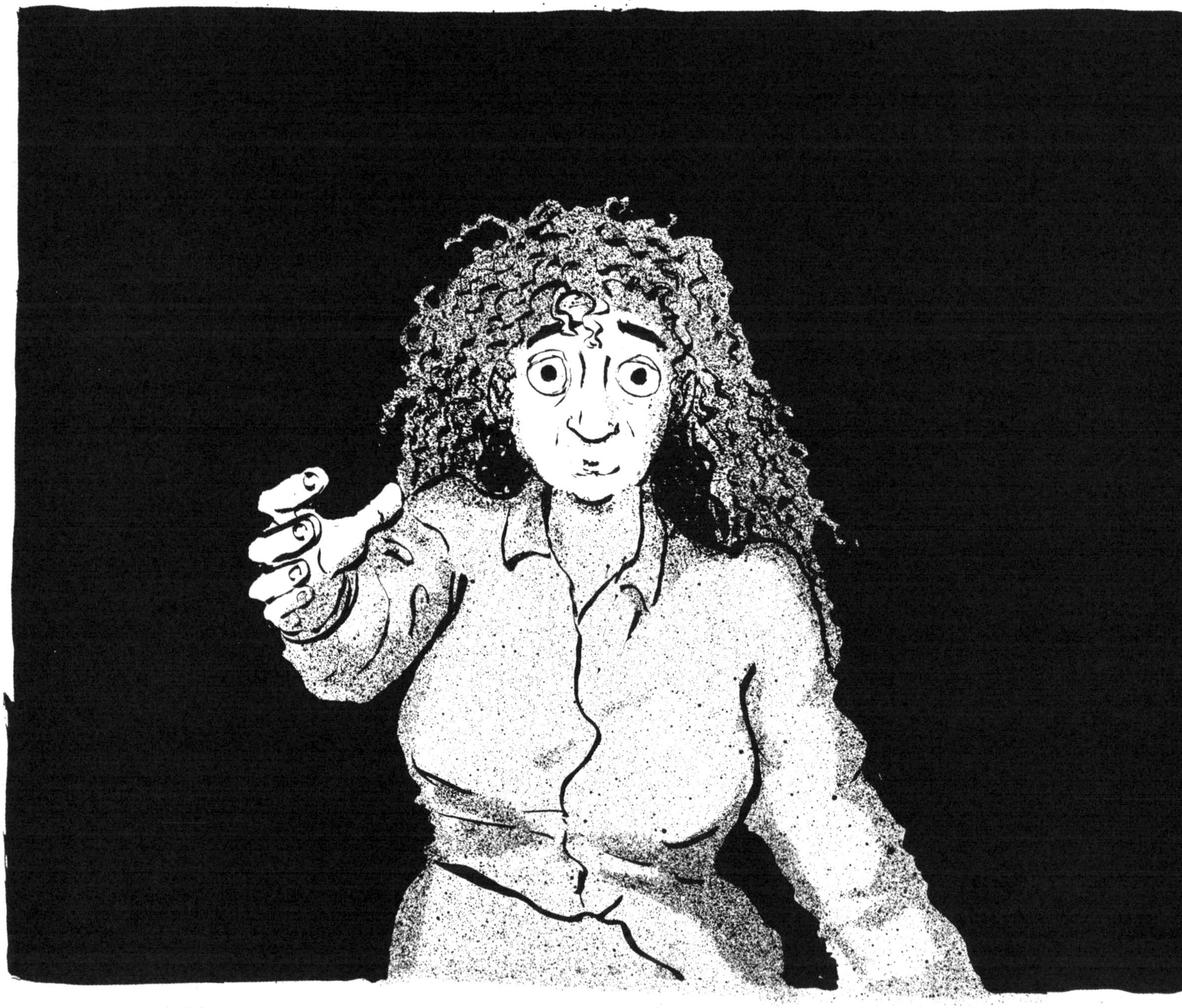

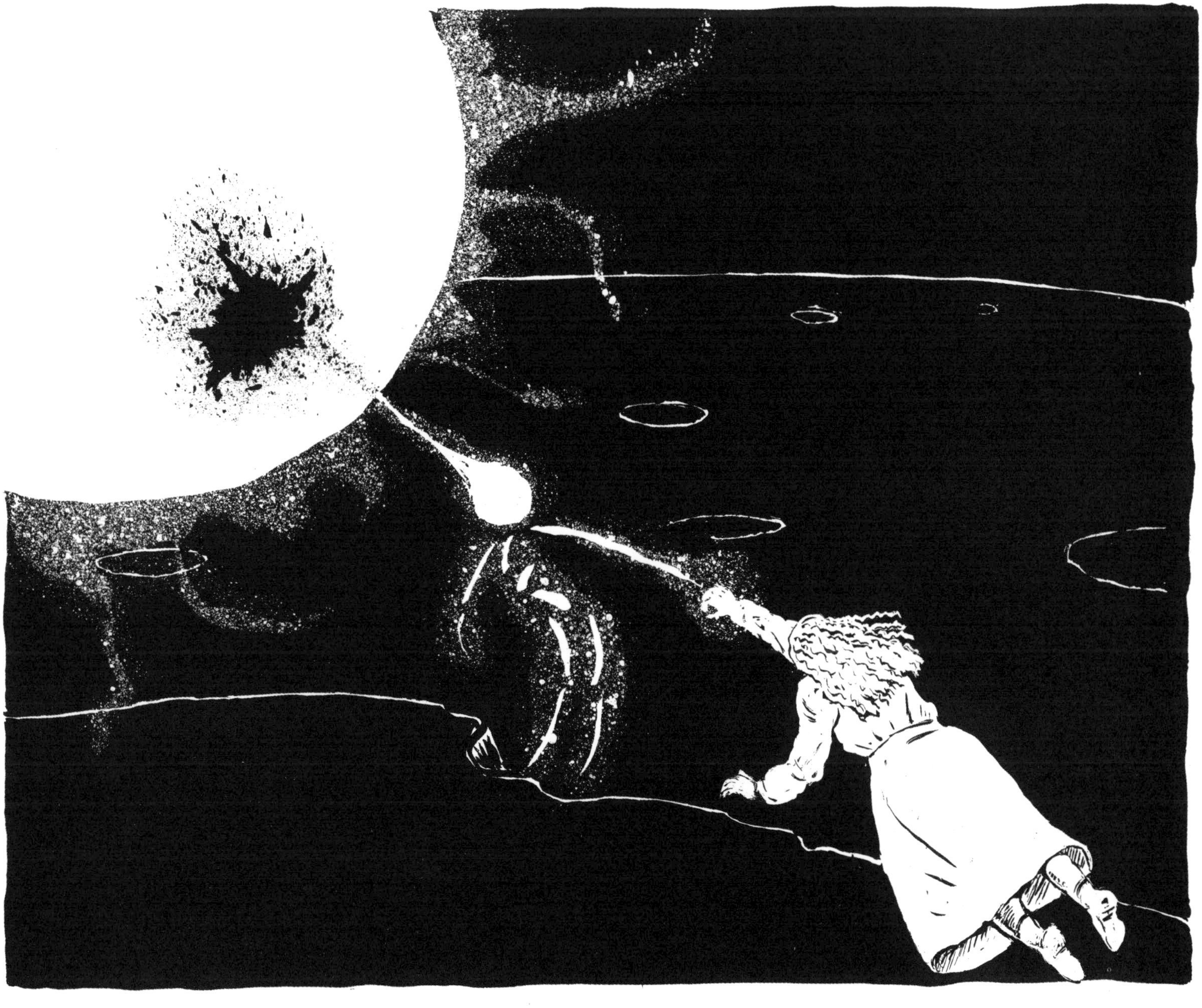

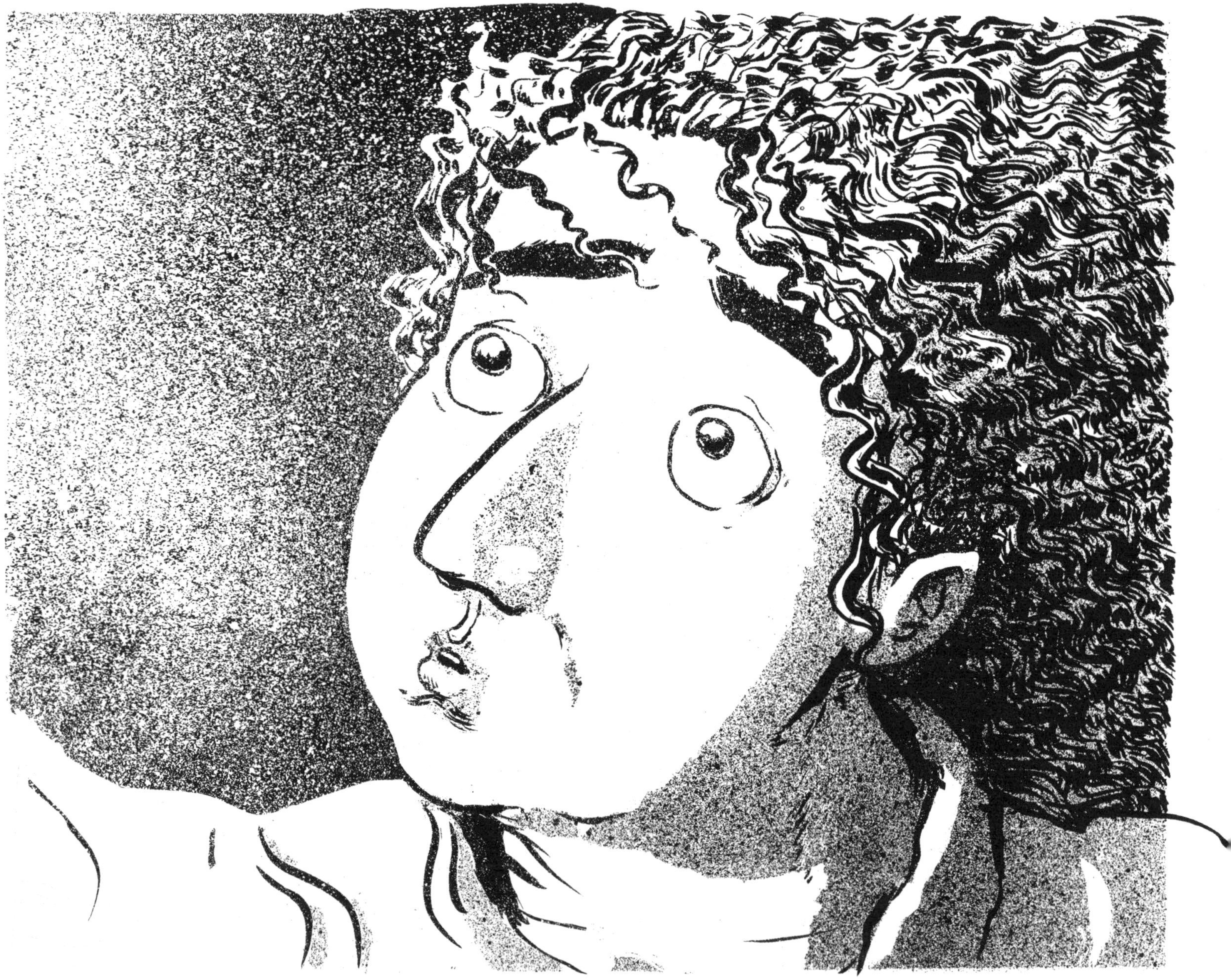

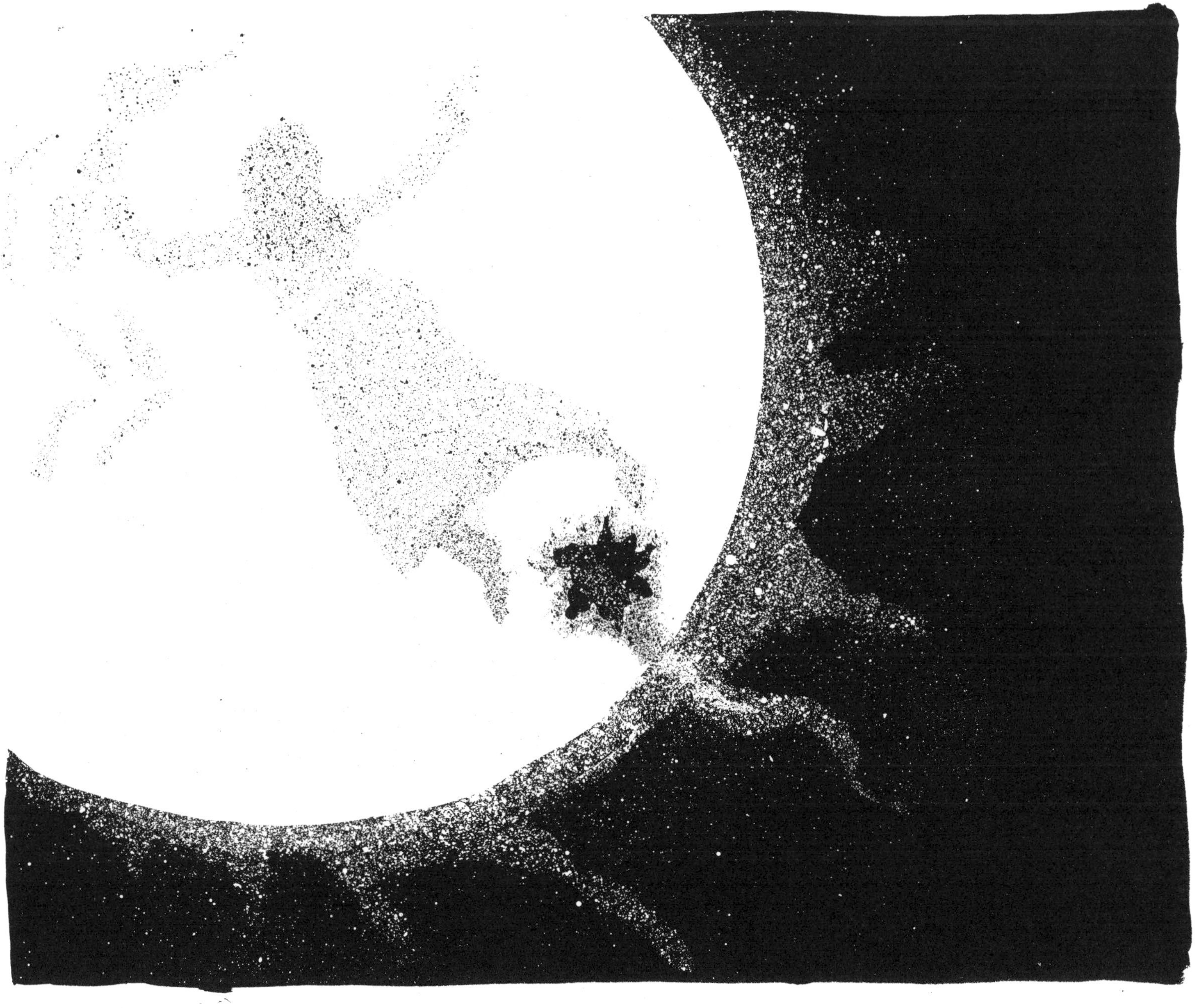

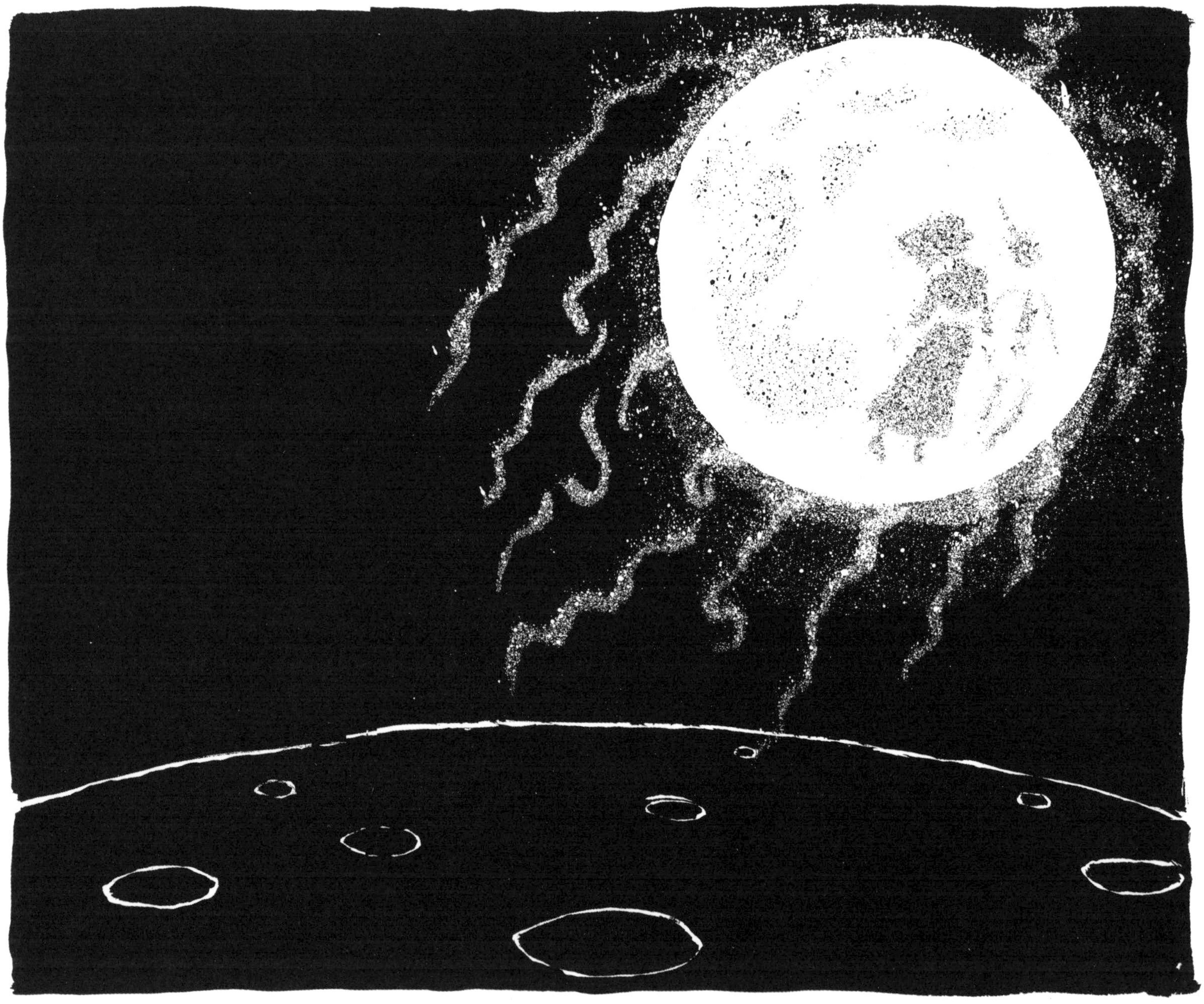

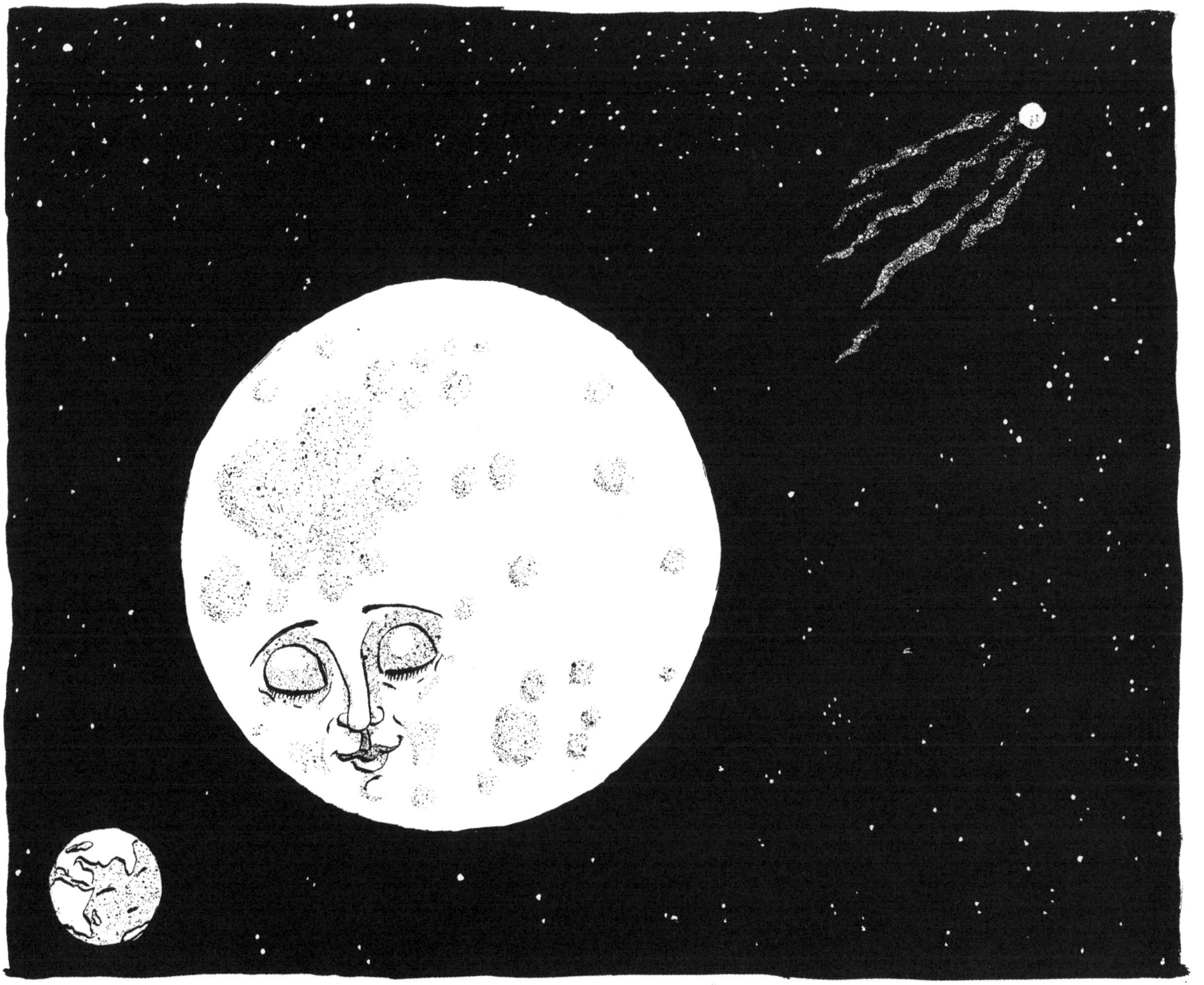

Scenes From
the Making of
"Lunatic"

I originally planned "Lunatic" as a much shorter story, laid out in panels like a conventio
comic. These were my first, rough "thumbnails" of the whole thing:

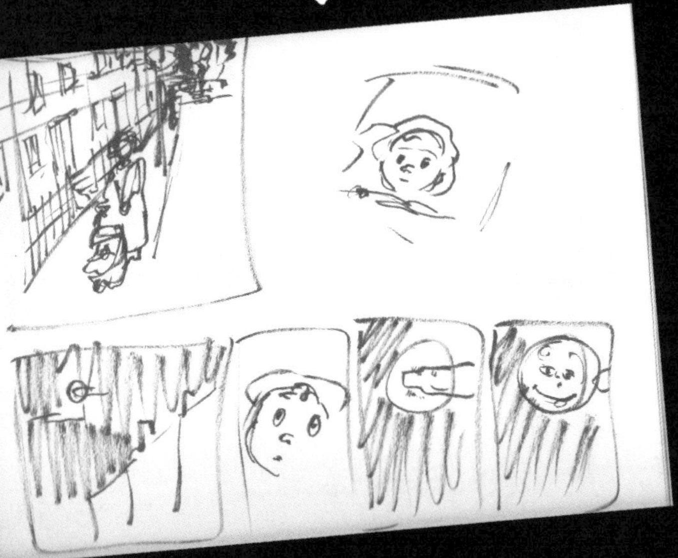

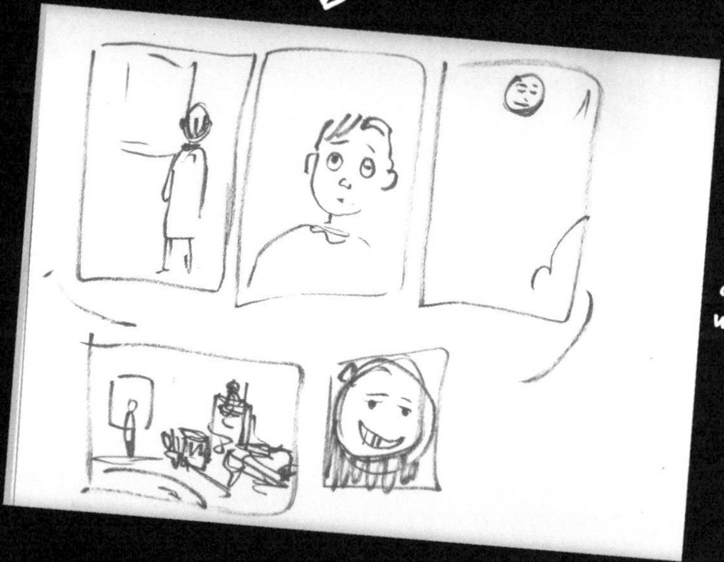

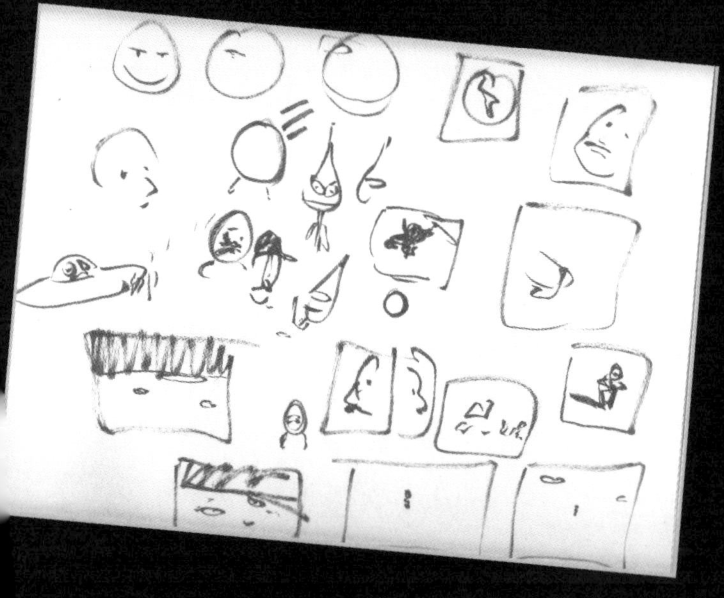

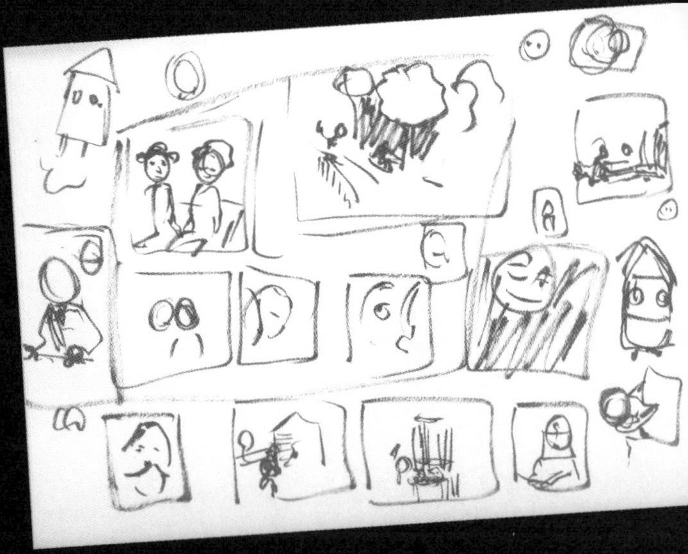

Eventually, I decided to try the "wordless book" format, with just o
image per page. I wanted each picture to have its own "presence."

Each chapter of the story shows a different phase in the character's life, so I wanted every chapter to have something different about it, a change in media. or a new stylistic approach:

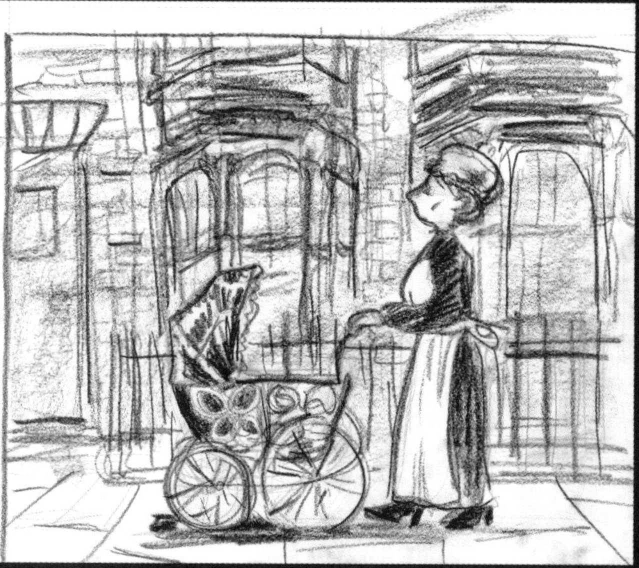

conté crayon sketch for page 2

The first chapter is drawn in a combination of conte crayon, india ink, and acrylic paint.

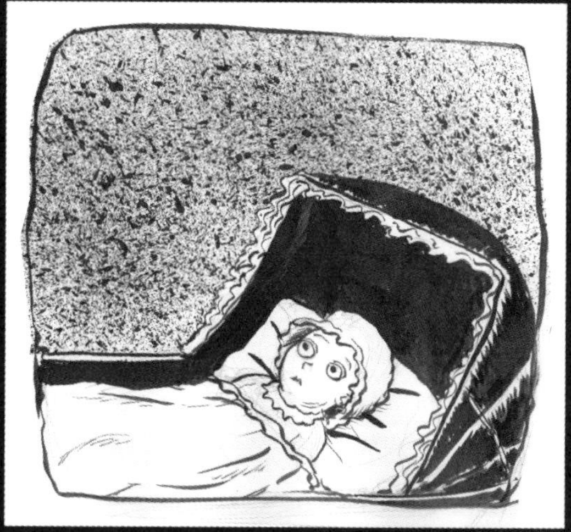

india ink - brush and toothbrush spatter

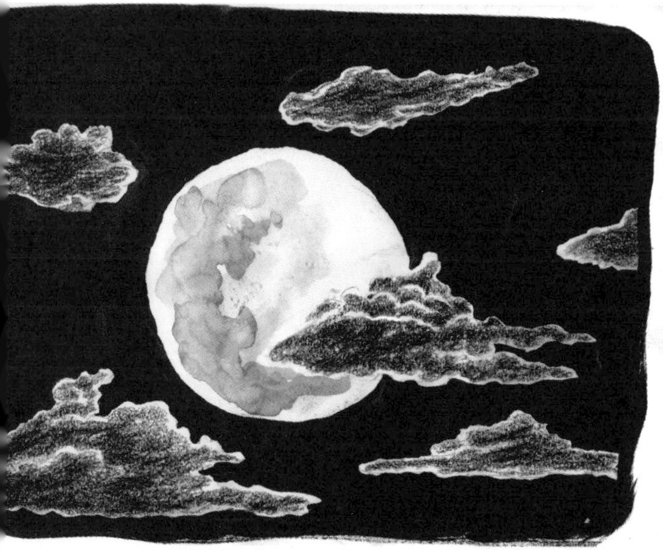

Some sketches and studies, trying out various media

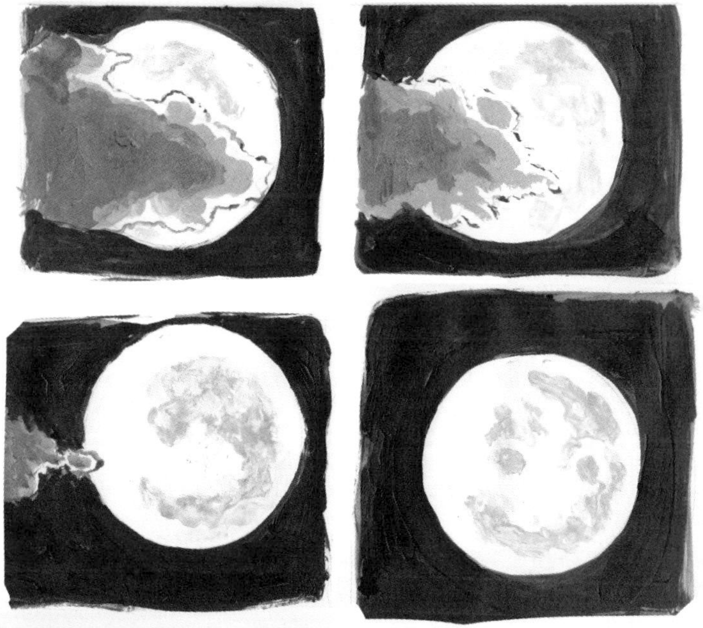

Chapter Two was drawn with nib pen and India ink, with ink washes (ink and water) on watercolor paper. I wanted the wash tones to be delicate, for the feel of a moonlit child's bedroom.

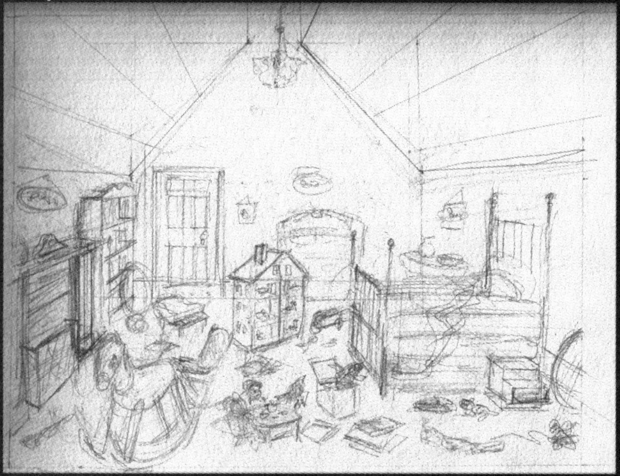

pencils ⤴

I inked this chapter with my left hand, though I'm right-handed. I like the "wavery" line, seems more playful.

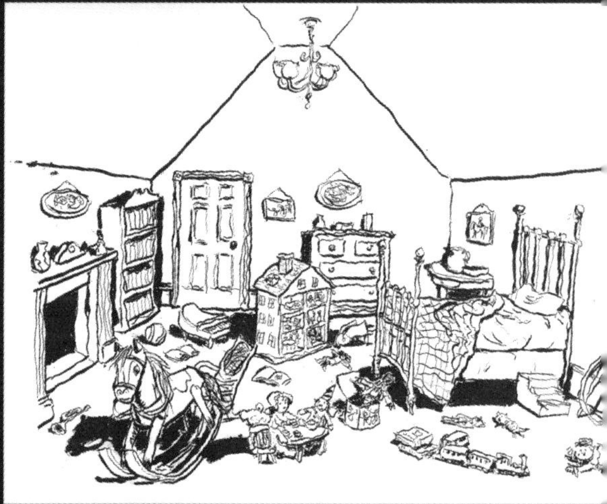

inks ⤴

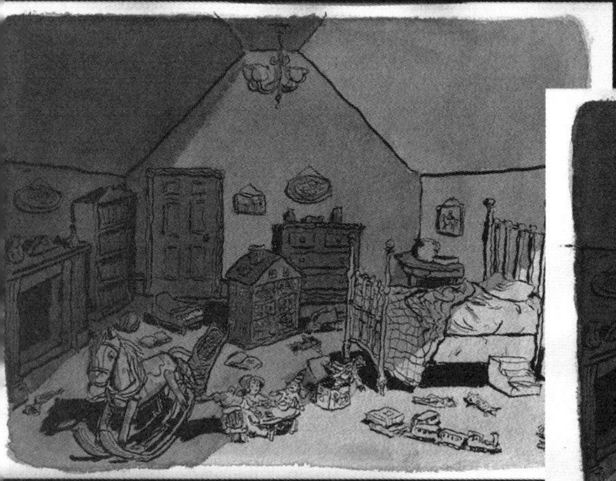

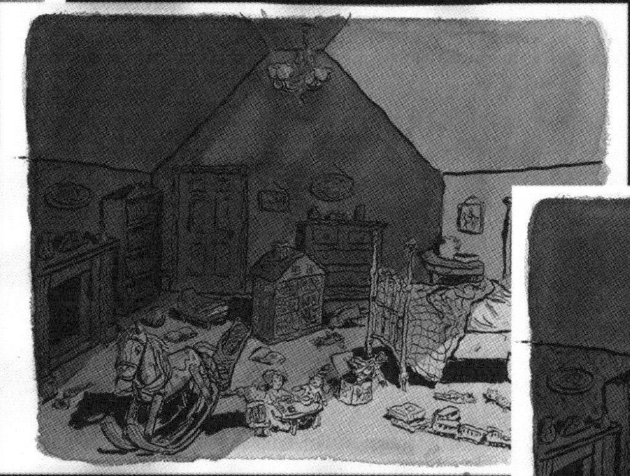

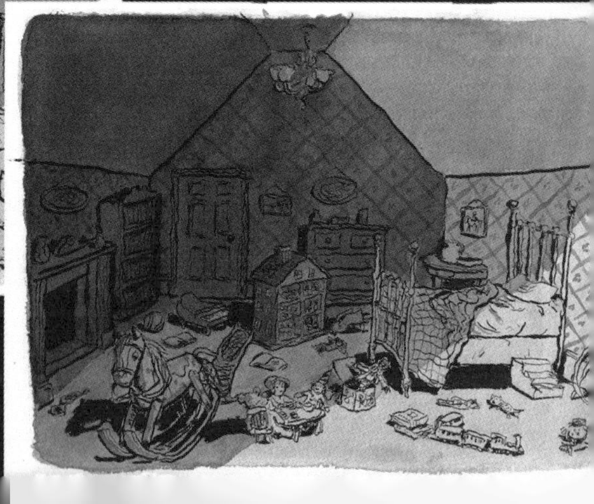

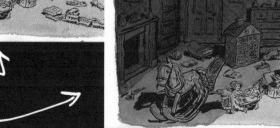

Then I applied the wash layers in stages, first to build the shadows, and then to add details like the wallpaper pattern.

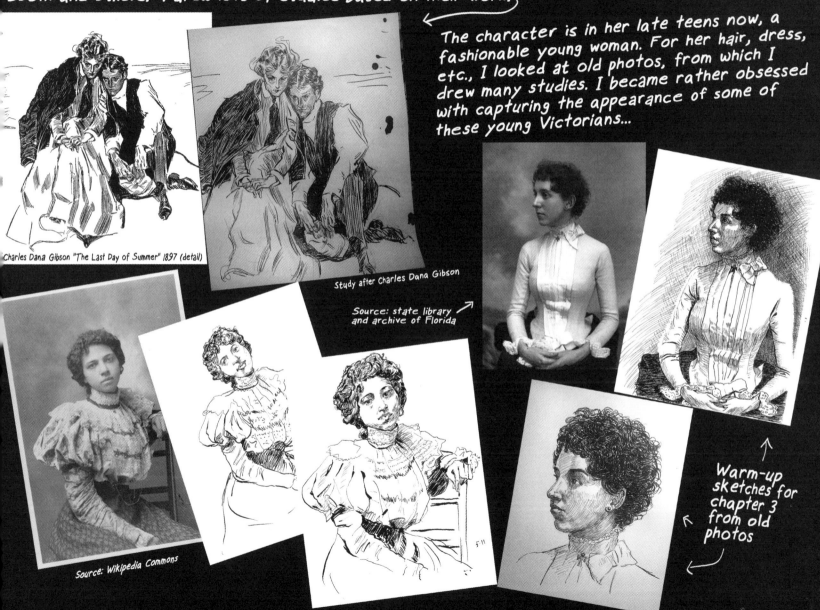

Chapter three was drawn in nib pen and india ink (no washes this time). The style is inspired by turn-of-the-century illustrators like Charles Dana Gibson, James Montgomery Flagg, Franklin Booth and others. I drew lots of studies based on their work.

The character is in her late teens now, a fashionable young woman. For her hair, dress, etc., I looked at old photos, from which I drew many studies. I became rather obsessed with capturing the appearance of some of these young Victorians...

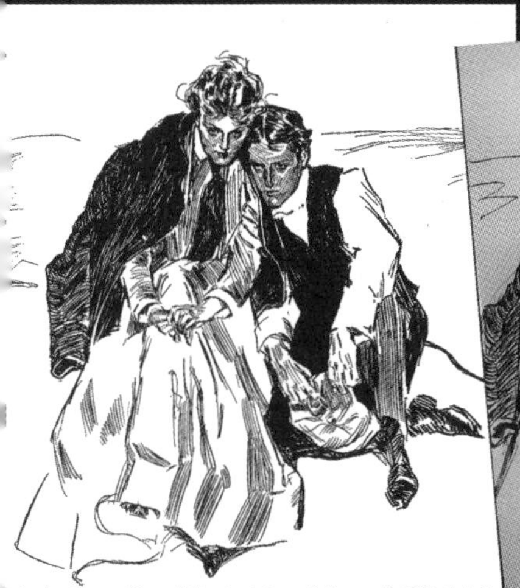

Charles Dana Gibson "The Last Day of Summer" 1897 (detail)

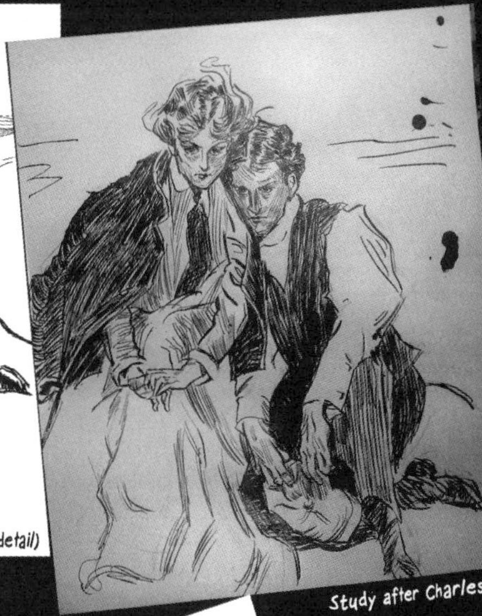

Study after Charles Dana Gibson

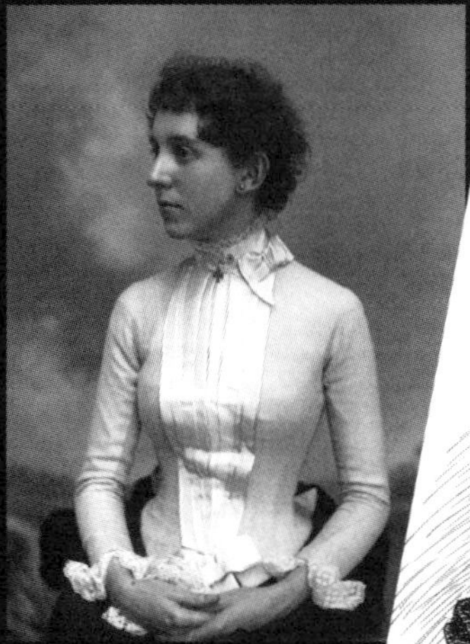

Source: state library and archive of Florida

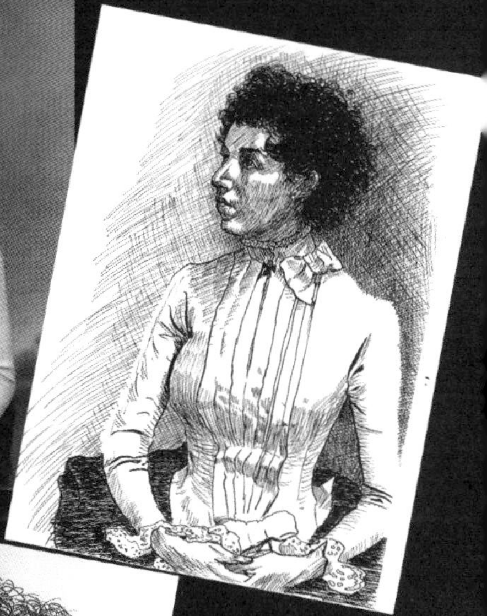

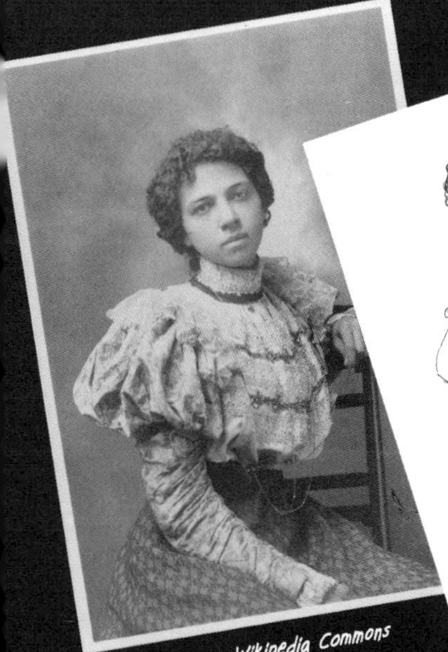

Source: Wikipedia Commons

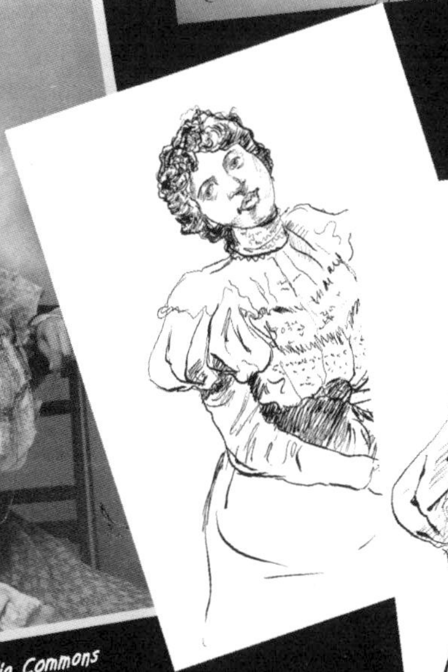

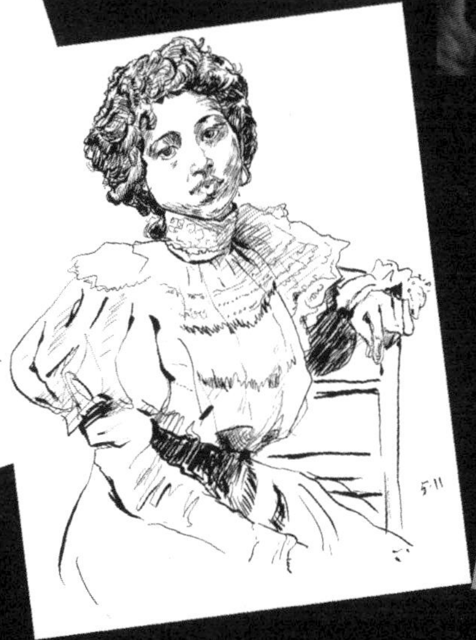

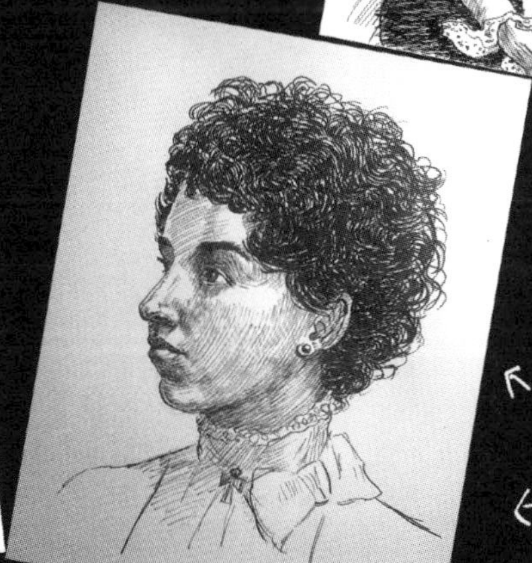

Warm-up sketches for chapter 3 from old photos

For chapter four, I used pencil and ink washes only, no straight black inks. I wanted to evoke fin-de-siecle French prints and drawings, by Bonnard, Toulouse-Lautrec and others. I love the soft tones of the lithographs, the way they place figures in space, and of course, the fashions.

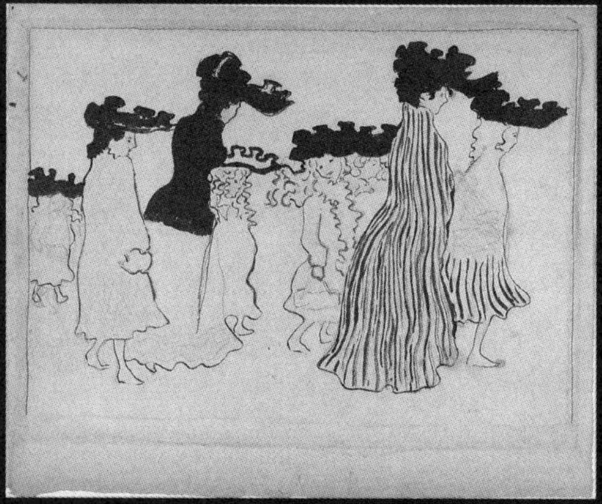

Pierre Bonnard, A Promenade in Fancy Hats, 1891/1893

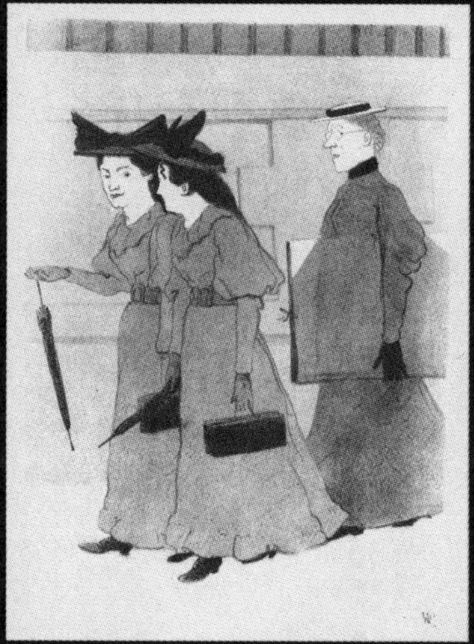

Hermann-Paul, La Vie de Madame Quelconque 1894

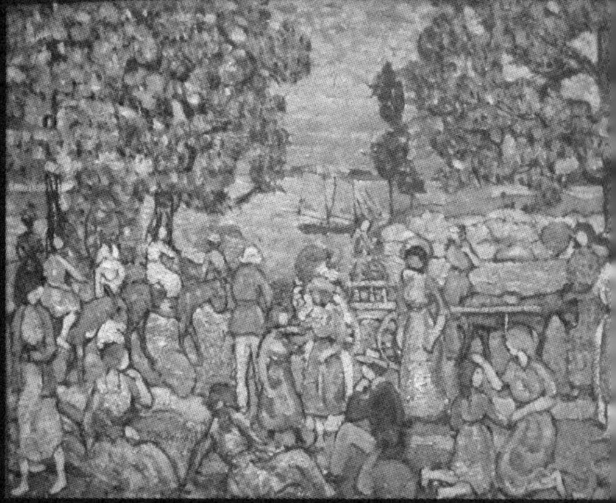

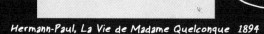

Maurice Prendergrast, On the Beach, No3,

(I also remembered the crowd scenes of American painter Maurice Prendergras

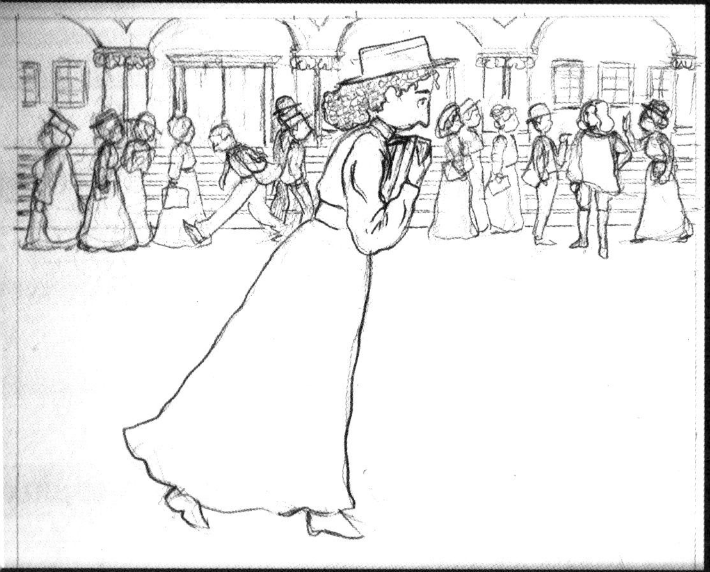

page 2 pencils

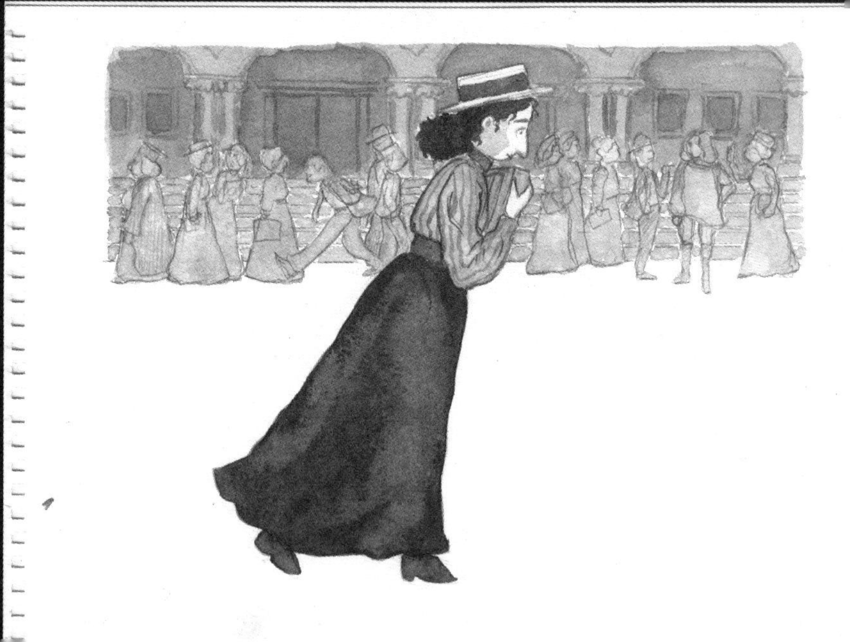

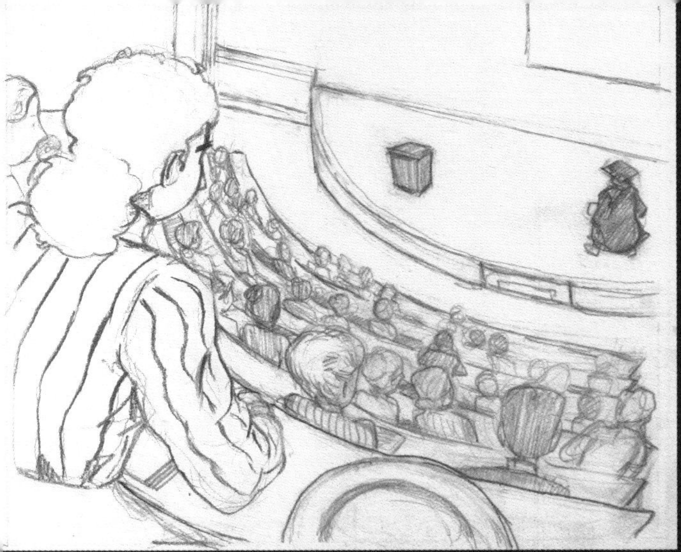

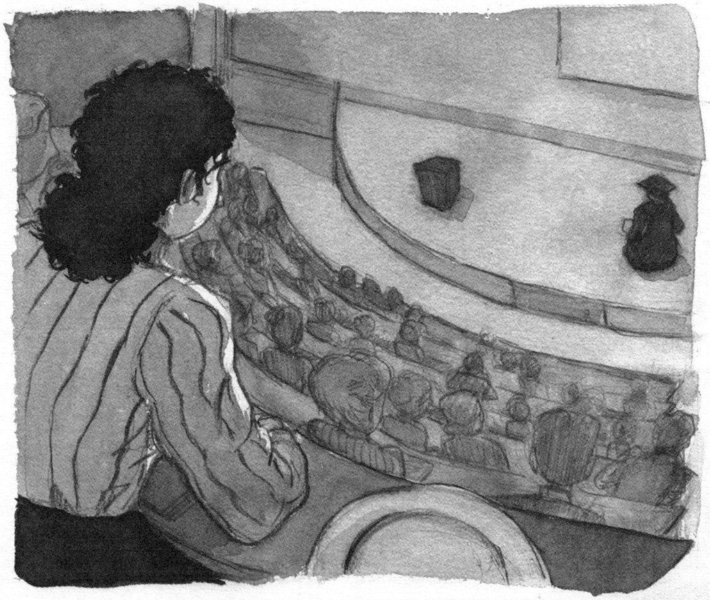

fter drawing page four, I decided I wanted to
ld the light of the magic lantern projector to
e image, so I drew a new layer on a separate
eet, and combined them in Photoshop.

Page 4, final:

This

plus this

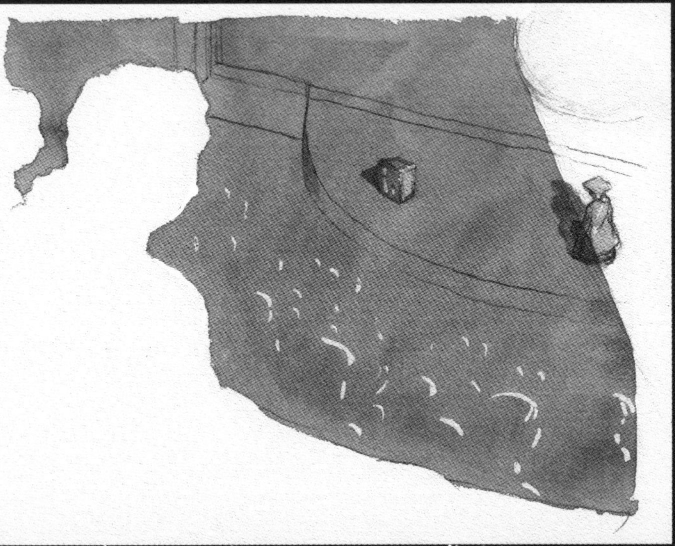

new layer, adding projector light

equals this

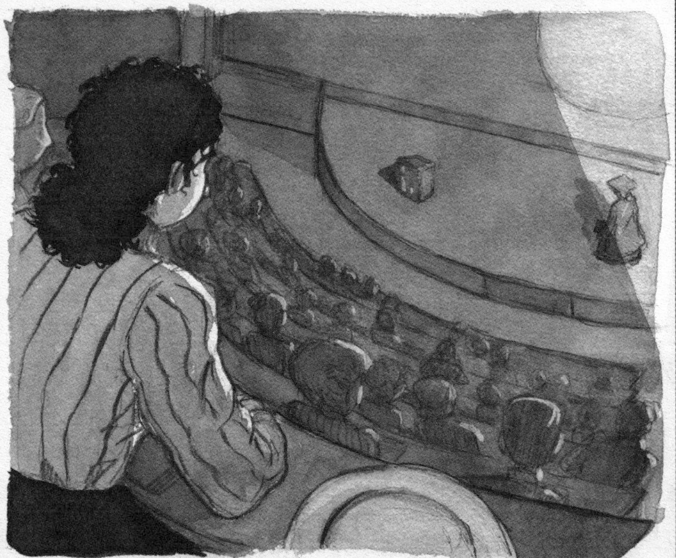

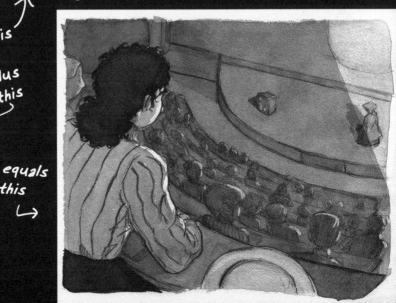

Chapter five is just three pages long, I thought it would be nice to vary the pace of the storytelling with some shorter sections (chapter six is just one page!) Drawing all those tall bookshelves in perspective took painstaking line-work. I drew the shading on separate pages, using a light table to match it with the lines, and put it all together in Photoshop.

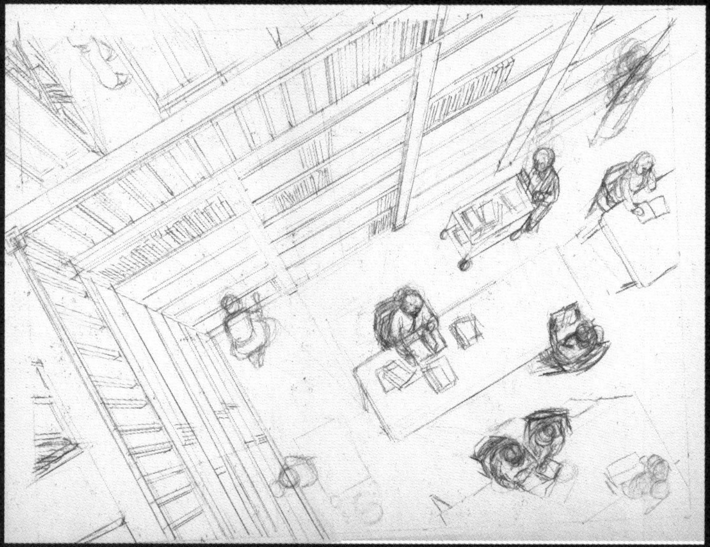

Pencils (non-photo blue)

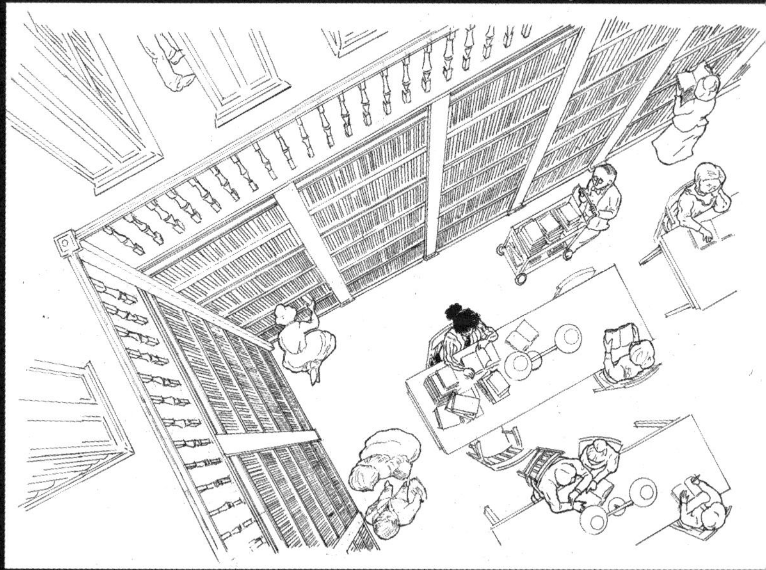

Inks (using a Rotring cartridge art pen)

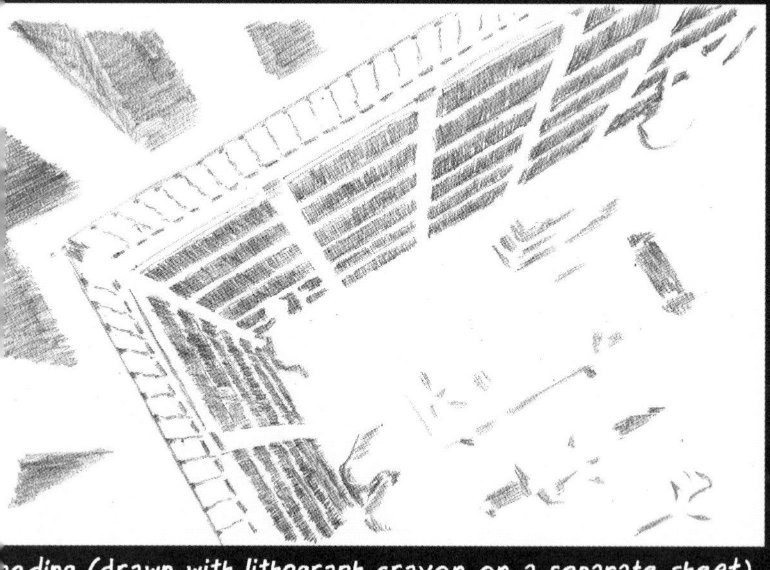

nading (drawn with lithograph crayon on a separate sheet)

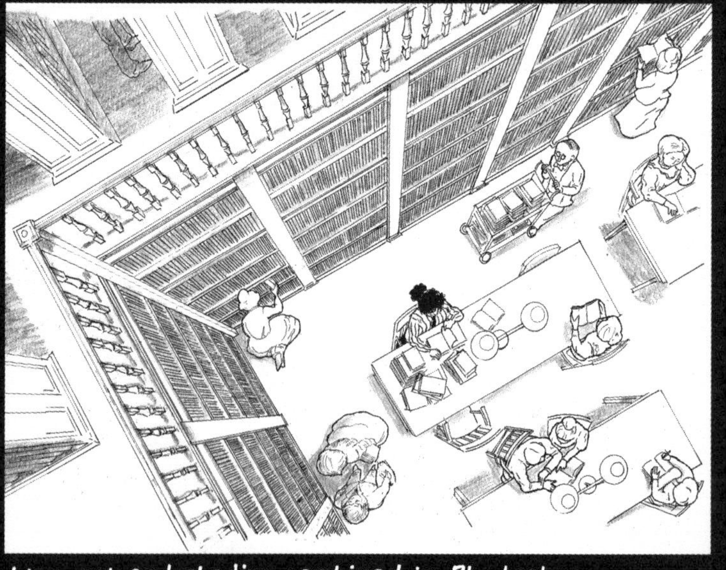

Line art and shading combined in Photoshop

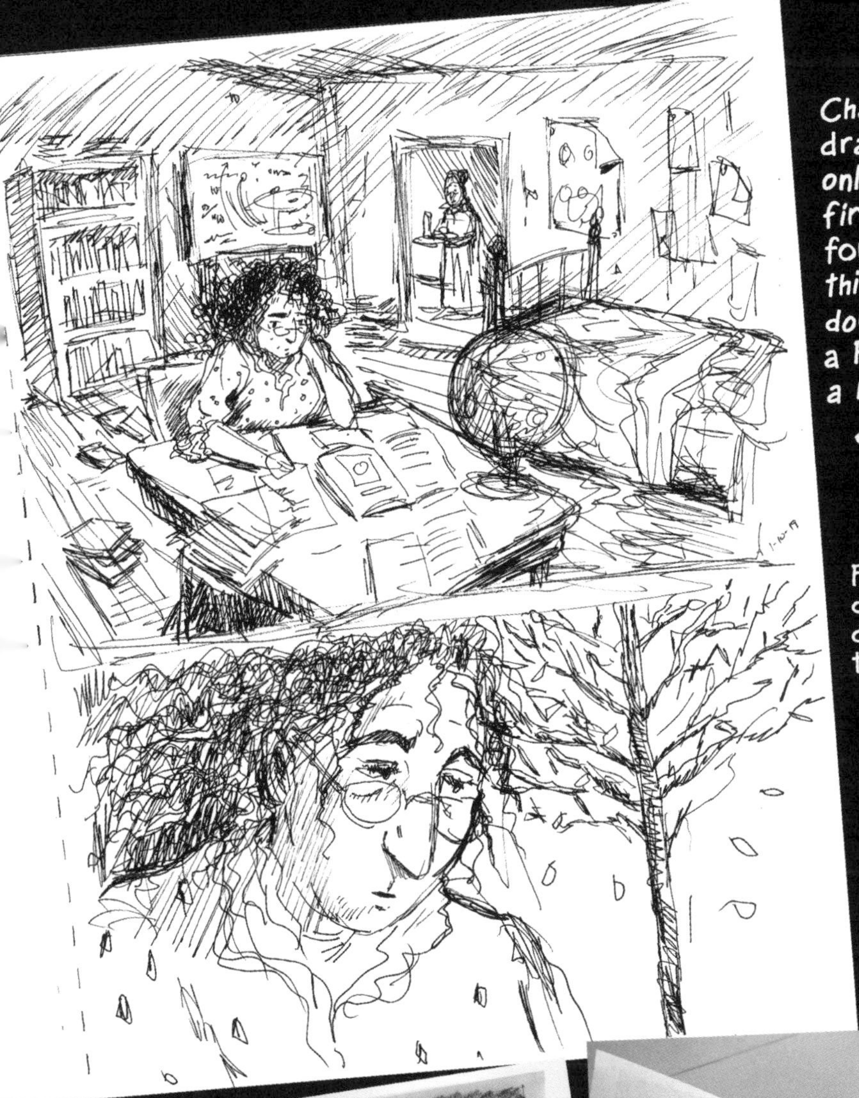

Chapter 7 was drawn in pencil only, but my first concept for it was this sketch, doodled with a Pilot pen at a meeting ⟵

For every chapter I first drew rough thumbnails ⟶

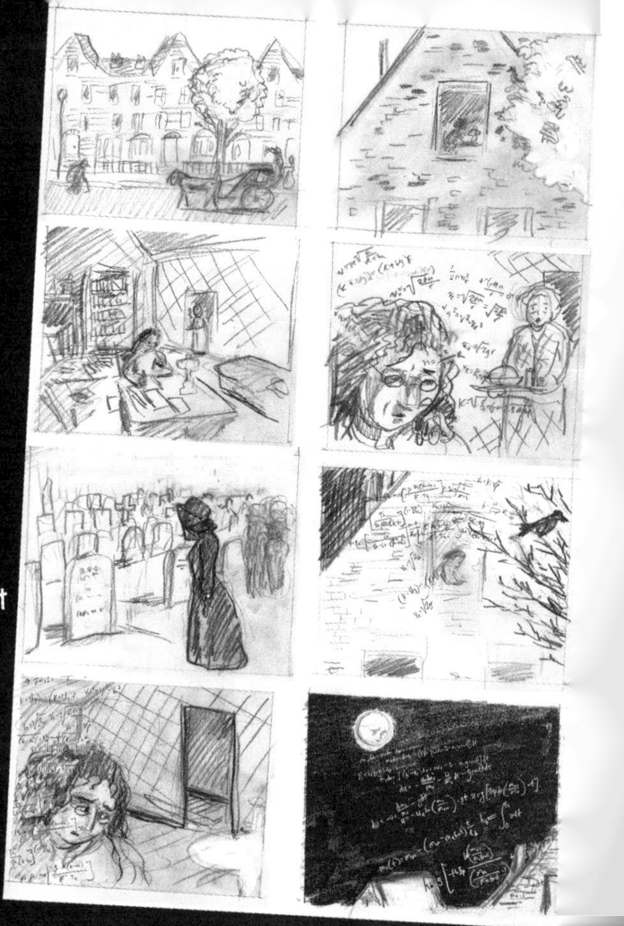

Which i could then print up as a little booklet, to judge the narrative flow.

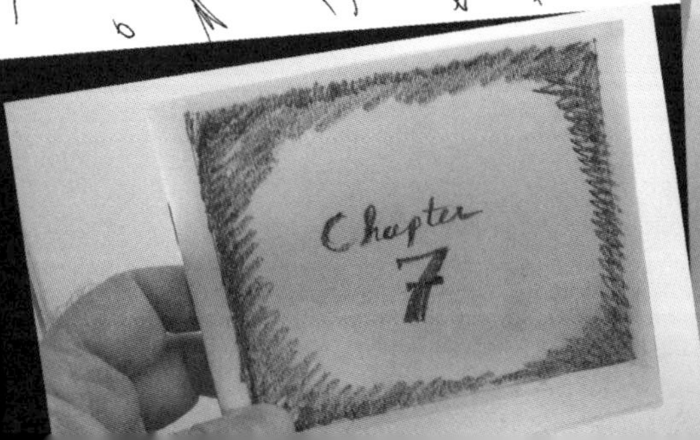
Chapter
7

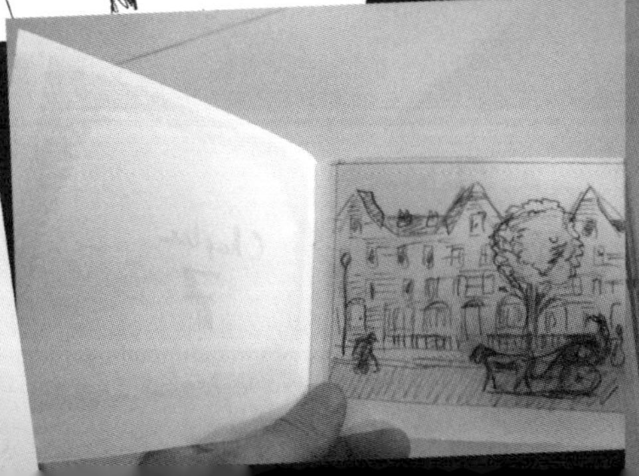

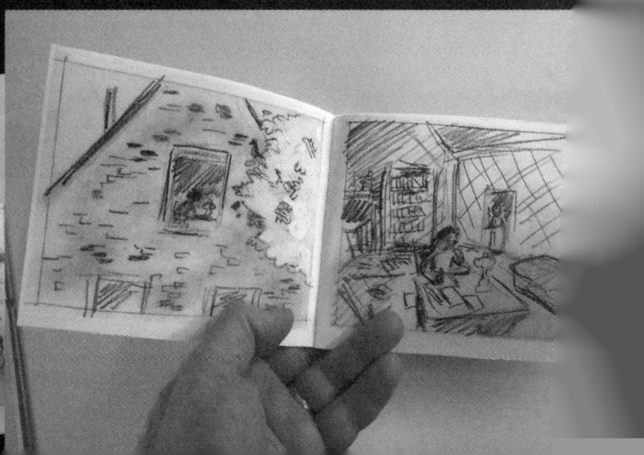

ery different than inks, with the ability to build, change and adjust by repainting over dry sections.

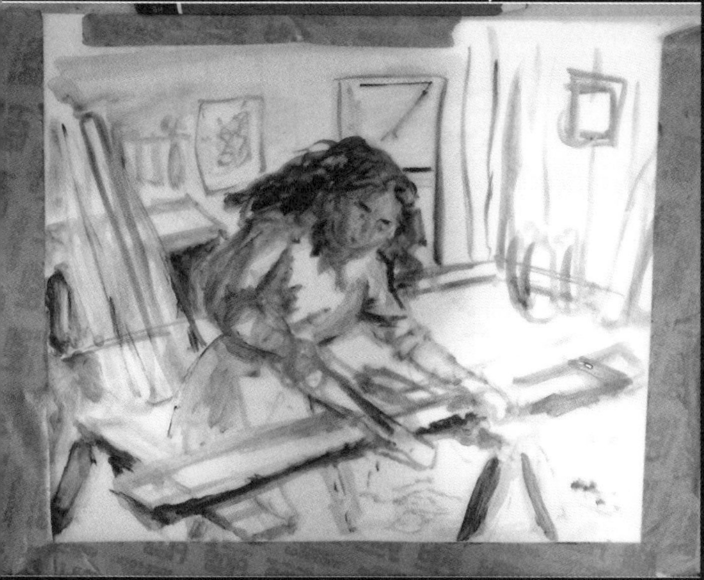

First, a loose sketch, with watery paints. ↵

Then firming up the lines and forms, putting in some shadows... ↪

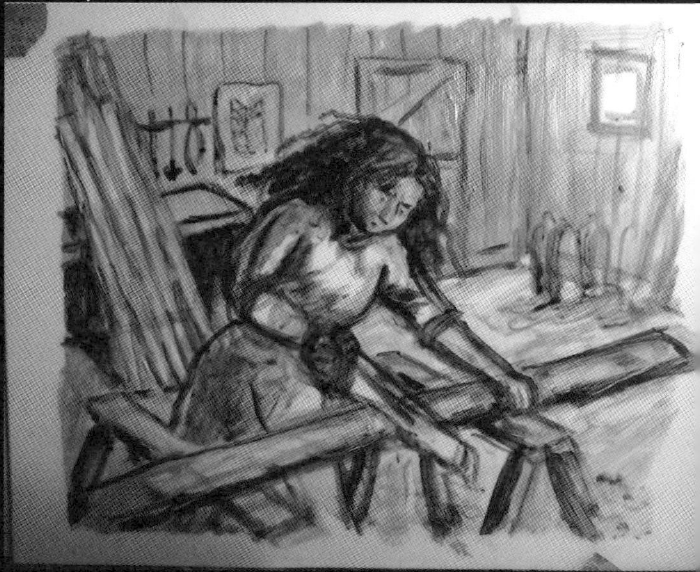

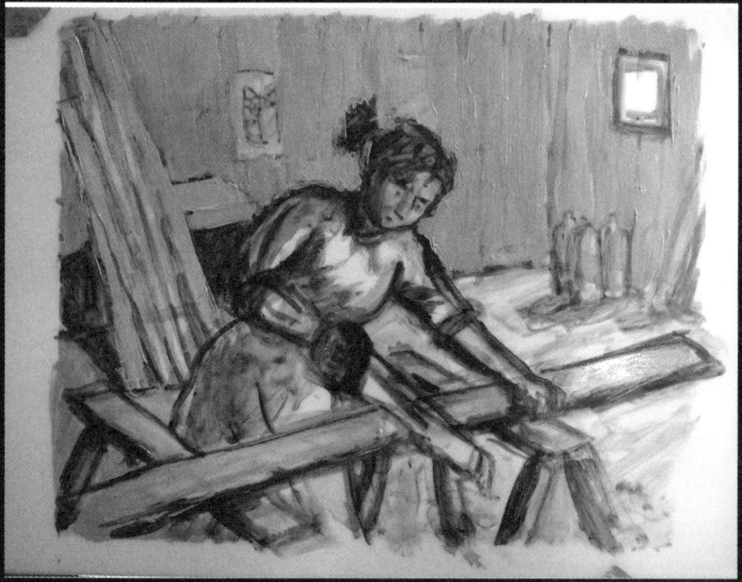

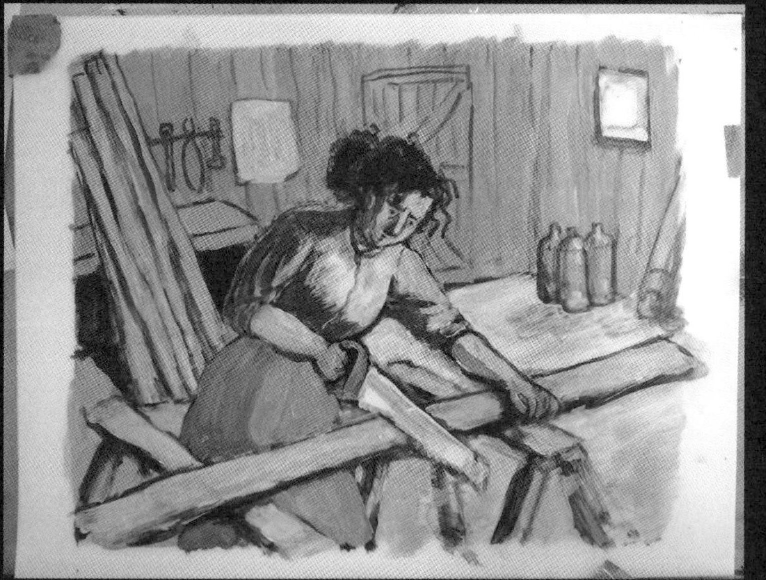

apter nine is drawn in brush and india ink, but for the last pages I added a technique I'd been
nting to try, using toothbrush/spatter to create textures and shading.

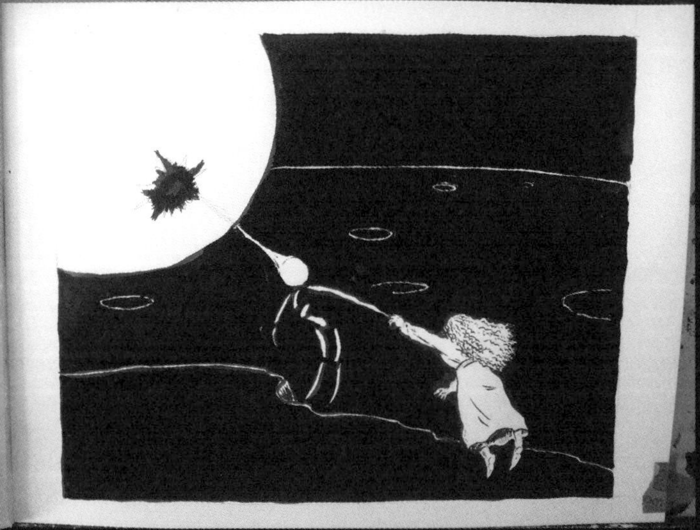

e's the page just inked, black ink on white paper.

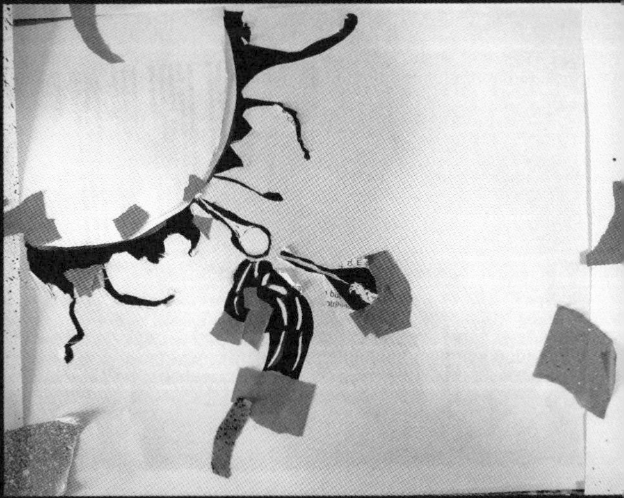

I cut stencils out of plain paper, using masking
in spots, to get the shapes just right.

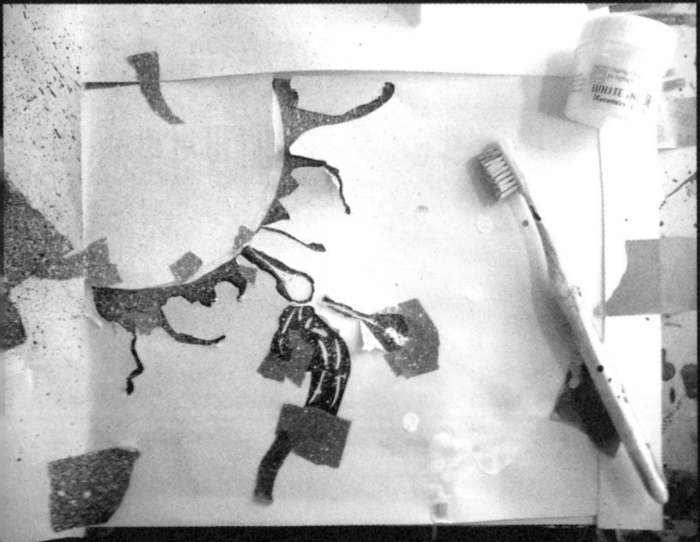

WHITE INK

toothbrush dipped in white ink is used to spatter
e unmasked areas of the paper (I flick the brush
th my thumb, wearing latex gloves).

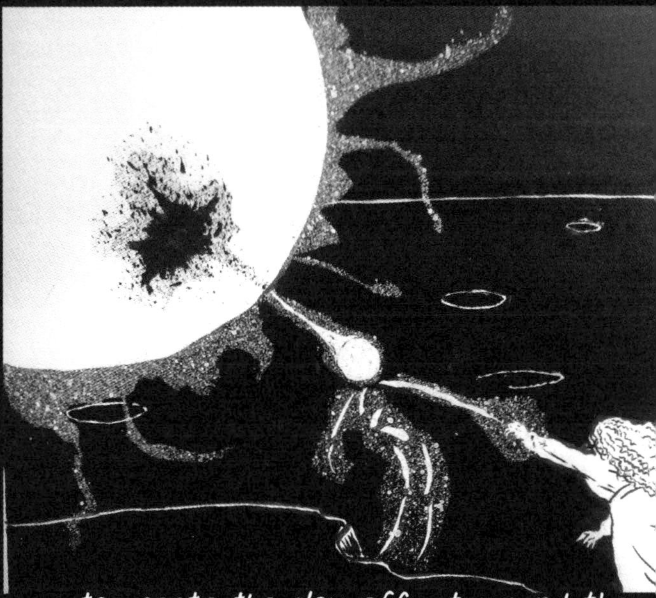

...to create the glow effect around the
object and figures.

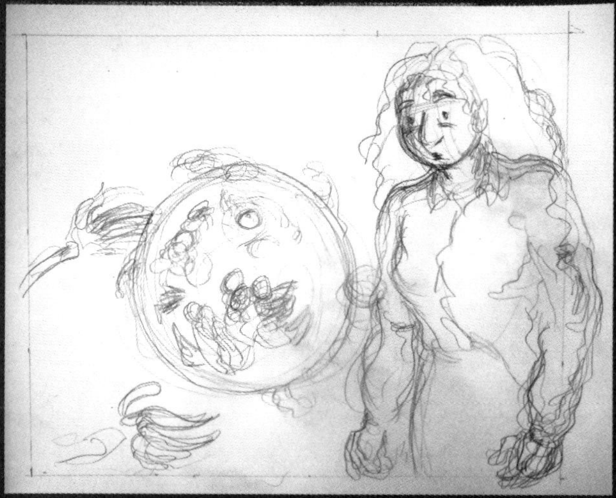

More spatter for chapter 9, this time to shade the figure. Here are pencils.

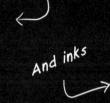

And inks

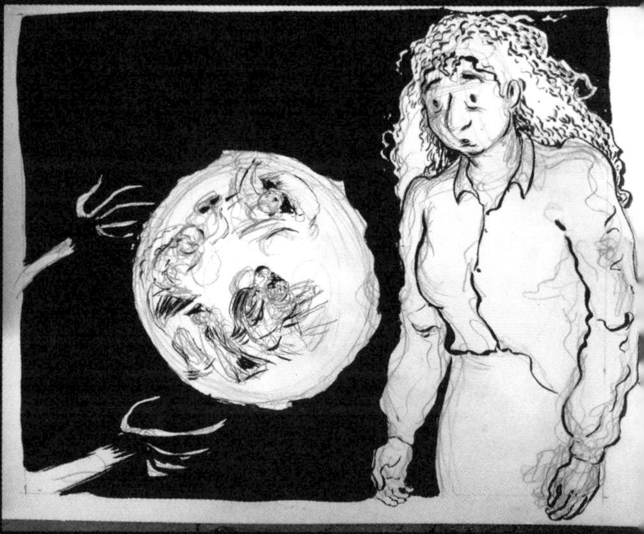

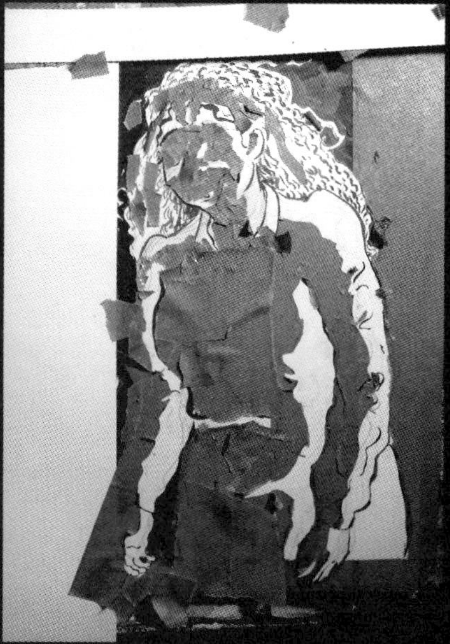

I use paper to mask off most of the page, and cut and tear pieces of tape to define the shaded areas on the figure.

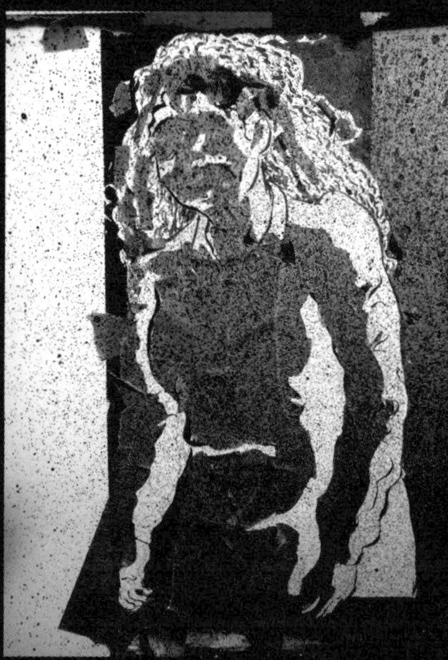

Then spatter with black ink.

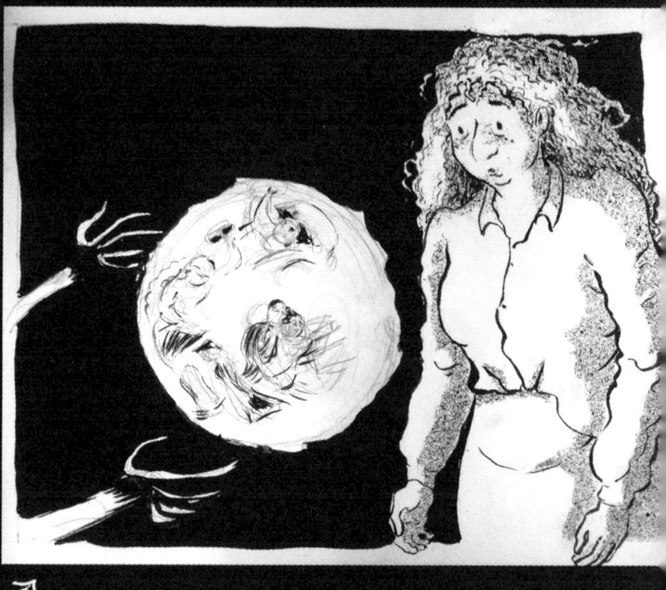

Results of the spatter, when the paper and tape are removed.

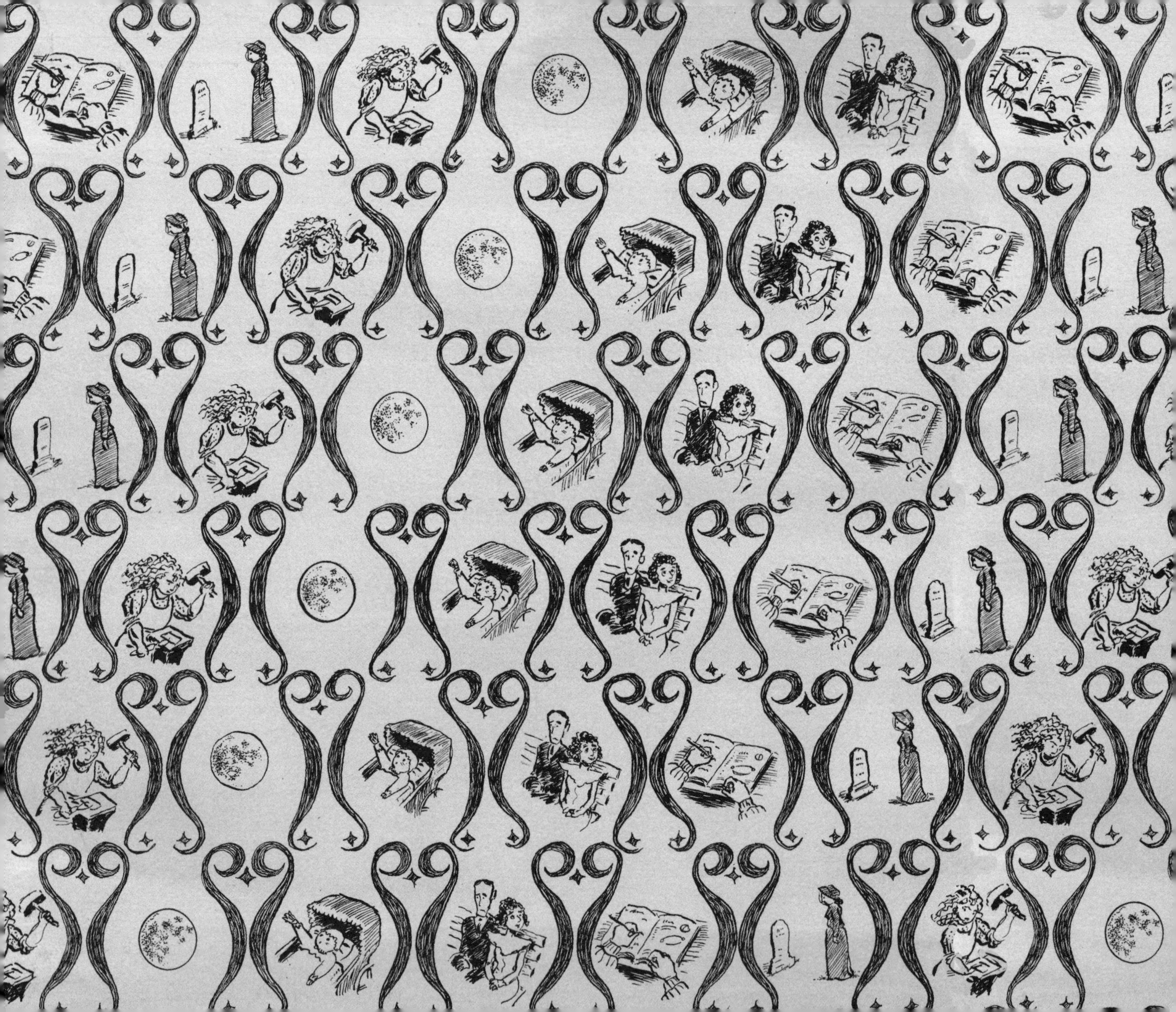